W9-CND-783

, 1938. Morning s...

NOTICE: Return or renew all library materials!
each Lost Book is $50.00.

The person charging this material is responsible for
its return to the library from which it was withdrawn
on or before the **Latest Date** stamped below.

Theft, mutilation, and underlining of books are reasons for disciplinary action and may result in dismissal from the University.
To renew call Telephone Center, 333-8400

UNIVERSITY OF ILLINOIS LIBRARY AT URBANA-CHAMPAIGN

6-/8-01
JUN 03 2016

APR 10 2003

1-11-2010
2-8-2009
JUL

JUN 24 2019

L161—O-1096

WITHDRAWN
University of
Illinois Library
at Urbana-Champaign

THE
PERCY GRAINGER
COMPANION

Percy and Rose Grainger, about 1910.

Other books written or edited by Lewis Foreman:
Havergal Brian: a collection of essays (1969)
The British Musical Renaissance: a guide to research (1972)
Discographies: a bibliography (1973)
Systematic Discography (1974)
*Factors Affecting the Preservation and Dissemination of
    Archive Sound Recordings* (1975)
British Music Now (1975)
Havergal Brian and the performance of his orchestral works (1976)
Edmund Rubbra: composer (1977)
Dermot O'Byrne: selected poems of Arnold Bax (1979)
Arthur Bliss:catalogue of the complete works (1980)

Books contributed to:
E. J. Moeran (Wild, 1974)
New Oxford History of Music, Vol X (1974)
The Music of Frank Bridge (Payne, Foreman, Bishop, 1976)
Havergal Brian and his Music (Nettel, 1976)
The Walled-In Garden (Hold, 1978)
Sources of Information on the European Communities (Palmer, 1979)

In memory of ELLA GRAINGER

FRONTISPIECE: *Percy Grainger in Australia, 1935(?)*

THE PERCY GRAINGER COMPANION

edited by LEWIS FOREMAN

THAMES PUBLISHING
London 1981

© Lewis Foreman 1981

chapter 5 © M Hartston Scott

chapter 12 © Ivar C Dorum

The contents of this book, or any part of them, may not be reproduced in any form whatsoever without written permission of the publishers.

Thames Publishing
14 Barlby Road, London W10 6AR

Printed and bound in England by Edgcott Press Ltd

BRITISH LIBRARY CATALOGUING IN PUBLICATION DATA

The Percy Grainger companion.
1. Grainger, Percy Aldridge
2. Composers — United States — History and criticism
3. Composers — Australia — History and criticism
I. Foreman, Lewis
780'.92'4   ML410.G7

ISBN 0-905210-12-3

780.923   music

G76f

CONTENTS

THE CONTRIBUTORS

*   *   *

ILLUSTRATIONS

I am very grateful to all who have supplied the illustrations for use in this book. It is fortunate that Percy Grainger himself was a keen photographer, not only being involved in the taking of photographs but accumulating those taken by others. We thus have preserved a wider and more vivid selection of prints to choose from than is the case with many composers.

Acknowledgements are due to the following:

Courtesy Stewart Manville and The Percy Grainger Library: *front dustjacket, front endpaper, frontispiece,* pp 24, 32, 47, 50, 62, 67, 83, 181, 202; the programmes reproduced on pp 20, 112, 199, 205 and the leaflet on p 199.

Collection Barry Ould: *half-title,* pp 10, 14, 18, 22, 45, 48, 102, 115, 116, 149 (and insets), 151, 167, 170, 184, *rear endpaper,* and *back of jacket;* and the handbill on p 17.

Ivar Dorum: pp 163, 164.

Collection The Delius Trust: pp 41, 43 (lower).

Lionel Carley: p 43 (top).

Leslie East: p 53.

Burnett Cross: pp 172, 173, 175.

Lewis Foreman: pp 29, 61, 105, 236.

The Borough of Grimsby (Hallgarth Collection): pp 58, 59.

Schott & Co: p 143, and many original scores published by them.

Grainger Museum, University of Melbourne: pp 145, 165.

David Tall: pp 60, 169, and many scores reproduced here in facsimile.

ACKNOWLEDGEMENTS

Many people have assisted in the preparation of this book, not least the authors of the various chapters, to whom a special word of thanks. The various officers of The Percy Grainger Society, too, have been most helpful, particularly David Tall, John Bird and Stephen Lloyd, who are also contributors, and Barry Ould, who supplied many of our best photographs (see list of illustrations).

Otherwise I have to thank Peter Anderson, Teresa Balough, Rachel Dugmore, Kay Dreyfus and Helen Griffiths (Grainger Museum), Jacqueline Kavanagh (BBC Written Archives), Harold Maxwell), Gill Newman, William Parsons (Library of Congress), Shirley Penrose (BBC Transcription Service), Miss Challice B Reed (Programme Information Office, BBC), Arthur Ridgewell, Miss J S Swithinbank (Welholme Galleries), Tony Trebble, Professor David Tunley, and Alan Woolgar (Schott & Co).

In respect of copyright material used in this book, thanks and acknowledgements are due to: Stewart Manville in respect of Percy Grainger's copyrights, which are copyright the Percy Grainger Library; the BBC for quotations from a BBC transcription disc, and from the *Radio Times,* as well as the material in Appendix III; chapters previously published are reproduced by permission of the editors of the journals from which they are taken—chapters 3 and 13 from *Recorded Sound* (courtesy Dr Anthony King, Director of the British Institute of Recorded Sound), chapter 12 from *Studies in Music* (courtesy Professor Sir Frank Callaway and Professor David Tunley and the University of Western Australia); and Appendix IV from *The Grainger Journal.* I am also grateful to the Delius Trust for material used in chapter 4, and to The Grainger Museum at the University of Melbourne. Chapter 5 is published by permission of Marjorie Hartston Scott.

The copyright music examples are reproduced by permission as follows:

Grainger Estate (The Percy Grainger Library); Ex 1 (p 65), Ex 6 (p 70), Ex 7 (p73), Ex 23 (p153);

By permission of the Percy Grainger Library and Schott & Co Ltd: Ex 2-5 (pp 68-69), Ex 12, *The Warriors* p 96, Ex 13 *Irish Tune from County Derry* (p119), Ex 15 *A Reiver's Neck Verse* (p126), Ex 16 *Willow Willow* (p130), Ex 18 *Country Gardens* (p137), Ex 20 *Shepherd's Hey* (p138), Ex 22 *To A Nordic Princess* (p148), and for the words of Grainger's folksong settings in chapter 10;

With acknowledgements to Oxford University Press: Ex 9 *Love Verses from 'The Song of Solomon'* (p86), Ex 11 *Tribute to Foster* (p93);

© 1924 Universal Edition Vienna, reprinted by permission: Ex 10 *Hill Song No 1* (p88);

By permission of Boosey and Hawkes Music Publishers Ltd: Ex 14 *Ramble on Love* (p120).

LEWIS FOREMAN
Rickmansworth
July 1981

CHAPTER ONE

Editor's Introduction

Lewis Foreman

PERCY Grainger was a giant in so many fields: as pianist, folksong collector, teacher, experimenter at the frontiers of new music—but above all as a composer of genius. Yet until recently Grainger was a shadowy figure to those not closely acquainted with his specialisms. His music is written, by and large, for forces outside the normal symphony orchestra, and most of his works are of comparatively short duration. His experiments, though foreshadowing many contemporary trends, are not likely to be generally appreciated, at least as far as his 'free music' is concerned. Yet his use of 'elastic scoring' and espousal of a wide range of percussion are very much of the moment. His personal magnetism as a performer is only partly to be experienced on the surviving recordings of his art as pianist, and most of these not in current record catalogues. What survived for many people were a number of short, popular works—*Molly on the Shore, Country Gardens, Shepherd's Hey* and others—and the legend. The two concertos Grainger was renowned for playing were Grieg's and the first Tchaikovsky. When in 1908, Basil Cameron, later a famous conductor, and a good friend, first saw Grainger it was 'when he strode onto the platform of Queen's Hall looking not the least bit like the general run of musicians of those days. He had a glorious mop of golden hair but he had the physique of an Olympic athlete and was obviously brimful of magnetic vitality . . . he was already recognised as one of the great pianists of the day.'[1] That is the main image of the Grainger legend: a golden Apollo of untiring energy.

In days when a blinkered musical establishment had a tight grip on the current scene, Grainger was somehow suspect—he did not slot into any convenient pigeon-hole, he wrote in no recognised form, no symphonies, concerti, chamber music or operas. He was not musically respectable. Before writing this introduction, it seemed a good idea to review the treatment of Grainger in some of the more important surveys of twentieth-century music, to see how their authors treated him. One was quite amazed to find that he does not appear at all in the indexes of distinguished studies by Paul Griffiths,[2] Arnold Whittall,[3] Jim Sampson[4] and Lawrence Davies,[5] nor in the *Music in the Modern Age* volume of Sternfeld's otherwise excellent *History of Music*[6] or the similar volume of the *New Oxford History of Music*[7].

Two factors have contributed to a significant revival in Grainger's fortunes over the last decade or so, and both, one is sure, would have pleased

11

CING PAGE: a golden Apollo.

him greatly. The first is the increasing performance of his music, not just the popular short orchestral pieces, but a broad sweep of what he wrote, and as it is music that only has to be heard to make its own way, it is a growing trend. This turn of the tide was heralded by the pioneering Percy Grainger Festival presented in London in 1970 by Bryan Fairfax, now a distinguished contributor to the present volume, whose chapter was written from his first-hand experience of choosing and preparing the music at that time. One thing is certainly clear: performance is vital to the assessment of Grainger; he cannot be properly judged by peering at his scores in libraries.

The second factor to underline the Grainger revival is the perception of his achievements as an Australian, by his fellow countrymen, notwithstanding his long domicile in the USA. Grainger's magpie accumulation of a vast archive relating to himself and his friends, and his building of his Museum at the University of Melbourne, is now bearing fruit in scholarly work at various Australian universities, examples of which will be found in the bibliography of the present volume. Additionally, the vision of the music department at the University of Western Australia in promoting the journal *Studies in Music* has provided a vehicle for publishing research that might have been sniffed at by European journals.

Furthermore, the material preserved by Grainger is of fundamental importance in researching the lives and music of his friends and contemporaries—including Grieg, Delius, Cyril Scott, Balfour Gardiner, Sparre Olsen and many American composers. In illuminating them he himself is illuminated in the reflected interest thus generated.

Now the need is for performance, and although much research of a biographical nature is still to be done, it is in the area of practical music-making and listening that help is most urgently required. It is this gap that the present team hope they have filled. This is a companion for performers: what to play, where to get it, how to do it. And for listeners: the background, what to listen for, what recordings and music to search out, the context of the music, what Grainger was driving at.

To put the musical discussion and appendices in context, several chapters of a personal and biographical nature were planned, and the whole is held together by Stephen Lloyd's brief sketch of Grainger's life, which users of different parts of the book may find worth a brief glance to provide a framework to any given enquiry.

In choosing the plan adopted, it has been necessary to adjudicate, particularly in the biographical chapters, between contributors whose essays have overlapped. A fairly liberal policy has been followed in retaining some duplication in the interest of the integrity of individual chapters, and the ease of the user wanting reference information rather than continuous narrative throughout the book. The occasional practice is also used of referring the reader to other parts of the companion by the use of footnotes. The index should be extensively used: it is intended to include everything in it that may be required, including all names and topics in the bibliography, in the illustrations and appendices, as well as in the text. As far as the musical chapters are concerned, contributors have, by and large, had to be selective in discussing the music, and any important works that they omitted are gathered up in Chapter 11.

Grainger is particularly well served by illustrations, both photographic and musical, and we have selected a generous cross-section of these and have aimed at presenting them in as good a quality as possible, in most cases direct from specially prepared prints taken from surviving negatives; in this respect a debt is due to John Bishop of Thames Publishing for being so sympathetic to this aspect of the scheme.

This book was first conceived when the present editor was working as music editor for Simon Publications in 1973, when it was announced on the jacket of Richard Shead's *Constant Lambert* as forthcoming under the editorship of Arthur Ridgewell. That scheme was frustrated by a number of the then intended contributors, who did not deliver their chapters, and by Simon Publications, who ceased to publish. Subsequently the rights in the project were acquired, taking over into the present book the chapters by Carley, Fairfax, Slattery and Payne which had been delivered promptly. Later their companions now published here were commissioned. Four contributions have been published before in the journal literature—those by Sir Peter Pears, Ivor Dorum, Burnett Cross and Stewart Manville—and the first and last have been revised for their appearance here. Acknowledgements appear elsewhere. The chapter by Cyril Scott comes from an unpublished typescript formerly in the Grainger collection in the Library of Congress, now in the Grainger Museum, Melbourne.

Now you have the facts; we hope we have communicated our enthusiasm: play the music, you cannot fail to find it invigorating, moving, rewarding.

CHAPTER TWO

Grainger 'In a Nutshell'

Stephen Lloyd

IN Kipling's novel *The Light that Failed* there is a prefatory poem to the ninth chapter that, not inappropriately, might well be taken to crystallise the polarity of Grainger's reputation even at some 20 or so years' distance from his death. One reads in *The Two Potters* of a craftsman declaring that were he to fashion out of common clay something 'in the shape of a god', then honour would be his, to which the rejoinder comes that if 'thy hand be not free from the taint of the soil . . . the greater shame to thee'.

Such has been the dichotomy of Grainger's public image. On the one hand he could be described, if a little extravagantly, by an acquaintance as 'this lovable man . . . an incarnated seraph, of perpetual youthfulness and golden good looks' who 'seemed to have descended to this earth apparelled in celestial strangeness'.[1] At the other extreme is to be found a complex and incongruous earth-bound figure whose contradictions of character and whose unconventional modes and eccentricities have frequently clouded any assessment of his artistic achievements.

His biographer, John Bird, who has sympathetically put these various imperfections and irregularities, including the more bizarre sexual aspects, into perspective, even goes so far as to suggest an admixture of genius and madness in Grainger's make-up.[2] But my purpose here is solely to indicate some of the more prominent milestones in this colourful career, to provide a context in which the remainder of this handbook may be read.

The Kipling analogy is apposite not only since he was a favourite poet of Grainger's, and the inspiration of about 40 works, but also because in the same volume the dedicatory verses with their refrain 'Mother o'mine' served as both an emotional and a musical motto in Grainger's life. Percy's attachment to his mother, much stronger even than was Kipling's, is just another extraordinary facet of the man. Rose Aldridge was born in Adelaide in 1861 to parents who in 1847 had emigrated from Kent to Australia. (The fact that Rose's mother asked to be lashed to the mast on the outward voyage in order to witness the ferocity of the elements hints at a precedent for Percy's spartan athletic feats.) Likewise, John Grainger, an architect and civil engineer whom Rose married in 1880, had also emigrated from England in 1877. Because of his work they moved after their marriage to Melbourne, where their only child, registered at birth as George Percy Grainger, was born on July 8 1882. It was, however, a broken marriage, with a drunken father often the instigator of violent scenes and a mother whose dominant,

15

ING PAGE: Grainger, early 1920s.

over-protective presence loomed large throughout Percy's life, even after her death, by which time he was 40.

Mother and son in fact became almost inseparable, and though he grew up with mutual love, he was subjected to the strictest maternal discipline, his punishment the whip. From her he received his first piano lessons at the age of five; at about the same time she introduced him to the Icelandic sagas and so gave him his intellectual Nordic bearings, and she would often sing to him the songs of Stephen Foster, a fond memory that bore musical fruit some years later.* When Percy was eight his parents separated, never to live together again. Eventually he adopted his mother's maiden name, calling himself Percy Aldridge Grainger.

At the age of ten, Percy took piano lessons with Louis Pabst and he made his public debut in July 1894 at the Melbourne Masonic Hall in a programme of Bach—an early enthusiasm. In May 1895 he left Australia with his mother for Germany, where on professional advice he was to continue his studies at the Hoch Conservatorium in Frankfurt. At that time Germany still attracted music students from far afield, including many from Britain, and Grainger's name was soon to become associated with three British students in particular—Roger Quilter, Cyril Scott, and Balfour Gardiner—and to a lesser degree with a fourth, Norman O'Neill, all being collectively known as the 'Frankfurt Group'.** Their ages spanned seven years, Grainger being the youngest by three, and it was probably their individuality of outlook rather than any musical unity that drew them together. And while they were to pursue different courses in later life, their friendships remained unimpaired. Scott was the group's avant-gardiste and, during their student days, the closest musically to Grainger. Both were innovators and enjoyed a fairly fluid interchange of new ideas and techniques.

Grainger soon fell out with his professor of composition and refused to take any more lessons with him. But he was fortunate instead in securing the teaching of an amateur musician, Karl Klimsch, for whom Grainger was to have a deep respect. It was Klimsch who opened his eyes to the beauties of folksong that was soon to form a central part of his compositional output.

A worsening of Rose Grainger's health soon necessitated a change of direction in Percy's career. As he wrote of his decision: 'my mother had become an invalid, constantly threatened with paralysis, & from then on my main anxiety was to be able to earn enough as a concert pianist . . . to secure for her a reasonable degree of comfort & security'. His ambitions as a composer were subordinated to his role as performer, and for fear that 'the radical nature' of his own compositions would 'stir up animosities' against him and threaten his earning power as a pianist he decided against the performance of 'the main body' of his works and similarly restricted their publication. Despite his professed dislike of both the piano and public performance he was in effect tied for life to the instrument. After her convalescence, he sailed in May 1901 with his mother for England to take up residence in London. He made his first public appearance there on June 11 in St James's Hall.

* See p 92.
** Cyril Scott writes about their Frankfurt days on p 51.

BECHSTEIN HALL.

Concert Direction E. L. ROBINSON

BEG TO ANNOUNCE A

Piano & Violoncello Recital

BY

PERCY GRAINGER

AND

HERMAN SANDBY

(THE DANISH 'CELLIST)

Monday, February 13th, at 8 o'clock.

VOCALIST:

Miss ADA CROSSLEY

Accompanist - Mr. HAMILTON HARTY.

BECHSTEIN GRAND PIANOFORTE.

TICKETS—Stalls (Reserved), 10 6 & 5 -; Balcony (Unreserved), 2 -
May be obtained from CHAPPELL's BOX OFFICE, Queen's Hall, and 50, New Bond Street, WHITEHEAD's Ticket Office, St. James's Hall; KEITH PROWSE & Co., 42, Poland Street, Oxford Street, W., 167 New Bond Street and Branches; MITCHELL, 33, Old Bond Street and Branches; LACON & OLLIER, 168 New Bond Street; CECIL ROY, 15, Sussex Place, 11, Post Street, S.W., and all Branches; J. B. CRAMER & Co., 126, Oxford Street, W.; Box Office Steinway Hall; ASHTON, 38, Old Bond Street and 35, Sloane Street, S.W.; ALFRED HAYS, 26, Old Bond Street; WEBSTER & WADDINGTON, Ltd., 302, Regent Street, W.; THE ARMY AND NAVY STORES, 105, Victoria Street, Westminster, S.W.; LEADER & Co., 14, Royal Arcade, Old Bond Street, W.; DISTRICT MESSENGER AND THEATRE TICKET Co., 195, Piccadilly, W., and Branches; CIVIL SERVICE SUPPLY STORES, 138, Queen Victoria Street, E.C.; Æolian Hall Box Office, 135-7, New Bond Street, W.; at the BOX OFFICE, BECHSTEIN HALL; and of
Concert Direction E. L. ROBINSON 7, Wigmore Street, Cavendish Square, W.

PERCY GRAINGER and HERMAN SANDBY.

..., Printers, 125 Farringdon Road, E.C.

...cert handbill, 1905.

During the early years of the century Grainger's schedule and reputation as a concert pianist rapidly expanded. He made his first solo appearance with an orchestra at Bath in February 1902, playing Tchaikovsky's First Piano Concerto. In addition to numerous recitals that year he toured the provinces in a concert party with Adelina Patti, and he gained an entrée into society, making the acquaintance of such figures as the painter and actor Ernest Thesiger, through whom he was introduced to John Singer Sargent. There was influential support from people like the financier William Gair Rathbone (dedicatee of *Handel in the Strand*) and the patroness and society hostess Mrs Lowrey. Needless to say, his golden Apollonian looks did much to enhance his society standing.

For a while he took on piano students. Such was the impression he created as a pianist that when Busoni heard him he invited Grainger to Berlin to study with him free of charge. In June 1903 he duly took up the invitation but his stay there was a short one and the relationship cooled. Later, in 1903, he embarked on an extensive concert tour of Australia, New Zealand and South Africa with Ada Crossley, and in 1905 he toured Denmark with recitals. His long-held desire to be free of the concert platform and to devote himself entirely to composition was never to be realised.

An important new direction in Grainger's career was largely sparked off by a lecture he attended in March 1905 given by Lucy Broadwood, secretary

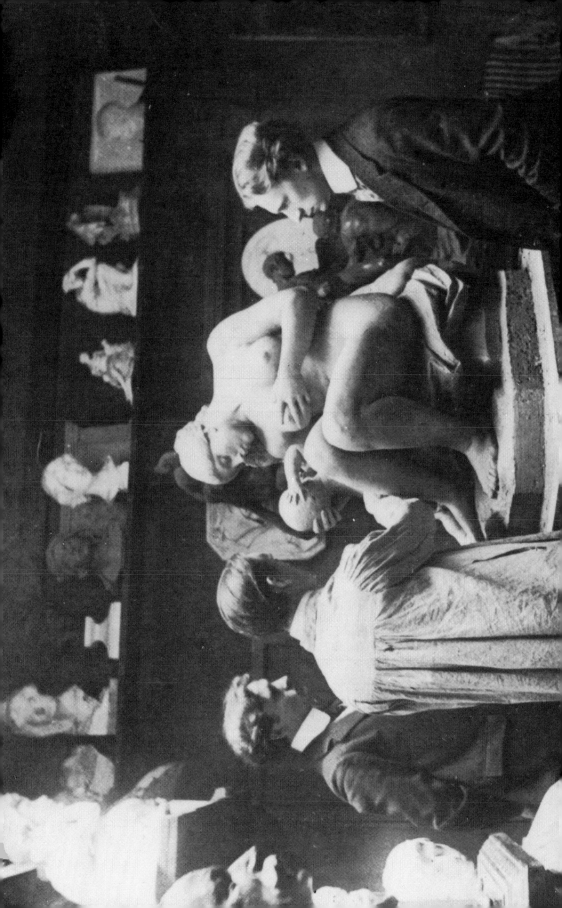

of the Folk-Song Society. In April and August he visited the Lincolnshire market town of Brigg to collect folksongs, among them the well-known *Brigg Fair,* of which he made a choral setting. He was soon collecting in earnest, using methods of notation that ensured a faithful adherence to every subtle variation and inflection in the songs—a sharp contrast to some of the approximations and distortions of previous collectors*. By 1906 he was using an Edison Bell phonograph in his work. He collected in Britain and abroad, especially Denmark, where he held in great respect the work of Evald Tang Kristensen, with whom he was later to gather folksongs. News of Grainger's pioneering work even reached Bartók, whose work in that field had begun at about the same time and who expressed a desire to correspond with Grainger on the subject, though his wish seems to have progressed no further. Grainger's extensive British folkmusic settings are 'lovingly and reverently dedicated to the memory of Edvard Grieg', with whom he enjoyed a close friendship in the last year of the Norwegian composer's life. They had first met (at Grieg's request) in May 1906 at the home of Sir Edgar Speyer, and Grieg had the warmest praise for Grainger's interpretations of his music. Grieg's death sadly robbed Grainger of the honour of playing the piano concerto at the Leeds Festival with the composer conducting, as had been planned.

In April 1907 there was another notable encounter when Grainger met Frederick Delius, whom he came to love and revere.** He showed him his choral setting of *Brigg Fair,* to some extent foreshadowing Delius's harmonisation of the folksong in his orchestral variations completed later that year and dedicated to Grainger, an honour reciprocated in the dedication of Grainger's magnum opus *The Warriors.* Delius had much respect for Grainger's art and it was he who was chiefly instrumental in persuading him to reverse his attitude towards the witholding of his works from public performance. Indeed, most of those initial fears were banished by the enormous impression his works created when presented in Balfour Gardiner's two series of choral and orchestral concerts in 1912 and 1913, in which they held a prominent position. So great was their impact that soon after the first series an all-Grainger concert was given before a packed Aeolian Hall in May 1912. In the first concert of Gardiner's first series (13 March 1912), as well as *Irish Tune from County Derry* and *We Have Fed Our Seas for a Thousand Years,* his *Father and Daughter* included a band of 30 mandoline and guitar players, and in the sensation that followed Grainger found his work twice encored and himself recalled a dozen times. One critic singled him out as 'not only a choral conductor of sheer genius but also a choral composer in a line by himself'.[3] Among other works included in the two series were *Colonial Song, Hill Song No 2,*[4] *English Dance* and *Green Bushes.*

Grainger's international reputation was at a peak when war broke out. If his reaction—leaving for America—was swift, his reason for going was characteristic: he feared that the possibility of being killed would thwart his cherished ambition of becoming the first Australian composer of worth. In

---

* See p 61.
** See ch 4, p 31.

19

FACING PAGE: Herman Sandby, Derwent Wood and Percy Grainger in Derwent Wood's Studio, Chelsea, ca 1904.

September 1914 he arrived in America, where he effectively made his home for the rest of his life. There he continued his parallel course as concert pianist and composer, with larger works like *The Warriors* and *In a Nutshell* receiving first performances. When America entered the war, Grainger, though a pacifist by nature, enlisted in the US Army—as a bandsman (2nd class) in the Coast Artillery Corps Band. There soon followed numerous war-aid concerts during which he introduced that perennial favourite *Country Gardens*.

In June 1918 he assumed full American citizenship, and when the war was over and he had been discharged from the Army he was back on the endless concert round-about with occasional conducting, teaching and lecturing.

The early post-war period was to be saddened by a serious deterioration in Rose Grainger's mental health, ultimately resulting in her suicide in April 1922. Percy was devastated. In an attempt to come to terms with it he threw himself into even harder work, including a European tour which took him to Denmark, where he did some folk-song collecting with Kristensen. He was able too, once again, to see friends from whom he had been separated by the war—Delius, the Frankfurt Group, and others.

In April 1924, taking a leaf no doubt out of Balfour Gardiner's book over a decade earlier, Grainger staged in America two ambitious concerts, largely conducted by him and including two Delius American first performances. Next month he left for Australia, chiefly to bury his mother's ashes but he

Programme of ship-board recital, 1929.

CHARITY CONCERT

IN AID OF
BRITISH & AMERICAN SEAMEN'S INSTITUTIONS

Held on board the Cunard Steam Ship Company's R.M.S. "Laconia"
(CAPTAIN : M. DOYLE)

In the MAIN LOUNGE - Friday, September 13th, 1929, at 9-00 p.m.

Chairman : BOYLSTON A. BEAL, Esq.

:: PROGRAMME ::

PART FIRST

Overture ... ... "Raymond" ... ... *Thomas*
LACONIA ORCHESTRA

Saxophone Solo ... "Valse Vanite" ... ... ——
Mr. T. HALLIS

Pianoforte Solo ... Three Folk Songs, *set by Percy Grainger*
(a) "Spoon River" (American Folk Dance)
(b) Irish Tune, from County Derry ...
(c) "The Hunter in his Career" (Old English)
Mr. PERCY GRAINGER

CHAIRMAN'S REMARKS   COLLECTION

PART SECOND

Pianoforte Solo ... ...
(a) "Juba Dance" (Canadian) ... *Nathaniel Dett*
(b) Colonial Song (a song of Australia) ...*Grainger*
(c) "Country Gardens" English Morris Dance...
set by Percy Grainger
Mr. PERCY GRAINGER

Selection ... ... "Pagliacci" ... ... *Leoncavallo*
LACONIA ORCHESTRA

STAR SPANGLED BANNER   GOD SAVE THE KING

TO BE FOLLOWED—TIME PERMITTING—BY
DANCING IN THE GARDEN LOUNGE

also gave some lecture-recitals there. That year too he became a vegetarian. He toured Australia again in 1926 and it was on the homeward stage that he met his future wife, the beautiful Swedish-born Ella Ström. Their wedding two years later was a typically unorthodox ceremony—on the stage of the Hollywood Bowl at the conclusion of a concert conducted by Percy and before a large paying audience*. The concert featured the first performance of his musical tribute to his wife, *To A Nordic Princess*. The couple were abroad together the following year and during their two months' stay in England there was a reunion of the Frankfurt Group (with the exception of Gardiner) in July at Harrogate, where their compositions featured prominently in a festival of British music organised by Percy Grainger and the conductor Basil Cameron.

Soon the Graingers were back in America, where a busy concert season awaited them and, as can be seen from the accompanying programme illustration, even on his return voyage Percy could not get away from the instrument that had, perforce, become his life's companion.

During the 'thirties and his remaining years he was engrossed with the idea of a museum which he built in the city of his birth. Its purpose was to provide as thorough a documentation as possible of his life, his friends, in fact of any influence on his artistic being. To this end, with an unbounded magpie instinct, he went to enormous trouble to amass a fascinating collection of music, paintings, letters, personal writing, books—even clothing. Much of his time and energy was expended on this project and the Grainger Museum was officially opened in 1939 (though the public at large were not admitted during his lifetime).

Another major project close to his heart on which he worked until his death in February 1961 was his concept of free-music. This provides further evidence, if it were needed, of his extraordinarily inventive mind, which even in his last years lent an interested ear to contemporary trends. Grainger was critical of the expense of the equipment used even in the 1950s for generating the new art of electronic music, picking up much of *his* 'equipment' in the streets for nothing. Basil Cameron recalled Ella Grainger describing 'how she and Percy used to go out in the evenings in their best clothes so that they shouldn't be arrested as suspicious characters while prowling around the dustbins and refuse heaps looking for odd bits of metal and of wood to fit into the free-music machines'[5]. With his free-music machines he had the technical assistance of Burnett Cross, a physics teacher.** This still remains a little-known part of Grainger's creativity.

The question is unavoidable: was Grainger's ultimately a 'light that failed'? Hardly. At times it may have shone intermittently and with less strength but certain areas, particularly folksong, he brilliantly illuminated as very few have done. One is reminded of that Grainger enthusiast Benjamin Britten's comment on hearing a broadcast of two of Grainger's folksong settings—'knocking all the V Williams and R O Morris arrangements into a cocked-hat'[6]. His music is deserving of a scrutiny equal to that given to his life. It still awaits a true assessment, but is gradually being accepted as a

---

*   See photographs, p 149
** Burnett Cross's own account of the free-music machine appears on p 171

At the microphone, Australia, late 1920s.

significant contribution to twentieth-century composition. One can only echo Donald Mitchell, who in 1966, after commenting on Grainger's 'inspired oddity', found he had 'made a singular contribution to 20th-century music which is not in general all that rich in high spirits and optimism'.[7]

CHAPTER THREE

A Personal Introduction to Percy Grainger

Sir Peter Pears[1]

I DID not know Percy Grainger intimately. I wish I had known him better. I first met him in 1936, when he was in his middle fifties and I was in my twenties, a member of the BBC Singers. Grainger was in London for a BBC concert of his music given by the BBC Orchestra and Chorus conducted jointly by Leslie Woodgate and himself. In the programme was a work which needed a tenor solo, and I was asked to undertake it. If they had thought it an important work, some outside singer would have been engaged. But it was not an enormous solo—just the piece for the likes of me: I was only in the BBC Singers, and delighted to earn a few guineas over and above my salary of £6 per week. The work of Grainger that I sang was *Love Verses from 'The Song of Solomon'*—a characteristic, charming piece of rhapsodic utterance, with some graceful phrases for solo voices. From the concert I also remember *The Marching Song of Democracy* and *Up-Country Song*. And there was *Tribute to Foster,* in which we all had to play the musical glasses: we had wine glasses half full of water, and we had to dip our fingers into the water and run them round the tops, and make melodious chords of F sharp major.

The occasion left me with one tangible souvenir which I have treasured ever since. Quite without asking, I was given by Percy Grainger a photo of himself with an extraordinarily kind inscription. That is in my experience an unusual acquisition: I have not generally been offered signed photographs of composers whose work I have performed. Indeed the only other one I remember receiving without solicitation was a photo of Shostakovich inscribed in barely legible Russian. That was very nice, but the photo itself shows Dmitri at his most tense and worried—not to say cross— so that I can hardly bear to look at it, much less display it. Percy Grainger was more photogenic than Shostakovich. His picture is much more agreeable to look at, being in fact the true likeness of a strikingly handsome and vivid man.

When Percy Grainger first came to England in the early years of the century, everyone fell for him: corn-coloured hair, bright blue eyes bursting with vitality, immensely enthusiastic, and a staggering pianist. Where had he, an Australian born in a suburb of Melbourne in July 1882, ever learnt to play the piano to such perfection? The answer to that question was also the most important, most powerful, most absorbing factor throughout Percy Grainger's life—it was his mother. And no one who talks about him can—or should—avoid talking about her.

Rosa Annie Aldridge was born in Adelaide, South Australia, in 1861.

Both her parents had gone there from Kent. Her early life is best told in her own words, written in 1916:

> I was born in a block of buildings in King William Street, Adelaide, South Australia, called in those days 'White's Rooms.' For a period my father used to engage celebrated artists to appear in concerts at these rooms; how long we lived in this house I don't know, nor do I remember my life there; but I have seen the building many times and have heard my parents speak of their life there. I was the eighth child of my parents, the third girl, and the baby for about eight years—when another boy was born and they called him Frank.

Two years later she put down some further notes:

> A short outline of my life—early memories from seventh year. Great love for and from Grandmother (my mother's mother) who made her room a fairyland for me. No unpleasant memory of her. She sang me old ditties, played with me, dressed dolls—men, women, children, soldiers, heroes and heroines. She died at the age of eighty-four.
>
> Experienced a fully happy childhood, great love for and from parents, brothers, sisters. Intense admiration for my mother and sister Clara. Great love of poetry, music, horses and most animals, birds and trees and flowers.
>
> Three happy school years, remembering no unpleasantness, no great friends at school, no enemies. Loved by head teacher. Petted and spoiled by men examiners, who gave me extra prizes. Loved acting and dancing. Always had a sweetheart, nothing serious. Cannot remember having any unpleasant experience before marriage. No quarrel with anyone at all. Always had the feeling of being liked and loved by men, women and children and animals.
>
> Married young. Impelled by fate to marry an Englishman whose physical attraction and mental outlook never appealed to me. Married life unhappy experiencing both physical and mental cruelty. Felt love for and from friends in Melbourne.
>
> The greatest feeling in my life—intense love and devotion for my beautiful boy whose physical beauty and genius was and is a great joy to me. He is to me like some glorious work of art, good to live with and look upon. I feel his genius is sacred to me and the world.

This passionate, devoted, possessive woman was to spend the whole of the rest of her life with her only child, Percy. She was never separated from him for more than a week or so at a time: the longest separations were about six weeks in 1904, and the last eight and a half weeks of her life. Then, after those weeks of separation, she made the separation a permanent one by taking her own life.

Mrs Grainger had more or less taught herself the piano. She sat beside Percy for at least two hours daily from his fifth to his tenth year, while he practised the piano. About that time her husband left her and went back to England. Then she had to earn a livelihood for herself and her son as a piano teacher — and very occasionally as a performer. Percy made his first public appearance at the age of 12 in Melbourne.

In 1895, when he was almost 13 and she was 33, they left Australia for Germany. She taught English while Percy studied music at Dr Hoch's Conservatory in Frankfurt. There he heard the sort of music that he had not heard in Melbourne — Wagner's music dramas, Brahms, Tchaikovsky, as well as Strauss and the younger men. Percy and his mother went often to the theatre, where they saw plays by Ibsen, Gerhart Hauptmann and Sudermann — to their intense pleasure. Percy spent his spare time painting and sketching, and cycling in the Taunus Mountains with his mother. For the first time he read Walt Whitman's *Leaves of Grass,* which became a leading artistic and spiritual influence in the life of both of them.

After four years in Frankfurt, Rosa had a serious breakdown in health. She was forced to lie still for months on end, nursed chiefly by Percy. It was then, at the age of 18 or 19, that he first began to earn the livelihood for his mother and himself as pianist, piano teacher, and accompanist.

In 1901 they came to England, and it became their home for 14 years. Rosa later said that England had left many happy but some unhappy memories. What were the unhappy ones, I wonder? Insular, exclusive, snobbish unkindness to the mother of a dazzling boy? Possibly — or was it just her husband turning up? At any rate, this was the beginning of Percy's international career. In the next years he was able to make close friends with fellow composers such as Cyril Scott, Roger Quilter, Balfour Gardiner, Frederick Delius, and also the man who became the father-figure Percy had lacked in his own life — Edvard Grieg.

Percy wrote much music in England, but one piece stands out. It is *Shepherd's Hey* — his setting of an English tune, with the genial introduction of a concertina in just the right place. It is perhaps the most English piece that he ever wrote, and in a small way it was to be his masterpiece. It is in fact a sort of microcosm of Grainger's contribution to music — extraordinary skill in orchestration, and marvellous feeling for rhythm and colour.

Percy Grainger had three different (though related) talents. He was a first-rate pianist, he was a composer, and he was a fixer — a disher-up of first-class quality. As an original composer he started early. There is no indication that he had any tuition in harmony until he reached Frankfurt and went to Dr Hoch's Conservatory. But there he would have been taught counterpoint and harmony in the traditional way.

What is very odd is that already in the 'nineties he had been attracted by the textures of Bach's scoring in the *St Matthew Passion* — the chamber (and at times almost solo) quality of the orchestral writing. Where can he have heard a performance of that nature in the 'nineties? (You have only to look at a score of one of the cantatas edited by Siegfried Ochs and published around 1910, with its direction for 14 first violins, 12 second violins, eight violas and six double-basses, to see how Johann Sebastian Bach was usually performed then.)

In a paper published in 1942 Percy Grainger appealed with eloquence for the proper proportions in performances of Bach and Handel. In Handel's and Bach's time the chorus for the *St Matthew Passion* and the *Messiah* would number not more than 30. (Even in the Handel commemorations of 1784 — 25 years after Handel's death — which have an appalling notoriety on account of the size of the forces involved—at least the proportions of the enormous forces were correct: that was 26 oboes, 26 bassoons, 12 trumpets, 48 first violins, and so on). Somewhere Percy Grainger heard a performance of the right weight — where the strings didn't drown the woodwind, and where the chorus didn't drown the lot — and it affected his own music profoundly. His two *Hill Songs* are scored for a large group of solo instruments, and many of his folksong arrangements use the same technique with a marvellous effect — beautifully calculated sounds for groups of instruments usual and unusual, like the concertina solo in the *Shepherd's Hey,* or the clarinet, horn and harmonium in *Shallow Brown.* He had an acute ear for orchestral sound. He may sometimes have miscalculated shape or structure in his own music, but he very seldom got the sound wrong.

I want to read you Percy Grainger's ideas of the 'Nature and purpose of music today' — written in the 1930s, contributed to a paper called *The Musical News.* It embodies Percy Grainger's deeply felt yearnings for music: and his quite characteristic originality — simple, direct and honest. It reveals what Percy Grainger aimed at in his own music:

> The other day I read in a quotation from the Chinese records of rights said to date from BC 2255 — that poetry is the expression of earnest thought, and singing is the prolonged utterance of that expression. That statement is just as true of the higher flights of Western music of today or yesterday as it presumably was of Chinese music long ago. I take it for granted that it is the office of the higher flights of music to uplift us, to emotionalise us, and to awaken and increase within us the well-springs of dreaminess, lovingness, and compassionateness — in other words to prepare our natures for some kind of angelic life, presumably here on earth. Also to turn our thoughts away from the worldly and practical things of life, those things that Walt Whitman calls 'a terrible doubt of appearance'.
>
> It seems evident to me that it is melody and harmony rather than rhythm that is empowered to turn our natures towards the angelic state. Now what do we mean by 'melody'? I think we all mean fundamentally the same thing by the term 'melody'. Even the most unmusical person will hardly speak of a melody on a bugle or a melody on a drum. So we may assume that even the popular conception of melody does not associate melody primarily with broken chords or with rhythm. Melody I take it is single-line sounds that follow that nature of the human voice — prolonged utterances — and it is these that we call melody.
>
> On the other hand, the dance-songs and the working-songs of the world have been comparatively rhythmical and unmelodic. Rhythm is a great energiser, a great slave-driver, and the lower types of mankind—the tyrants, the greedy ones, the business-minded people — have not been slow to sense the practical advantage to be drawn from rhythmically regular music as an energising action bearing force. When those hard-headed practical people want young men to go out and get themselves killed, they play marches to them, and they encourage sailors and road workers to sing at their jobs in order that the maximum of hard work may be forthcoming as economically as possible. The practical-minded people welcome any type of music that will encourage them — as well as others — to dance rather than dream, to act rather than think.
>
> Don't I see proofs of this in my own royalty returns? We composers know that with rare exceptions our rhythmic compositions sell by the thousands, while our melodic compositions sell by the tens or the hundreds.

Grainger goes on to talk about the orgy of rhythmic music in jazz and classical fields in the 'twenties and early 'thirties. He speaks about the case of Frederick Delius as showing the typical position of an exalted, incurable dreamer during an era in which the economics of selling music depend on its rhythmic appeal:

> Here is a composer who has written nothing that could be described as light or popular, nothing spectacular, nothing to appeal to virtuoso conductors or soloists, few songs, piano pieces, or solos of any kind that amount to anything. Most of his

representative compositions are long, vague, expensive, and troublesome to perform. But they certainly are the prolonged expression of earnest thought and they certainly are melodious, harmonious, uplifting and spiritualising. As Delius has been blind in paradise for the last ten years and as he is mainly dependent on the proceeds of his compositions for his wherewithal, it is consoling to those of us who consider him the great living composer to hear that his royalties have never been so big as during the last two years.

He was a person who had tremendous enthusiasms, was Percy Grainger — quite unafraid to speak out his enthusiasms for those people who were quite unfashionable or who hadn't been heard of. He greatly admired Cyril Scott. In the early part of the century Scott's music was widely acclaimed. His *Piano Sonata,* composed about 1904, was much performed in Europe by the composer and others. It is full of highly irregular rhythms, which later began to appear in the works of Stravinsky and Hindemith. So of course Grainger saw in Cyril Scott's work a direct influence. He was also devoted to the music of the 17th century — the English chamber music of Lawes, Purcell and Jenkins. And he edited quite a considerable quantity of 14th- and 15th-century music.

Among his most ambitious pieces is *The Power of Rome and the Christian Heart.* It is, I think, representative of the bigger forms that he attempted. It is written for a large band — a really very large band with all sorts of clarinets, saxophones, and the rest. Few people can write for brass like Percy Grainger, and this piece in particular shows a marvellous feeling for it. And all this is augmented with an organ part. The piece begins with an extremely soft organ introduction. This slowly works up to a theme which the composer calls the *Theme of the lonely man,* and then we hear the *Power of Rome* theme. At the end the organ finishes the work very softly, as it had begun.

I think Percy Grainger's biggest achievement, however, is in the realm of folk-music arrangements. He was obviously in love with folk-song. Was it his colonial upbringing — by no means without music, but perhaps lacking in indigenous folk-music — that filled him with the passion for the musical roots of Northern Europe, of Great Britain and Scandinavia in particular. In the early years of the century Grainger plunged into the collection of folk-music with the utmost zeal. He was the first (or very nearly the first) to use the phonograph and gramophone in collecting folk-songs. And his enthusiasm inspired the first class of folk-singing in a British music festival.

This was at Brigg in Lincolnshire in 1905. Grainger had become friends with Gervase Elwes, the great English tenor, whom many composers adored and wrote music for: Vaughan Williams, Cyril Scott, and Quilter in particular. Elwes was a well-to-do county-family man, and used to sponsor local musical gatherings. I quote from *Gervase Elwes; the story of his life* by his wife:

> Percy Grainger was always to the fore, bubbling with enthusiasm and vitality. He invariably had some composition, which often took the form of a part song. He would then firmly take the meeting in hand, circulate copies of the piece, force everybody to take part, and then conduct the whole show and get a rousing result. The professional singers did not have it by any means all their own way. Some of them could not read music at sight nearly as well as the amateurs. In particular Margaret Massingbird, her sister Susan Lushington, and her sister-in-law Diana Montgomery, were towers of strength, owing, as they explained to me, to their having been trained by the 'tonic sol-fa method.'[2]

There is a fascinating description of Percy Grainger collecting folksongs in Lincolnshire in 1905, when he was a guest of the Elwes family. After the success of the festival, when the first prize for folksong was won by Joseph Taylor, Percy said:

> The results are so rousing that I am going to see I get a week off sometime in the summer and do a sort of bike tour through Lincolnshire gathering tunes. I risk asking you all this because one can ask folk-song lovers to do anything, and I dare say Linc'll prove rich. Anyway, you must feel proud at the jolly results your forethought of this year rounded up.[3]

That was typical of the way Grainger collected folksongs. On this occasion he and Gervase Elwes's sons scoured the countryside of Lincolnshire. First they hunted up all the folksong singers of the previous festival: some of them had quite large repertoires of songs. And Percy never had the slightest hesitation in pumping anybody he came across. He would go up to a man ploughing and ask him if he knew any songs: and often the man would stand and sing a song in the most natural way in the world. He also began to use the phonograph at this time to record songs. Percy used to jot down the tunes on bits of paper. At other times he drew: he drew the Brigg workhouse—where he had found a most charming old gentleman, a real product of Lincolnshire, whom he then 'brought in to lunch with us, and who sat at table with us and our party without a trace of shyness'.

At the Brigg Festival concert in spring of 1906 the main feature of the programme consisted of Percy's setting of some of the enchanting folksongs that he had collected the previous summer. Gervase Elwes sang *Brigg Fair* with the combined choirs. A little later Percy Grainger and Gervase Elwes combined in a recital at the Aeolian Hall, which the *Daily Telegraph* described as a concert of pure delight from start to finish.

The man who won the prize at the Brigg Festival, Joseph Taylor, became quite famous and at Percy Grainger's suggestion the Gramophone Company

Brochure advertising the Gramophone Company records of folksongs, 1908. (For the front cover of this document see p 236.)

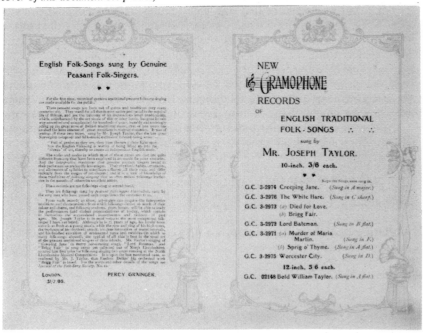

got him to make some commercial records. He recorded both *Brigg Fair* and *Died for Love,* both of which Percy Grainger had collected. Taylor recorded only two verses of *Brigg Fair* because he couldn't remember the rest of the words. Nevertheless, Joseph Taylor made a tremendous impression on people. He was about 75 when he made his records, but his voice had lasted marvellously. He was famous for his interpolated turns and ornaments — and it was one of the facets of folk-song that fascinated Percy Grainger. Grainger was attracted by the personality of a singer, by what he did, his characteristics, voice, and his own particular personal quirks and fancies. He himself after all was a marvellous performer and he was interested from the performer's point of view in folksongs.

None of the other great folk-song collectors felt this in quite the same way. Both Vaughan Williams and Cecil Sharp, for instance, were concerned in rescuing lost music. They wanted to re-incorporate it into the musical life of the country. They wanted all the schools to sing it, and therefore wanted to provide the young singers with accompaniments that could be played by their brothers and sisters, so that this music should get into the bloodstream of us all again. Percy Grainger was also fascinated by this music — he adored the music, in fact — but he was interested most of all in variations introduced by one performer or another. He copied down every single variation he met with.

His notation seeks to make it quite clear on the page how the singer would sing the song. As one first looks at Grainger's notations of folksongs, they look wildly edited, because there are hair-pin markings, commas and pauses all the time. But that was the way he thought it was being sung to him. Grainger wasn't thinking in terms of classes of children singing it, or simple people singing it. He wasn't trying to get it into a usable shape so much as wanting to set it down precisely as he had heard it, and nearly all his arrangements of folksongs had this quality of improvisation and freedom about them.

This links up in an interesting way with what Grainger said about rhythm in his *Musical News* article quoted earlier. It wasn't at all a strait-jacket, four-in-a-bar kind of intent he had: folk-singing — it was much freer than that. When he wanted a rhythmic piece of course he was perfectly capable of writing it. But his folk-song arrangements were really made, as I understand it, for skilled professionals. One of the most beautiful of all was in fact done for Gervase Elwes — *Six Dukes went a-fishin'.* I will conclude with another quotation from the life of Gervase Elwes. Toward the end of his life he had the great pleasure of having him occasionally as a guest. One of these visits gave him an image of the man that I shall always treasure:

> Percy could never walk downstairs. He had to come bounding down several steps at a time and take a great leap to the bottom. Unfortunately he did it once too often during this visit, sprained his ankle, and had to lie up while I applied hot fomentations at intervals. While thus confined to the house, people were collected from all over the place and brought into his room to sing, as he lay in bed listening and writing down the tunes. One day I went in and found a row of ten singers at least sitting in a circle round the room. Before his foot was really well again he left for a concert tour in Denmark. Despising my offer of the station bus, he leaped on a bicycle and pedalled away with one foot in the air.[4]

CHAPTER FOUR

Impulsive Friend: Grainger and Delius

Lionel Carley

Your things lie so near to my own feelings in life & art that I feel them myself to be a stronger indication of what I feel & stand for than my own things—
Grainger to Delius, 18 September, 1912.

THE summer of 1907 was for Percy Grainger a particularly happy period of his life, spending part of it, as he did, in Norway as Edvard Grieg's guest at the composer's home, Troldhaugen. Grainger, who had been introduced to Grieg in London only the previous year, was now just 25, and some of the boundless energy packed into his slight frame was spent that summer in swimming daily in the fjord, rowing the Griegs across to the opposite shore, or simply walking in the hills that he so much loved. The two men would rehearse the A minor concerto and then go off for long walks together in the surrounding countryside.

The concerto was to be given at the Leeds Festival in October, with Grainger taking the solo role and Grieg conducting, and Grieg was already delighted with his new friend's interpretation of the work. At other times Grainger worked alone at his own compositions, in the tiny log cabin on the shore, just below the house—that hallowed retreat where Grieg had composed many of his great works. The evenings would be spent in the house itself and more often than not Grainger would play for the Griegs: some of the composer's own pieces, but mainly Bach, Brahms and Chopin—and some English folk-songs which Grainger had brought with him and which had excited Grieg's interest.

He had also brought with him from London the score of Delius's *Appalachia,* which Delius had made him promise to show Grieg. This time Delius himself had been unable to spend the summer in Norway, although only a month earlier he had told Grainger: 'I won't swear that I shan't turn up on the steamer when you go to Bergen. If Grieg were only young & well enough to go into the hills we might have a lovely time.'. Delius had long loved the immense peace and beauty of the Norwegian summer mountainscape, remembering with nostalgia the short, light nights and the 'feeling of nature' that he so much admired in the best works of Grieg. 'You have it too', he wrote, '& I think we all 3 have something in common'. Delius's feeling for Norway was, I think, best to be expressed in a letter he wrote to another friend some years later: 'I ... should never think of settling too far ...

from my beloved Norway & the light summer nights & all the poetry & melancholy of the Northern summer & the high mountain plateaus where humans are rare & more individual than in any other country in the world; & where they also have deeper & more silent feelings than any other people'.[1]

Grieg was keenly interested in *Appalachia*, studying the score often during the course of Grainger's stay and listening appreciatively while Grainger played to him extracts from the work; and he was delighted when his guest proposed to write and ask Delius to send over a further copy of the score for him. Grieg would often talk of Delius, always in terms of admiration and affection, for by now they had been intimate friends for almost 20 years. He would, too, recount to Grainger tales of the walking tours that he, Delius and other friends had in the past undertaken together in the Norwegian mountains. However, within a month of Grainger's departure for Denmark, Grieg had died. Grainger had been his last guest and in all probability *Appalachia* the last major new work he had studied.

Inevitably, Grainger was deeply upset over Grieg's death, his attitude to the composer having been one of adulation tempered with an almost filial affection. Perhaps fortunately for his own psychological needs, there was

now a successor to whom this kind of feeling could be transferred: Delius himself, whom he had first met in London in April that year. The qualifications were there in plenty. Delius was old enough to be his father—20 years older, in fact (with the early separation of his parents Grainger had grown up virtually fatherless). Delius had, too, a gift for inspiring close friendships, Grainger soon recognising in him a 'joyous & affirmative nature'. He was, furthermore, a man of notable taste and discernment where the arts generally were concerned, numbering artists of the calibre of Edvard Munch, Rodin and, earlier, Gauguin among his friends. His taste for Nordic life and culture was enthusiastically echoed by Grainger, and the two men were soon to plan (although not ultimately to effect) a joint walking-tour in Norway in 1908. Above all he was a composer of considerable originality, writing, as one conductor had put it, 'sounds which none before him has heard'.

As for Grainger, Delius saw in him a gifted musician who was endowed with a particularly attractive personality: impulsive in his affections, he was striking in appearance and sparkling in company. Writing to his wife shortly after the first meeting, Delius described Grainger as 'a most charming man & more gifted than [Cyril] Scott & less affected, an Australian, you would like him immensely. We all meet at his house on Thursday for music. My concerto & *Appalachia*. ...He is impulsive & nice.'[2] Grieg himself had been unable to resist Grainger's warmth and friendliness at Troldhaugen. 'Grainger was a splendid fellow!' he wrote to his friend, Julius Röntgen. '*How* he played and *how* dear and kind he was!'[3]

It was easy enough, then, to be charmed by Grainger. How much easier still to fall under the spell of his child-like adulation, to be flattered by his praise—praise which could be as naively expressed as it was deeply felt. It could perhaps be said that Delius, without children of his own, needed Grainger almost as much as Grainger needed him. Certainly, when illness and a bitterly early old age were later to take their toll of him, his reliance on the younger man was to grow, both in musicianly and sentimental terms.

Grainger's first contact with Delius's music had come, it seems, in 1906, before he met the man himself, when he saw the full score of *Appalachia* lying on Robin Legge's piano in Chelsea, and he 'started to read the first, a cappella outburst'. 'I was amazed to find that anything so like my own chordal style existed. It struck my mother the same way: "What piece of yours is that?" she called from the next room, taking for granted it was mine, yet not able to recognise it".'

As for Delius's perception and appreciation of Grainger's musicianship, this was certainly in evidence as early as that summer of 1907. His orchestral tour-de-force, *Paris*, had already been arranged for two pianos by Julius Buths, and now Delius wanted a straightforward arrangement for piano: 'I have proposed you to my Editors & if the work interests you perhaps you might undertake it'.[4] He must already have seen the score, published in 1906, of Grainger's fine arrangement of the folksong *Brigg Fair*, even if he had not had an opportunity to hear the work, for by the end of the summer of 1907 his own rhapsodic orchestral variations, based on the same tune, had been completed.

Grainger first heard Delius's *Brigg Fair* at one of its several English performances in 1908 and found it 'adorable', but at the time he was quite

ING PAGE: Percy Grainger with Edvard and Nina Grieg, and Julius Röntgen at dhaugen, August 1907.

unaware of Delius's intention to dedicate the work to him: 'I never told you my deep delight at & thankfulness for your dedication of Brigg Fair to me', he wrote to Delius early in 1911. 'I had no idea you intended doing so & I am delighted & proud to see my name above that glorious poetic work.' As for *Appalachia,* after hearing a full performance of the work for the second time, he told Delius: 'Not only I alone, but every each young composer chap I met that day there all breathed the same phrase: "pure genius".'

Both composers in fact did what they could to promote performances of each other's music. Delius was able to stipulate that some of Grainger's work should be played at the first Festival of the Musical League in 1909, and some time later we find him urging his friend Hermann Suter, conductor at Basel, to perform Grainger's *English Dance.* He was probably instrumental in securing Beecham's performance of the work in February, 1912, at a concert which included his own *Walk to the Paradise Garden.* This latter piece Grainger found quite overwhelming: 'I never loved anything more in my life. You are certainly the greatest living genius & one of the greatest & most adorably touching souls that ever lived. I found that stuff of yours *perfect* in every deepest sense.' Adding: 'Beecham did my thing like a *God*', he signed himself 'Your loving thankful friend'.

Presumably, too, Grainger had Delius to thank for a performing engagement shortly afterwards at Elberfeld, since the conductor of the Elberfeld Concert Society was Hans Haym, an intimate of Delius's, having pioneered his works in Germany.[5] In 1913 we find Delius trying to engineer a performance of some Grainger by Schwickerath in Munich, and later still, on hearing that Schreker was to give his *Father and Daughter* for chorus and orchestra with the Vienna Philharmonic, Grainger suspected Delius's hand at work and wrote: 'Is this due to you, dear friend? If so, a *thousand deepest* thanks.' By now he had got to know *On hearing the first Cuckoo in Spring* and his tribute to the composer was both profound and generous: 'The mood of it & lots of the Dance Rhapsody feel closer to me personally than my own work does, it utterly voices what I most inwardly long to hear expressed or to express'.

Grainger, too, was active in promoting Delius. On a Dutch concert tour, for example, early in 1911, he took the newly-published score of *Brigg Fair* along to Mengelberg, 'but was glad to hear that he knew it well already'. His advocacy of the Piano Concerto is well known; it remained a standard work in Grainger's repertoire throughout his performing life and he gave it all over the world. How odd, then, to find that he did not take it up seriously until the beginning of 1913, when his mother wrote to Jelka Delius to say that Grainger was 'now going to learn it'. In fact it was not till March that year that he even heard a performance of the work, by Evelyn Suart. 'We enjoyed yr concerto . . .', wrote Rose Grainger afterwards, 'but I think it required a Man's power in the loud parts. Percy is practising it at this moment, & it suits him well, he has so much real strength; I long to hear him do it with orchestra.'

They were soon contracting for performances of the work both in England and abroad, although the outbreak of war the following year was to put paid to some promising ventures. However, Grainger performed it under Beecham in April 1914 and felt 'very happy' in it. 'It is a work one loves more & more as one knows it longer.' His agent wrote to Mengelberg to tell the conductor of Grainger's wish to undertake the concerto when next in Holland, and Grainger too urged Delius: 'When you see conductors abroad with whom you would like me to do the work I wish you would mention the matter to them, as I very much want to play it *everywhere* I can. You are now getting so universally loved & honored everywhere & the time seems to me just ripe for the lovely concerto to come into its own.'

Such letters gave Delius a lot of pleasure: 'You are always the one who sends me such good news from England—I love your impulsive letters—they are so entirely yourself & just like your music which you know I love so much. I feel we have an enormous lot in common & that you understand better than anyone what I am trying to do.'

Rose Grainger corresponded quite frequently with the Deliuses, and a clue to one facet of her son's personality is readily supplied by her letters. 'Dear little Beecham', she writes, 'was here last night & was telling Percy all his plans, wonderful aren't they?' And in 1917, after her son had joined the US Army as a bandsman (2nd class!), we find her writing to Delius in the following terms: 'Percy read me your dear letter to him & we both shed a few tears & felt very grateful & touched by your & your dear wife's affection for him. He loves you and admires you and your work so enormously . . . You can imagine how I hope this wicked, cruel war will end, & how I hope my beloved one's life will be spared so that he can go on doing more of the work he loves & which gives so much joy to his fellow-beings.'

There was a degree of preciousness—for want of a better word—in Rose Grainger that could scarcely have failed to have an effect on her son. She was, after all, his constant and solicitous companion until he was over 40 and there was no question of marriage until after she was gone. The maternal apron-strings were tied about an uncomplaining son. In fact quite the reverse, Grainger willingly acquiescing while his mother took the lead in promoting his career. And with so much vested in her it is no wonder that when her untimely death came, he was left shocked, alone and vulnerable. From very early on the precious quality of Grainger's prose left very little doubt as to where it had derived from: 'Isn't it too sad, darling sweet little Grieg's death? I had such an unspeakably happy & uplifting time with them.' His letters to the Deliuses, as to other intimate friends, are liberally peppered with terms of endearment, from 'dearest friend' to 'darling Delius'; and he would, for example, sign off with 'Reverently & lovingly yours', 'Ever worshippingly', or on one occasion 'With thousands of untold loving and admiratious thots'.

It would, however, be too easy to make fun of Grainger on this account. His language was in a sense the penalty of that excessively maternal environment and anyway had its compensations in turns of expression that were fresh, original and felicitious, as students of his scores will know. The contrast with Delius's written style is particularly striking. Delius was never able to write really informally and his English often seems quite antiquated: something that tended to be reflected in his own operatic libretti. There was a dry, laconic quality in his prose expression, and his frequently stilted sentences do not often achieve any real rhythm or flow. Grainger himself noticed Delius's odd 'lack of ear' for language: 'His German & Scandinavian were as motheaten as his English. I think he grew up in a home where no language was mastered.'[6]

With the advent of war the Graingers, mother and son, decided to leave England for America, and in October 1914 they were settling down in New York, soon urging the Deliuses to follow them. Grainger rapidly established himself as a concert pianist, to the extent of being able to tell Delius in April 1915: 'My pianistic success here has been simply *tremendous,* & next winter I shall be having almost more to do than I can manage'. In the space of seven years following his arrival, quite apart from swiftly achieving the status of a 'star' performer, he joined the US Army, became a naturalised American and, finally, bought the house at White Plains which was to remain his home until his death in 1961.

He soon became aware that in contrast to the position in Europe, Delius was little-known in America: 'I don't think your things are being pushed here at all'. However, thanks to his own meteoric rise to American fame, he was soon able with relish to set about promoting Delius. Grainger had, of course, one quality which Delius—at least by comparison—lacked: he was an inveterate and energetic self-publicist. Why not? He had rare enough talents to promote after all. And why not by extension publicise the genius of Delius, who seemed rapidly to be becoming his *alter ego?*

In 1915 he expertly and artfully combined the two crusades. Booked to play the Delius concerto in November with the New York Philharmonic, he wrote to Delius some time in advance. Some form of publicity could usefully be placed in the American press. This Grainger would see to, and he therefore asked Delius to send him a letter along the following lines: 'It is a great joy for me that it will be *you* who will introduce my Piano Concerto to America. Your perfect performance of my work at the various Festivals remain in my memory as singularly satisfying feats, of true interpretative genius. I only wish I could be in New York to hear you do it! You are that rare phenomenon: a musician who is equally great as a creator and as an executant.' Grainger continued:'Could you write me this, or something *short* similar (laying the jam on pretty thick as I have, as U.S.A. needs this!) in a letter, so that I could show it in your writing *if need be?* If you would do me this kindness, kindly let these sentences occur on pages the whole of which could be perused by outsiders, if need be!'

There can be no doubt that Grainger expended a great deal of time and selfless effort on Delius's behalf in America. 'I want to do my part in establishing you here as one of the greatest of the greatest', he told Delius at the outset of his crusade; and before long his efforts were well under way and bearing fruit. He wrote articles for the musical papers, referring to Delius wherever possible, although he soon wisely dropped his initial references to the composer as being 'Anglo-German'.[7] He badgered Delius's American publishers for scores, which he had soon found were almost unobtainable on the other side of the Atlantic. He wrote to Europe and to Delius himself for printed music. A piece of advice he gave to Delius was for the composer to get his publishers to cut down the exceptionally high performing fees they were charging for his works. He got in touch with conductors such as Damrosch, Stransky and Stokowski, Stock in Chicago, Oberhoffer in Minneapolis, and Tandler in Los Angeles, with the result that they all agreed to play works by

Delius. He sent the young Stokowski, already a 'big bug here', a score of the *Dance Rhapsody* and was delighted when Stokowski immediately agreed to do it in October 1915. However, Stokowski unfortunately had to put off the work, apparently on account of his failure to procure a baritone oboe from Paris in time for the performance, but it is interesting to note that about a year later he was able to inform a correspondent that he knew most of the scores of Delius's orchestral works and that having been unable to obtain a full score of *A Mass of Life,* he had been studying for a week the piano score of this 'monumental work' with deep interest. 'Percy Grainger and I', he wrote, 'have often discussed Delius, and I am hoping soon to hear him play his piano concerto'.[8]

At the beginning of the war the Deliuses, too, seriously considered going to America. Initially they were particularly encouraged to do so by the Graingers themselves: 'We wish you were both over here, now', Rose Grainger had written in that first October. 'We like New York & Boston very much.' And in November Grainger assured Delius: 'We were ... beside ourselves with joy at the thought of your coming over here! What times we could have together, it would be divine. Europe is no place to stay in any more.' He discussed transatlantic routes, New York hotels and concert possibilities. Delius obviously had it in mind to conduct some of his own works, but perhaps fortunately, in view of his inadequacy in this sphere, he was warned by Grainger that Americans apparently did not particularly go in for conductor-composers. However, 'we are *longing for you both to come* & do so hope you really will', he asserted; ' ... you could push your immortal works by coming and incidentally rejoice our hearts'.

In fact, Grainger was no doubt guilty of raising the Deliuses' hopes too high, for by the middle of 1915 he was now warning his friend not to risk crossing the Atlantic until the war was over: 'What is a year sooner or later compared with the preciousness of your life?' By the summer of 1916 Delius was growing more persistent, Grainger, however, finding further reasons for counselling delay, at least until the war was over. Above all, Delius's music was more or less sold out in America (during the war further stocks could not be procured from Europe), so that if he came over there would be a brief boom, with people trying to buy his scores and failing, 'and the whole enthusiasm would not come to its full blossoming'.

Delius had still not relinquished the dream of a return to America in 1917, hoping that both Muck and Stokowski would perform *A Mass of Life* during the coming season, and fully intending to be present. He even cherished the idea that the Metropolitan Opera might give *A Village Romeo and Juliet* in the autumn; he and Jelka would stay in New York for a while. But by that summer Grainger was in the army, writing at about the time of his enlistment: 'Everything is uncertain now & I don't know whether I shall have to go to Canada or England or where. Should anything happen to me, & you & I not meet again, know that I have loved you & yr art truly, have realized that you are one of the greatest musical geniuses of all time, & have responded to you passionately, both on artistic & personal lines ... I did not write, because all was so uncertain, I did not know how to advise you re a visit to U.S.A.' Grainger had joined the army only two weeks after hearing of his father's death. In fact his father had been ill for years and, paralysed as he was, needed constant nursing and medical attention. His death was obviously a release for the son, who in spite of the long family separation had supported him financially through a particularly prolonged and costly illness.

The Deliuses accepted Grainger's appraisal of the situation without demur, Jelka understanding well that no better-informed advice could come from elsewhere. 'Grainger is a genius for practical Art-exploitation', she wrote to her friend Marie Clews in October 1916. Marie was the wealthy wife of Delius's American sculptor friend Henry Clews, and although both were now living mainly in France, they too were in touch with influential friends on the American musical scene on Delius's behalf.

Delius returned to the American theme in the summer of 1918: 'We are seriously thinking of coming to America in the Autumn'. Again the project foundered, but Grainger soon reverted to all the old enthusiasm. 'I think the time will be ripe for you next season (winter 1919-20) . . . They are just ready for you now, and I believe you would meet with a ripping reception if you came then.' Unfortunately, the war had taxed Delius heavily in financial terms and his health was now giving him more cause for concern. The dream slowly receded and by 1924, when Grainger made a final bid to get the Deliuses to join him, offering to help pay for the trip across and placing his house at their disposal, it was all too late. Delius would never be able to return to the land where in his younger days, long ago, he had spent perhaps the most carefree time of his life.

America was not of course the making of Grainger, for by 1914 he had already well established a name for himself in Europe. But because of the war he was for the first time able to put down roots and at least for a while to enjoy a temporary break from the exhausting round of concert tours which had taken him around much of the world since the beginning of the century. However, it was not in his nature to stay still for long, and he was soon engaged on tours across the length and breadth of North America. The Delius concerto figured largely in his programmes and, as in Europe, he would be off to hear performances of Delius's works whenever he had the opportunity.

Grainger always maintained that his concert tours were undertaken with the express intention of making sufficient money in as short a time as possible to enable him to retire and devote himself to composition; but he was perfectly aware now that this could yet take years and that his urge to compose demanded some sort of response, however heavy the demands such a response might make on his time and energy. Inevitably he was to complain of overwork, telling Delius in September 1916: 'Bringing out a new orchestral Suite (4 movements), 10 new piano pieces, 4 pieces for 2 pianos, & 2 other trifles is no light matter when one designs all one's own covers & has a vast pianistic winter ahead . . . I am very hard at work on my *The Warriors* long orchestral piece, to be dedicated to you if I like it well enough.' Early the following summer, after hearing this, his largest work, in rehearsal, he wrote to tell Delius: 'in many ways, I look upon it as my best orchestral work in large form, & feel it is truly emotional & also truly orchestral in feeling. Therefore I am dedicating it to you, hoping you will find things to like in the work when you hear it. With it goes the deep and true love & reverence for you & your touching art that I have felt ever since coming in contact with both. The thrills I have felt through our music, dear friend, have been some of the deepest & keenest feelings of my life.'

Overworked he may have been, but he was happy in America, as his decision to take out American citizenship in June 1918 indicates. 'I just love my life here', he wrote to Delius at the end of that year; 'I have never been so happy, hopeful and satisfied anywhere'. And he had developed a real interest in American music: 'In 5 or 10 years time it will be in full blast compositionally. John Alden Carpenter and Howard Brockway are real geniuses to my mind, and there are 3 negro composers of the real stuff in smaller forms: W N Cook, Dett and Diton.'

In August 1918, Delius drew up a will in which Grainger was named as one of three executors, the others being Balfour Gardiner and Philip Heseltine. Henry and Marie Clews were witnesses. Later superseded, this will directed that in the event of the simultaneous deaths of Delius and his wife, a fund was to be created from which awards of £200 a year were to be made to young English composers.

The 1920s brought in musical terms a new dimension to the relationship between Delius and Grainger. This was initiated by Grainger, writing in 1921 from the home at White Plains into which he and his mother had recently moved:

> Has your 1st Dance Rhapsody ever been arranged for 2 pianos? I love it most of *all* modern works, and long to arrange it for 2 pianos. I think I arrange mighty well for 2 pianos (have had lots of practice the last few years) and could make a really fine job of it. But I don't want to do it if it's already been done. I would be willing to hand it over to your publishers and do not want any payment for my arrangement. I just *long to see such a modern classic as that piece is available for 2 pianos*—which I regard as a good study-medium for modern works.

It would have been difficult for Delius not to accept this generous offer; and the arrangement was in fact completed in 1922 and published the following year, Delius finding it 'so wonderfully good'.[9]

In London late in 1922, still distressed by his mother's death, Grainger heard Delius's *The Song of the High Hills* for the first time and was deeply affected by it. A source of inspiration for the piece had lain in his own similarly-named work, the *Hill Song No 1*. 'I think it is one of my works in which I have expressed myself most completely', Delius told him. 'When you tell me that on hearing it your great sorrow was appeased, then I feel that that is the highest appreciation possible'. Before long Delius had given him a copy of the score and Grainger was again at work on an arrangement for two pianos, which he completed in December 1923.[10] Two years later, incidentally, Grainger was able to tell Delius that he had contracted to conduct the work in Los Angeles. The only other arrangement of Delius known to have been made by Grainger was of the *Air and Dance,* this time for piano solo.[11]

One of the several post-war meetings of the two men was in Frankfurt, where the Deliuses spent much of the winter of 1922/3. Delius was at this time still under the misapprehension that he had been born in 1863—a year later than his actual birthdate, as he was shortly to discover—and friendly musicians, poets and painters in Frankfurt arranged to give a chamber concert for him in celebration of his 60th birthday. Grainger was one of the performers and played several of his own works. He was, too, involved in a second celebratory concert.

While in Frankfurt, Delius arranged for the publication of Grainger's *Marching Song of Democracy* and *Hill Song No 1,* and attended rehearsals of some of his friend's works, including *The Warriors.* They were together often, and Delius's enthusiasm for Grainger's playing was boundless:

> How kind of you to offer to play for me! I will tell you quite frankly that I very seldom have had such pleasure from piano playing as I have from yours. I find it so extremely musical, masterly, and without the slightest affectation or pose. Your delicate nuancing is quite a revelation to me: for years I have heard nothing but thump, thump, thump! I can only say that you cannot play too often for me, and I am only afraid of abusing your kindness.
>
> Do come again soon and pay me a lot more Grieg, some of which I do not even known and some more Bach—I got such a thrill over the Bach the other night and Jelka loved it so much too!

Delius's signature was appended to this letter which, like all the composer's letters from now on, was written by dictation to his wife.

The Deliuses were to spend part of the summer of 1923 at their chalet in the Norwegian mountains, and they pleaded to Grainger to join them there.[12] Jelka wrote to him at the end of April: 'Fred says he will not invite another guest to Lesjaskog—if he cannot have you, he will have nobody, but he feels you will come'. Come he did, and during the course of his stay he actually composed late in July a little of the incidental music to *Hassan.* Delius's score was virtually complete, but Basil Dean, who was to present Flecker's play with Delius's music at His Majesty's Theatre in September, wanted some three minutes more music for a ballet section. Grainger familiarised himself with the rest of the score and then composed and scored the short passage required. According to Grainger himself, this was the sum of his contribution to *Hassan.*[13]

Grainger's physical abilities, too, were put to good use at Lesjaskog, for he helped to carry Delius on an improvised litter up to one of the mountain summits nearby. In the grandeur of the Norwegian fell landscape the composer, whose eyesight was declining, was able to drink in the view of the sun setting over the distant mountains, an experience he was never to have again. Jelka helped too, but acknowledged that 'without your glorious energy and devotion Fred would never have been taken to the top'. A letter she wrote to Marie Clews on 4 August describes the experience:

> We have the visit of Percy Grainger, who is such a dear and delightful friend, and so devoted to Fred. Just fancy, what he did: Fred was *longing* to go up the mountain side and up a high mountain back of our hut, because there is a heavenly view on the High Snow-mountains and a great solitude with no human trace up there. So Percy arranged a chair[14] and two poles thro' it and straps and ropes for us all three, Percy in front, Senta and I at the back, all strapped in like horses and so we carried Fred up to the top and down again. With wraps and overcoat, our lunch etc. to carry it was an awfully heavy job. But we could not get any Norwegians to do it. It took us 7½ hours, as we had to rest so often and we had to go over stones and rocks, up the steep mountain, thro' snowfields, rainclouds, bogs, becks—a tremendous job. I cannot boast for myself as Percy and Senta had the heaviest carrying; but being quite out of training I found it all I could do. But we came home in triumph at 9 p.m. having been watched from below with telescopes and

Percy Grainger and Frederick Delius outside 12 Domplatz, Frankfurt,
5 April 1923. (Snapshot by Butzie Schumaker.)

marvelled at by the inhabitants, Fred very cold and tired, but all the better for the beloved mountain-air and sight and we all rather stiff but alright next day.

After an extended stay in Europe, Grainger was planning to return to America, with the prospect of a lonely homecoming to White Plains and memories of his mother. After having spent so much time together with him since the spring, the Deliuses greatly missed him when he had gone, and Jelka was moved to write: 'We do belong together all three, and Fred loves you and your music so intensely, as nobody else's'. One wonders to what extent during these months Jelka Delius was helping to fill, knowingly or not, the psychological gap left by Rose Grainger's death. She had, after all, considerable strength of character and great resilience—without her love and attention during the last years, Delius would never have lasted so long. She told Grainger gently but firmly that although it would be difficult for him, he would have to work himself out of his loneliness and worry. Although Grainger hated the idea of returning to the empty house at White Plains, he was unwilling to come and live with his friends at Grez-sur-Loing. Delius had offered to employ him in any capacity which would have allowed both men to continue writing their music, but Grainger, wisely conscious of his own need for some sort of independence, declined.

Hassan, in its first London production in September 1923, did enormously well and more than anything else helped to set the Deliuses on an even keel financially. *'Our* ballet piece was a *great success',* wrote Delius, on returning to Grez from London, adding: 'In the ballet you brought in that rhythmical vigour which contrasted so well to the first part. I wish you could have heard it. It really came off splendidly'.

Thanks, no doubt, mainly to the additional income from *Hassan,* the Deliuses were able to spend the winter of 1923/4 relatively comfortably on the Italian and French Rivieras. They wrote to Grainger in January: 'We are sitting in the sunshine on the terrace of our Villa overlooking the beautiful bay of Rapallo and talking of you, and we were wondering whether *ever* any other composer had met with a colleague and friend like you, so devoted and interested in his friend's work and understanding it thro' his own genius'.

News of Grainger's success in America as a conductor cheered the Deliuses in the spring of 1924, part of which they spent uneasily at a German spa looking for a cure for Delius's incipient blindness and paralysis. Returning there the following spring their greater—if short-lived—optimism was compounded by news from Grainger announcing his intention of coming to stay with them at Grez in the summer. It is odd to think that after all this time Grainger had still not visited them at their home in the French countryside. Before the war they had only met when the Deliuses visited England, and afterwards, apparently, only in Germany and Norway. Jelka grasped at Grainger's coming like a straw in the wind. The worry and anxiety she now constantly faced with her physically helpless husband and the round of doctors and cures were taking their toll of her. It was a lonely responsibility and she often felt dispirited and distressed at what she felt was her inadequacy to discharge it fully, to minister to all Delius's needs. What she described as Grainger's 'enlivening and sympathetic' presence would be a tremendous gift to her and his musical help a tonic to Delius. She was not to be

OVE: The chair adapted by Grainger to carry Delius to the top of Hørda-Lia in 1923.
...otographed by Lionel Carley at Øverli farm, Lesjaskog, May 1976.)

... Ström, Jelka Delius and Percy
...inger, Grez-sur-Loing, 1927.

disappointed and Grainger brightened the August of 1925 for them immensely. Balfour Gardiner came too and together these friends played two-piano and piano-duet arrangements of Delius's works to the increasingly housebound composer. Grainger left at the end of the month and on the day of his departure Jelka wrote to Marie Clews: 'He has been delightful'. A few days later she sat down to thank him for having come:

> Needless to say we missed you terribly; I thought I missed you most, but Fred missed you so much too . . . it is absolutely certain now that this great festival of friendship and music did him no end of good. He even once or twice has *seen* some little movement, or a figure going by like a shadow.
> There are no words that could express my gratefulness for this beautiful gift of your precious time you so generously gave us. No help could have been better or more welcome; it has been one of the beautiful things in life.

Grainger now had to give to his relationship with Delius more than he could ever hope to take from it, and it is to his eternal credit that over the following years he was to make further summer visits to Grez and to write frequent letters, while many of the Deliuses' former friends quietly faded into the background. The old pleasures had to be diluted to accommodate the needs of the invalid and Grainger's undimmed energies to be subdued to the increasingly clinical routine of the household. The hours devoted to playing to Delius were innumerable, like the miles covered pushing his friend in a wheelchair along the country roads out of Grez.

Sentimentally Grainger's life was taking a new turn and in 1927, in company with Balfour Gardiner, he brought Ella Ström, his future wife, to Grez for a first memorable visit. They married in 1928, Grainger finding in this vivacious and artistic woman a settling influence he had needed for some years. She, no less than Jelka, was to prove an ideal choice as a musician's wife, accepting the subordination of a part of her own artistic personality to a talent that was greater than her own, and spending the rest of her life helping to perform and promote her husband's music.

When separated from Grainger the Deliuses could now be reminded of his musicianship by purely mechanical means. They had one of the best gramophones available and on this they could play the records he brought or sent to them, not only of his own music but of Joseph Taylor's singing and, too, of more popular American pieces that he apparently sometimes included. They had a radio that was sufficiently powerful for them to pick up broadcasts from English as well as from other European stations, and Jelka would go carefully through the *Radio Times* each week, noting concerts of interest and even taking cuttings of details of Grainger broadcasts which she would send to White Plains to add to their friend's enormous collection of references to performances of his own works.

For a time they were loaned by the Aeolian Company a splendid Duo-Art reproducing piano, on which they were able to play rolls made by Grainger both of his own and Delius's works. They were able to listen several times to *The Warriors,* but their greatest pleasure undoubtedly lay in Grainger's recordings, made with fellow-pianist Ralph Leopold, of *Brigg Fair* and *North Country Sketches.* Both were marvellously performed, so sensitively indeed that it might be said that the orchestral colouring and texture of the works are hardly missed, particularly perhaps in *Brigg Fair;* and it is good

FACING PAGE: Percy Grainger, Balfour Gardiner and Ella Ström, Grez-sur-Loing, 1

news that they have been re-recorded for the gramophone, to reach the wider audience they deserve. It seems that a projected piano-roll recording by Grainger of the first *Dance Rhapsody* never materialised, and the only other Grainger/Delius legacy we have in this sphere is a curious one: the piano arrangement, by Otto Singer, of the orchestral score of Delius's Piano Concerto. There can be little doubt that Grainger must have intended this to be married to the solo part, but there is no evidence to suggest that he ever cut the complementary roll—a sad consideration when one remembers that the Delius concerto came second only to that of Grieg in his repertoire and that his personal identification with it was so close.[15] There is, incidentally, an interesting echo of Delius's endorsement of Grainger's first American performance of the Piano Concerto (I refer to that already-noted eulogy written at Grainger's request in 1915) in a similar request to the composer in 1928 to write to the Aeolian Company in praise of the *Brigg Fair* and *North Country Sketches* rolls. This requirement was fulfilled by the Deliuses with enthusiasm.

Grainger's assessment of Delius's genius remained quite undiluted in its commitment and fervour. 'In my judgement', he wrote in 1927, 'Delius looms not only as undoubtedly the greatest of all living composers, not only as the greatest British composer of any period, but as one of the five or six transcending creative musical giants of all time—alongside Bach, Handel, Beethoven, Chopin and Wagner'.[16]

It was in 1928 that the last subtle change in the ever-dynamic relationship between Percy Grainger and the Deliuses was ushered in. The 'calm and almost posthumous existence' that Jelka had wryly acknowledged she and her husband were leading by the beginning of that year was transformed when in August a shy young musician from Yorkshire volunteered to come to Grez to help Delius write by dictation the music that some people, not least the composer himself, knew was still in him.

Eric Fenby was in his early twenties and had felt, just as Grainger had felt a score of years before him, an extraordinary kinship with and reverence for Delius's music from the moment he first heard it. But he met at Grez someone who was vastly different from the man Grainger had met for the first time in London so much earlier. Delius's gradual physical breakdown had somehow brought with it a harder edge to his character—a cutting edge that was certainly unattractive to those who had seen it developing. In his younger days Delius could certainly find harsh words, although more usually expressed in private, for the humbug and the charlatan—two favourite terms of his—but Grainger's memories of him were essentially of his predominantly sunny side. He found Delius's outstanding qualities to be 'his playfulness and gaiety, & his mischievousness'.

Delius's spirit during those last years was indomitable and in a sense heroic on a grand scale, and his mind was to remain alert almost to the end. Yet he could be cruel or caustic. In 1929, for example, after listening to the performance of *A Mass of Life* at Beecham's Delius Festival in London, he calmly announced to an artist who was sketching him: 'Henry Wood would ruin it—he is finished'.[17] And yet it had been Wood who had first championed his work in England. Whether this kind of harshness can be explained as a direct result of his illness, or whether it was perhaps

FACING PAGE: Delius and Grainger, Grez-sur-Loing, late 19

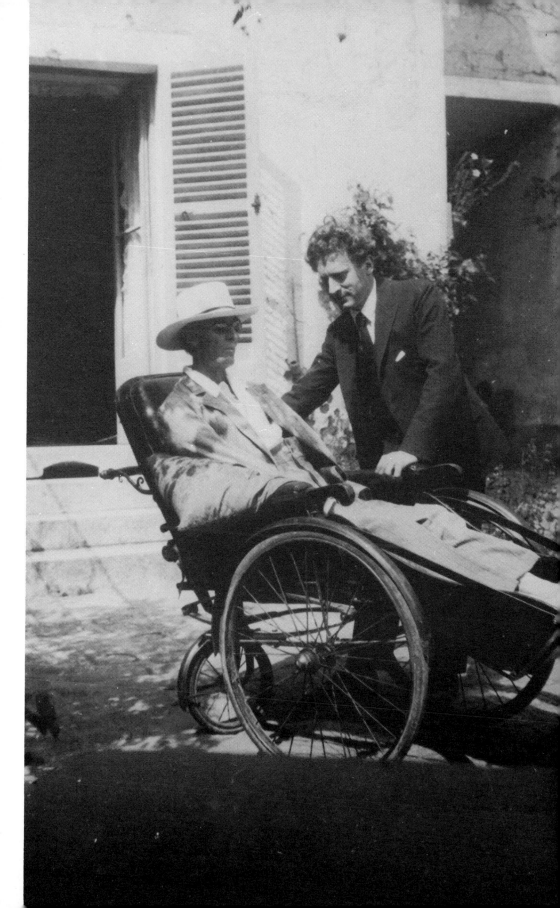

more of a psychological phenomenon, almost deliberately cultivated in compensation for the wasting of purely physical faculties, may one day be discussed more fully. But it was a part of the later Delius that Grainger was never seriously to resent or feel the need to accept with anything other than good grace.

Fenby now took on the role that Jelka had inwardly hoped Grainger might still play, and after intense initial difficulties began to live out an unparalleled labour of love that was to last until Delius's death and, indeed, long beyond. Slowly and painfully, after years of silence, Delius began to compose again. Grainger came to stay for a while in the summer of 1929, working at Grez on his *Hill Song No 2* and playing duets with Fenby to the Deliuses. He was conscious that in some ways he was not actually needed any more, but his principal reaction to this was one of pleasure that Delius could now be so relatively active again. Delius's growing acerbity was occasionally in evidence. 'Before you came to Grez', Grainger wrote later to Fenby:

Fred always behaved nicely to me & Balfour. But with you there he behaved abominably. And I was *so delighted* to see it. It showed *how much he valued yr devotion & help*. His behaviour to B. and me clearly said: "You boys could only give me 2 days or 10 days at a time. Now I have a young friend who gives me *all* his time. To Hell with you!" That *bragging* attitude showed me that he was still young & happy in his mind.

Delius would poke fun at Grainger's vegetarian and teetotal diet: 'Why don't you enjoy a nice mug of ale and a good beefsteak? Why don't you enjoy yourself while you can?' Grainger inevitably gave as good as he got and arguments would be more impassioned than they had been in the past. But neither man took such things seriously for long. Jelka, sensitive to undercurrents in the relationship, wrote: 'One talks sometimes of such nonsensical things . . . but these are only *words* and underneath that which we really think and feel goes on subconsciously'.

Grainger had changed too, and was much more preoccupied with matters affecting his own career—a further reason for being glad that Fenby was relieving him so effectively of the responsibilities he had always felt towards the Deliuses. He felt that in a way he had 'behaved badly' to Delius and in one of the last extant letters that he wrote to his friends, in 1932, he tried to explain more fully his feelings:

The full measure of my love and reverence for you & your art is not evident when I am with you, because of my annoying ways and manners and my argumentativeness. What I feel is not well expressed in my daily behaviour and particularly has this been the case of late years.

Jelka, in replying, showed that she fully understood the reasons for this 'argumentativeness':

Your thoughtful and deeply affectionate letter went right to our hearts. It is true that in the throes of a real meeting one is often curiously aloof and unmanageable and that in one's solitude [one] often feels so much nearer to those one loves and always *will* love deep down in one's nature.

In 1934 Delius died. Grainger was dismayed that the house at Grez was sold after Jelka's death the following year, having felt strongly that it should have been turned into a 'Delius Museum', with everything being kept just as

nger in the Delius's garden at Grez, 1925 (?).

it was when the composer was alive. However, his own collection of Delius letters, scores and iconographic material greatly increased after his friend's death, and much of this is now housed at the Grainger Centre in Melbourne, although there are papers of interest at White Plains as well as in the Delius Trust's London archive and in the Library of Congress.*[18] We can leave to Grainger himself the last word:

> Delius was, above all things, extremely *playful* and an inveterate tease. Delius was a man of leisure (so that he had plenty of time for fun), a man of cosmopolitan experience from his birth (so that he never took any customs or opinions too seriously) and always a man of simple practical sense. He had a very fatherly streak in his nature and liked to be *helpful*—I have seldom met anyone more helpful and benevolent. His and my relations to each other seemed to me singularly satisfying—at least they always were to me. Although he was 20 years older than I, there never seemed to me any age discrepancy between us. Maybe this was partly because I was developed as a composer so very early (at the age of 16) while Delius was so late in developing as a composer. Thus we both of us reached our compositional maturity at about the same time—around 1898 . . . Our relationship was . . . always *mutually* helpful and life-giving.[19]

* See David Tall's chapter on Sources for Grainger Research, p 203.

ABOVE: Grainger rowing on the Loing at Grez, 1925 (

CHAPTER FIVE

Grainger and Frankfurt

Cyril Scott

Between 1916 and 1961 the composer Cyril Scott published a number of accounts of memories of Percy Grainger and the 'Frankfurt Gang' during his student days at the turn of the century. Among the Grainger papers at the Library of Congress (now in process of being transferred to the Grainger Museum in Melbourne) is an 83-page unpublished manuscript on this subject. The following has been selected from this source, which is dated October 1936. Percy Grainger and his friends were still alive when this was written; Scott's tenses have been retained as in the original.

Percy Grainger is one of those men who does not believe in silence; he believes in truth, with its admixture of the pleasant and the unpleasant, the intimate and the impersonal. But then Grainger possesses an almost phenomenal love of detail. For this reason, where on countless points other men would be silent, he is discursive. His compositions are headed with prefatory letter-press. He even notes in his diary the precise hour that visitors arrive and leave him. The time of an arriving or departing train which bears one of his many guests is a circumstance worthy of note in his detail-loving brain.

Grainger's pronounced love of detail is highly significant and much contributes to an understanding of his lovable yet many-sided and complicated personality. Unless this love of detail in his character be fully recognised and comprehended, Grainger may go down to posterity as one of the most egotistical composers of the present epoch. For the man who is not content to immortalise himself solely through his works but must needs subsidise a museum largely to that end is, apart from other considerations, in serious danger of being deemed an egotist. Yet the following must not be overlooked; in addition to his intense love of detail, which, as I have shown, accounts for much, there is also his intense love for the country of his birth, which, in his case, amounts well-nigh to a passion.

When I first met Grainger, some forty years ago, I regarded this exaggerated patriotism as merely a youthful enthusiasm to be out-grown as the years went by. But I was doomed to be wrong. Although Grainger has in the interim become an American citizen, his love for Australia and its enrichment is as passionate as when he was but fourteen years old.

It was not long before young Grainger appeared at my rooms one afternoon with a composition under his arm; this he proceeded to play to me with considerable enthusiasm and a fine command of the piano. It proved to be Handelian in character, and that is all about it that I can remember. One of the remarkable features about Grainger's Muse is the fact that he reached a great measure of maturity while still in his teens. The next composition of his that I was destined to see was already 'Graingerian': he had, in short, achieved his own individual style in a phenominally short time.

Then he discovered Kipling, and, as I have written elsewhere, that author and poet exercised a marked influence on his creative output. His song *The Men of the Sea,* which he wrote a year or two later, remains across the years not only a most beautiful composition, but breathes the true Kipling-spirit to perfection. No poet and composer have been so suitably 'wedded' since Heine and Schumann, than Kipling and Grainger. Kipling transformed the colloquial into poetry; Grainger transformed what may be termed the colloquial in music into a work of art. Unlike some composers, he has no fear of the flagrantly melodic and the obvious; he believes in making a direct appeal and giving the listener something to catch hold of at the outset.

Grainger shared, at any rate latterly, neither affection nor admiration for Iwan Knorr, his composition professor; he maintained that Knorr imparted to him little of value, and that it was really 'old Klimsch', Karl Klimsch, an amateur musician, who greatly influenced Grainger, who taught him how to compose. The old man said in effect 'say what you have to say plainly and directly, and avoid all messing about.' I remember a fragment for string quartet which he wrote at the time and called *Der Pfeifende Reiter* ('The Whistling Horseman'), there being something distinctly equestrian about its rhythm. It was a lively, inspiring affair of a somewhat obvious type; but the curious part about it was that its bass sounded all wrong to our then unmodernised ears. Knorr, somewhat amused, more or less dismissed it as bad nonsense, and even I, admirer of Grainger that I was, seem to recollect remonstrating with him. But undaunted he stuck to his guns, and was not to be deflected from the particular path he had chosen for himself.

Meanwhile, Grainger was working to become a pianist under the guidance of Professor James Kwast. I always remember this bearded little man as wearing a light buff-coloured suit of which the trousers had so materially shrunk that he was obliged to let them down to their fullest capacity. This gave him a fullness in the seat and a shortness in the leg which suggested an elephant's posterior. Indeed, apart from Herr (Lazzaro) Uzielli and Professor Hugo Becker, the cellist, I must say all the professors at the Conservatoire showed a lamentable taste in dress, and perhaps the worst example was the Herr Direktor himself. Over his light, bile-coloured trousers and waistcoat, he would wear a long black frock coat that flapped about as he shuffled along and which appeared to have no lining.

Grainger, under the tuition of Kwast, was soon proficient enough to play Mozart's A major Piano Concerto with orchestra at one of the Conservatoire concerts.

There was one composition, I remember, that he brought me which he had called *The Long Serpent* after the Viking boat which figures in Longfellow's epic (for Grainger had acquired an admiration for Longfellow as well as for Kipling.) This composition, which certainly had a marine flavour about it, gave me a sort of forbidden pleasure in that I greatly liked it but at the same time regarded it as frivolous and undignified. The curious thing in connection with it, however, was the fact that, in Grainger's own words, it was inspired by the Pilgrim's Chorus from *Tannhauser*. I remember this admission on Grainger's part gave me intense amusement, for I could see no resemblance between the two 'tunes'. Wagner's was sedate and tinctured with religiosity, Grainger's jocose and horn-pipish.

When Grainger settled in England it was characteristic of his generous nature to see how he could help his friends along the path to fame in company with himself. I had composed a bravura piece for piano called *An English Waltz* and no sooner had he contrived to get himself engaged for a

Cyril Scott, Roger Quilter and Percy Grainger at the Harrogate Festival, 1929.

tour with the celebrated singer Adelina Patti, than he arranged to play the waltz in question.

Meanwhile, Grainger and Quilter had collected a bevy of people together to sing his choruses, one of which was called *The Londonderry Air.* These choral practices took place in an elegant drawing-room overlooking the Thames, and one of the singers was Balfour Gardiner. I mention him especially because he averred that the only way he could contrive to sing his particular part was to stop up his ears so as not to be put off his shot by the others singing theirs.

Grainger influenced me, not so much by the colour and texture of his music as by his ideas. To him I first certainly owed the idea of writing in irregular rhythm. Why should a piece be in $\frac{4}{4}$, $\frac{3}{4}$ or $\frac{6}{8}$ time? Why should it not be in various times, a $\frac{3}{4}$ bar followed by a $\frac{5}{8}$, a $\frac{5}{4}$ or what-not? Why, in fact, should there not be a sort of prose-music just as there is a free-verse type of poetry in contradistinction to that written in regular metre? This, in fact, was the theory Grainger expounded to me. He even went so far as to picture a mechanical device which would obviate the necessity for bar-lines altogether, in that each orchestral player would simply play from a strip of music passing across a given space at a given time, somewhat after the fashion of a pianola roll.

And as regards Grainger's manifold arrangements of folk-songs, granted that through them he has reaped a somewhat inconvenient reputation, there is no doubt he was an inventor along this line of musical activity and treated his material in a manner no one to my knowledge had ever treated it previously. What with his particular employment of polyphony and his very individual harmonies the folksong underwent a new birth at his hands.

Then there is his treatment of that old form the passacaglia, which he employs in his most original orchestral work, *Green Bushes*—also a folk tune. Then there is *Father and Daughter,* that most original and thrilling work for male quintet, chorus and orchestra, including guitars. I shall never forget the effect this produced when first performed at the Balfour Gardiner Concerts. The climax was electrifying, and one can only feel a deep regret that the work has been so seldom performed since.

Although Grainger's chief emotional characteristic is his pronounced virility, yet at moments he can be very gentle and touching, as in his *Died for Love* and *My Robin is to the Greenwood Gone.* Another work in which the gentler side of his nature becomes apparent is his *Song of Solomon,* a choral composition replete with melodic beauty of a touching and appealing type. There is no false orientalism or cheap local colour in this work—devices to which a mediocre composer might have had recourse—but it breathes the true spirit of the words in a way that is completely satisfying to one's artistic imagination. It shows convincingly that Grainger *can* create melodies of his own, and however often he may elect to arrange already-made melodies in the form of folksongs, they are not indispensable to him.

Grainger is the first composer to combine a direct appeal to the masses and great artistic capability. He is the composer *par excellence* of democracy, of the People.

* See Grainger's letter to Herman Sandby, p 158-159.

CHAPTER SIX

Grainger and Folksong

David Tall

PERCY Grainger began to collect folksongs at Brigg in Lincolnshire in 1905. In short, intensive bursts over the next five years he collected and transcribed well over 300 songs and assembled a collection of 216 Edison cylinders, many of them containing material that he never transferred to written notation. He added a few Maori and Polynesian recordings in 1909 and a handful of American notations in the following decade. Later, his other major collection was to consist of over 170 Danish notations, also taken, in the 1920s, with the aid of a phonograph.[1]

Grainger's interest in folksong was first aroused when he was a young student at Frankfurt. At 15 years of age, in the autumn of 1897, he began to study counterpoint with Iwan Knorr, whose appointment at the Hoch Conservatoire had been secured on the recommendation of no less a personage than Johannes Brahms, on the strength of Knorr's *Variations on a Ukranian Folksong*. Grainger gave no credit for his love of folksong to Knorr; their personalities clashed from the start and the young student resolutely insisted that he learnt nothing from his official teacher.

Instead he sought solace and advice from Karl Klimsch, a musical amateur of substantial means who invited Grainger and his friends regularly to his house. Klimsch also happened to be a close personal friend of Knorr; the latter had written a set of variations on a theme of Klimsch which had been published by Breitkopf and Härtel. To his credit, Klimsch was able to retain a balanced view of the relationship between Grainger and his teacher and took the young student in hand, giving him forthright advice in the art of composition.

It was Klimsch who introduced Grainger to folksong,[2] perhaps with the veiled intention of effecting a reconciliation between him and his teacher. During the period of intense disagreement between Grainger and Knorr, Klimsch showed him a copy of *Songs of the North*, a collection of Scottish traditional and folksongs edited in 'drawing-room' style by A C MacLeod and Harold Boulton, with music arranged by Malcolm Lawson. This was a workmanlike collection of pieces for voice (or voices) and piano which Klimsch had discovered during a holiday in Scotland.

Folk melodies appealed to Grainger straight away. They served as a vehicle and a necessary restraint on his extravagant musical imagination. In February 1899 he set 26 melodies from Augener's collection *English Folksongs and Popular Tunes*. Presumably this was under the auspices of Klimsch for at this time he was not working with Knorr.

In a sense, Grainger was firmly in the European tradition of Haydn, Beethoven and Brahms with their respective collections of folksong settings. He was later to pay tribute to Haydn[3] as a source of inspiration for his uninhibited fast numbers, such as *Shepherd's Hey*, and to Brahms[4] for the glowing harmonies of *Sussex Mummers' Christmas Carol*. But there was another side of his personality that was developing and would have a significant role to play when he came to collecting folksongs for himself. This was the pioneering Australian sense of involvement, experiment and enterprise. Already he had ideas of 'free-music', devoid of melodic and rhythmic restrictions. In his *Song of Solomon* he had used natural irregular speech-rhythms to set the words. His Australian background also freed him of the influence of English church music and the tyranny of the church modes which conditioned the expectations of the early British folksong collectors.[5]

At the turn of the century, however, Grainger's first face-to-face contact with a folksinger was still five years away. During this time he composed a number of vocal and choral works based on folk or traditional melodies from published sources. In 1900 he set 14 pieces from *Songs of the North*, in a style which showed a harmonic touch on a totally higher plane than the published settings which he used as a model. In 1901 came the Scotch *Ye Banks & Braes o' Bonnie Doon*, the English *Three Ravens* and in 1902 the *Irish Tune from County Derry*.

A student friend, the Danish cellist Herman Sandby, had already introduced him to Danish folksong and by 1902 they were performing a *Scandinavian Suite* for cello and piano set by Grainger and fingered by Sandby. It featured melodies from Sweden, Norway and Denmark. One of the movements, *Song of Vermeland*, was subsequently set by Grainger for chorus. By 1904 he had composed another nine settings, comprising two Welsh, four English, one Irish and two Scotch melodies from existing published collections. His sources were only loosely what might be called 'folksong'; one was a melody[6] by the Elizabethan madrigalist Thomas Morley.

In 1904 the Vincent Music Co. of London published six folksettings[7]: the *Irish Tune, Song of Vermeland, Men of Harlech, The Camp (Y Gadlys), Sir Eglamore, The Hunter in His Career*. When Grainger attended a lecture[8] on folksong by Lucy Broadwood on 14th March, 1905, he was already a force to be reckoned with.

He was captivated by Lucy Broadwood's presentation and her simple, unaffected performance of the melodies she herself had collected.[9] He resolved to have a go himself, and four short weeks later came the event that was to change his life; he attended the North Lincolnshire Musical Competition Festival at Brigg. Here he took down his first published folksong notations[10] and was to return again to take down upwards of a hundred melodies in the traditional way, by ear.

That summer he toured Denmark again with Sandby, who introduced him to the Faeroe Island folksong collector Hjalmar Thuren. Fired with enthusiasm by Thuren's collection, he set about sketching arrangements of two of his melodies, subsequently completed and published.[11] Thuren also told him of the Danish folk-lorist Evald Tang Kristensen. Grainger was later to recall Thuren's words:[12]

> Evald Tang Kristensen seems to me the folk gatherer who best has known how to keep alive in his notings-down those rhythmic unregularnesses, personal oddnesses, and the old time modal folk-scales that mean so much in the songs of the Danish country folk.

But the hoped-for meeting with Kristensen did not materialise for another 17 years.

Returning to England, Grainger cast his eyes over his own folk notations and began to use them in his settings. His 'Yule Gift' that year to his mother included his first two arrangements of melodies heard firsthand from the singer: *I'm Seventeen Come Sunday* and *Marching Tune*, both for chorus and brass. These and three others—*Brigg Fair, The Gipsy's Wedding Day* and *Six Dukes Went A-Fishin'*—were completed in time for a highly acclaimed performance at the Brigg Festival on 7th May, 1906.

Three weeks later Grainger met Edvard Grieg in London. His way had been prepared by the ever-active Sandby, who had sent copies of his early published compositions to the older composer. So began a friendship of uncommon warmth and closeness that was only to be rudely terminated by Grieg's death, on 4th September, 1907. In his last letter[13] to Grainger, Grieg accepted the dedication of the 'British Folk-Music Settings' which became his memorial 'lovingly and reverently dedicated to the memory of Edvard Grieg' when they were first published in 1911.

At first Grainger was pulled in opposite directions in his folksong activities. In a letter to Cecil Sharp on 2nd November, 1906, he wrote:[14]

> I am very keen that the tunes I collect (barring now and then a choral setting or 2) should be publicly presented in as merely scientific a form as possible for the time being. I don't wish to come forward as an arranger yet awhile altho' in 15 to 20 years time I hope to myself publish a folk music book; settings, etc.

He was to wait only five years before launching his folksong settings in earnest; meanwhile, he published just two sets of folk notations. The first consisted of four songs noted in Brigg on that first visit, 11th April, 1905. These appeared in the *Journal of the Folk-Song Society* with the tunes taken down by ear by Grainger and the words noted by others.[15]

The gulf between him and his peers subtly showed itself in the first comment on his first noted song. 'This absurd production', wrote Kidson, referring to the words of *T'Owd Yowe Wi' One Horn*, 'has at least what appears to be a very early air associated with it'.

Grainger never demeaned his folksingers in this way; he always treated his 'kings and queens of song' with the utmost respect and human understanding. Of Joseph Taylor, his favourite folksinger, he wrote: 'He is a courteous, genial, typical English countryman, and a perfect artist in the purest possible style of folk-song singing'. His pen-portraits of the singers could be direct and honest, yet with a measure of common humanity that raised his descriptions to the level of poetic prose. Of George Gouldthorpe he observed:[16]

> His personality, looks, and art are a curious blend of sweetness and grim pathos. Though his face and figure are gaunt and sharp cornered, and his singing voice somewhat grating, he yet contrives to breath a spirit of almost caressing tenderness into all he does, says, or sings; even if a hint of tragic undercurrent be ever present also. A life of drudgery, ending in old age, in want and hardship, has not shorn his manners of a degree of human nobility and dignity, exceptional among English peasants; nor can any situation rob him of his refreshing (unconscious) Lincolnshire independence. His child-like mind, and his unworldly nature, seemingly void of all bitterness, singularly fit him to voice the purity and sweetness of folk-art.

The young Australian found it easy to identify with his folk-singers. Where

English gentlemen collectors heard the modes of the Church, he heard a 'single, loose-knit modal folk-song scale' with mutable third, sixth and seventh, and noted certain regularities in the use of these intervals.[17] His earlier experiments in speech rhythms enabled him to recognise the irregular rhythms of the singers and yet he was able to see underlying patterns in their irregularities from verse to verse. His perception of these subtleties was greatly enhanced by the simple expedient of using an Edison phonograph, so that he could not only listen to the same performance several times but he was able to slow the machine down and capture detail that was impossible to grasp at normal speed.

Grainger's innovatory use of recording equipment was amazing in that no-one had seriously done it in England before. It was not for the want of public knowledge of the idea that the method had not been utilised. In his inaugural address to the Folk-Song Society on its formation in 1898, Sir Hubert Parry had stressed the need for accurate recording, preferably with the wax cylinder phonograph.[18] At Lucy Broadwood's lecture there was an extended discussion[19] that centred on recording: 'I could almost wish for the first time in my life for a gramophone', stated the chairman, W H Cummings. 'I should like them to be noted down with all their errors, and not have them changed according to the good taste, or the bad taste, or the whim or humour

of those who take them down'. John Fuller Maitland responded:

I think the Chairman's suggestion of the gramophone is most excellent. If the Folk-Song Society were rich enough we would buy one at once. But we should have put it in a back parlour for I fear the country folk would be so flabbergasted by the performance of the gramophone, to begin with, that they would be afraid to sing.

The Folk-Song Society never did buy the gramophone. In 1906 it was the 24-year-old Grainger who strode into Lincolnshire with his newly acquired phonograph. 'When I first started collecting with the phonograph', he later wrote[20]

I was surprised to find how readily the old singers took to singing into the machine. Many of them were familiar with gramophones and phonographs in public houses and elsewhere, and all were agog to have their own singing recorded, while their delight at hearing their own voices, and their distress at detecting their errors reproduced in the machine, was quite touching.

His first cylinder was cut at Brigg on 26th July, 1906 and that summer, in a few short days, he cut 55 more. Several further expeditions came later. On the 4th, 5th, 6th of April, 1908, he recorded 48 cylinders in Gloucestershire, aided by Eliza Wedgwood, and on 25th to 27th May, 1908, he cut another 66, again in his beloved Lincolnshire. The vast majority of his 216 English folksong cylinders were taken in these three short periods of activity. The rest were isolated recordings made at various times between 1906 and 1909 in London, Gloucester and Lincolnshire.

He was to hektograph many items from his collection and circulate them round his friends. The method involved writing with special ink on special paper to produce a master which was pressed onto a gelatine surface, leaving a mirror image; plain paper pressed on to the gelatine was then imprinted

OVE: The market at Brigg, 1906.
ING PAGE: George Gouldthorpe, Percy Grainger, Joseph Leaning, Joseph Taylor and ~rge Wray; Brigg Manor House, 1906.

INDEX TO GRAINGER'S PHONOGRAPH CYLINDERS (page 3)

Cyl.No.	Title,Folksong	Sung by etc.)	No in G'sCEY	No in J.12
45	The Rainbow,1st perf.2nd½	George R. Orton,Brigg4,8,06	115	4
	Spencer the Rover	Ditto	145	
	Artichokes & Cauliflowers	Ditto	106	
	Geordie	Joseph Taylor, 4,8,06	137	9
46	The Rainbow(2nd perf.)	George R. Orton ,Ditto	115	4
47	Young Barker	Ditto	107	
	Artichokes and Cauliflowers,(2nd record)Ditto		106	
	Green Bushes,	Joseph Taylor Ditto	282	
48	I'm 17 Come Sunday(1st ½)	Fred Atkinson,Brigg 31,7,06	125	
49	I'm 17 Come Sunday (2nd½)	Ditto	125	
	The Lost Lady Found(1st½)	Ditto	44	
50	The Lost Lady Found(2nd½)	Ditto	44	
51	Six Dukes Went A Fishing(1st½)	Joseph Leaning Brigg 4,8,06	104	2
52	Six Dukes(2nd ½)	Ditto	104	2
	Time to Remember the Poor (2 perfs.)	Ditto	197	
53	Creeping Jane(1st½)	Ditto	294	
54	Creeping Jane(2nd½)	Ditto	294	
	The Sheffield Highwayman	George Wray,same date	300	
55	Lord Bateman(1st½)	Joseph Leaning Ditto	173	
56	The Nutting Girl	Ditto	253	
57	The North Country Maid	Ditto	116	
	Digging Turf Land	Ditto	296	
58	The Old Mare (B of "Green Bushes")	Ditto	273	
59	Old Friend Gardner and Ploughman(1st½)	Ditto	286	
60	Old Friend Gardner and Ploughman(2nd½)	Ditto	286	
61	The Shark, or How Gallantly	George Wray,Brigg, 4,8,06	267	
	Green Bushes	Joseph Leaning Ditto	100	
	General Wolfe(Bold)	Ditto	101	
	Green Bushes(2nd perf.)	Ditto	100	
62	Wharncliffe Highwood	Ditto	252	
	The Nutting Girl(last verse)	Ditto	253	
63	The Pretty Maid Milking Her Cow	Ditto	120	
	Come All you Jolly Ploughboys (Here's April, Here's May)	Ditto	255	
64	The Poacher	Ditto	287	
65	Where are you going to My Pretty Maid	J. Taylor,4,8,06	289	
	Ditto (1st verse)	Edgar Hyldon,ditto	290	
66	I'm 17 Come Sunday	Ditto	132	
	The Spotted Cow	Ditto	291	
67	The Sprig of Thyme	Joseph Taylor,4,8,06	122	
	Green Bushes(1st verse)	Joseph Leaning ditto	100	
68	Rufford Park Poachers	Jos. Taylor ditto	117	
	I'm 17 Come Sunday	Joseph Leaning Ditto	130	
	The Banks of Sweet Dundee	Ditto	278	
69	Liston(It's on the Monday Morning) (Wrongly called"Dublin Bay"?) (1st performance)	Mr. Dean(Hibaldstow) Brigg25,5,08		¶(See foreword to Lincolnshire Posy"
70	Lisbon (2nd perf.	Ditto		
71	Brigg Fair2 performances	Ditto		
	Henry Martin(3rd cyl.)	Septimus Love,25,5,08(Brigg)		
	The Tree on The Hill (3rd cyl.)	Ditto		
72	Henry Martin(1st cyl.)	Ditto		
73	Henry Martin(2nd cyl.)	Ditto		
74	The Tree on The Hill (1st cyl.)	Ditto		
75	The Tree on The Hill(2nd cyl.	Ditto		
76	Riley(1st performance)	Geo. R. Orton,Brigg 25,5,08		

A page from Grainger's own list of his folk-song recordings.

with a copy of the original. In total Grainger produced just over 200 hektograph masters. These included just three of his first hundred tunes noted by ear (although many were retaken with the phonograph at a later time). There were then two separate sets, numbers 100 to 200 and 201 to 300, each with a careful listing of the singers, their ages, occupations and towns of origin.

A selection of these notations were polished for his second, and most impressive, publication[21] in the *Journal of the Folk-Song Society* of 1908. He gave practical hints for the use of the phonograph, a number of profound yet simple observations on folksong, tender portraits of his singers and deeply considered notations of 27 songs bristling with detailed annotations. Sixteen were taken with the aid of the phonograph, sometimes recorded several times over. Seventeen came from Lincolnshire, one from Wimbledon, and the remainder were sea chanties taken down by ear in association with Charles Rosher, H E Piggott and Everard Feilding. The editing committee condemned themselves in their conservative comments:

In considering Mr Grainger's theories, which are based on most careful observations, we wish to point out that the general experience of collectors goes to show that English singers most rarely alter their mode in singing the same song. About the value of the phonograph as an aid to collecting there can be no doubt; whether it is sufficiently perfect as yet to be preferred to the human ear is still a disputable point. Similar and careful records and

Grainger contributes to the Journal of the Folk-Song Society, 1908.

The following repeats of portions of verses occur:
In record B: last quarter of (1), last half of (3), last half of (4). (6) is incomplete.

204

In record C: last half of (4). (5) is sung without any repetition, and after its last note Mr. Wray adds (in speaking voice) " must yield."

In record C a distinct F♯ is heard in place of those notes marked *, and a questionable F♯ in place of those marked **. There are also occasional F♯'s in record B, occurring, like those in record C, in the lower octave, but never in the higher. Otherwise the three records resemble one another closely in all important points.

The order of taking the records was as follows: B, A, C. They were all made on the same day. Thus Mr. Wray's pure Dorian performance (record A) occurred between the two in mongrel scales.

These three records are an instance of the gain occasionally to be had of taking several records of the complete song. Thus, had I taken but record A, I should have had no indication of Mr. Wray's tendency (twice out of thrice), to sing the song in a blended Mixolydian and Dorian scale, whereas, had I taken records B and C, but not A, I should have lacked an instance of his having once sung the song in the Dorian mode throughout. Without record B there would be no account of his habit of occasionally repeating the last quarter of a verse, while record C alone contains the spoken repetition of the last few words of the song, so characteristic of folk-singers in general, and Mr. Wray in particular.

I am well aware that many of the minute rhythmic irregularities of the above (such as the ⅜-bars) are mere wayward and theoretically unimportant lengthenings and shortenings of rhythms fundamentally regular. Nevertheless their presence added to the extreme quaintness of Mr. Wray's rendering, and I feel there may be value in as literal as possible a translation into musical notation of all his details. To compass this I screwed down the speed regulator of the phonograph until the record sounded an octave below its original pitch, and, accordingly, at half its original tempo. Thus, the metronome rate that had originally fitted to the crochets now beat to the quavers. At this degree of slowness it was far easier to arrive at a clearer consciousness of the pitch and duration of many of the quick notes of the song.

Thus a note to which the metronome beat a tick and a half was determinable as having the duration of three semiquavers; three notes of even length to which the metronome beat two ticks (the second tick falling midway between the second and third note), being quaver triplets, etc., etc.

Despite all this care, however, I fear that the rhythms of the above can lay claim to only approximate exactitude.

At verse four: " my head in camp did fall " (note that Lord Melbourne is still alive in verse five!), is an amusing corruption of " my aide-de-camp did fall," as collected by Miss Lucy Broadwood (see " The Duke of Marlborough," *Folk-Song Journal*,

205

No. 4, p. 157). No doubt the rhythmic stock of the above version has originally been as regular as that of Mr. Burstow's (both variants of the same tune), Mr. Wray's song being an instance of a rhapsodic mode of performance grafted upon an underlying regular rhythmic structure. The first impression from Mr. Wray's singing of " Lord Melbourne " is that of a half-extemporized recitation. Nevertheless a comparison of the three phonograph records shows that he repeats his irregularities with great uniformity in different performances. –P. G.

Mr. H. E. D. Hammond has noted a Dorian variant of the tune in Worcestershire, where the singer called the hero " Lord Marlborough." The Worcestershire air is very much like the Mixolydian tune noted by me in Sussex, except for the Dorian minor third. The version in Barrett's *English Folk-Songs* (see " Marlboro' ") which the editor states " is preserved in the Eastern Counties," is a curious blend of the Sussex air and the Lincolnshire air, the second half of the tune having the minor third, and several characteristics in common with Mr. Wray's second strain.–L. E. B.

13–'MERICAN FRIGATE; OR, PAUL JONES.

Sung by Mr. George Wray,
Phonographed and noted by Percy Grainger.   at Brigg, Lincolnshire, July 28th, 1906.
Sung in B. Fast. M.M. ♩ = about 192. *Energetic and pattering.*

206

207

Percy Grainger and A J Knocks, Otaki (New Zealand), 16 September 1924.

analysis of the performances of trained singers and instrumentalists would therefore be of great value in helping to determine this.

The committee never instituted such recordings or analysis. Instead they poured cool doubts on some of Grainger's observations. Of his irregular limpid rhythms in his notation of *Rufford Park Poachers*, for instance, Fuller Maitland responded:[22]

> The bars of ⅜ time are probably due to an exaggerated accent being put on the third note of a bar of ²⁄₄ time. The bars of ¾ time are clearly uniform in design with these, and the whole tune points to a perfectly regular original in ²⁄₄ time.

Faced with such comments, despite being elected to the committee himself, Grainger's activities in folksong collecting slowed dramatically. About 50 of his cylinders remained untranscribed and his collection lay incomplete.

In 1909, on a concert tour of Australasia, he met A J Knocks in New Zealand. Knocks had already used a phonograph to record Polynesian and Maori music. Seven of his cylinders found their way into Grainger's collection —five of Raratongan music and two of Maori origin[23]. Grainger himself made a small number of recordings and six Maori cylinders from 26th January, 1909, are preserved. He also transcribed three native Australian tunes[24] in Melbourne some time in May from a phonograph cylinder recorded by Baldwin Spencer in 1901. Evidently the musicians of the new world were not as inhibited in their use of recording devices as the British had been!

On his return to England he added only nine more cylinders to his collection, once more from Eliza Wedgwood in Gloucestershire. Only a few sporadic additions were made after that, all taken down by ear, usually prompted by someone else, for instance joint work with Edith Lyttelton in Kent (1909) and W B Reynolds in Ulster (1911/12). He also learnt that a number of commercial records made of Joseph Taylor's singing by the Gramophone Company in 1908 had not sold well.

He turned his attention to original composition and in 1911 began publishing his settings with Schott of London. He had steadily built up a number of these compositions over the years and now polished them to go into print. Paradoxically, none of his most popular settings used tunes of his own discovery. *Shepherd's Hey* and the later *Country Gardens* came from Cecil Sharp in 1908, *Molly on the Shore* was taken from Stanford's complete edition of Irish Music. In other cases he wove variants of his own finding into settings based on other published melodies, such as *Green Bushes* and *Scotch Strathspey and Reel*. In his slower settings he was often able to imbue great inspiration into a tune obtained from a published collection, as in *The Irish Tune from County Derry* or *Willow, Willow*. But a tune noted by himself usually brought out a great depth of feeling, as witnessed by *Shallow Brown* or *Brigg Fair*, and a phonographed melody was capable of inspiring great poignancy, such as *Six Dukes Went A-Fishin'* and *Died for Love*. He rarely failed to compose a setting of great quality when he had the inspiration of the phonograph to keep his imagination alive.

In 1914 he emigrated to America and his folksong collecting, already dormant, virtually ceased. He never looked for English folksongs in America, as did Cecil Sharp. Only a few melodies survive from his American years[25]— four negro songs from 1914 and two from 1919. There are also a few items of correspondence enclosing tunes from other sources. One of these, *Spoon*

River, was passed on to him from a Captain Robinson by way of the poet Edgar Lee Masters; it formed the basis of his one and only American Folk-Music Setting in a projected sequence that was never extended.

Instead he concentrated on large orchestral works and playing the piano. He also joined the army for a period in 1917/19. Here he gained experience of scoring for wind band and produced his famous piano setting of *Country Gardens* which was to give him a sizeable income for the rest of his life. He later offered a large share of the royalties to Cecil Sharp, who had collected the tune, but Sharp refused, though he relented just before his death; the money was used to bring out a posthumous edition of his English folksongs collected in the Appalachian mountains of America. In this way Grainger demonstrated his true humanity, setting aside petty quarrels for the sake of his indebtedness to Sharp for the use of his melody.

After being released from the army he set about his earlier sketches of compositions and tried to ginger up his flagging inspiration in composition. A number of folksettings come from this period.

In 1922 his mother committed suicide. Grainger was distraught. He frantically tried to complete all his sketches to demonstrate that he was the great Australian composer that his mother wished him to be: it was hopeless. In a state of agitation and sadness he left for his first tour of Europe since his emigration to America eight years before. A new source of inspiration came to him that heralded his second great period of folksong collecting: he finally met Evald Tang Kristensen, now nearly 80 years old. The two of them travelled through Jutland with Grainger's phonograph. They collected 80 melodies in August 1922 which Grainger subsequently transcribed; in September 1925 a second tour gave rise to the Danish melodies he numbered 81 to 172. From a third trip, in October 1927, the fruits were less bountiful. The Grainger Museum[26] contains only a single manuscript book with melody number 177 and a version of 159.

Grainger made several poignant settings from this material, including *The Power of Love* and *Lord Peter's Stable-Boy,* in memory of his mother. To Herman Sandby he dedicated *The Nightingale and Two Sisters* with the legend 'through whom I learned to know and love Danish folk music as long ago as 1900'. The *Jutish Medley* he dedicated to Kristensen, 'in deep worth-prizement and fond friendship'.

In Kristensen he saw a man who had had a struggle similar to that he had encountered himself, and he helped the Dane triumphantly to conquer his opposition through the use of his phonograph. 'The phonograph', wrote Grainger,

> which does not lie, made two facts stand out very clearly; firstly how very true to nature Evald Tang Kristensen's notings-down had been from the very start; secondly how un-called-for and knowledgeless had been the belittlings of his musical notings-down by those Danish "connoisseurs" of the seventies who dubbed as "wrongly noted" those very traits in his melodies that were strikingly typical of the middle ages and of the Danish country-side and hence of the rarest worth.[27]

Grainger could have said the same of his own work. He remained isolated from the English folksong movement; in the remaining years of his life he made a few more British and Danish settings, including his masterpiece *The Lincolnshire Posy* for wind band, but he collected no more.

His vigorous nature never allowed him to rest, although his original con-

Ex 1: Grainger's transcription of 'Sekar Gadung'.

tributions to music were drying up. Instead he worked at transcriptions and more arrangements. On his trips to Australia in the 'thirties he was to meet more ethnic music in the Pacific. He transcribed the Javanese *Sekar Gadung* in 1932/3 aided by Norman Voelcker, and then in 1935 the Balinese *Gamelan Anklung* (helped by James Scott-Power) and the Jalatarangan *Bahiriyale V. Palaniyandi*. All three were taken from gramophone records. An African tune and a piano transcription of a Chinese melody *Beautiful Fresh Flower* (harmonised by Joseph Yasser) complete the Grainger canon.

His interest in the ethnic folk-art of the Pacific extended far beyond the music; he collected artefacts, mixed freely with the natives, wore grass skirts and learned to make up their intricate decorative beadwork. He was one of the first true ethnologists to look beyond the surface sheen to the very soul of the people by taking part in their lives. One of the stated aims of his museum in Melbourne is as a centre for ethnic study in the Pacific.

As he grew old he attempted to set his folk notations in order. The Library of Congress transferred his cylinders to disc and later to tape. The original Danish cylinders were deposited in the Folkeminde Samling of the Kongelige Bibliotek (Royal Library) of Copenhagen. But when Grainger later required copies of his Danish recordings they were made by a small Danish firm and found to be full of flaws.[28] One hopes that the original cylinders are in a better state.

In 1936 Grainger returned to his most famous folk notation of all, *Brigg Fair*. At the request of the Scottish Students' Song Book Committee he prepared a version for *Student Songs for Camp and College*[29]. He based it on two different gramophone recordings made back in 1908 by the Gramophone Company. It is instructive to compare the final version with Joseph Taylor's two performances, for he sings different decorations to the melody in different places on the two takes. Grainger selects the 'best bits' of each in the time-honoured manner of the folksong-collector rather than by sticking to a single performance, like a scientist. Always a pragmatist, his scholarship in notation is modified to the best practical solution for performance.

He never solved the practical problems of how to notate his melodies. The more irregular of his notations are fearfully difficult to read, with their strange time signatures and precise detail discovered only through slowing down the recording and comparing it with the slow tick of a metronome to find the time. At one stage he considered an imaginative notation in which the pitch was represented as usual by the height in a stave but the length of each note was represented by the horizontal length of the symbol. It was not far from here to his graphs of 'free-music'.

Since his death, various scholars have attempted to resolve the problems and collate his complete collection. The Grainger Museum remains the central source of material[30]. It contains the English melodies numbers 1 to 92 (July to November 1905) in a single book, with a second book containing texts and a few melodies. The hektograph notations of melodies 100 to 300 are complete and then there is a jumble of envelopes containing folksongs numbered (with gaps) up to 388. Some of the latter have texts only, sent to Grainger by interested parties. These, together with the untranscribed portion of the recorded cylinders, constitute the Grainger English Music Collection. Copies are to be found in various libraries around the world, including the Elder Conservatorium in Adelaide, Cecil Sharp House in London and the British Institute of Recorded Sound, which all have copies of the hektographs. The latter also has copies of English tunes 301 to 339 and the Danish melodies. The originals of the Danish transcriptions are in the Grainger Museum. Other libraries have collections in various states of completeness.

Technically we can never have the Grainger collection precisely as he wanted it. He was given to reconsidering his recordings and often made a number of alterations to his hektograph versions before they appeared in the *Journal of the Folk-Song Society* or as the basis for one of his settings. There are also occasional discrepancies between his recordings and his notations

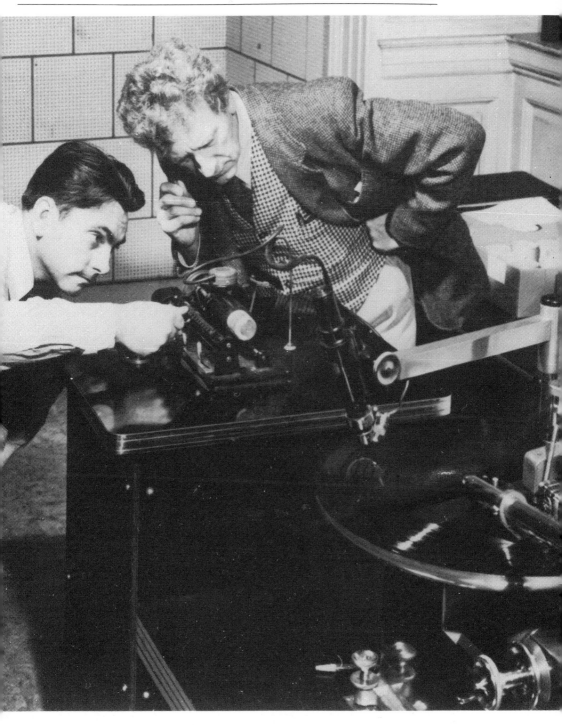

:ording Grainger's priceless cylinder recordings.

which doubtless he would have refined before publication.

What we have of his collection, however, is a sufficient legacy to realise the possible potential of his work. In 1968, *Twenty One Lincolnshire Folk Songs* appeared in a practical edition, edited for Oxford University Press by Patrick O'Shaughnessy. All are from Grainger's collection, as are three in *More Folk Songs from Lincolnshire*, which appeared from the same source in 1971.

Ten songs and one chanty appeared in the 1974 issue of the *Folk Music Journal*, scrupulously edited by R S Thomson. Then in 1975, Patrick O' Shaughnessy released 48 more in two volumes of *Yellow Belly Ballads* published by Lincolnshire and Humberside Arts. A number of the latter are taken from tapes of Grainger's cylinders, including several which Grainger never transcribed himself. Patrick O'Shaughnessy tells graphically of the frustration and difficulties associated with listening to the crackling and much deteriorated tracks from those wax cylinders.

At this time it is part of the grand plan of the Grainger Museum to see their collection properly catalogued, edited and published, but that may yet be some time away. Grainger is at last being given belated recognition for his far-sightedness. The original gramophone records of Joseph Taylor and a selection of phonograph tracks were reissued on a long-playing record (Leader Sound: LEA 4050) in England in 1972. Every new book on folk-song now has the obligatory reference to Grainger's pioneering spirit, prompted largely by the insight of his fellow countryman A L Lloyd in *Folk Song in England* in 1967 and the biography by John Bird.

Grainger himself should be given the last word on the subject, in an extended quotation from his preface to *Bold William Taylor* of 1952:

> The traditions of English folksinging can easily be acquired by listening to the phonograph & gramophone records of the singing of genuine folksingers, such as the records of Joseph Taylor's folk-singing put out by the London Gramophone Co.
>
> In nothing do the traditions of English folksinging show themselves more strongly than in the matter of the allotment of syllables to music. The folksong tradition demands clear articulation of intervals—similar to the articulation achieved by the Dolmetsch family when playing pre-Bach English string fantasies. Most folksingers are inclined to avoid slurs (more than one note to a syllable of text), preferring to add 'nonsense syllables' to the words of their songs, so that each note of the melody has a syllable of text to itself. Thus what a singer ignorant of the folksong tradition would sing as follows:

Ex 2:

She dressed ___ her-self ___ in ___ man's ap - pa - rel

becomes in a well-traditioned folksinger's mouth:

Ex 3:

She dressed ___ her-sed-delf id - den man's ap - pa - ril

A typical case of the lavish use of 'nonsense syllables' is the following phrase of the song *The American Stranger* as sung by Mr George Wray of Barton-on-Humber, Lincolnshire, England:

Ex 4:

for ter cree-oose in the chad-da-nid-dle of Old Eng-ge-land's fame

This becomes lifeless & inarticulate if sung in the 'art-song' manner with slurs:

Ex 5:

for to cruise in the chan - nel — of Old Eng - land's fame

To sing a Lincolnshire folksong such as *Bold William Taylor* without the folksingers' dialect & without the nonsense syllables & other details of English folksong traditions is as inartistic as it would be to sing Wagner with Italian operatic traditions, or to sing *Rigoletto* with Wagnerian operatic traditions. Singers should wake up to the fact that such a folksong as *Bold William Taylor*, shorn of its local dialect, loses its charm as surely as would *Kathleen Mavourneen, Comin' Through The Rye* or an American negro spiritual if sung in 'Standard Southern English'.

The greatest crime against folksong is to 'middle-class' it—to sing it with a 'white collar' voice production & other townified suggestions. Whether it be true or not that the ballads originated in the knightly & aristocratic world, one thing is certain: they have come down to us solely as an adjunct of rural life & are drenched through & through with rural feelings & traditions.

In her PhD thesis of 1979, Dr Jane O'Brien has edited and catalogued the first 99 notations and suggested a conjectural numbering of the whole collection from 1 to 413. This follows a projected reorganisation begun by Grainger in 1940 but never completed. He had drastically reorganised numbers 1-99, deleting certain songs copied from printed collections, some of doubtful origin and a few whose publication had been refused by the Scottish singer Mr R McLeod. These were replaced by songs collected by ear in 1905 and a few phonographed in 1908. Songs 100-300 are as in the hektographed collection, 301-339 are the Gloucestershire songs, and the remainder, ingeniously conjectured by Dr O'Brien, include titles and words of untranscribed items in the phonograph collection. Many of these appear never to have been committed to paper by Grainger, some have words only or music only, and several were noted by others. Dr O'Brien's thesis marks the most significant step forward in understanding the Grainger English folksong collection.

Ex 6: Grainger's sketch for 'Sea Song' (1907), written out for pianola or mechanically-played organ.

CHAPTER SEVEN

Orchestral Music

Bryan Fairfax

TECHNIQUE AND STYLE

AT the time of his death, Grainger's manuscripts included hundreds of sketches of works which were not only incomplete in themselves but were often only fragments of projected series. *Train Music, Sea Music* and *Desert Music,* fascinating conceptions as musico-philosophical studies, remained as fragments, even though they were often re-worked over periods of years. Nor did Grainger attempt to hide the often incredible amount of time during which even brief works were gestated. *Shepherd's Hey,* for example, was begun in 1908 and 'ended' in 1911, while *Country Gardens,* which was 'rough-sketched' in 1908, was not 'worked-out' for piano until 1918.

Indeed, *Country Gardens* had its origin as an improvisation on an English folk-dance. With so much of the work completed almost in an instant, therefore, it is surprising that its written-down version occupied a disproportionate amount of time. The reason may be found if we examine the difference between a piece which is improvised and strongly influenced by the environmental situation at that very moment, and a piece composed in the style of an improvisation but which has to stand exposure to vastly differing situations.

Grainger was not a noted exponent of the former. The improvisation did not appear as an item in his concert programmes, notwithstanding the origin of *Country Gardens,* which was made up in a spirit of bravura for fellow troops when he served in the US army during the First World War. He was, however, a master of the composed 'improvisation', of which the spontaneity was a projection of his own personality and musical predilections. For all their freshness and immediacy of expression, Grainger shaped and polished his miniatures with the care and precision of a diamond-cutter.

For Grainger the search was for a musical expression of the essence of the image which came to his mind. Hence, *Train Music* was born of a desire for a music to be created not only out of the sounds and rhythms of a moving train, but of its smell, heat, material, invincible 'onward-rushing' (Grainger's words), changes of scene, climate and weather en route, heroic non-complaining in the service of mankind, and its consummate weight when at rest. A glorious totality; an essence transmuted into sound.

In the train-inspired music of Honegger *(Pacific 231)* and Villa-Lobos *(The Little Train)* both composers limited themselves to the direct musical associations of the sounds and rhythms of a train; they settled for less but did produce the works. Grainger's project was too expansive and consequently remained incomplete. However, we have his sketches for the opening bars of the work, the orchestration indicating an ensemble of about 150 players. Of these, 100 are strings and no fewer than 38 are woodwinds.

It is especially interesting to see the large number of double-reeds which Grainger listed: eight oboes, four English horns, six bassoons and two double-bassoons. He particularly favoured this quality of sound. The original scoring of *Hill Song No 1* was entirely for wind instruments with emphasis on the double-reed sound, a texture only slightly reduced in the revised and final version. In the score he asks for the oboes and sarrusophones (an all-metal, oboe-type instrument) to be played with hard reeds so that the tone would have a strong, nasal quality (a sound which it is almost impossible to persuade a professional player to make).

A similar tone-quality for *Train Music,* allied to continual changes of time-signature and a percussive density of sound, shows that he was thinking along radically different lines to the prevailing late-romanticism of those Edwardian times. The linear style is completely athematic in its restlessly bounding contrapuntal lines, and the harmony, atonal and with grinding dissonances, intensifies the overall rhythmic texture. A distinct parallel with certain episodes of *The Rite of Spring* is evident. Although Grainger worked on these sketches from 1901-07 he failed to precede Stravinsky with a completed work, although in the conception of a music derived from elemental and barbarous forces he may be said, in principle, to have done so.

Train Music originated during a journey in 1900 in a very rough and clangorous Italian train. Together with *Charging Irishrey A and B,* from a similar journey in Ireland, the total duration would have been about ten minutes. *Sea Song* (1907), however, is a completed work, albeit an experiment in free-flowing rhythms which, at Grainger's suggested tempo, would last about 15 seconds. A seating plan for the eight solo players indicates that there was every intention that the piece was intended for performance. Two versions were made: the first in 14 irregular bars and the second in a ¾ time-signature throughout, a re-grouping of only 12 bars. The latter smooths out all the rhythmic character—probably easier to read, but depriving the rhythmic nuances of an appropriate expressive notation, Grainger making his point by providing two versions for comparison.

Train Music and *Sea Song* are the merest fragments and yet, in a sense special to Grainger. It can be fully justified to examine them in the light of his total output. Grainger took a somewhat proprietorial attitude to those ideas which he felt were original to himself. None more so than in the matter of irregular barring, of which he was such an early exponent; he recalled how Cyril Scott had written to him asking permission to use 'his' innovatory technique of irregular barring. Towards the end of his life, Grainger considered the fate of his compositions—the larger ones neglected and the miniatures mostly overdone—and attempted to find a total assessment of what he had achieved. Rather tragically he said that his achievement was as an innovator—tragically, because no composer really wants the principles of his works to be remembered rather than the works themselves, and also because this has not actually been the case.

In spite of his flair for publicity, a charismatic personality which attracted

Ex 7: Opening page of Grainger's 'Train Music' in full score.

attention, and the undeniable prognostications contained within his music, he was almost completely non-influential. His irregular barring, it may be accepted, was found expedient by Scott to express his already pliable rhythmic style, but although Grainger evolved the principle years ahead of Stravinsky it remained, until 1911 and *The Rite of Spring,* an idea *in vacuo.*

Many of his projected ideas were of a conceptual nature, and were really awaiting the development of his 'free-music'. As it was, his classical background persuaded him to think in a fundamentally conventional way where

73

normal instruments were concerned, notwithstanding his originality in certain effects—nasal reed-tone and 'stomping' piano style, for example. His attempt to develop music along lines which did not conform to established orders of harmony and melody was the primary cause of the disillusionment which became manifest during his middle years.

If *Train Music,* and similar music, were in themselves a practical failure, we can see elsewhere that they nevertheless contributed to the overall character of his work. Although he was not the product of academic training (even his piano studies were to a large extent self-sufficient), Grainger was a man of wide aesthetic and intellectual interests, perhaps even too wide for the moderate degree of discipline which his mercurial temperament was prepared to devote to them. He was by nature a primitive. Few men can get the hang of what it is to be a savage, yet he could extol the beauty and simplicity of their lives, appreciate the unfathomable mystery of their beliefs and see these qualities as a communication with universal values at the deepest level.

Even so, no matter how deep one's empathy with different races and traditions—and Grainger's were as wide as sincerity could allow—one's racial origin is the overpowering influence. His European cultural background was a subjective barrier which did not accord with his artistic desire to devour an infinite variety of things in his creative maw. So long as traditional musical values were present he felt obliged to use them, and for this reason his music does not always sound as revolutionary as in principle it is. To offset this cultural influence with something innate to his personality, he maintained a life-long devotion to his conception of 'free-music': music not bounded by any limitations, either aesthetic or practical; music which was free of restrictions and therefore free to proceed in any direction which the imagination itself takes. Free-music would allow absolute freedom of pitch, tonal quality and rhythm, as well as allowing unlimited sound-combinations.

The ideal medium through which free-music would be realised would not be written notation and the middle-man performer, but instead it would be created direct by the composer onto a machine—an extraordinarily prophetic hint of electronic music. Unhampered by the rudimentary choice of merely 12 tones and a necessity to consider the limitations of instruments and their performers, the composer would be entirely free to set down the products of his imagination. He was also willing to admit the element of chance and improvisation, of which we have evidence as early as 1913 in his *Random Round* and *The Warriors,* so it is clear that Grainger was proposing fundamental changes in aesthetics and techniques, even more radical than those undertaken by Schönberg.

Schönberg achieved almost total realisation of his aims simply by an unwavering concentration upon essentials, but Grainger's only partial achievement was the result of diversity. Inevitably one must compare the overwhelming reality of Schönberg's mind and his critical capacity, which tended to reject more than it would accept, with Grainger's beatific vision of a world of sound, peopled with men and women who creatively enjoyed their natural artistic gifts, and a critical instinct which rejected only that which suggested any form of monopoly (tone and form structures, interpretation, etc) however loosely the term might be applied. Such 'monopolies' were 'un-democratic', as he would say.

But, regrettably perhaps, success is often in proportion to the degree to which an artist monopolises his own points of view and artistic criteria to the exclusion of other people's. This does seem to be the only way in which the creative mind can cut through limitless and enticing influences in order to achieve conclusions. Grainger was, however, prey to every 'democratic' influence which came to him; he *made* himself subject to such influences, even seeking them out. It was impossible for him to bring everything on which he ventured to a conculsion.

Further to the analogy with Schönberg we can see that, whereas Schönberg substantiated trends which had already been progressively gaining ground during a comparatively lengthy period, Grainger was 'kicking out into space' in a way which men had hitherto reserved for momentary fantasies and not usually as the basis for formulated works of art. Grainger saw art as life (hence the extraordinary vitality of his finest works), not as a phenomenon isolated in its own world of values; the prodigious range of life became the crucible for his own art.

He endeavoured to enshrine everything that evoked life: the clothes that once contained the body, the letter, the mind, the language, the nationhood, the structures and machines, the endeavour, and the song the mystery of mankind. He built and financed a museum which contains clothes of people he knew and wished to be remembered; letters were filed and his own often written in triplicate (he was an avid user of the old gum duplicator). He studied the languages of neglected cultures. He has written movingly of the fiery roar of a trans-continental train which passed him in the night as he hiked alone across an Australian desert, and was willing to seek the aid of the machine to produce his own music; and he recorded the voices of ordinary people, whose songs were an expression of lives that should not be forgotten.

It is significant that his notation of those songs was true in the minutest detail to the living performance. He was not for regularising the rhythm, or tidying up the melodic decorations by omitting them altogether. The inflexibility of our notational system obliged him to add his own indications of pitch variations and rhythmic pliance. He always saw art in relation to humanity, and in a world that now realises the prime urgency of actually maintaining life, let alone enriching it, it is for Grainger's love of life in the embodiment of man that he will, in turn, be remembered. When examining his music in more detail this will be a theme that will constantly recur.

ELASTIC SCORING

A unique feature of Grainger's instrumental writing lies in the principle of what he calls 'elastic scoring'. By this he means that any of his works scored in this way can be performed by any number and type of instrument, from two or three up to full symphony ('massed') orchestra.

Not all his works are designed in this way. The two *Hill Songs*, *The Warriors* and the suite *In a Nutshell*, for example, have stipulated instrumentation, although there are some indications for *ad lib* instruments. But those which are produced with elastic scoring appear with a bewildering range of

75

alternatives. A typical example is *The Lost Lady Found,* set either for mixed chorus and small orchestra, for small mixed chorus and large chamber music, for a single voice (or unison chorus) and small orchestra, for large chamber music, or for piano; all these possibilities are contained in the one printed score. In these works Grainger states in an introduction (which also appears in other scores) that he is not concerned with prescribed tone-colours, only that the balance between the parts should be correct.*

This comment, it is also stated, is directed to amateur and school orchestras so as to accommodate almost any combination of players on almost any instruments. In particular he wanted to make it possible for the maximum number of people to enjoy ensemble playing, and 'to promote a more hospitable attitude towards inexperienced music-makers'.

Grainger's conception of the small ensemble of diverse instrumentation was a reaction to the overblown, statutory orchestra of the late-Romantic period. In this respect his advocacy was prophetic of the wide diversity of instrumentation to be found in scores of the latter part of the 20th century. His ideal was not the scaled-down symphony orchestra but unique choices of instruments of every type. If this selection should come by chance according to the available players, well and good.

The choice of combinations for *Spoon River* (1929) is clearly itemised, A to E, in the score:

A. Three or more single instruments (he suggests two pianos and a harmonium, to which can be added any orchestral instruments).
B. Piano, harmonium and three or more strings.
C. Large Room-music (ie, chamber-music in which the string parts should be played solo; again there is a wide range of suggested instruments, included saxophone, harmonium and a variety of tuned percussion).
D. Massed pianos and pipe-organ or massed harmoniums (he suggests that these instruments may be 'massed to any extent—the more the mellower'; which proposes a fascinating sound that few people must have heard).
E. Symphony Orchestra or Massed Orchestra (the latter being Grainger's preferred 'Englished' term).

Such is the flexibility of notation that the one score is equally applicable to all the above combinations. Grainger's elastic scoring lies not only in the scoring itself but in the ingenious way in which he has laid out the printed page. The entire score is printed in C, although transposing instruments have their parts printed in the appropriate keys. The main sections of the orchestra—woodwinds, brass, percussion and strings—are each condensed usually to two staves, treble and bass, and can easily be read on the piano if required.

Less convenient, although highly characteristic of his frequent comments throughout his scores, are the comic-strip 'balloons' which emanate from a particular melodic line and contain indications as to instrumentation. For a

---

* Grainger's actual statement appears in part on p 139

conductor to read this and be able to assess exactly who plays what in a complex score such as *The Warriors,* calls for a Holmesian skill in detection rather than musicianship. However, the *total* effect is perfectly clear without implanting a rigid orchestration.

In a sense his elastic scoring is not as miraculous as might be imagined for it is assumed that at least one piano, and possibly a second piano and a harmonium, will be ever-present to fill in, in the 18th-century continuo style, for any instrumental part which is weak or absent. Where Grainger does show insight is in his unfussy confidence in setting a rustic tune in a robust style and leaving the decision as to instrumentation to the democratic judgement of the performers. *Spoon River* (duration about 4½ minutes) was an American fiddle-tune of which he said, 'My setting (begun March 10 1919; ended February 1 1929) aims at preserving a pioneer blend of lonesome wistfulness and sturdy persistence'. The powerfully rhythmic tune, similar to a Scottish reel-tune, is treated in Grainger's accumulative style in which continual accretions of chromatic harmony and contrapuntal textures virtually explode to conclude the piece: vitality overthrowing itself.

Harvest Hymn (duration c.3½ minutes; composed 1905 and 1932) is gentler stuff and again designed for elastic scoring: 'Two instruments up to massed orchestra, with or without voice or voices'. The vocal part, as is so often the case with Grainger, does not have any words; instead he adds the following note: '(sing) "La", "la", or any other suitable meaningless syllable to each note. If you don't like meaningless syllables, make up your own text.'

A hymn-style often tends to flavour the character of his slower music; in *Harvest Hymn*, as one might expect, it is the predominant feature. The opening phrase of 16 bars was sketched in 1905 and the symmetrical construction of four-times-four bars gives it an authentic hymnal quality. It is, in fact, an excellent hymn-tune, with just a touch of the community song to take it out of the cloisters and place it more suitably in the open air.

Although it is an amusing suggestion that the singers might make up their own text, it is a shame that Grainger did not find, or produce, some really stirring words. The tune is a fine and simple one and *Harvest Hymn* could well have become a useful and popular addition to the repertoire.

THE 'PIONEER' STYLE

The elastic scoring and the no-nonsense 'pioneer' style of many of his pieces contribute to the immediacy with which they communicate to performer and listener. Clearly this spontaneity was not merely the result of exercising certain compositional techniques. Rather did the spontaneity emanate from a deeply-felt conviction that sensitive willingness to participate could leave the music free to take care of itself. Not many of his instrumental works are suitable for unskilled performers. Even those which in the main are relatively easy can contain lines requiring high technical ability. But he was always willing to include a part that almost anybody might be able to cope with, be it whistling, simple time-beating or strumming a guitar.

The tuned wine-glasses played by the chorus in *Tribute to Foster* utilise a party trick that everybody can do and yet, together with the richly woven vocal lines, they produce an altogether ravishing sound*. In other works, such as *Father and Daughter,* there are parts for massed guitars and mandolins in which only a few simple chords need be prepared before even a novice can take part. Grainger's personal enthusiasm during the preparation of his own concerts would encourage people from every type of job and profession, including musicians and distinguished public figures, to join the fray and take a strumming part in some of the items in the programme.

Grainger was true to his word in wanting everybody to take part in ensemble music, not only by supplying playable music but also in expressing a genuine appreciation of talent in its natural, untrained state. In his preface to *Lincolnshire Posy,* packed full of wistful anecdotes about his collecting of the original folk-songs, he dedicated this masterful work 'to the folk singers who sang so sweetly to me'—as ever, beautifully expressed in words that are exactly right. Grainger is not irrational in his praise; he claims nothing that they cannot do. How truly sounds the description 'sweetly' for a voice probably of limited range and of no great power. And how can one resist the idea of someone singing 'to me'? A minimal audience that only the amateur can afford to entertain.

His capacity to accept any situation on its own terms, provided that it was an expression of sincerely felt inner conviction, is a vital clue to the vast range, and often conflicting elements, of his artistic tenets. His 'universalist approach' to all music from all places and all times is now a distinctive quality in all forms of art. In Grainger's time it would be readily accepted on humanitarian grounds but dismissed artistically as being without focal point. Critical selectivity was the core of 19th-century aestheticism and still lamentably prevalent among devotees of 'appreciation' and those dwindling generations of professional musicians whose early training was in that tradition. Grainger, accustomed to an exceptionally liberal environment from childhood, was a complete radical. Within the small family home in Brighton (Melbourne) the arts of music, painting and literature, and the customs and languages of widely differing peoples, were studied and enjoyed with complete independence from traditional prejudices. His mother, on one hand a harsh disciplinarian and excessively determined to succeed through her son's career, was on the other hand equally capable of joining with his artistic pursuits. She played piano duets with him and supplied the musical comradeship that he would have otherwise got at an academy but along with its established taboos. With skill and imagination, four hands and one or two pianos can satisfy almost any musical desire, and the use of this instrument and the principle of adaptation and transcription remained with him for life.

Because of the special nature of his precocious aesthetic awareness his first contact with traditionally accepted values was highly disturbing to him. He was unhappy, not to say dissatisfied, with his professors at Dr Hoch's Conservatory in Frankfurt. He insisted that he learnt more from an elderly amateur musician** who, with canny mistrust of the customary musical edifices of the mid-1890s, advised him always to get straight to the subject of his composition and to stop when the work had run its full course.

Nor were his brief studies with Busoni an improvement. Although he was admired by his fellow-students, young and still sensitive to art as life rather than as propoganda, he clashed with Busoni's theocratical outlook. Thus it was that an important element of Grainger's musical art was closely akin to the spirit of the pioneers—to accept a given situation (and here is implied a musical one) and to make do, to avoid petty restrictions and favour activity and spontaneity.

EARLY EXPERIMENTS

These continual brushes with authority were to weaken him in the long run. No man with such an extrovert character can feel content in the 'unofficial' status which he assumed with regard to academic circles. He was reluctant to pursue his career to the centres of musical tradition—Paris, Berlin, Vienna—and inaugurated an endless pioneering of outlying cultural communities, which though admirable as a philosophy was but merely shifting sands for the professional musician. The pace became too hot, no doubt because it was ultimately unsatisfying, to continue to produce such star-turn pieces as *Country Gardens, Handel in the Strand* and other sensationally popular works. In the late 1920s and 1930s he turned to research in Gothic music and undertook lecturing in what might be described as demonstration recitals, again showing his originality by using a vast array of percussion, and gravitating towards mechanico-electronic music, 'free-music', an aspect of his art in which he was virtually alone. Free-music he held to be the most significant part of his life's work. Although he had reached a highly developed syntax for this type of music and had produced a few experimental test-runs, positive creative work had not began before he died.

However, as early as 1901 he had experimented with the principle of free-music via a mechanical medium. He constructed a small box which was to be placed on the piano before the pianist. At one end of the box was a small spool loaded with a long roll of paper, upon which was drawn the five lines of the stave along its full length; random notes at random distances were written upon the stave. The roll of inscribed paper was passed horizontally under a vertical black thread and the roll was wound onto another spool, rather like the film in a camera. The performer in this little experiment was to turn the take-up spool with one hand and with the other hand play the notes as they passed under the black thread.

By 1914 another experiment produced a very endearing work, a musical game in fact, in which the principle of chance elements made a remarkably early debut. *Random Round* is a 'join-in-when-you-like Round for a few voices and tone-tools (instruments), backgrounded (accompanied) with guitars'.

It consists of an introduction ('fore-play'), three episodes referred to as A, B and C, and two bridge passages, also lettered. All sections can be repeated as often as desired. There are rules to the game and a provision for absolutely anybody to take part; hand-clapping and whistling, for example, can be introduced as surprisingly effective ideas. But above all, you can sing or play when or however you will.

The basically simple material devolves upon two splendid little tunes

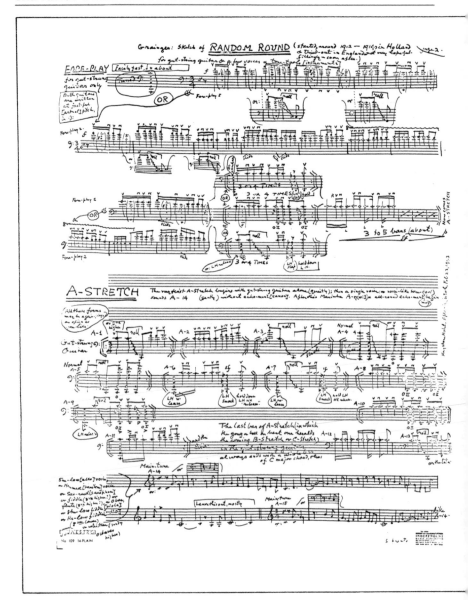

Ex 8: Grainger's sketches of 'Random Round'.

(wordless): one in triple measure, with a frequent incursion of duple cross-rhythm, and the other in $\frac{5}{4}$. The bridge passages introduce a quite different harmonic and melodic flavour, with one of them containing a free *rallentando* which, when heard against the otherwise strict tempo, produces the truly liberating effect which a *rallentando* seeks to convey.

Each participant has a sheet of music containing the above-mentioned sections, each being identified by a letter. The whole performance is guided by a person holding up one large sheet of cardboard after another, upon each being written one of the identifying letters, and by the 'band-boss' (conductor), who keeps the beat going, indicates some dynamic levels and attempts to perform instant-composition by bringing in certain groups or inviting them to drop out. Having tried the possibilities he periodically bangs a gong, or blows a referee's whistle, to give a one-bar warning before a new section, now disclosed on another card, is to commence. The whole is capable of an infinitely variable arrangement of sections and combinations of instruments and voices. A 'cat-and-dog-fight' among all participants by way of a climax is Grainger's dig at academic formal structure with its obligatory climax. Not only does the piece anticipate an entirely new aesthetic but it can prove to be immensely attractive in performance.

ORCHESTRATION

In an introduction, already referred to, which appears in a number of his scores, Grainger makes very positive statements as to his attitude towards the content of the orchestra. He does not rebel against the conventional symphony orchestra; he only asks that a more varied and imaginative use be made of available instruments—instruments of all types—and differing numbers and combinations of those instruments. In particular, he asks that there should be no hard and fast conception of what constitutes an orchestra. He suggests that all performers, especially those in their teens, should be encouraged to take part in performances which can experiment with varied instrumental combinations. All instruments should be welcome: saxophone, sarrusophone, harmonium, piano, dulcitone, marimba, staff bells, guitar, ukelele, banjo, mandolin, and so on. Although these comments were put to paper in 1929, and the '20s were not lacking in experimentation of this sort, Grainger had first put the principle into practice some 30 years earlier.

He recalled Bach's attitude: 'He seems to have been willing to experiment with all the instruments known to him and to arrange and re-arrange all kinds of works for all sorts of combinations of those instruments. It is easy to guess what liberal uses he would have made of the marvellous instruments of today.' Further on he adds: 'Salvation Army Booth objected to the devil having all the good tunes. I object to jazz and vaudeville having all the best instruments.' Were Grainger a young man living today one might well conjecture what a vigorous part he would play in the use of electronically modified instrumental sound.

Before the turn of the century he had made contact with the Pacific cultures, which, he insisted, should be primary influences in Australian culture, in preference to the transplanted European tradition. The gamelan ensemble of Indonesia he regarded as the most perfect of all instrumental ensembles, and he sought to include our nearest instrumental equivalents—bells, marimbas, xylophones—in his own orchestral works. They are an essential part of *The Warriors, In a Nutshell* and *Tribute to Foster* anticipating by almost half a century future predilection for a quantity and variety of percussion.

His comment on conductors who habitually ignored the percussion requirements of a score recreates for us an interesting historical fact. Although a conductor would hesitate to remove, say, two horns or a harp from a score, he would be less concerned about allocating only two percussionists (the 19th-century norm) to a work needing four to eight players. In defence of the conductor we must admit that eight players would be a unique demand for those times.

Grainger, as already shown, admired practically all instruments (although I have not come across a single reference by him to the harmonica, or mouth-organ) but his special favourites appear to have been the harmonium (reed-organ)—'the most sensitively and intimately expressive of all instruments'—and the saxophone—'if not the loveliest of all wind instruments it certainly is one of the loveliest; human, voice-like, heart-revealing'.

He included the harmonium, or at least recommended it, in nearly all his works. Even the big-tone pieces could be given with massed harmoniums (consider the practical problems in such an idea), but in the sweet and refined texture of *Love Verses from 'The Song of Solomon'*, with only 13 players, the presence of the harmonium is heard at its best. The nostalgic voice-from-the-past tone of the instrument is a perfect tonal reflection of human feelings that once existed. In another work, the Passacaglia on *Green Bushes,* pungent rhythmic patterns are at times stridently supported by a dispassionately sustained tang from the harmonium's chord-clusters.

Also in this work there are parts for soprano and baritone saxophones. The small ensemble of 20 to 22 instruments, including eight solo strings, gains immeasurably in resonance and incisive articulation from their presence. The baritone saxophone, in particular, lends character to the lower voices more effectively than the usual suave tone of the cello/bass combination. Both *Hill Songs* include saxophones in the scoring. In *Hill Song No 1,* a work which required much re-scoring by Grainger, the presence of saxophones is less successful against the strings than in *Green Bushes,* the strings sounding redundant against the overweight tone of the winds. But in the *Hill Song No 2* the scintillating orchestration, this time exclusively for wind instruments, again uses the saxophones to achieve a glowing 'voice-like' timbre. Wind instrumentation is not always distinguished for this quality; what is achieved in clarity can at times be accompanied by a certain dryness. *Hill Song No 2* ranks among the most outstanding instrumental textures of the 20th century. *Lincolnshire Posy,* scored for winds and one of his finest works, again used saxophones.

Another instrument specially favoured by Grainger was the guitar; he was continually advocating its use. *The* people's instrument of today, it is hard to realise that it was once neglected. Grainger saw the guitar not as a handful of contrapuntal strings but—reasonably when you come to think of it—as a bat; even an oar. He suggested that it be played 'Australian' fashion; that is, the neck sloping to the floor and the left hand grasping the neck from above. The strings would be tuned to a chord so that a harmony could be produced at the position of any fret. With the guitars divided into groups, and each group provided with a different tuning, it was possible to utilise the guitars over changes of key and with varied chord structures with only a minimum of preparation for the players. The strings were merely strummed with the right hand; changes of chords were produced not with the fingers but by the whole hand clenched across the finger-board.

The description sounds a little crude, but the musical effect was not so.

82

Such is the thoroughly good nature of the music that a performance reveals a sense of bounding rhythm and vitality.

For his concerts, Grainger would assemble groups of friends, musical but not necessarily musicians, to take part in these guitar bands. No doubt it all sounds rather primitive, especially when an alternative band of guitars is required, as in *Father and Daughter,* to overcome the set tuning of the strings to obtain additional harmonies. But the artistic result was justification enough. The earthy rhythmic pulsations of massed guitars has a special

83

)VE: Guitar duet–Grainger and Henry Cowell.

quality which Grainger fully realised with vivid effect. *Random Round*, with its background of guitars, is also entirely successful in this style of guitar writing. Although the style was an expedient at the time, Grainger turned a limitation into an artistic and cultural innovation.

SELECTED WORKS

Grainger's total output contains a considerable number of works, many of which appear in a number of different versions made by the composer himself. Some of these he referred to as merely 'dished up'; even so they occupy their own numbered places in a series such as British Folk-Music Settings, so the 40-odd items in that series contain nothing like that number of original works.

He was systematic about cataloguing his works (such as his hand-written notebooks in which he wrote down the folksongs he collected) and pains-taking in preserving all manner of things. It is therefore sad that his own published music should now have reached a state of confusion in which publishers are often unaware of the quantity, even existence, of their stocks of his music. More than one consignment to the flames has cleared shelves of 'dead stock'. Publishers cannot be blamed, however, for their investment must have been heavy, as were their losses. Who would have thought that Grainger, whose music sold in millions of copies, could ever have been a publisher's risk?

The situation at present for those who wish to perform his music is confusing, both through the profusion of Grainger's own editions and through the running down of publishers' stock. This makes it difficult to determine readily the suitability of his music for inclusion in today's prog-rammes, much of it being brief and not in accordance with the 'weight' of our concert programmes. The following works discussed here have been chosen, therefore, because of their suitability for modern programmes, though all his works can be placed with some imagination. *Random Round*, to give an example, would require some thought and energy to get organised but for the right occasion it has the potential to make it a unique event.

The order in which the following works appear is rather an arbitrary one, and certainly not preferential. The date-order of the main composition of each work has been decided upon for there are stylistic qualities developing which we should become aware of, even if processes of later re-scoring might not make this so valuable an arrangement. Practically every work contains *ad lib* instruments and/or alternatives of one sort or another. For reasonable brevity, therefore, the basic instrumentation is given, but reference to the score itself will reveal possibilities which might make even these details more adaptable to a given situation. It is all very flexible.

One aspect, that of the percussion section, should be clarified now. In addition to conventional percussion (side drum, bass drum, cymbals, triangle, etc.) Grainger used an *ad lib* percussion orchestra, a European version of the Indonesian 'gamelan' ensemble, in four of these works—the *Marching Song of Democracy, Tribute to Foster, The Warriors* and the suite *In a Nutshell*. The effect is fascinating but skilful, and musicianly players are essential for it is difficult to balance and the shades are subtle. It is almost

Percy and Ella Grainger playing percussion, 1952(?).

inevitable that some pruning will have to be undertaken in this section (who can afford, even find, the maximum ten players for the *Marching Song of Democracy?*) and Grainger indicates the *ad lib* instruments and gives practical advice as to the best distribution of available players, so examination of the score is essential.

The figures laid out below each title are as follows:— 1111-1100 means one each of flute, oboe, clarinet, bassoon—horn, trumpet, no trombone and no tuba. Piccolo, cor anglais, bass clarinet and double bassoon when present are included in the figures. Other abbreviations are:—t = tympani, p = percussion, hp = harp, pno = piano, xyl = yxlophone, cel = celesta, glock = glockenspiel, harm = harmonium.

Ex 9: From the published vocal score of 'Love Verses from "The Song of Solomon" ' (with acknowledgements to Oxford University Press).

LOVE VERSES FROM 'THE SONG OF SOLOMON'

1899/1900; rescored 1931
1111-1100, string quintet (single or massed)
harmonium (single or massed) or pipe organ
mezzo-soprano and tenor soli and mixed chorus, or four soli

When performed with four solo voices (SATB) and 12 solo instruments this exquisite little work achieves a degree of sensitive intimacy that places it more within the realm of *lieder* than instrumental choral music. For this reason it is more appropriate to its underlying character to perform it with solo rather than 'massed' voices and instruments.

The confidence and quiet affection expressed in these love verses are, of course, redolent of the years of a man's maturity. Extraordinary therefore that the young Grainger, still not yet 18 years of age, should have selected them. Even more remarkable is the benign mellowness of his setting. This aspect of tender love might suggest an influence of the Victorian ballad, but such is the originality of the freely germinating melodic line and the complete absence of metric pulse that any associations of this sort are submerged by the unique qualities of the work itself. Also the instrumentation, though preceded by Wagner's *Siegfried Idyll*, is quite independent of the standard Romantic orchestra.

Grainger's freedom in varying the time-signatures contributes to the flowing character of this work. Mostly they vary in the number of crotchets, or quarter-notes, to the bar (2, 3, or 4) but there is a central episode of 28 bars which contains 20 changes of time-signature and includes smaller divisions into quaver, or eighth-note, signatures of $\frac{5}{8}$ ($2\frac{1}{4}$ as Grainger wrote it) and $\frac{3}{8}$. The whole passage has a degree of flexibility that is gratifying to the singer, for the rhythmic shape accords exactly with the natural expression of the words.

Here, as in the *Nocturne* section of *Tribute to Foster* of many years later, Grainger's writing for the voices is sumptuously rich but never cloying nor inflated. The purity of the somewhat contrapuntal strands of melody, their spacing and independence, keep the texture open. A golden resonance prevails.

HILL SONG No 1

1901-02, final rescoring 1923
2312-1100 euphonium t (also plays cymbals) harm. pno.
soprano and alto saxophones
string septet (2 violins, 2 violas, 2 cellos, 1 bass)
(for 22 or 23 players, the single horn being ad lib)

HILL SONG No 2

1907
3363-2200 4 saxophones (SATB), cymbal.
Additonal instrumentation is also suggested for full wind band (adding trombones, tuba, etc) and for symphony orchestra (without trombones, tuba or violins)

*Ex 10: From the published full score of 'Hill Song No 1' © 1924, Universal Edition, Vi
Reprinted by permission .*

Grainger considered the first of his two *Hill Songs* to be his finest work. By any estimation they both rank among the foremost works of their kind. To be specific, the second *Hill Song* for 24 wind instruments, together with the *Lincolnshire Posy* for symphonic wind ensemble, are unsurpassed in the repertoire for this most difficult of combinations: the all-wind ensemble. For plasticity and sheer range of sounds one must look to the *Symphonies of Wind Instruments* by Stravinsky and, of course, the three great wind serenades of Mozart for suitable comparisons.

The two *Hill Songs* are closely related—indeed, the second is mainly a condensed version of the first, its extraordinary vivid, poetically brief imagery being as no more than a stanza to the epic qualities of the earlier prototype. The second is easier to listen to and in the utter clarity of its scoring certainly the easier to perform. But this is not to suggest that it is either a simplified or an improved version. Both must be considered as independent works deriving from a common source of inspiration—hill country—and utilising certain motives which the composer symbolised with it.

As usual with Grainger, none of this music is in any way representative of specific places or events but 'arose out of thoughts about and longings for the wildness of hill countries, hill people and hill music (such as the Scottish Highlands, the Himalayas and the bagpipes)'. It recalls the famous phrase from Beethoven's *Pastoral Symphony,* 'more a matter of feeling', but unlike that work of masterly organisation Grainger allows his evocative works to flow unpredictably with the rise and fall of the land, the changing weather and light, and perhaps with one's fluctuating energy: 'In fast walking measure' (crotchet = 116) in No 1 and 'Fierce and keen, at fast walking speed' (crotchet = 120) for No 2. The pace is invigorating and the sounds bright and gusty.

The original scoring of No 1 (1902) was for an extraordinary choice of instruments for that time. With rare emphasis on the tone of double-reed instruments it was for 2 piccolos, 6 oboes, 6 cor anglais, 6 bassoons and 1 double-bassoon. It might well be considered for resuscitation for it was probably never performed in this way by the composer, as he felt that it was not 'feasible'. However, some 20 years later he produced the scoring shown above. As given it is based on two alternatives suggested by the composer: an oboe and a bass clarinet to replace two sarrusophones (sopranino in E flat and tenor in B flat) as affording easier choices in most cases. But the sarrusophones (double-reed instruments like metal oboes) would fulfil the composer's wishes more authentically providing the performance as a whole followed his directions:—

> All the double reeds . . . should be played with a very stiff reed, so as to produce a wild, nasal, 'bagpipe' quality of tone. The gentle emasculated tone-quality produced by soft reeds (as normally used by most players) is utterly out of place in this composition. The saxophones should produce as reedy a tone as possible.
>
> Do not try to subdue the naturally robust saxophone and sarrusophone tone down to the volume of a clarinet or an oboe; the office of the saxophones and sarrusophones is to provide a tonal strength mid-way between the volume of the woodwind and the volume of the brass.
>
> All reed instruments should play with plenty of vibrato, particularly in the expressivo passages.

89

... which clearly raise some debatable points for both listeners and for players.

Hill Song No 1 contains 397 bars, while No 2 has 141 bars. Both are very free in their barring, particularly No 1, which in addition to changing the crotchet beats has frequent time-signatures of $\frac{3}{8}$, $\frac{5}{8}$, $\frac{7}{8}$, $\frac{1}{4}$ and $\frac{5}{16}$; exceptional for the time. The effect, however, is not to create violently rhythmic patterns (eg Stravinsky and Copland) but to remove the regularity of an insidious metrical pulse. The music flows lyrically, so that distinctly rhythmic cells are heard the more vividly.

The first of the two works poses major problems of balance similar to those of Schönberg's *Chamber Symphony,* but the expressiveness called for from each player requires greater individuality, more eloquent response to its infinite subtleties than with Schönberg's more classically conceived work. *Hill Song No 1* is the type of work which one tends to idealise in the 'perfect' performance. Grainger would have it treated with robust good sense, but its contrapuntal complexity in fuller passages and the elusive poetry of solo phrases are not readily commanded. Grainger had recourse to bracketing principal phrases in the score and in the parts as well (Schönberg's device), so he was fully aware of this particular problem. The strings, though only seven in number, and the piano too are responsible not only for an enrichment, but also for a thickening of the texture; it is significant that the second of the *Hill Songs* for wind alone, dispenses with the use of bracketing phrases altogether.

The 'sound' of each work is quite different from the other. The first, with its darknesses and at times troubled moods, created by hybrid instrumentation; a soft cushion of strings evokes the warm glow, humid and exotic, of Capricorn. *Hill Song No 2* is all tang. Not quite summer, we have to walk briskly in the clear, bright air.

Their typical 'sounds' are projected into the larger scale of their form. No 2 is based on the quicker music (the 'first speed' of No 1) which it sustains unbroken until a peaceful epilogue. No 1, on the other hand, is more complex in a structure where thematic material is also related to temporal factors. Schematically it can be analysed as follows:

Introduction	1st speed In fast walking measure
EXPOSITION 1 bar 46	2nd speed Slowly flowing and very wayward
Transition bar 249	3rd speed Very fast
EXPOSITION II bar 286	1st speed (as above)
Epilogue bar c.368	long *rallentando*

The two *Hill Songs* may be considered as the works most closely reflecting the composer's innermost character, the first of them doing so the more fully. They are gay and reflective in turn; zestful, with enormous reserves of physical and mental energy, yet infinitely tender; they have the courage to throw away a phrase but at other times to cocoon a melody, even a fragment of one, in sentimental feeling. It is not surprising therefore that they are the only works in which he shows continuity and develops a theme, for the subject is, in fact, the composer himself.

ENGLISH DANCE
dedicated to Cyril Scott
1899-1909, rescored 1924-25
3323-4332 t, p (3), organ, piano, strings

The title is misleading. It is not a dance at all and is not to be associated with the genre of which *Country Gardens,* a 'handkerchief dance', is an example. As with so many of Grainger's descriptive titles, it is more an expression of the composer's feelings towards the subject than a literal portrayal. In his introductory note to the score he wrote that he wanted to express 'a certain bodily keenness and rollicking abandonment that I found typical and enthralling in English national life'.

He goes on by referring to the high average speed of their walking in the streets, the vivid sporting activities of football and sprinting, newspaper boys swerving about on 'low bicycles', and also to 'a profusion of express trains hurtling through the dark, factories clanging and blazing by night, and numberless kindred exhilarating showings'. Yet none of these points are specifically illustrated musically; it is the 'keenness' and rather dizzy activity which is the key to this work.

In this preface, as in others (*Spoon River,* etc), Grainger draws attention to 'texture' rather than to 'colour' in regard both to material and orchestration. Bach is given as his example. An immediate impression on looking through the score is that it does possess a baroque quality of overall patterning and contrapuntal structure. A melodic phrase, stated by the organ in the first eight bars, establishes a pattern of running quavers, a dotted rhythm and a general intervallic freedom which permeate virtually the entire work. In as much as these features can be used generically it can be said that the *English Dance* possesses thematic ideas. However, these are not developed into self-contained melodic themes; there is no big central theme. Grainger describes this as 'flow of the form, the eschewal of small contrasts and the uniformity of almost unbroken peg-away even rhythms'. He contrasts this with the classical conceptions of characterisation, variety and 'human' touch.

In the methods of scoring he states 'the somewhat grey and certainly monotonous* scheme of Bach's colouring (as, for example, in the first chorus of the *St Matthew Passion*) has been preferred to the more heterogeneous, shorter-breathed, broken-up brush-work of modern orchestration habits'. In taking only this one aspect of *English Dance* it is certainly at the opposite pole to orchestral pointillism.

Notwithstanding his avoidance of 'colour' the work is certainly colourful in its display of sparkling virtuosity. As with Berlioz, such virtuosity is achieved not by making daunting technical demands upon the players but rather by an underlying vitality in rhythmic drive and crispness of utterance. Sensual it is not, but Grainger may have underestimated the undeniable appeal of rapidly changing instrumentation, albeit within his scheme of uniform materials, and its attendant variety.

The profusion of contrapuntal activity and the avoidance of a major

---

* Fowler points out that it is only in its secondary sense that monotonous implies same or tedious; its primary meaning refers to pitch or tone, to which Grainger relates texture.

central theme make it a difficult work to bring off. All too easily the effect could be a cornucopia of musical activity. Grainger made frequent use of placing phrases between brackets which should be brought out, but very often such phrases, only marginally assisted by their orchestration, are difficult to isolate in performance. One can only say that such problems are not necessarily those of the composer but remain as a challenge to the orchestra and its conductor.

English Dance is a gargantuan essay in sustained musical energy and might be compared to the first movement of Nielsen's Second Symphony, though not, of course, to its choleric temperament. In a meticulous performance its effect is breathtaking.

TRIBUTE TO FOSTER
1913-14; scored 1931
3232-4331, t, p (4-9), harm, hp, strings, five solo voices (SSTTB), solo piano, mixed chorus (also playing musical glasses)*
(the variable number of percussionists refers to *ad lib* tuned percussion)

A childhood memory of Grainger's was of his mother singing him to sleep with Stephen Foster's *Camptown Races*—a rather stimulating ditty one would have thought for this hour of night. However, his mother must have sung it in a very relaxed manner for he recollects the song as being more like a lullaby. Grainger retained his admiration of Foster—'one of the most tender, touching and subtle melodists and poets of all time; a mystic dreamer no less than a whimsical humorist'—and when he came to write his tribute he used Foster's melody, both in its original tempo and as a lullaby. The latter occupies a quiet middle section, producing an overall ternary form. This and *The Warriors* are his only two works which contain distinctly constrasting middle sections.

In spite of the familiarity of Foster's melody, its accordance with Grainger's style enables one to accept it unhesitatingly as an original work and not merely as an arrangement; to say the least, it is a transcription of the highest order. The piano plays a prominent part and its performer must attain to soloist standard; it appears to symbolise the composer's presence during the enactment of the tribute.

The piano starts the work off (F sharp major) with the pattering of busy semi-quavers which are present throughout the greater part of the work, thus setting a mood of fluttering excitement. The tune is then announced (surprisingly in E flat), again by the piano, in a brilliantly filled-in version which abounds in jazzy syncopations and arabesques (to be used later for the jaunty 'Doodah' phrase). With the entry of a solo baritone voice singing Foster's words this alternates with the chorus and biting orchestral accompaniment to the end of the first part. Mention should be made of an odd little interlude in which the piano seems to extemporise on its opening statement of the song and runs around in arabesques of ever-decreasing circles, tying

---

* *These are wineglasses of varying sizes which are fine-tuned by adding water to them, see pp 23, 77-78, 249*

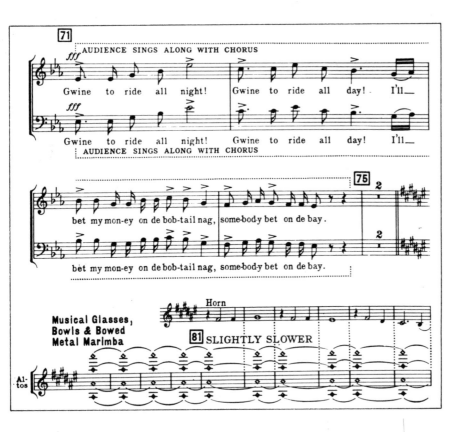

Ex 11: From the published vocal score of Grainger's 'Tribute to Foster' (with acknowledgements to Oxford University Press).

up fingers and thumbs in a way such as Chico Marx might have done.

Activity dies down and against quietly reiterated B flats on the piano the alto members of the chorus set up the exquisite humming of musical glasses. Horns play a hymn-like fragment of the tune, sopranos then set their glasses ringing, and from a delicious aura of mixed major-minor tonalities the *Nocturne* emerges.

It is impossible to describe the sheer beauty of the sounds which emanate during this section of the work. Though not exclusively created by the choir of glasses, their presence is sufficiently telling, and their sound so rarely heard, that only through actual performance can the effect be fully realised. The widely-spaced F sharp major chord which is distributed throughout the musical glasses is founded on especially deep tones which can only be produced by huge vase-like glassware of about quart size. At a later stage of the *Nocturne,* two out-of-tune tones, foreign to the key, are introduced to add to the prevailing hallucinatory quality.

As the chorus is fully occupied in playing the glasses, the vocal parts are given to five soloists. Here the vocal writing achieves remarkable intensity—a passion all the more moving for a purity in the part-writing, which reminds us of Grainger's study of the early polyphonic composers. The words of this section were supplied by Grainger himself—in a skilful reconstruction of Foster's style. Unprintably sentimental they may be, yet touching and nostalgic in Grainger's setting.

The piano soloist, who, during the *Nocturne* has been occupied 'inside' the instrument and playing upon the undamped strings with soft mallets, again introduces the *Allegro* theme. This is a shortened version of the first section and it leads into an extended coda. In this coda, conflicting fragments of melody are heard on the trumpet and clarinet, whose players are directed to adopt tempi independent of the main one. The total effect is of numerous half-heard songs recalled from past memory, all buoyantly jumbled together and symbolising man's eternal solace through song. This musical 'dissolve' gradually fades and we are left with a single clarinet contentedly tooting while some distant side-drum, as if oblivious of all else, taps out its own jaunty rhythm *a niente.*

THE WARRIORS: MUSIC FOR AN IMAGINARY BALLET
dedicated to Frederick Delius
1913-16
3433-6431 t, p(3), xyl, block, cel, hp (2), pno(3), strings
Two (or one) assistant conductors
Tuned percussion (additional to above percussion): 4-5 players
(wooden and steel marimbas, tubular bells, staff bells)
Off-stage brass: 2220 (or can be drawn from the orchestra)
(*includes heckelphone *ad lib)*

This is Grainger's largest work. It is said that Sir Thomas Beecham suggested to Grainger that as his music was of such a physical nature they might collaborate on a ballet, for which Beecham would supply the scenario. Grainger was greatly stimulated by the idea and almost immediately began jotting down some sketches. As the promised scenario never materialised and Grainger's enthusiasm never waned, the work was eventually completed for an 'imaginary' ballet.

Not unexpectedly, therefore, the ballet has 'no definite program or plot' underlying the music and 'certain mind-pictures set it going'. Nevertheless, it has the essential dramatic and mobile elements required for a ballet. A creative choreographer would be freed of a stipulated scenario and would, no doubt, impose his personal visual realisation upon the score; but Grainger's vision of consummate humanity is a splendid theme.

By 'warriors' he implies a glorification of humanity. Apart from its limited meaning of those involved in actual warfare, we are all warriors by nature of our very striving in life; getting through many a day calls for the courage and chivalry of a warrior. His love of humanity and, incidentally, his keen observation of racial types, is conveyed in this extract from the programme note contained in the score:

> ... the old Greek heroes with fluttering horse-haired helms; shiny black Zulus, their perfect limbs lit with fire-red blossoms; flaxen-haired Vikings clad in scarlet and sky-blue; lithe bright Amazons in windswept garments side by side with squat Greenland women in ornately patterned furs; Red Indians resplendent in bead-heavy dresses and negrito Fijians terrible with sharks' teeth ornaments, their woolly hair dyed pale ochre with lime: graceful cannibal Polynesians of both sexes, their golden skins wreathed with flowers and winding tendrils;—these and all the rest arm in arm in a united show of gay and innocent pride and animal spirits, fierce and exultant.

The large orchestra creates a vast concourse of sound. Spacious, brightly coloured, dome-like, it engulfs the auditorium. Without recourse to electronics it produces its own stereophonic quality. Pungent rhythmic figures are outlined by the pianos, which also serve to produce strangely elliptical effects when used in conjuction with the large array of percussion. The atmosphere is charged with mercurial excitement right from the outset of the work.

It is broadly ternary in form (only in *Tribute to Foster* do we find another of his works which contains a contrasting middle section), but with several sub-divisions in each section. The thematic material of the first part does not constitute any formal arrangement of first or second subject but is a stream of related and interchangeable phrases. They are treated with continual development by sequence and fragmentation and re-arrangement. Though they can be generally described as simple, diatonic and folk-dance in character, their setting is highly chromatic, both in harmony and orchestration.

It is interesting to compare this work with Stravinsky's *Rite of Spring*, which might possibly have influenced Grainger. They are both substantial and, of course, ballets and both have a large orchestra as a major distinguishing feature—Stravinsky with the larger wind section and Grainger using more percussion (in fact, a complete percussion 'orchestra'). Although Mahler and Strauss had used orchestras as large, their effect was to extend the tonal qualities of the classical orchestra. But Stravinsky and Grainger use their orchestras to create a deliberately stylised and bizarre orchestralism. It is the sound itself which is of predominant importance.

Both have as a central theme the re-enactment of communal celebration, but whereas Stravinsky suggests a pre-civilised community and barbaric rites of an elemental kind, Grainger's subjects have the finesse of a sophisticated society. Stravinsky found for the expression of his 'rite' a musical language both poignantly expressive of man's tentative emergence and of unprecedented barbarity when once he had established his place on earth: Grainger's 'people' have passed this stage and reached the security and plenty of an exotic earthly paradise where love, art and an affirmative well-being abound.

The middle section of *The Warriors* is therefore unexpected. A slow and passionate melody is heard on the strings, an anguished lament for some lost and only partly-remembered bliss, against which an off-stage brass group states themes from the beginning of the work in ringing fanfares. All this is preceded and concluded by mystic washes of sound from the tuned percus-

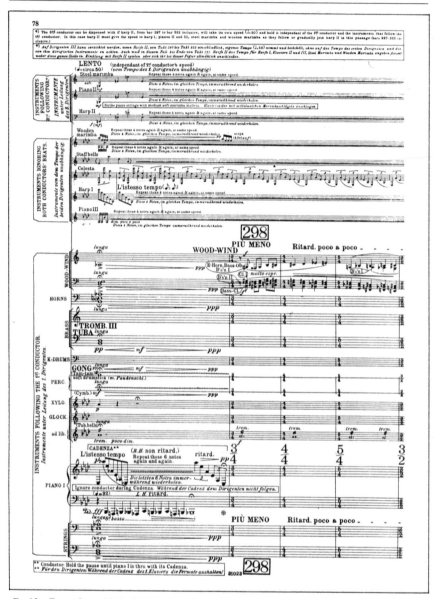

Ex 12: From the published full score of 'The Warriors'.

sion, celesta, harps and pianos and containing the rare and lovely sound of a 'languishing' melody played by the heckelphone (best described as a bass-oboe). One or, preferably, two extra conductors are required for this section. It is masterful in conception and prodigious in execution.

The final *Allegro,* based on material from the first part, though entirely re-worked, has as its main feature the off-stage theme but now vastly augmented. The scoring, excepting the lighter-toned celesta, harps, etc, is

96

for the entire orchestra. In the concluding break-away *Presto* the xylophone part, desperately busy with running four-note chords, is marked: 'The actual notes do not matter; anything of this sort will do equally well'—an extraordinary admission for those times.

As in the *Rite of Spring* and its extraordinary terse eruption in the final bar, *The Warriors* also suddenly halts in its head-long dash; there is a staggering silence and with four rock-heavy steps the music crashes to its end.

'IN A NUTSHELL': SUITE
1914-16

3333-4331 t, p (3-7), hp, cel, pno, strings
(tuned percussion is a flexible element)

1. Arrival Platform Humlet, 1908-12, scored 1916.
2. Gay but wistful, 1912, scored 1915/16.
3. Pastoral, 1915-16, scored 1916.
4. The Gum-suckers March, 1905,14, scored 1914.

The full score has a six-page preface in which the composer describes the percussion instruments, with detailed advice as to the distribution of the percussion between four to eight players (additional to the 3-7 players for the conventional untuned percussion). The material for each movement is discussed, together with dates and places of composition.
1. *Arrival Platform Humlet,* an enigmatic title best explained by Grainger's own words:

> Awaiting the arrival of belated train bringing one's sweetheart from foreign parts, great fun! The sort of thing one hums to oneself as an accompaniment to one's tramping feet as one happily, excitedly paces up and down the arrival platform. The final swirl does not depict the incoming of the expected train. The humlet is not programme music in any sense. It is marching music composed in an exultant mood in a railway station, but does not portray the station itself, its contents, or any event. There are next to no chords in this composition, it being conceived almost exclusively in single line (unaccompanied unison or octave). There are likewise no 'themes' (in the sense of often-repeated motives), as the movement from start to finish is just an unbroken stretch of constantly varied melody with very few repetitions of any of its phrases.

The tempo is described as 'with healthy and somewhat fierce "go" '—'fierce' being a quality of mood and character which he much admired. The opening theme, featuring the woodwinds, is indicated 'nasal, reedy and snarling'. As previously mentioned, this is an instrumental quality difficult to obtain from professional players, who naturally wish to guard their reputations for performances of classical style. Nevertheless, performed according to Grainger's suggestion it is an exhilarating sound. Throughout the movement, continual accretions of rapid phrases come and go, rather like a reel in its persistence. It is a unique sound to hear a full symphony orchestra gyrating wildly throughout five-octave unisons.

2. *Gay but wistful* is a 'tune in a popular London style'. Grainger writes that this movement is 'an attempt to write an air with a Music Hall flavour embodying that London blend of gaiety with wistfulness so familiar in the performances of George Grossmith Jnr., and other vaudeville artists'.

For this movement only the steel marimba and glockenspiel are retained from the tuned percussion. The tempo is a gracefully flowing $\frac{6}{8}$: a movement of old-world charm reminiscent of Elgar's 'salon' style. The scoring is delicately shaded, with occasional use of solo strings. The mood is relaxed and decidedly 'wistful'.

3. The *Pastoral* could stand as a tone-poem in its own right, and is one of Grainger's principal works. With a duration of just over nine minutes it is comparatively lengthy for a single movement. The full orchestration is again used but with only three of the tuned percussion: steel marimba, glockenspiel and staff bells.

The texture is rich and succulent—the burgeoning countryside in full summer—yet displaying frequent moments of intimate chamber-music proportions. Almost throughout a solo string sextet (2 violins, 2 violas and 2 cellos) is set aside from the main body of strings and used with solo woodwind, and myriad pointillistic effects from the tuned percussion, harp, celesta and piano.

The piano fulfils a concertante role, part-solo and part-orchestral. There is a notable episode in which the piano plays in a tempo independent of the orchestra 'waywardly', the bar-lines not concurring with the rest of the score. A short cadenza is accompanied by reiterated octaves on the steel marimba ('keep on steadily at the same speed without following conductor') while another short cadenza, for harp, celesta and piano, requires the players to follow one another from the cues printed in their parts and without reference to the conductor. The piano closes the movement by playing upon three strings (their dampers silently raised by pressing down the appropriate keys) with a soft mallet. Against lugubriously close harmony on four muted horns the sustained sound of F, G flat, A, C and C sharp is collectively mysterious and sinister.

The overall progress of the movement is disturbing. From a 'restful and dreamy' theme played by unaccompanied oboe, the acme of the pastoral idiom, the texture becomes complex then restless in extraordinary atonally juxtaposed sets of moving triads. A climax suffused in dissolving chromaticism completely removes the pastoral cliche with which the movement commenced.

Grainger's evocation of the countryside is an unusual one for he is concerned with its mystery; its nature, its people and its infinite past emerge and overwhelm everything. The traditional views of pastoralism—everlasting and benign beauty, the merry dancing peasant—do not figure. Rather do we have the hidden secret power of an independent force often alien to man, its laws unfathomable yet eternally questioned by him. We may choose to count only the sunniest hours, yet the inexorability of their passage is a fundamentally sinister phenomenon. This is the sentiment which Grainger evokes in the *Pastoral;* a study of nature as original in conception as, for example, Strauss's profound insight into the deeper qualities of Don Juan's character.

4. *The Gum-suckers March.* 'Gum-sucker' is a nick-name for an Australian hailing from the state of Victoria, the home state of the composer. The leaves of the "gum" (Eucalyptus) trees are very refreshing to suck in the parching Summer weather.

The lively march tune, 'at quick walking speed', completely diatonic, is refreshing indeed. The full percussion section is used again in this movement and mostly tutti. The climatic end of the movement, and the whole suite, is a veritable paean of jingling sounds against which Grainger places the main theme from an earlier work, a piece which Sir Thomas Beecham chose to distinguish as the worst in the world—the *Colonial Song.* In its original setting this melody had a distinctly 'sentimental' quality (and nice that is too when tenderly expressed) but at this quick walking speed it strides heroically above the orchestra.

This suite is superbly balanced in its four movements and contains in the *Pastoral* an outstanding essay in orchestral textures, expanded harmonic freedom and an early hint at the artistic viability of improvisatory and chance elements.

MARCHING SONG OF DEMOCRACY
dedicated to Rose Grainger
1901-17
3233-4332, t, p (2-10), pno(s), organ, strings
mixed chorus (wordless)
(tuned percussion is a flexible element)

Rose Grainger, the composer's mother, was, given the phenomenal receptivity of her son, chiefly responsible for his very early traditional acceptance of a wide range of art-forms in many cultural manifestations. Apart from music he was skilled in painting (there are a number of sketches and attractive watercolours from his youth) and at expressing himself in words. In the latter respect he could convey a splendid racy disposition and an infectious enthusiasm. His frequent use of the hyphen and his 'englished' terminonogy (eg 'tone-wrought' for composed), though sometimes strained to an extent which amounted to self-parody, succeeded in establishing a distinctive and idiomatic 'graingerism': no small feat in the use of language.

With so many talents he could have easily slipped into the self-contained world of the dilettante. Instead, Grainger was supremely appreciative of, indeed dependent upon, the living world of mankind. Had he lived into these times he might well have been in the vanguard of appealing for the rights of the common man. Few people have expressed their affection for mankind more 'lovingly' (a favourite word of his) than Grainger, and the perfection with which he conveyed their expressions of inner feelings through song and dance is attributable to that affection.

From an early age he was highly sensitive to human dignity and was an upholder of the democratic principles which defend our rights. He was ever as alert to its presence as to its perils; it existed in polyphony but not in homophony, in elastic scoring, in wordless song, in directions like 'any notes will do' when in fact that was so, and a refusal to accept the arts as a monopoly of an elite professionalism. It was an amateur who helped him formulate his musical aesthetic when struggling amid alien academicism in Frankfurt, and Walt Whitman, that unique amalgam of peasant reasoning and skilled literacy, who crystalised his social philosophy.

When a boy of 16 or 17, Grainger was struck by the truth contained in Whitman's *Leaves of Grass* that of all the poetry and music coming to America from Europe 'is there one that is consistent with these United States . . . is there one whose underlying basis is not a denial and insult to democracy?' And Grainger saw this as applying no less to Australia, 'and I felt a keen longing to play my part in the creation of music that should reflect the easy-going, happy-go-lucky, yet robust hopefulness and undisciplined individualistic energy of the athletic out-of-door Anglo-Saxon newer nations'. His benign nationalism was truly democratic, 'heroic but not martial, exultant but not provocative, passionate but not dramatic, energetic but not fierce, athletic but not competitive'.

Marching Song of Democracy was therefore a desire to express a healthy affirmation of life and to praise the goodness of communal effort and the pioneering spirit—an Australian *Gloria*. The original plan, that it should be for voices and whistlers, surprisingly was in 1901. It was conceived as a song to sing and whistle while 'marching along in the open air'. Although its final form was as a concert piece, it nevertheless retained the open-air spirit of the original idea. It is his major choral work.

The wordless syllables for the chorus seem, on paper, to be slightly ludicrous—'Ta da di da ra; dum pum pum pum; dam pam pam pa; ti da ti pa, pom pom pa'—but in performance they are extraordinarily effective. They possess the two primary requirements of any vocale: a predominance of vowel sound and distinct consonants for rhythm and emphasis. They 'sing' beautifully. At one stage he advises the singers, 'Don't tire yourselves over this; keep fresh for what's to come!' and then later on, 'Now's your time to sing up!' At the end of the work the voices vie with the brass in a fanfare motive; 'detached, rhythmic' is the style and 'tam pam pam pa' does this most effectively.

It is marching in spirit, but not a real march. The varying time-signatures of 2, 3, 4 and 5 in a bar avoid any jack-boot metre. An episode in $\frac{2}{2}$ and $\frac{3}{2}$ has a flowing lyricism in contrast to the quarter-note values which otherwise prevail. To describe it as a *Gloria* is entirely fitting; it is indeed a song of praise. The immense swing of the first part, the fresh lyricism of the middle section and the gathering surge of power which sweeps on to an ecstatic conclusion stamp this work with a convincing mastery of technique and expression. Though literally a secular work, it undeniably expresses a deep faith in mankind and an innocent, though nonetheless true, justice.

LINCOLNSHIRE POSY
'Dedicated to the folksingers who sang so sweetly to me'
3363-4331 (2), 5 saxophones (SAATB)
baritone, euphonium, string bass(es), t, p (2-3)
(tuned percussion at the very end *ad lib*)

Lisbon (Dublin Bay);
Horkstow Grange;
Rufford Park Poachers;
The Brisk Young Sailor;
Lord Melbourne;
The Lost Lady Found.

Grainger himself collected the first five songs by noting them down direct from their folksingers during 1905-06. *The Lost Lady Found* (which is the same tune as *Green Bushes*) he used with acknowledgement from the collection of Lucy Broadwood. Most of the actual composition for this suite was done during the 1930s, although some sketches dating from the years of collection were also used.

The songs which he collected were noted down with meticulous care for the rhythmic, dynamic and pitch details of the singers' performances. One can see in the example of his notation of *Rufford Park Poachers,* shown in the preface to the score, the extent to which he was prepared to annotate these songs, most notably in their rhythm, for it is rare to see constantly changing time-signatures in the notation of British folk-music. Far from being an exercise merely in musical detection, Grainger's aesthetic discoveries as to how people 'felt' music, when too often the conscious musician can only 'compose' it, were a profound influence on his own creative work.

In *Lincolnshire Posy* Grainger clearly gets to the root of every song and transcribes it into symphonic utterance. The wind orchestra sounds strangely and appropriately archaic in these settings—the medieval parallel chording of *Lisbon;* the extraordinary wailing as *Rufford Park Poachers* begins; the barbaric war-song of *Lord Melbourne,* with the brass fiercely sounding like Roman 'buccinae'.

Neither does Grainger try to score off these old melodies—he sees in them such fulfilled expression as one can only learn from—nor does he cosset them like curious song-birds. The work succeeds because of a sincerity which eschews the big rhetorical statement. Its charm, grave dignity and buoyant rhythms place it in descent of that greatest folk-inspired genre—the 17th-century suite.

Percy Grainger, Fort Hamilton, South Brooklyn, New York, summer 1917.

CHAPTER EIGHT

Music for Wind Instruments

Thomas C Slattery

AT the turn of this century, Percy Grainger was internationally acclaimed as a distinguished pianist, and by 1915 his compositions for orchestra were the most frequently performed in London of all works by composers of the British Empire. Grainger's reputation as a concert pianist and a 'genial composer of pleasant music in specialized vein'[1] unfortunately obscured his unique work in the wind medium. Before most composers were attracted to the sonorities produced by consorts of wind instruments, Grainger had written *Hill Song No 1* (1901-02), followed in 1907 by *Hill Song No 2*.

Hill Song No 1 has proved to be one of Grainger's most unusual scores for wind instruments. Scored for 2 piccolos, 6 oboes, 6 cor anglais, 6 bassoons, and 1 double-bassoon, it remained unperformed until 1969,[2] not only because of its unprecedented instrumentation but for its rhythmic complexity as well. Its unconventional barring is explained in a note appended to the first page of the autograph score:[3]

> The dividing of this piece into bars does not imply that the first beat of each, or any, bar shall receive greater pulse or accent than the beats inside the bar. The divisions are made only for the sake of facility in reading.

In 1921 Grainger transcribed it for chamber orchestra and, through Frederick Delius's influence, it found publication three years later.[4] The orchestral transfer was literal, although the barring had been simplified by dividing bars of $\frac{13}{8}$ into smaller units of $\frac{3}{4}$, $\frac{3}{4}$, $\frac{7}{8}$, while bars of $\frac{10}{8}$ became measures of $\frac{2\frac{1}{2}}{4}$, $\frac{2\frac{1}{2}}{4}$, and $\frac{5}{8}$.

Grainger's fascination with reed instruments led to an arrangement with Boosey of London in 1904-05, whereby he borrowed from them a different instrument weekly. His interest in reeds was already established prior to *Hill Song No 1,* for he was later to write:

> I was in love with the double-reeds (oboe, English horn, etc.) as the wildest & fiercest of musical tone-types. In 1900 I had heard a very harsh-toned rustic oboe (piffero) in Italy, some extremely nasal Egyptian double reeds at the Paris Exhibition and bagpipes in the Scottish Highlands.[5]

His experimentation with Boosey's instruments led directly to his second large wind piece, *Hill Song No 2*. A characteristic of nearly all his subsequent instrumental works, that is the scoring for complete families of instruments, chronologically begins with this composition.[6] After *Hill Song No 2* was tried out at a rehearsal in London in 1911, a slight revision was undertaken, though its first public performance did not occur until the Festival of British Music in Royal Hall, Harrogate, on July 25, 1929, Basil Cameron conducting.[7] A further revision preceded its American premiere under Colonel Francis Resta at the West Point Military Academy on April 25, 1940. Two further changes were made, in 1942 and 1946.[8] There is no question that the second *Hill Song* was a particular favourite of the composer. Following the 1940 West Point performance, Grainger noted in his daybook: 'Hill Song No 2, perhaps the pleasantest compositional surprise my life'.

From his earliest writing for winds, through *Lincolnshire Posy*, and later with arrangements and transcriptions for smaller mixed groups, Grainger created an unparalleled legacy of wind music. Richard Franko Goldman has stated:

> The 20th century has seen a strong renewal of interest in writing for wind instruments; the reed instruments in particular have been the objects of much thoughtful attention. In general this interest and attention have not tended toward a search for rarer and more exciting colour effects, but rather toward a rediscovery of a genuine wind-type of line.[9]

In his writing for winds, Percy Grainger achieved not only a genuine wind-type of line, but discovered colours and sonorities which only recently have become accepted as part of the composer's language. Therefore, the two *Hill Songs* might be respectively classified as antithesis and synthesis: the first being boldly experimental, contrasting traditional wind writing, while the second presents a more refined approach to scoring. The first *Hill Song* was only the beginning of a set of pieces Grainger was planning, for on the frontispiece of the autograph score he states: 'N.B. This is merely an exploration of musically-hilly ways, a gathering of types for future Hill Songs, a Catalogue'.

The cornerstones of Grainger's wind reputation most certainly rest on the *Hill Songs* and the popular *Lincolnshire Posy*. Although Grainger transcribed many of his pieces from one medium to another, with the exception of piano reductions, no attempt was made to disturb the original character of these models. The full range of his orchestrative pallette and his fund of compositional techniques are vividly displayed in these works.

It is difficult to label and catagorize Grainger's work as compositional periods are not applicable. Almost any general statement made about his music can be refuted by citing abundant examples of decidedly the opposite. Perhaps what can be uncompromisingly stated is that he was an innovator who wrote music to be performed.

The influences which led Grainger to write for particular combinations of instruments, however, clearly fall into periods. From 1901 to 1914 (London years), chamber music recitals held in the salons where he performed led to the creation of mixed wind combinations, and later his time in the United States Army (1917-1919) produced some of his finest band scores. Associations with American summer music-camps in the 1930s and early 1940s produced transcriptions of traditional music for saxophones, clarinets, and mixed wind groups. It is to his credit, and to the performer's benefit, that Grainger's instrumental lines prove so musically satisfying. 'I have never written a part', he explained, 'that I did not sing myself'.

CONCERT OF APRIL 26th 1925[1] (All-Grainger Program)

My works to be presented will be seen to date from 1898 to 1912. Owing to my very slow methods of composition, based upon frequent experimentation and again and again repeated rescorings, most of the many chamber works I have begun in more recent years are not yet ready for performance, though I hope to bring them forward in later room-music concerts. My experiments with large chamber combinations and the blending of voices, reeds, guitars, strings, concertina or harmonium, percussion, etc., in proportions and choice of performers varying with each composition, began around 1899 and thus antedated by several years the European Continental renaissance of larger chamber groupings that came to a head with Arnold Schoenberg's "Kammersymphonie" (1906). What chiefly actuated me was my fondness for the individualistic quality obtainable with solo (as contrasted with massed) parts and the intensity, for climaxes and out-bursts, that can be had, in rooms and quite small halls, of the nasal or reedy resonance of wood-winds (why should the oboe, for instance, always be heard *only* as a *distant-sounding* instrument—which is the impression it makes in larger concert halls?). This intensity of *quality* obtainable with large room-music blends has, in the case of the normal symphony orchestration, to be replaced by *quantity*, owing to the obliterating over-weight of greatly massed strings and to the exigencies of large halls in which only the blare of the brass is sufficiently incisive for truly climactic moments—a factor that seemed to me to tend towards poverty of color choices and loss of instrumental individualisticness.

SUNDAY EVENING, APRIL 26, 1925
at 8.15 P. M.

Grainger's Room-Music Concert

Performers

Conductors: Frank Kasschau, Percy Grainger
Pianists: Ernest Hutcheson, Ralph Leopold, Percy Grainger
Guitarists: Ralph Leopold, Percy Grainger
Kasschau's Solo Choir (Conductor: Frank Kasschau)

SOPRANOS	CONTRALTOS
Marie Langdon Andrews	Florence Prommelt
Mildred M. Ross	Marian Adam

TENORS	BARITONES	BASSES
Samuel E. Craig	John P. Hamilton	Elmer Ross
George E. Bennett	Charles Southwick	Wallace Cannon

24 MEMBERS of the NEW YORK PHILHARMONIC ORCHESTRA

PROGRAM

1 ENGLISH DANCE (composed 1899-1909).
   PERCY ALDRIDGE GRAINGER
   (Born Brighton, Vic., Australia, 1882)
   For 6 hands at 2 pianos.
   ERNEST HUTCHESON, RALPH LEOPOLD, PERCY GRAINGER

2 HILL SONG No. 1 (composed 1901-1902) . . . . GRAINGER
   For piccolo, flute, oboe, English horn, bassoon, double-bassoon, sopranino sarrusophone, heckelphone, soprano saxophone, alto saxophone, horn, trumpet, euphonium, kettle-drums, cymbals, harmonium, piano, 2 violins, 2 violas, 2 cellos, bass.
   Conductor: PERCY GRAINGER

3 KIPLING SETTINGS (composed 1898-1908) . . . . GRAINGER
   Poems of India and the Jungle (by permission of the author, Mr. Rudyard Kipling) set for voices, accompanied and unaccompanied.
   (In order that the continuity of this cycle may not be broken the audience is requested not to applaud until the end of the final number.)
   (a) The Fall of the Stone (mixed voices and 15 instruments).
   (b) Night-Song in the Jungle (men's voices, unaccompanied).
   (c) Morning-Song in the Jungle (mixed voices, unaccompanied).
   (d) Hunting-Song of the Seeonee Pack (men's voices, unaccompanied).
   (e) The Peora Hunt (mixed voices and 9 instruments).
   (f) "Tiger! Tiger!" (men's voices, unaccompanied).
   (g) Mowgli's Song against People (mixed voices and 12 instruments).
   KASSCHAU'S SOLO CHOIR (Conductor: FRANK KASSCHAU)

4 (a) *"MY ROBIN IS TO THE GREENWOOD GONE"
   (composed 1912) . . . . GRAINGER
   A ramble upon an old English tune for flute, English horn and 6 strings.
   Conductor: PERCY GRAINGER

   (b) *SCOTCH STRATHSPEY AND REEL, INLAID WITH SEVERAL SCOTCH AND IRISH TUNES AND A SEA-CHANTY (composed 1901-1911) . . . . GRAINGER
   For 4 men's voices, 5 wood-winds, xylophone, harmonium, 2 guitars and 8 strings.
   Conductor: FRANK KASSCHAU

STEINWAY PIANOS, ESTEY HARMONIUM used.

---

*None of the compositions on the above program are based on folk-music or popular melodies except those two marked with a star.

...inger concert at the Little Theatre, 238 W44th St., New York: Sunday evening 26 April 1923 ...15 pm.

Chronologically juxtaposed between the two *Hill Songs* lies *Lads of Wamphray*, Grainger's first work for the wind band.[10] This was completed in 1905 and performed that year by John Mackenzie and the Band of His Majesty's Coldstream Guards. Although the two *Hill Songs* and *Lads of Wamphray* might be considered as the first major band works of the 20th century, 'these works were not published, however, until much later, and the credit for being the first available and universally recognized original band work of the century must unquestionably go to the Holst Suite'.[11]

Lads of Wamphray was based on a folk poem of the same title taken from Sir Walter Scott's *Minstrelsy of the Scottish Border* and, unlike so many of Grainger's later band scores, utilised no folk material or traditional tunes. After a revision to accommodate the instrumentation of American bands, it found publication in 1941.[12]

With the exception of two folk-tunes Percy arranged for voice and accompanying brass instruments,[13] his next work with a large body of wind instruments occurred while he was a member of a United States Army Band. *Colonial Song,* scored for military band in 1918, was originally a piano piece written as a 1911 'Yule Gift' for his mother. Listed in his own files as 'Nr. 1' of a projected series of 'Sentimentals', it remains the lone contribution to that category. The harmonic structure of *Colonial Song* is less complex than *Lads of Wamphray* and, with the exception of the opening statement, the texture seems contrived and unoriginal. An interesting feature of the score, which was to become a Grainger trademark, is the manner in which its crescendo and diminuendo are constructed:

> To ensure a wide range of tone-strength differentiation I applied to large chamber music what I would call Wagner's 'organ registration type of scoring'. That is to say: where waxing and waning tone-strengths are desired in one and the same tone-strand (voice or part) they are attained not merely by changing dynamics in the instruments playing the total tone-strand, but also by adding extra instruments to the tone-strand where a loudening of the tone is desired & by withdrawing the extra instruments where a softening of the tone is intended.[14]

In a letter to Dr Frederick Fennell, Grainger explained that his *Colonial Song* was 'an attempt to write a melody as typical of the Australian countryside as Stephen Foster's exquisite songs are typical of rural America'.[15] Although no folk-tune material was used, the influence of the American Negro spiritual *Nobody Knows the Trouble I've Seen* is evident in the opening measures.

The *Children's March, Over the Hills and Far Away* was also a product of his Army career and 'especially written to use all the forces of the Coast Artillery Corps Band in which I was serving in 1918'.[16] It was one of the earliest wind scores calling for a piano as an integral part of the sonority. Because of the nature of the Army organization for which it was written, parts are sufficiently 'cued' to eliminate the piano. The original scoring, however, was conceived with the piano in mind.

A new type of scoring for the wind band originated with this composition. For the first time the low reeds were used effectively to balance the reed choir against the brass. Individual and carefully conceived percussion writing brings the three sections of the wind band to a balanced whole. Parts for the bassoon, English horn, contrabassoon, and bass clarinet are exploited for their particular sonority rather than for their individual range. The roots of the distinctive orchestration which characterized Grainger's later wind compositions may be found in this score. Sarrusophone parts are used with an optional substitution by bassoons or saxophones.[17]

The military band to which Grainger found himself assigned provided a valuable opportunity to experiment freely with his writing for winds and percussion. His arrangement of Debussy's *Bruyères* for ten instruments and harmonium is inscribed 'Fort Jay, September, 1918'. Through his adaptation of folk-tunes, Grainger received his greatest popularity as a composer and, while in the Army, he produced some of his finest settings for military band.

Now, over 60 years after its publication, the *Irish Tune from County Derry* remains a basic part of the wind band's repertoire. The simple and direct approach to idiomatic wind-writing introduced in this setting produced sonorities which were revolutionary in wind-band scores. Appearing in 1918 as No 20 of his *British Folk-Music Settings,* this arrangement was preceded by settings of the same tune for mixed chorus, piano solo, and for horns and strings. With the exception of the final 16 bars, the tune is presented in a simple manner with no more than six voice-strands appearing at one time. By combining the various lines among the different instrumental families, a richness of sound is achieved which today remains unique in scores for the wind band.

Shepherd's Hey, also scored for military band in 1918 and published on the reverse side of *Irish Tune,* was designated No 21 of the *British Folk-Music Settings.* Grainger was indebted to Cecil Sharp for collecting this traditional English Morris tune.[18] In its rhythmical make-up and lack of unusual sonorities, this score sharply contrasts with that of the *Irish Tune.* A cleverly syncopated countermelody grows out of the opening statement and propels the rhythmic drive of this dance to its climax. Solo intruments take on the characteristics of the original dancers, who would spontaneously enter and leave the dance as their energies dictated. Percussion instruments of a fixed pitch are used in abundance and contribute a unique timbre to the score.

Two years following the unusually productive 1918, Grainger completed the last band score of his Army period. *Molly on the Shore,* scored in 1920, was based on two Cork reel tunes, *Temple Hill* and *Molly on the Shore.* Their source was *The Complete Petrie Collection of Ancient Irish Music.*[19] The original setting dates from 1907, when Grainger scored them for string quartet as a birthday gift to his mother. Although the string quartet version was a public success, the military band arrangement did not receive wide acceptance. It is similar to *Shepherd's Hey* in its rhythmical design and clever (almost whimsical) handling of the borrowed material. Chromatic progressions and deft changes of instrumental colour make it a charming addition to the literature and point to it as a direct link and precedent to *Lincolnshire Posy.* Its 195-bar length was unusual for Grainger's folk settings of this period.

By 1949, Schott & Co of London issued four of Grainger's compositions arranged for traditional brass band. Of these four, *Irish Tune from County Derry, Mock Morris, Shepherd's Hey* and *The Duke of Marlborough,* only the last-named was appearing in print for the first time. The remaining three had existed in varying arrangements.

Grainger's finest achievement in wind instrument writing was *Lincolnshire Posy*. It was completed in 1937 and premiered on March 7 of that year at the Eighth Annual Convention of the American Bandmasters Association in Milwaukee, Wisconsin. This single work carefully documents Grainger's ideas on rhythm, harmony, and orchestration in settings of Lincolnshire songs he collected in 1905 and 1906. *Lincolnshire Posy*[20] must be considered an original work, although it draws its thematic material exclusively from English folk-songs. The originality in their adaptation to wind instruments sets them apart from mere arrangements. In programme notes he prepared for the published edition, Grainger explained his intentions:

> Each number is intended to be a kind of musical portrait of the singer who sang its underlying melody . . . a musical portrait of the singer's personality no less than of his habits of song . . . his regular or irregular wonts of rhythm, his preference for gaunt or ornately arabesqued delivery, his contrasts of legato and staccato, his tendency towards breadth or delicacy of tone.[21]

The band at the premiere was conducted by Grainger, and composed of local professional musicians who had a great deal of difficulty with the performance. In the subsequent published score, Grainger reacted to their inadequacies by appending a note to bandleaders explaining that the only players likely to balk at those rhythms were seasoned professional bandsmen, 'who think more of their beer than of their music'.

In 1941 Grainger arranged his *Immovable Do* for military band. The resulting transcription was successfully made by converting the original mixed chorus lines to appropriate instruments. Though not developing the rich sonorities of his earlier *Irish Tune, Immovable Do* used similar orchestrative techniques. Both pieces are models of simple but effective writing.

Grainger's last original work for band was *The Power of Rome and the Christian Heart*. It was commissioned in 1947 to commemorate the 25th anniversary of the League of Composers, and was in honour of the 70th birthday of Edwin Franko Goldman. It is his largest wind score and calls for an organ to supplement the wind complement. This work does not possess the colour which was characteristic of his earlier writing, although a striking similarity in harmonic devices exists between it and *Lincolnshire Posy*. The *Power of Rome,* first begun in 1918, was completed in 1943 for an expanded orchestral wind section, strings, and organ. Faced with the deadline of the commission and nothing yet on paper, Grainger decided to rescore it for the occasion. Openly admitting what he had done, he explained: 'As it takes me about 20 years to finish a tone-work, the best thing I could do was to fix up my *Power of Rome* so it could be played without strings'.[22]

Grainger's 1949 adaptation of the Scottish folk tune, *Ye Banks and Braes o'Bonnie Doon,* was an all-purpose publication. The score contains an overlapping instrumentation which permits the performance for almost any combination of reed and brass choirs, as well as for wind band.

Grainger's final work for the band was also a folk-tune setting: *Let's Dance Gay in Green Meadow* was first sketched in 1905, but not completed until 1954. This unusual seven-bar dance tune, the last bar serving as the anacrusis to the first had been collected in 1922 by Grainger and the Danish folklorist, Hjalmar Thuren.

Following Grainger's death in 1961, several scores for the wind band appeared in arrangments by others. In 1962, Richard Franko Goldman published his arrangement of *Handel in the Strand* and in 1965 his version of *Sussex Mummers' Christmas Carol* was released. *Spoon River,* originally completed in 1929 with a first performance by the Goldman Band, was re-edited by Glenn C Bainum and published in 1967. Mr Bainum's editing of *Let's Dance Gay in Green Meadow* found a publisher in 1969.[23]

In addition to the two aforementioned selections for voice or chorus and brass, Grainger contributed three additional works for chorus utilising the wind band as an accompanying body. *Sir Eglamore,* written for double mixed chorus and band, was completed in 1912, followed by *The Bride's Tragedy,* a ballad for double chorus and band, in 1914. *The Widow's Party,* scored for men's chorus and band, appeared in 1923.

The *Marching Song of Democracy,* published originally for orchestra and chorus in 1916, was arranged for band and chorus by the composer in 1948. Late in 1946, *Under a Bridge,* a Danish folksong he had collected in 1922, was cast for mezzo-soprano, baritone, flute, trumpet, piano, and keyboard percussion.

A relatively unknown aspect of Grainger's contributions to the wind band is his arranging of the music of J S Bach, Antonio de Cabezón, Gabriel Fauré, Cèsar Franck, Guillaume de Machaut, John Dowland, and Josquin des Prés, along with selected items from his English Gothic Music Series. These arrangements date from 1931 to 1943, and though they remain in manuscript, most were conducted by the composer at American festivals. In many instances these arrangements were first conceived for smaller wind choirs with parts being added to accommodate band performances.

Only two of the many scores Grainger produced fall into the classification of chamber music 'exclusively for wind instruments'. Both were written prior to 1907 and possess the distinctive rich sound which is characteristic of Grainger's early wind offerings.

Walking Tune was written for woodwind quintet in 1905 and published in 1912. It was based on a tune written during a three-day walking trip Grainger made in the Scottish Highlands in the summer of 1900. This score is one of the loveliest of Grainger's original wind pieces. At the insistence of Stokowski in 1940, Grainger expanded the score to embrace an orchestral wind section. It was not to be included in a subsequent recording Stokowski made of Grainger's music.

In 1907 Grainger prepared the folksong *Died for Love,* which he had collected from Joseph Taylor, for voice, flute, clarinet, and bassoon. This short, transparent piece consists of a simple 20-bar Dorian tune, supported polyphonically by the instruments quite independent of the vocal line. Although the composer later rearranged the accompaniment for strings, piano, and other instrumental combinations, the original setting remains the most popular orchestration and the one which Grainger himself preferred.

A larger body of literature exists for chamber music which includes wind instruments as an integral part of the structure. One of the earliest of these was the old English tune *The Three Ravens,* in a setting for baritone solo, mixed chorus, and five clarinets (optional flute for first clarinet). It was written in 1902, although not published until 1950, and received the 41st position in Grainger's *British Folk-Music Settings.* Also designated as No 41[24] was *Bold William Taylor,* written in 1908 for voice, two clarinets, harmonium, and six strings. The following year, Grainger arranged his popular *Shepherd's Hey* for flute, clarinet, horn, concertina, and eight strings. It was this setting which became one of his earliest successes. Combining vocal and instrumental lines was a preferred technique and one which was to consistently occupy Grainger's attention.

Directly following *Shepherd's Hey* and the second *Hill Song* was the unusual *Scotch Strathspey and Reel,* written in 1911 for ' room-music 20-some'.[25] Sketches exist for a variety of instrumental combinations but the double reed and concertino (optional harmonium) sound dominated his thinking and the British folk-tunes were preserved in this unusual and delightful framework.

Perhaps the best adaptation of a non-original tune for chamber music proportions was *My Robin is to the Greenwood Gone,* completed in 1912. Grainger described it as: 'A room-music ramble upon the first 4 bars of the old tune of that name for flute, English horn, and 6 strings'. He extended the tune, added superb counter-themes, and produced a piece which is among his best offerings of the period. His most successful works from both popular and musical points of view were most often those which he based on a borrowed tune or phrase.

The years Grainger spent teaching and performing at various summer music camps in America, the most notable being the Interlochen Music Camp in Michigan, produced a large number of pieces for homogeneous wind groups. The most common groupings were saxophone choir, clarinet choir, and brass choir. The general category 'Arrangements for Wind Instruments' contains the greatest number of entries; the largest is those arranged for saxophones.

In 1937, Grainger arranged the folk tune *Lisbon* for woodwind quintet. It was based on chorus sketches dating from March, 1906, and eventually rescored and published under the title of *Dublin Bay,* as the first movement of *Lincolnshire Posy.* In 1943, Grainger scored it for six saxophones. This setting, in addition to saxophone arrangements of *Immovable Do* and *The Merry King,* are the best-known of his works arranged for saxophones. The last two were completed in 1939.

The Merry King began as a sketch for chorus in 1905 after Grainger captured it near Wimbledon in an early folk-hunt. It is similar to *Shepherd's Hey* in its instrumentation and history. In 1938 and 1939 he reworked it for chamber winds which included three clarinets, flute, bass clarinet, baritone saxophone, contrabassoon, trumpet, horn and piano. It appeared as *British Folk Music Setting,* No 39; a piano version that same year is recorded as No 38.

Especially when working with folk-tunes, Grainger would seemingly transfer selections indiscriminately from one medium to another, but whenever he cast folk-tunes for wind they would become a permanent part of his programming.

Transcriptions for saxophone choir include three short works of J S Bach, three numbers from the *English Gothic Music* series, prepared jointly with Dom Anselm Hughes, the three works mentioned above, and one transcription each from the works of Antonio de Cabezón, Alfonso Ferrabosco, John Jenkins, Claude Le Jeune, William Lawes, Guillaume de Machaut, Herman Sandby, and Josquin des Prés. In arrangements for clarinet choir, two *English Gothic Music* pieces are listed, as is a single work from each of the following composers: J S Bach, John Jenkins, Claude Le Jeune, William Lawes, Alessandro Scarlatti, and Adrian Willaert. The arrangements for brass groups include single works of J S Bach, Alfonso Ferrabosco, Claude Le Jeune, Guillaume de Machaut, Josquin des Prés, Adrian Willaert, and *The Annunciation Carol* from his *English Gothic Music* series.

The traditional pieces which Grainger arranged and rearranged for varying wind combinations occupied the greatest share of his compositional time following the completion of *Lincolnshire Posy*. None of these arrangements ever reached publication, although they were programmed many times when Grainger appeared at summer music camps or with school groups in concert. This manuscript series, entitled *Grainger's Chosen Gems for Winds,* was available in blueprint reproductions from the composer and their use encouraged whenever he chanced to find an audience. The basic categories for which he wrote were: brass choir, saxophone choir, clarinet choir, combined saxophone and clarinet choirs, small wind groups of unlike timbres, and military band. Many pieces appear in transcription in more one section of the series.

As an orchestrator and arranger for winds, Grainger holds a unique position in 20th-century music. He was constantly experimenting with instrumental combinations and he strongly favoured reed instruments. He was critical of his original offerings, but the two *Hill Songs* and *Lincolnshire Posy* remained for him, and his public, testimonies to his creative talents. In 1957 he wrote to a friend in Sweden, stating:

> As to the public dislike of all my music except for 5 or 6 little pieces, I think I understand that pretty clearly. In my own compositions (those in which I have not used folksongs) the melodic invention is pretty poor. Also the emotional background is not of a kind to interest most people . . . But who cares about the 9th century, which is the period of my chief inspiration? . . . Most people want their folksongs middle class.[26]

When considering Grainger as an original composer, his significance is not because he initiated particular techniques, but rather that he embraced new ideas and changes. From his childhood visions of 'free music', through his scholarly notation of folksongs, his solo wind chamber pieces, his experiments with improvisation, the editing of old music, and his experiments with electronic music, Grainger's thoughts, as documented in his writings and his compositions, were always advanced. His concept of woodwind families and woodwind sounds was the beginning of the emergence of a standardization of instrumentation for the wind band. No single composer has done more in this century for the wind band medium.

STEINWAY HALL

Lower Seymour Street, W.

MR. PERCY

GRAINGER

(The young Australian Pianist

WILL GIVE HIS

FIRST

Pianoforte Recital

In LONDON

(Under the Direction of Miss ALICE E. JOSEPH)

ON

Tuesday, October 29th, 1901,

At THREE o'clock.

Stalls, Reserved, 7s. 6d.   Area, Unreserved, 3s.

Balcony, Unreserved, 1s.

Tickets to be obtained of Mr. PERCY GRAINGER, 61 Gloucester Place,
Kensington, W.; of Mr. Mickey, Box Office, St. James's Hall;
Mr. Whitehead, Box Office, St. James's Hall; Ticket Agencies,
and of

Miss ALICE E. JOSEPH,

Opera and Concert Agency.

7a, Hanover Street, Regent Street, W.

J. MILES & CO. LTD. WARDOUR ST. W.   [For Programme P.T.O.

PROGRAMME.

a. PRELUDE and FUGUE, A minor   . . *Bach—Lust*

b. INTERMEZZO, Op. 116, No. 6 ⎫
   INTERMEZZO, Op. 119, No. 2 ⎬ . . *Joh. Brahms*
   CAPRICCIO, Op. 76, No. 2 ⎪
   INTERMEZZO, Op. 117, No. 1 ⎭

c. BALLADE, Op. 24   . . . . *Edv. Grieg*

d. CAPRICCIO ⎫
   PASTORALE ⎬ . . . . . *Scarlatti*
   DEUX ETUDES CONCERTANTES *Frédéric d'Erlanger*

e. PRELUDE, Op. 28, No. 9 ⎫
   ETUDE, Op. 25, No. 10 ⎬ . . . . *Chopin*
   ETUDE, A flat ⎭
   "VALSE DES FLEURS" (Suite Casse-Noisette)
                       Tschaikowsky—Grainger

An early London recital programme.

112

CHAPTER NINE

Grainger and the Piano

Ronald Stevenson

PERCY'S 'Graingerness' was first manifested in a piano piece he composed in Frankfurt on July 24 1898, at the age of 16. Its title is the first of his Graingerisms: *Saxon Twi-Play*. Whether that refers to the street sword-play of German youths or to the 'chopsticks' play of two hands on the keyboard, is open to conjecture. Though the title is in English (if idiosyncratic), the tempo and interpretative directions are in Italian (albeit just as idiosyncratic). In the unpublished MS I consulted in the Grainger House, White Plains, NY, in May 1976, there is a unique marking in the last section of the piece: *excell al presto*. The 'excell' is obviously a mis-spelling of *accel*: Percy had so little feeling for Italian that maybe it's just as well he chose to use colloquial English for tempo and expression markings on his later compositions.

There is no reason why an English-speaking composer should not use English expression-marks (Britten, for instance, probably taking Grainger's lead, used them increasingly), any more than Beethoven should not use German directions, as he did in his late piano sonatas. But British snobbism is such that Beethoven's German (sometimes drawing on a vocabulary unfamiliar to non-Germans, as in the word *ermattet*—'exhausted', in op 110) is revered, whereas Grainger's English is deemed 'funny'. Racy it certainly is. In the very year that Grainger wrote his *Saxon Twi-Play*, MacDowell published his *Sea Pieces*; and they employ English very freely—for instance 'well bound' for *legatissimo*, 'hold' for *tenuto*, and so on. MacDowell's example may have encouraged Grainger to use English terms instead of Italian—though, paradoxically, in the unpublished MS of Grainger's transcription of Byrd's *The Carman's Whistle* (made between 1942-1951) he employs a good many Italian expressions. (Grainger was nothing if not paradoxical.)

His first employment of his idiosyncratic English in published music was in his *Paraphrase on Tchaikovsky's Flower Waltz* (published in London in 1905) which includes such Graingerisms as 'harped' for *arpeggiando* and 'louden lots' for *crescendo molto*; and, at the end, bears the characteristic legend '20.4.04.S.S. 'Sophocles' '. But what a Graingeresque slip of the pen—a *glissando* rather than a slip!—to write 'excel to presto', for that is what he was doing all his life.

Grainger's unique contribution to the concert platform and to its repertory was that he brought the outdoors spirit into it. How did he do this? A curious thing is that, alone among the great composer/pianists, apart from transcriptions, he never wrote anything initially for piano. All his best-known compositions were originally conceived for other instrumentation. He claimed that he only made piano versions at the behest of his publishers. I suggest that he brought the open-air spirit into the concert hall because he was the only concert pianist who made music in the same way that a folk-singer makes his: naturally, untrammelled by notation.

Indeed, he once applied the same method to his own piano-playing as he did in recording folk-singers on the Edison phonograph, and then notating their performance. He improvised his *Lullaby* from *Tribute to Foster* on a Duo-Art Pianola and notated the rendition, thereby reversing the usual procedure of performing from a slavish reading from the printed page. In his notes to this published piece he states his objective of 'preserving, as it were photographically, all the rhythmic irregularities of an individual rendering' and adds that it is 'not intended to be followed slavishly, note for note, by other players'.

But it wasn't only in rhythmic freedom that Grainger's pianism emulated the folk-singer's: I believe he based *every* aspect of his playing and piano-writing on the folk-musician's model. In his essay 'The Impress of Personality in Unwritten Music'[1] he writes of the 'non-legato tendencies' of folk-singers, who 'use their breath, more as some birds and animals do, in short stabs and gushes of quickly contrasted, twittering, pattering and coughing sounds which (to my ears, at least) are as beautiful as they are amusing'. He noted similar tendencies in British and Scandinavian folk-fiddlers, 'who are as fond of twiddles and quirks as are the old singers, and do not try to exchange the "up and down" physical nature of the bow for the attainment of a continuous tone'.

Like the folk-musician, Grainger sought to *speak* in music. Indeed, it would be true to say that he was the only concert pianist who was also a folk-musician. Röntgen described him as 'a folkloristic genius'.[2] Grainger had absorbed so much folk-music that he was a folk-musician. So he articulated as a folk-musician does. In the piano, despite his love-hate relationship with it, he had in some ways an ideal medium, because it is essentially a *non-legato* instrument.

Grainger's folk-like articulation was often achieved, especially in passages marked 'roughly', by unusual fingering, such as what he termed 'bunched' fingering, meaning the use of the middle finger with the index finger wrapped over it and supported by the thumb under it, for increased strength. On a black key, four fingers would be used. Another unorthodox technique to achieve greater articulation was the use of uniform fingerings for double 6ths (eg $\frac{4}{1}$ $\frac{4}{1}$ $\frac{4}{1}$ in the right hand). In the note to his arrangement of *Shepherd's Hey* he demonstrates his opposition to the Matthay 'relaxation methods' by urging the student to practise in 'the most mercilessly energetic, taxing and exhausting way possible' and claims that 'if the attack of double notes (sixths and octaves) is energetic enough, the relaxation (between attacks) would look after itself'. He adds, 'you do not have to tell a man to sleep who has just walked 65 miles without stopping'. The instruction for the double sixths is to play with 'stiff fingers, stiff wrist'! All this does not deny that Grainger could be as elegant as any pianist when he chose; just as his wardrobe contained Savile Row suits, however much his

FACING PAGE: a late study of Grainger at the piano.

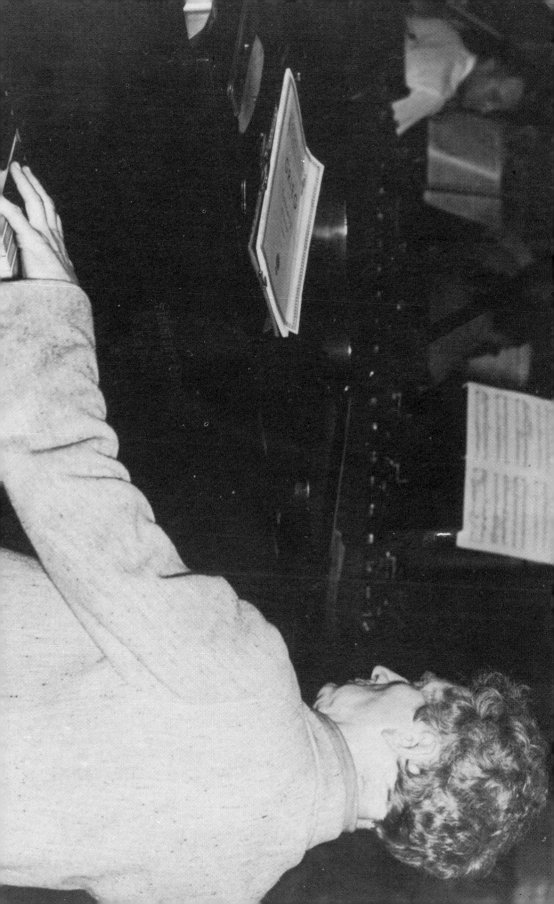

Percy and Ella, mid 1950s.

preferred garb was an open-neck blue shirt, white 'duck' house-painter's trousers, a sports jacket and his old army boots.

In his published *Guide to Virtuosity*,[3] we see how other aspects of his pianism were based on the human voice. His phrasing, for instance. He advises that, to compensate for decrease of intensity of tone towards the keyboard treble, a *rising* melody should be played *crescendo*, a *falling* one *diminuendo*. Short pauses on melodic climaxes—especially in *pp*—should simulate the singer's *mezza voce* or *falsetto*.

Grainger achieved dynamic contrasts through *quantity* of tone, not *quality*. (Here he agrees with Sir James Jeans in asserting that if a note is played by 100 different pianists with the same tone-strength it will have the same quality). His speciality was what, in the *Guide to Virtuosity,* he calls 'simultaneous tone-strength differentiation': the bringing out of middle melodies. More of this later.

The *Guide* also presents his ideas on pedalling. He had many uses of the damper-pedal. Apart from 'syncopated' pedalling (probably the invention of Anton Rubinstein), he frequently used half-pedalling for clarification of harmony through partly-sustained tone—like the sun bursting through a mist. And he often employed *vibrato* pedalling—a 'fluttering' of the foot on the damper pedal—to achieve a graded *diminuendo*.

He is unique in having used the middle, or *sostenuto*, pedal in *all* his piano-writing—even in song accompaniments. This enables a single note or a single chord to be sustained while other notes are played without pedal or with the damper and/or the 'soft' pedal. Thus, bass notes in the middle pedal function as the organ pedal-board; or, if in the middle register, they function as sustained horn-chords, increasing the quasi-orchestral possibilities of the piano. The *fons et origo* of Grainger's use of the middle pedal was Section 4 of the First Appendix to Volume I of the Busoni edition of Bach's *Well-tempered Clavier*[4]: 'On the Transcription of Bach's Organ-works for the Pianoforte'. In the summer of 1903 Grainger studied Bach-Busoni transcriptions with Busoni in Berlin, and the use of the middle pedal would certainly be an integral part of those lessons. Grainger was the only Busoni pupil who developed his master's technique of middle-pedalling.[5]

In the Grainger Museum in Melbourne in June 1980, I discussed with Libby Wright her researches on Grainger's re-workings of Bach transcriptions by Tausig and by Busoni. The Bach transcriptions Grainger played were really Bach-Tausig-Busoni-Grainger. To make a generalisation, I would say that Busoni's transcriptions were like Rembrandtesque engravings from a master painting, whereas Grainger's were like the painting made into a poster. One style employed finesse, elegance: the other, the broad brush stroke. Busoni's transcriptions sound splendid (unless you disagree with his aesthetic) in such a hall as London's Wigmore (seating about 500); Grainger's would sound sumptuous in a large American amphitheatre. And yet Grainger described himself as 'a pianist for the village hall' and Busoni as 'pianist for the metropolis' (but that was when Grainger had abandoned any ambition he ever may have had as a virtuoso, totally at loggerheads with the streamlined concert-world of the Horovitzian era).

Grainger used the 'soft' pedal not only in *piano* but in *forte*, just as Grieg achieved repressed passion in writing for string orchestra by using the mutes in *forte* passages. Grainger used the three pedals often simultaneously: the 'soft' and middle pedals pedipulated by the left foot, slewed round so that the toe worked the middle pedal and the heel the 'soft' pedal.

Grainger's two-piano edition of the Grieg Concerto[6] is an exemplary piece of editing. He prints Grieg's original solo piano part, with addenda, sometimes initialled 'P.G.' and sometimes 'P.G.—E.G.'—indicating either his own re-writings or re-writings that he discussed with Grieg and that had Grieg's approval. The arpeggio-passage beginning in the 15th measure after the '*In tempo I*' in the first movement's cadenza (after the last bass chromatic run) is a brilliant example of Grainger's pianistic invention. Grieg's original gives a four-note arpeggio to each hand alternately: Grainger's revision preserves the same text, note for note, but divides the arpeggi between the hands, each hand playing only one note at a time— single notes alternating in an electrifying cascade, suggesting a diabolical Hardanger fiddler's super-athletic bowing.

Grainger was so concerned with amateur music-making that he made many versions of his music for beginners, the more advanced and the really advanced: sometimes calling for three pianists at one piano (*Zanzibar Boat Song*) and four pianists at two pianos—what he termed 'piano team-work' (his transcription of Bach's A minor Fugue from Book I of the '48'). These ideas of piano pedagogy were ahead of their time. They certainly were designed to inculcate the musicality that only ensemble-work can provide: a feature often absent from piano lessons. Sometimes, as in his Children's March *Over the Hills and Far Away* (which he described in his summer school teaching-lists as 'easy'), he overestimated the tyro, as did Villa Lobos, occasionally, in his *Guida Prattica*. This was why I welcomed the commission to edit *The Young Pianist's Grainger* for Schott.[7]

In my researches in the Grainger House, White Plains, in 1976, I unearthed a piano solo version by Grainger (dated July 2, 1901, London) of *The 'Rag'-Time Girl*.[8] This was based on an American popular song sung to Grainger by his Frankfurt friend Carlo Fischer. It was the first of a number of compositions based on, or influenced by, Black American music. From 1903 to 1909 he worked intermittently on another such popular song of the time, *In Dahomey* (still in MS). In 1905 Stanford suggested to his former student Coleridge-Taylor that he send his *Twenty-four Negro Melodies* to Grainger. The first all-negro vocal ensemble to tour the world were the Jubilee Singers of Fisk University, Nashville, Tennessee. Their history and repertoire was published in London.[9] Towards the end of the last century they spread the fame of the negro spiritual. But neither their published songs, nor Coleridge-Taylor's piano transcriptions of spirituals, reproduced the vocal registration of the negro performance-style. In 1911 Grainger *did* reproduce that style in his (still unpublished) *Who built de Ark?* for "leader" (rich middle voice), 3 accompanying male voices and guitar. Grainger's friend (and fellow Busoni student) Natalie Curtis Burlin was the first to record, on Edison phonograph, traditional old plantation songs as sung by negroes. From these recordings she made as exact a music notation as possible. These were published as *Negro Folk-Songs*.[10] They show how the 'lead' voice was never on top but, pitch-wise, in the *middle* of the ensemble—just as in Grainger's *Who built de Ark?* Now in the very year that Grainger wrote that

Ex 13:

PERCY ALDRIDGE GRAINGER.

BRITISH FOLK-MUSIC SETTINGS.

(*Lovingly and reverently dedicated to the memory of Edward Grieg.*)

Nº 6. IRISH TUNE FROM COUNTY DERRY.

(Name unknown.)

(By kind permission of Mʳ Alfred Perceval Graves.)

Collected by Miss J. Ross, of N. T. Limavady, Londonderry.
printed in The Petrie Collection of the Ancient Music of Ireland. (Dublin 1855.)

Dished up for piano from his setting of the same
for unaccompanied mixed chorus Nº 5 of this lot.

for setting for string
see Nº 15 of this lot

by

Percy Aldridge Grainger.

Begun: October, 1902.
ended: July, 1911.

The tune is thro'out printed in bigger notes.

SLOWISH, but not dragged, and wayward in time. M.M. ♪ = between 72 and 104.
(*Rubato il tempo, e non troppo lento.*)

ROSENKAVALIER RAMBLE   Strauss-Grainger   Ronald Stevenson's working copy
additional fingering by RS

A. 7899 F.

spiritual-setting (1911) he published two piano pieces—*Irish Tune from County Derry* and *Sussex Mummers' Christmas Carol*—which both put the tune in the tenor, embedded in the harmonic texture in the same way as a negro's 'lead' voice is in the vocal ensemble. My contention is that the negro style of harmony influenced Grainger's characteristic layout of keyboard texture: which means that not only his phrasing and articulation were based on folk performance practices but so was his *harmonic thinking*. Interesting that he told Natalie Curtis Burlin that he considered Black American harmony 'the most perfect part-singing in the world'.[11]

In 1913 Grainger made a concert tour of Russia. The Liszt pupil Siloti conducted for him and programmed Grainger's newly published string orchestra version of the *Irish Tune from County Derry*. Siloti liked it so well that, not knowing Grainger had himself published a piano version of it, he published one of his own. The difference between the Grainger and Siloti versions is revealing: Siloti puts the tune on top throughout; Grainger's harmonisation is pure 'negro spiritual'. (I mean in layout; I don't of course mean the *melodic* material sounds 'negroid'.)

Grainger's most sumptuous piano work is his *Ramble on the Rosenkavalier Love-Duet*.[12] This employs the full range of his pianism. It is the most fastidiously notated piano-writing in the whole virtuoso literature. (Yes, it even exceeds the fastidiousness of Godowsky, for Godowsky never notated such detailed pedalling as Grainger and never notated for middle pedal.) If the performer follows all the instructions faithfully—fingering, dynamics, phrasing, pedalling—he will not need to seek for an interpretation. The interpretation in this case *is* the notation.

There is so much to say about Grainger's piano-writing that I had better give a brief résumé of his pianistic innovations, rather than get lost in the thicket of his numerous works. He innovated direct contact with the piano strings in his *Pastoral*[13]: he specifies a marimba mallet to strike a bass string at the end of the piece—thereby making the so-called *avante-garde* of half-a-century later seem the *derrière-garde* they were (and are).

Use of the *fist* was another innovation. Near the end of the concert version of *Country Gardens*[14] he calls for the right hand to be clenched in a boxer's 'fist', the thumb-knuckle playing B flat and the little finger knuckle playing the E flat a fourth higher, to get the hammered sonority he requires, which fingers alone could not achieve.

I have a photocopy of Grainger's working copy of the first edition of Cyril Scott's Piano Sonata. At the black-key *glissando,* Grainger has added a self-instruction: to pin a silk handkerchief on an elastic band into his breast pocket; to whip it out and play the *gliss* with the handkerchief over his fingers, then release it and the elastic would return it to the pocket! Funny—yes, Harpo Marx-like—but *practical*.

His 'orchestration' of piano-writing is richly colourful. In *Blithe Bells*[15] (a free ramble, or fantasy, on Bach's *Sheep may Safely Graze*) he imitates sheeps bells in high treble 10ths. His transcription of Gershwin's *Love Walked In*[16] evokes musical glasses by 2-note treble *tremoli*, containing the tune and a descant—the *tremoli* termed 'woggles'. His American folk-dance *Spoon River*[17] captures the 'seesaw' of folk-fiddle bowing in the chopped-up interplay of the two hands. A fife-and-drum band is strongly suggested in his

Scots folk-song setting *O gin I were where Gowrie rins*:[18] the fife simulated by 'twiddly' ornamentation. The MS of this piece is a re-working of one of his Scots folksong settings of 1900, as he writes in his note 'remembered (no doubt, inaccurately) Oct 21, 1954'.

Another seven years and Grainger was dead—if one can say that about such a spirit. As he wrote on that early piano piece *Saxon Twi-Play,* he did indeed 'excel to the end'.

Grainger's Songs

David Wilson-Johnson

Shallow Brown was the first Grainger song I heard and I thought its intensity was amazing. After working on a few songs for the Balfour Gardiner Centenary, I was led to work more generally on the 'Frankfurters' and as a result I went into all Grainger's songs. The first time I sang in an all-Grainger programme was at the 1978 Holland Festival, and it was the first of many happy encounters with Percy Grainger. While his vocal lines have the simplicity of folksongs and would stand by themselves, they are actually enhanced by the accompaniments Grainger provides. This is not always the case with folksong arrangements, which can so easily be uncumbered with their settings. Working on most folksong arrangements, I try to start with the tune sung in isolation, but with Grainger there must be a different approach: it is the harmonic basis which gives the impetus to the performance, and here the problems begin. The performer must be a kind of arbitrator—balancing the simplicity of the actual folk-melody and the harmonic spiciness added to it. Nature versus Art.

Most of Grainger's best songs are folksongs. He did not seem to be particularly concerned with words outside the folk context. He was not one who could take a great poet and make something smaller out of it, as a lot of other people managed to. His choice of verse-setting is often strange.

Perhaps it would be useful first of all to list the songs in chronological order, and then discuss representative examples.

1898	*Secret of the Sea* (Longfellow) June 19
	You Wild and Mossy Mountains (Burns) Oct 27/28
	Evan Banks (Burns) Nov 1st
	O Willow, Willow (1st setting) Nov 2nd
	Afton Water (Burns) Nov 2-4
	The Sea Wife (Kipling) Nov 10-11
1899	Early settings (25 extant) Jan 17-29
	Anchor Song Feb 7
	First Chantey Feb 7/8
	Song of Autumn (Gordon) Feb 20
	Young British Soldier Feb 21
	Soldier, Soldier (extension of '1st setting') Feb 23
	Ballad of the Clampherdown July 15 (more added 1901)

	Ride with an Idle Whip Aug 13
	Men of the Sea Nov 14
	Merciful Town (1899?)
	Ganges Pilot (1899?)
1900	*Songs of the North* (12 for voice and piano)
1901	*Dedication* March 27/30
	Love Song of Har Dyal Sept 12
	Ragtime Girl
	Sailor's Chanty (?1901)
1903	*Twa Corbies* Feb 25-28
1906	*Widow's Party*
1906-7	*Died for Love* (ended Dec 18)
1908	*Reiver's Neck-Verse* (Swinburne) 24 Feb-8 March
1908	*Bold William Taylor* April 4-Aug 8
1910	*Shallow Brown* Aug-Dec 17
1902-1911	*Willow, Willow* (2nd setting)
1905-1912	*Six Dukes Went a-fishin'*
1913	*Colonial Song* (2 voices and piano)
1907-1920	*Sprig of Thyme* (ended May 13)
1920	*Pretty Maid Milkin her Cow* Sept 14
	British Waterside Sept 22-23
1920-1921	*Creeping Jane* (ended June 28)
1922	*The Power of Love* Sept 3-6
1923	*Husband and Wife*
1925	*Old Woman at the Christening* (man's voice, piano, horn, Oct 10-14)
1910-1938	*Lost Lady Found*
1938	*Harvest Hymn* (voice and piano duet)
1901-1940	*Early One Morning* (Oct 16 1901-Aug 4 1940)
1944	*Farewell to an Atoll* (Ella Grainger) Oct 2-4
1946	*Hard-Hearted Barbra Ellen* (written out Feb 16)
1948	*Honey-Pot Bee* (Ella Grainger) Feb 1
1954	*David of the White Rock* Aug 5-6

I find the songs often lie awkwardly on the voice. They call for well-integrated head and chest registers. One also needs to remember that, although they do transpose, they can lose quite a lot of colour or take on quite a different colour in a new key. But it is sometimes necessary for a baritone to bring them down a third or a fourth. *Six Dukes* is a good example because the original printed version was obviously for a tenor; it still works well when 'key-shifted'. It has to come down quite a long way because it must sound easy. It is rather like a Schubert song in this respect. If you transpose it down from a tenor to a baritone key, say down a minor third, it may still sound too high. So don't be afraid to bring it down perhaps a fourth or a fifth even. It make make the folk melody sound much simpler and more natural—less 'art song-y'.

The accompaniments are *so* important and Grainger's orchestrations are very exciting. For example *Willow, Willow* in its various versions is hauntingly beautiful. The version for piano alone can sound a little bland, and such rich harmonic texture certainly needs very careful handling by an accompanist. Songs like *Shallow Brown* are really quite impossible without the full instrumental textures. And anyway, the orchestral versions are much easier to sing!

Among the earlier, original songs, *A Song of Autumn* and *Dedication* are good, and well worth airing. Though not published by Schirmer until 1923, *A Song of Autumn* dates from the composer's late teens. He uses a simple harmonic idiom, and writes a simple but effecting song; the vocal line just a continuous flow of quavers. The words by Adam Lindsay Gordon—'where shall we go for our garlands glad at the falling of the year'—have dated far more than the music and for that reason it has rarely been performed. It may be 'key-shifted' but it is not really necessary because it lies in the middle of either a baritone or a tenor voice. In contrast, *Dedication* is a stirring piece, written at 19 years old.

A Reiver's Neck-Verse is another original song, the text taken from the third series of Swinburne's *Poems and Ballads*:

> Some die singing,
>   and some die swinging,
>   and weel mot a' they be;
> Some die playing,
>   and some die praying,
>   and I wot sae win-na we,
>   my dear, and I wot sae winna we.
>
> Some die sailing,
>   and some die wailing,
>   and some die fair and free;
> Some die flyting,
>   and some die fighting,
>   but I for a fause love's fee,
>   my dear, but I for a fause love's fee.
>
> Some die laughing,
>   and some die quaffing,
>   and some die high on tree:
> Some die spinning,
>   and some die sinning,
>   but fagot and fire for ye,
>   my dear, faggot and fire for ye.
>
> Some die weeping,
>   and some die sleeping,
>   and some die under sea:
> Some die ganging,
>   and some die hanging,
>   and a time of a tow for me,
>   my dear, a time of a tow for me.

A good, though not great, song which transposes well. I do it in B flat; I have also done it in C. Such 'key-shifting' in performance can be very awkward unless you have an accompanist able and willing to transpose (and there are not many of those around!) 'Key-shifting' Grainger's harmonic richness and his fistfuls of chords can be a rather daunting task. At the end, Grainger offers an alternative vocal line. They both work very well:

Ex 15: *Closing bars of 'A Reiver's Neck-Verse', with alternative vocal line.*

I think Grainger had probably been working with a very loud tenor. It is a fairly loud tenor song and is more operatic in many ways: a big song and calls for a big tone from both participants.

There is ample time for colouring the words: they're marvellous words to sing. Lots of scope for 'Some die playing, some die praying, some die sailing, some die wailing, some die far and free, and some die flyting, some die fighting, some die laughing . . .' It's a fine vehicle for a singer with many vocal colours at his disposal, and a much more straightforward song in many ways than the folksong arrangements that follow.

This brings us to a sequence of magnificent folksong settings, which by his treatment Grainger makes entirely his own. First, chronologically, is *Bold William Taylor*:

> I'll sing you a song about two lovers,
> O from Lichfield town they came;
> O the young man's name was William Taylor,
> the maiden's name was Sally Gray.
>
> Now for a soldier William's listed,
> for a soldier he has gone;
> he's gone and left sweet lovely Sally
> for to sigh & for to mourn . . .
>
> Sally's parents they controlled her—
> filled her heart full of grief and woe;
> and then at last she vowed and said
> for a soldier she would go.

She dressed herself in man's apparel,
man's apparel she put on;
and for to seek bold William Taylor,
and for to seek him she has gone.

One day as she was exercising,
exercising amongst the rest;
with a silver chain hung down her waistcoat,
and there he spied her lily-white breast.

And then the Captain he stepped up to her,
asked her what had brought her there:
'I've come to seek my own true lover,
he has proved to me so vere (severe)'.

'If you've come to seek your own true lover,
pray tell to me his name'.
'His name it is bold William Taylor,
O from Lichfield town he came'.

'If his name it is bold William Taylor,
and he had proved to you so vere,
he's got married to an Irish lady,
he got married the other year.

'If you rise early in the morning,
early by the break of day,
there you shall spy bold William Taylor,
walking with this lady gay'.

Then she rose early in the morning,
early by the break of day,
and there she spied bold William Taylor,
walking with this lady gay.

And then she called for a brace of pistols,
a brace of pistols at her command,
and there she shot bold William Taylor,
with his bride at his right hand.

And then the Captain he was well pleased,
was well pleased what she had done;
and there he made her a great commander
aboard of a ship, over all his men.

It is a wonderful song but very awkward word-wise. It is dictated by the
strange stresses of the Lincolnshire dialect. The simple tune does not really
work with the piano; the orchestrated version is so much richer. It
exemplifies a typical pattern in Grainger's settings by starting very simply
and getting more and more intense as it progresses. One has to take some
account of the use of dialect, and Grainger would have said it was essential.
But today I find it can get in the way and may sound stilted. I just do not
know quite how far one wants to take it, and one can overdo it. I remember
talking to Sir Peter Pears about it and he said: 'I notice it on the page, but I

don't think anybody would notice it in the air'. I think this is probably the key and the way to do it.

This brings us to *Shallow Brown*, which Grainger always refers to as a 'chanty'. Grainger tells us the voice part may be sung: by 1 man's voice (singing both 'solo' and 'chorus'); or by 2 men's voices (1st voice sings 'solo', 2nd voice sings 'chorus'); or by 1 woman's voice (singing 'solo') and 1 man's voice (singing 'chorus'); or by 1 man's voice (singing 'solo') and a male unison chorus (singing 'chorus'); or by a mixed unison chorus (women's voices singing 'solo', men's voices singing 'chorus').

> Shaller Brown, you're goin'ter leave me,
>   Shaller, Shaller Brown;
> Shaller Brown, you're goin'ter leave me,
>   Shaller, Shaller Brown.
>
> Shaller Brown, don't ne'er deceive me,
>   Shaller, Shaller Brown;
> Shaller Brown, don't ne'er deceive me,
>   Shaller, Shaller Brown.
>
> You're goin' away accrost the ocean,
>   Shaller, Shaller Brown;
> You're going' away accrost the ocean,
>   Shaller, Shaller Brown.

[*Slightly slower: piercingly, lingeringly. Dwell threateningly on each note, growing steadily towards top of phrase*].

> You'll ever be my heart's devotion,
>   Shaller, Shaller Brown;
> You'll ever be my heart's devotion,
>   Shaller, Shaller Brown.
>
> For your return my heart is burning,
>   Shaller, Shaller Brown;
> For your return my heart is burning,
>   Shaller, Shaller Brown.
>
> Shaller Brown, you're goin'ter leave me,
>   Shaller, Shaller Brown;
> Shaller Brown don't ne'er deceive me,
>   Shaller, Shaller Brown.

Grainger's minimum orchestra is: clarinet, bassoon, horn (or alto saxophone), euphonium (or 2nd horn, or 2nd alto saxophone), harmonium, piano and 7 strings (2 violins, 2 violas, 2 cellos, bass). To these 13 instruments may be added any or all of the following: piccolo, flute, double-bassoon, 2 mandolins, 2 mandolas, 2 ukeles, 4 guitars, more strings.

Grainger tells us that 'the song was supposed to be sung by a woman standing on the quay to Shallow Brown as his ship was weighing anchor'. [I do] 'not know why Brown was called "Shallow"—unless it was that he was shallow in his heart', as he added. 'My setting (composed in 1910) aims to convey a suggestion of wafted, wind-borne, surging sounds heard at sea.'

This is a song that is magnificently effective from the audience's point of view but is awkward in some ways because of the scoring; a song which is made by the crescendi. Again it does not work nearly so well with the piano, although in the orchestral version a piano part is actually still a primary participant. *Shallow Brown* is such a passionate piece that it is difficult to follow in a programme.

Willow, Willow is actually Grainger's second attempt to set this folksong:

> The poor soul sat sighing by a sycamore tree,
>> Sing willow willow willow:
> With his hand in his bosom and his head upon his knee.
>> O willow willow willow willow,
>> O willow willow willow willow
>> Shall be my garland;
> Sing all a green willow, willow willow willow;
>> aye me the green willow must be my garland.
>
> He sighed in his singing, and made a great moan
>> Sing willow willow willow:
> I am dead to all pleasure, my true love she is gone.
>> O willow willow willow willow,
>> O willow willow willow willow
>> Shall be my garland;
> Sing all a green willow, willow willow willow;
>> aye me the green willow must be my garland.
>
> Take this for my farewell and latest adieu
>> Sing willow willow willow,
> Write this on my tomb, that in love I was true.
>> O willow willow willow willow,
>> O willow willow willow willow
>> Shall be my garland;
> Sing all a green willow, willow willow willow;
>> aye me the green willow must be my garland.

It is rather different from the other settings of around the same time, because he has taken it from a printed source and not from having heard it. This does make a difference to the song. We haven't got the awkwardness of the language as in, say, 'Wunst I had a sprig of thyme'. The accompaniment is sparse, just chords to start with. The interpreter has to decide how dramatically he should sing 'O willow, willow, willow, willow'. It's always a problem: it can so easily go over the top. I think it is probably better suited to higher and lighter voices. Again, it works much better in its orchestral context or certainly in the version with guitar and string quartet. How simple can one make such a song when it develops such a rich harmonic idiom? We have heavily expressive chord progressions and at 'Write this on my tomb, that in love I was true', this amazingly effective chord:

Ex 16 'Willow Willow'.

It follows the typical Grainger pattern: simple at the beginning and more complex as it moves on, as the composer imposes his personality on the material. And it has a very effective ending when performed with the guitar and a string quartet.

How involved with the character should the singer become? Avoid the temptation to over-identify with the poor maid. Perhaps the voice sings it simply throughout and the pianist underplays the intense chromaticism in the accompaniment. It is difficult, just a matter of taste, but a most beautiful song.

Six Dukes Went A-fishin has become very familiar in Sir Peter Pears' recording:

Six Dukes went afishin' don (down) by yon sea-saed (sea-side);

won (one) of them spied a dead body } lain by the water saed (side).
goin floatiddin (floating) with the tide.

They won said to itch (each) other the-ese (these) words A've (I've) heard them sa (say):
'It's the Ro-e-yull (Royal) Duke of Grant am (Grantham) what the tide 'as e weshed awa (has washed away).'

Tha (they) tok (took) him up to Portsmoth (Portsmouth), to a place where he was non (known);
from there up to London, to the place where he was born.

Tha-a (they) tok (took) ot (out) his bowils (bowels) and stretch-ed ot (out) his fe-et (feet),
and they balm-ed his body with rosis (roses) se (so) sweet,

He no (now) lies betwixt two towers, he no (now) lies in cold cla (clay),
when the Ro-e-yull (Royal) Queen of Grant'am went weepin' awa (away).

Here the problem of dialect is most acute. In the printed copies Grainger even lays out a rhyming scheme:

VOWEL SOUNDS, ETC.

a = *a* in German *hat*	*ò* = *o* in *cold*	*ú* = *u* in *put*
ä = *a* in *father*	*ó* = *o* in *nor*	*r* = so-called "*burred r*," that is,
ã = *a* in *bare*	*ō* = *oo* in *food*	the *r* is mute and the tip of the tongue
é = *er* in *her*	*ö* = *u* in *put*	is "inverted" (curled up and back)
ē = *ee* in *green*	*o* = *o* in *cod*	while pronouncing the foregoing
		vowel.

To throw further light on the dialect sounds, I add the following hints:

The vowel *ã* in *ãfishin'*, *sã*, *awã*, *thã*, *plãce*, *thã-a*, *rãed*, *clã*, should be exactly like the first of the two vowel sounds in the diphthongs *there, hair, bare*. It is rather like the vowel sound in *add, sat, swam, placid, that, razzle, clad*, lengthened, and rather like the *ä* in German *mädchen*. *a* in *thã-a*, *Grãnt'am*, *'as, ãnd* should be like the vowel in German *hat, land*.

dön	should rhyme with	*bone*	*fē-et* should rhyme with	*he eat or he bet*	*Lòn(don)* should sound like *loon*, but with the
seā...*we are*			*nön*...*lawn*		vowel short and lax,
bódy...*gaudy*			*rosis*................................*no biz (business)*		instead of long and
wäter...*barter*			*saēd* should sound like *side*, but with the		tense
öther...................German *butter* (as far as the			second vowel sound lengthened		*thã-a* should sound somewhat like *there*, but
vowels go)			*wön*..*worn*		with greater separation of the 2 vowel sounds
thé-ese...............................*He Es(mond)*			*words*.........................*cods*, but with the		*ot* should sound like *out*
ä've..*curve*			o " inverted "		
Grãnt(ham).....................*aunt* (Southern			*Rö-èyull*.......................*royal*, but with the		*where*...........................*weir*
pronunciation)			second vowel sound lengthened		*sé*..................................*sir*
weshed..*meshed*			*e*..*err*		
tok...*Luke*			*up*................... *'oop (hoop)*, but with the		*no*...............................*no*
(Ports)möth......................................*oath*			vowel short and lax,		
öt...*boot*			instead of long and		*tòwers*......................*towers* (men on a
böwils..*no wills*			tense		tow-path)

Grainger writes in the score 'Very simple and with a child-like unconscious pathos'. It was written for Gervase Elwes, and I can see that his very mellow tenor would have been the ideal voice for it. Again, it is so simple: a small tune—two phrases really—but again, it gets so rich harmonically. The whole idea 'They took out his bowels and stretched out his feet'—very naive but vivid words and they receive colourful harmonic treatment. 'And they balmed his body with roses so sweet' ... wonderful harmonic touches there. It always is, I think, in performance, tellingly *ben sentito*. Again, the problem is—does one make a meal out of it? Does one make a large song out of it? One's esteem for the song would lead one to make it enormous. One should just sing it as the highlight of the evening. It usually is. The last verse has an amazing poignancy 'He now lies in cold clay ...'. There is an *enormous* crescendo on 'weeping', but avoid any hint of the operatic. The whole verse starts and ends piano. It calls for an increase of intensity, not really of dynamic.

Breathing in such a song is very important. I think the answer is to take as much time as one can, certainly in that last phrase. It's such a beautiful phrase, it needs stretching; and don't be afraid to take breaths anywhere. As with all breaths, take them out of the previous note rather than the new one. On the last page, for example, 'He now lies betwixt two towers, He now lies in cold clay' (breath), 'When the royal Queen of Grantham' (big breath) 'went weeping' (breath optional) 'away'. The continual changing of time signatures, too, might worry the inexperienced. Some of the other songs are even more complicated, and one sings them almost as if they were unbarred. Sing with the stress of the words. Beautiful things like 'and they balmed his body with r-o-s-e-s so sweet', when the voice has the semiquaver at the end against the quavers of the piano. It's a beautiful phrase which just falls into the cadence; it's all dictated by the words, and their natural stress. That's probably the thing to remember, they are folksongs, so the narrative matters most.

How much one wants to characterize the participants in the story can also be an interpreter's problem. Is the actual singer a character in the drama or is he an observer? In some ways it can be so poignant if he is just an onlooker. How far does he experience the emotion he is singing about? The accompaniments are so subjective and so intense harmonically, but one should not assume that the vocal line has to be equally intense. I think it has to be simple, and that the harmonic intensity is the continuous undertow. Again, it's all too easy to go over the top and harangue the audience—'Look, I've noticed this harmonic point and by God you're going to notice it too!' To understate the vocal line can be strangely more expressive.

Grainger's emotional associations with many of these settings undoubtedly have to do with his memories of the folk singers who sang them. *Six Dukes* was sung to Grainger by George Gouldthorpe, of whom he notes in the score:

> Was a never-to-be-forgotten noble, touching and lovable being, and a born artist. He was a lime-burner. His personality, looks and art were a curious blend of sweetness and grim pathos. Though his face and figure were gaunt and sharp-cornered and his singing voice somewhat grating, he contrived to breathe a spirit of almost caressing tenderness into all he did, said and sang: though a hint of tragic undercurrent was ever present also. A life of drudgery, ending in old age in want and the workhouse, had not shorn his manners of a degree of humble nobility and dignity, exceptional even among English peasants: nor could any situation rob him of his refreshing (unconscious) Lincolnshire independence. His child-like mind, and his unworldly nature, seemingly void of even the capacity for bitterness, singularly fitted him to voice the purity and sweetness of folk-art. He gave out his tunes in all possible gauntness and plainness, for the most part in broad even notes: the touching charm of his singing lay largely in the simplicity of his versions of songs and the richness of his dialect, which in every-day speech might be hard to beat, and which he did not eliminate from his singing as much as most folksingers do.

This influences the way Grainger envisaged the music being performed:

> The tune and dialect in this setting closely follows my notation from phonograph records I took of Mr Gouldthorpe's singing. This mixture of dialect and standard English pronunciation is typical of the old singers I have collected from: they are trying to sing English and the lovely dialect sounds creep in and enrich unawares.

One needs to be very careful with this today because 'standard mumerset' will not do.

Now *The Sprig of Thyme:*

> Wunst (once) I had a sprig of thyme,
> it prospered by night and by day
> till a false young man came acourtin'te (to) me,
> and he stole all this thyme away.
>
> The gardiner was standiddn (standing) by;
> I bade him che-oose (choose) for me:
> He chose me the lily and the violet and the pink,
> but I really did refuse them all three.
>
> Thyme it is the prettiest thing,
> and time it e will grow on,
> and time it'll bring all things to an end
> addend (and) so doz (does) my time grow on.

> It's very well drinkin' ale
> and it's very well drinkin' wine:
> but it's far better sittin' by a young man's side
> that has won this heart of mine.

This is a masterpiece. The problem again is the Lincolnshire dialect and how far one goes in performing it. Is it 'Once I had' or 'Wunst'? How far do we go in the concert-hall context, when accompanied by a Steinway grand? The performer has to bridge the considerable culture gap between the wastes of Brigg and, say, the Queen Elizabeth Hall. But a magnificent song, and again so simple.

There's a slight sexual problem, too. One never quite knows how far to take the characterization. It's the same as with the *Willow Song*. How does a male singer put over a song sung by a female which has probably been transmitted by a male singer anyway and then worked out by Grainger? I can only touch on such problems.

There are slight awkwardnesses in the accompaniments when Grainger asks for silent bars: 'Press down silently the sustaining pedal'. This effect only works on pianos with a third pedal. Harmonically it again becomes very rich. Things like 'And Time it'll bring all things to an end' is an amazing bar, and is one of the passages to relish harmonically. It has a tremendous yearning, a stretched-out legato feel. One never knows how much legato to use in singing a folk-song. To what extent is Grainger in the *bel-canto* tradition? For this reason it *can* be very awkward to do in concert programmes. If it were in a folksong programme, one would try to get all the inflections.

Speak the words—on a finely-spun legato line. That's the way I've always tried to do it. But there's always a problem where there's such a long dramatic passage as 'and time it'll bring all things to an end' which just has to be legato and needs long breaths. It's a taxing song, one of the most taxing, and Grainger is very explicit in the copy; he's written every single direction in. It is slightly awkward in its lengths of phrase. They're almost too short in some ways. You either breath all the time and stop the momentum, or you breath infrequently and risk running out in the process. The last phrase is an exception. 'It's far better sitting by a young man's side that has won this heart of mine', which would be wonderful to do in one breath but it's far too long, unless you put a spurt on and lose the pathos of it!

It's difficult to pin down, just what is the essence of this or that particular Grainger song. The answer only comes in performance and with an audience present. That was brought home to me when I was singing in Amsterdam to a Dutch audience, most of whom understood English. They listened so well, far better than many English-speaking audiences, to the actual inflections of the words, and somehow the whole folk-idiom was easier to transmit because it was further removed, I suppose. I felt I was communicating a whole atmosphere, rather than the quirkness of dialect words.

The Pretty Maid Milking the Cow

> It was early one fine summer's mornin'
> when the birds sat and sung od-den (on) each bow,
> I heard a young damsel thus sing-in',
> thed-den (then) as she sat milk-in' her cow.

133

> She sang with a voice so melodious,
>   which made me scarce able to go
> For my heart it e was smoth-er'd e with sorrow,
>   by the pretty maid milk-in' her cow.

This maintains the high standard of its predecessors, but again there are similar problems. At what speed does it go? The speed of the words almost dictates a fairly fast approach but it says 'slowly flowing'. And as we go on through the piece it follows a familiar pattern, becoming much more adventurous harmonically. 'She sang with a voice so melodious which made me scarce able to go, for my heart it was so smothered with sorrow'—we have to stretch that a lot. But as soon as we start stretching it we upset the balance of the song. So the tempo is more difficult to establish. When I've done this—and we have done it on all sorts of occasions—I have varied my approach. I've tried it fast, slow, very legato, with as few words as we can and lots of vowel sounds, and with as many words, many consonants and as much conversation in it (again a straight folksong delivery). What does one do, for example, with a pause on the word 'cow', when there is a rich harmonic cadence going on underneath? This is a long way removed from the folk-song he started with. In fact he progresses in the space of three pages from the very simple folksong to something much deeper. It's almost too short to be an art song. And particularly in this song the vocal line is taken over by the accompaniment.

Finally, *British Waterside*, or *The Jolly Sailor*, collected by Grainger from Samuel Stokes at Retford in Nottinghamshire in August 1906:

> Down beyond the British waterside,
>   as I walked along,
> I over-heard a fair maid,
>   she was singing a song.
> The song that she did sing,
>   and the words repelid (replied) she;
> 'Of all the lads in Engeland
>   is the sailor lad for me'.

> You may know a jolly sailor lad
>   as he walks down the street,
> He is so neat in his clothing,
>   and so tight on his feet.
> His teeth are white as ivory
>   and his eyes black as shoes;
> You may know a jolly sailor boy
>   by the way that he goes.

> North Yarmouth is a pretty place,
>   it shines where it stands;
> The more I look upon it
>   the more my heart burns.
> If I was at North Yarmouth
>   I should think myself at home,
> For there I have sweethearts
>   and here I have got none.

I'll go down yon British waterside
   and build my love a tou-er (tower)
Where the lords, dukes and skewiers (squires)
   may all it admire.
The King can but love the Queen,
   and I can but do the same;
But you shall be the shepherdess
   and-ell (and) I will be your swain.

This is a fast one and has a difficult piano part. It works very well in performance. It is, I find, difficult to sing. It lies awkwardly again because, although it's fast, it must be rhythmically exact and punchy. 'The more my heart burns'—there is a lot of syncopation, and the accompaniment is always trying to elbow the voice from its position of supremacy. The balance can be a problem.

This song is particularly useful to break up a Grainger group, partly because the majority of the songs are slow. It's the scherzo movement in a group, the third of five or the fourth of six. This one can be very conversational. There is fine imagery, for example, 'I will go down to yon British waterside and build my love a tower'. Don't be afraid of the symbolism in that phrase. Yet it's also a falsely naive piece: 'The King can but love the Queen and I can but do the same, for you shall be the shepherdess and'll I will be your swain'. Again it is so clearly marked strictly in time but in performance one either has to temper this last phrase with a dynamic range which actually brings the audience in, or slow down. Otherwise it's very difficult just to get the words over, and a lot of it is lost. Sometimes it's difficult to get the sense over because the words of the song dictate a much slower speed than the piano part would suggest.

It is only comparatively recently that the power of these five songs has been generally appreciated. Possibly part of the problem was that until recently Grainger wasn't perhaps quite respectable. The musical establishment did not look favourably on Percy Grainger. And yet one cannot pin down why, and his critics would not elaborate as to why they would not. He just was not quite the thing. Sooner or later the songs of English composers are going to be taken out of the closet and people will sing them with the passion that they demand, rather than the English watercolour voice and even more watercolour accompaniments which have unfortunately become the tradition. If you look at the songs that were being written around 1900, you see they are full-blooded things. Somervell's *Maud* is a good example, a wonderful cycle, but it has to be *sung*. You can't pussyfoot your way around such works. It's an enormous cycle and needs the full operatic works. English song needs that, I think. And now, at last, there are many English singers who can do it. The problem is that English song got stuck in the Vaughan Williams tradition, which was a fraction too respectable and a fraction too un-idiomatic as far as the vocal writing was concerned. The art of performing English song got stuck with it too. Percy Grainger's folk-song arrangements are not part of that tradition; they are intensely passionate songs and need singing as such.

To choose a Grainger group—usually five, never more than six—I think one might start with *Pretty Maid Milking her Cow;* it engages the audience with the singer. Then possibly *Sprig of Thyme, British Waterside, Willow, Willow* probably and *Six Dukes*. Always end with *Six Dukes*. You certainly can't follow it.

CHAPTER ELEVEN

Miscellaneous Works

Lewis Foreman

Percy Grainger's popularity as a composer, particularly in the era of
recordings and the radio, has tended to revolve around five short works:
Molly on the Shore, Country Gardens, Shepherd's Hey, Mock Morris and
Handel in the Strand. They were conceived in that order over the period
1907 to 1911, although arranged and rearranged, in common with most of
Grainger's other works, over the larger part of his active creative life.

Molly on the Shore sets the pattern of a short popular piece that was
followed in the succeeding pieces in the genre. It was variously designated by
Grainger as BFMS (British Folk-Music Setting) No 1 (string quartet or
string orchestra, violin and piano, full orchestra or theatre orchestra, two
pianos four hands), as No 19 (piano solo) or as No 23 (for band). *Molly on
the Shore* is actually an Irish reel, and with it Grainger incorporates a second
similar tune called 'Temple Hill'. These tunes were not collected by
Grainger himself, but were taken from the second volume of *The Complete
Petrie Collection of Irish Music,* in which they are tunes number 901 and
902. This collection was edited by Sir Charles Stanford, and Grainger's use
of the tunes may be yet another evidence of Stanford's sympathetic and
friendly attitude towards the young composer in the early years of the
century.

Country Gardens began life as an arrangement of a morris dance collected
by Cecil Sharp, which Sharp sent to Grainger suggesting it would arrange
well. Grainger himself drew attention to the fact that *Country Gardens* is a
variant of *The Vicar of Bray:*

Ex 17:

Vicar of Bray

Ex 18:   Country Gardens

The work was sketched for 'two whistlers and a few instruments' in 1908 but
was not finalised, in the piano-solo version, for a decade, being first
published (as BFMS No 22) for either piano solo or two pianos, four hands,
in 1919. Later, other arrangements by other hands (for orchestra, military

137

band and other forces) appeared. It was recorded by the pianist Mark Hambourg under the title *The Handkerchief Dance*[1]. Its popularity in America dates from the rallies to sell war bonds towards the end of the First World War, when Grainger, then a US Army bandsman, would improvise on it at the piano. Its ensuing popularity demanded that he notate it and it is reputed to have been one of his publisher's best-sellers, selling over 30,000 copies a year.[2]

Shepherd's Hey, subtitled 'English Morris Dance', was also collected by Sharp. Grainger utilised four variants in his treatment, and pointed out it was but a variant of the familiar folk-song *The Keel Row:*

Ex 19:

The Keel Row

Ex 20:

Shepherd's Hey

The word 'Hey' denotes a particular movement in morris dancing.

Mock Morris is different from its predecessors in that, while the rhythmic cast of the piece is Morris-like, neither of the tunes nor the detailed shape of the whole keep strictly to the morris-dance shape.

The tune of bars 9 to 12 Grainger admitted to unwittingly 'cribbing from an early *Magnificat* of Cyril Scott's':

Ex 21:

Scott used the phrase again in the piano piece *Chimes,* Op 40 No 2. *Mock Morris* is designated as 'Room-Music Tit-Bits No 1', and it is inscribed as a 'Birthday-Gift, Mother 3.7.'10'. It, too, exists in various arrangements, from solo piano, through string sextet and string orchestra to full orchestra, together with versions by others for brass band, theatre orchestra, even recorder and piano.

Handel in the Strand ('Room-Music Tit-Bits No 2') was originally entitled *Clog Dance,* but its dedicatee, the banker William Gair Rathbone, who had befriended Grainger, suggested the evocative title eventually used. He felt that the music 'seemed to reflect both Handel and English Musical Comedy', the home of the latter being The Strand in London's West End. Grainger tells us that in bars 1 to 16, and their repetition at bars 47 to 60, he 'made use of matter from some variations' he wrote 'on Handel's "Harmonious Blacksmith" tune'. Again it is variously arranged.

Spoon River, in terms of its scale and the melodic interest, is really another essay in the style of the popular scores already discussed. But in many ways it transcends them, and much more epitomises Grainger's philosophy of elastic scoring.

Grainger's American Folk-Music Settings are only three in number, and all are different versions of this tune: No 1 for piano solo, No 2 for 'elastic scoring', and No 3 for two pianos, four hands. We will primarily concern ourselves here with the second.

'American Folk-Dance set for Elastic Scoring (from 3 single instruments up to massed orchestra)' reads the subtitle of the published score. Grainger, in his usual manner, also gives us this background to the tune set:

> A Captain Charles H Robinson heard a tune called 'Spoon River' played by a rustic fiddler at a country dance at Bradford, Illinois (USA), in 1857.
>
> When Edgar Lee Masters' *Spoon River Anthology* appeared in 1914, Captain Robinson (then nearly 90 years old) was struck by the likeness of the two titles—that of the tune and that of the poem-book—and he sent the 'Spoon River' tune to Masters who passed it on to me. The tune is very archaic in character; typically American, yet akin to certain Scottish and English dance-tune types.[2]

Grainger scored it during April and May 1929. The published orchestral score is prefaced by a lengthy essay addressed 'To conductors and to those forming, or in charge of, amateur orchestras, high school, college and music school orchestras and chamber-music bodies'. Grainger has a lot to say (three pages of a large score printed in small type), and does in fact reprint the same essay in the front of other scores published soon after. We may get the flavour from his opening remarks:

> My 'elastic scoring' grows naturally out of two roots:
>
> 1. That my music tells its story mainly by means of *intervals* and the liveliness of the part-writing, rather than by means of tone-color, and is therefore well fitted to be played by almost any small, large or medium-sized combination of instruments, provided a proper *balance of tone* is kept.
>
> 2. That I wish to play my part in the radical experimentation with orchestral and chamber-music blends that seems bound to happen as a result of the ever wider spreading democratization of all forms of music.
>
> As long as a really satisfactory balance of tone is preserved (so that the voices that make up the musical texture are clearly heard, one against the other, in the intended proportions) I do not care whether one of my 'elastically scored' pieces is played by 4 or 40 or 400 players, or any number in between; whether trumpet parts are played on trumpets or soprano saxophones, French horn parts played on French horns or E flat altos or alto saxophones, trombone parts played on trombones or tenor saxophones or C Melody saxophones; whether string parts are played by the instruments prescribed or by mandolins, mandolas, ukeleles, guitars, banjos, balalaikas, etc.; whether harmonium parts are played on harmoniums (reed-organs) or pipe-organs; whether wood-wind instruments take part or whether a harmonium (reed-organ) or 2nd piano part is substituted for them. I do not even care whether the players are skilful or unskilful, as long as they play well enough to sound the right intervals and keep the afore-said tonal balance—and as long as they play badly enough to *still enjoy playing*.

There is much more, concerning orchestral experimentation, orchestral use of keyboard and saxophones, remarks about percussion and tuneful percussion and finally tonal balance in string sections.

Grainger presents what he calls a 'full compressed orchestral score', which lays out the sections of his orchestra in broad bands, though without a stave necessarily being allotted to each instrument. The brass, for example ('trumpet (Bb) (or soprano saxophone) horn (F) (or Eb alto horn or alto saxophone) 3 trombones and tuba *ad lib'*) is often written on one line.

The most interesting groups (and the ones that give Grainger's score his characteristic orchestral sound) are the tuned percussion and the keyboard instruments. The first of these includes, as well as xylophone and glockenspiel, wooden marimba, steel marimba, staff bells, and tubular chimes *ad lib*. The keyboards are Grainger's favourite harmonium (or pipe-organ) and piano together with the harp. A note indicates that there is available a second piano part 'that contains all voices, chords etc., lacking in Piano I & harmonium or pipe-organ. This Piano II part may be used to replace missing instruments or support weak ones.'

His tempo indications are usually evocative of what Grainger wants, none more so than here. It reads 'Sturdily, not too fast; with "pioneer" keeping-on-ness (no change of speed thru-out)', and translates in more traditional terms as *Allegro non troppo, ma molto energico.*

To Grainger, who utilised folk or quasi-folk tunes in many of his works, the passacaglia, a form in which he could repeat the tunes while developing or varying their treatment, was one on which he was always likely to embark in substantial works. The repeated presentation of simple material which is characterised by ever more powerful harmonic and contrapuntal treatment, is the most noticeable feature of the solo-song settings of folksongs by Grainger, and is also the underlying technique in the more complex instrumental settings, and in particular *Green Bushes: Passacaglia on an English Folksong.*

Green Bushes, a piece lasting about 8½ minutes, is a fine example of Grainger at his invigorating best. It was originally written in London and Denmark between November 1905 and September 1906, but was not rescored in its final form, for 22 single instruments or orchestra, until 1921, and was published thus in 1931. It is designated BFMS No 12 and is dedicated* in Danish to Karen Holten, his 'playmate over the hills' of the Edwardian period. The 16-bar tune is also the basis of the last movement of *Lincolnshire Posy,* when it is called *The Lost Lady Found.* Grainger wrote an extended programme note for this work which eloquently deals with sources and technique together:

> Among country-side folksingers in England, *Green Bushes* was one of the best known of folksongs—and well it deserved to be, with its raciness, its fresh grace, its manly, clear-cut lines. The tune has also been noted in Ireland (see Nos 368, 369, 370 of the *Complete Petrie Collection*) and in the United States (by Mr Cecil J Sharp, in the Southern Appalachian Mountains).
>
> My setting is mainly based, with Mr Cecil J Sharp's kind permission, on a version of *Green Bushes* noted by him from the singing of Mrs Louie Hooper of Hambridge, Somerset, England. To a lesser extent I have used a variant of the same tune that I noted from the singing of Mr Joseph Leaning of Barton-on-Humber, Lincolnshire, England.
>
> *Green Bushes* strikes me as being a typical dance-folksong—a type of song come down to us from the time when sung melodies, rather than instrumental music, held country-side dancers together. It seems to breathe that lovely passion for the dance that swept like a fire over Europe in the middle ages—seems brimful

---

* It actually reads: 'Kameraten Karen Holten kjælighedsfuldt tilegnet, til Minde om Svinkløvs Glæder'.

of all the youthful joy and tender romance that so naturally seek an outlet in dancing.

An unbroken keeping-on-ness of the dance-urge was, of course, the first need in a dance-folksong, so such tunes had to be equipped with many verses (20 to 100, or more) so that the tune could be sung (of course without any break between verses) as long as the dance was desired to last.

In setting such dance-folksongs (indeed, in setting *all* dance music) I feel that the unbroken and somewhat monotonous keeping-on-ness of the original should be preserved above all else. To this end I consider the passacaglia form as fitting as I consider the variation form unfitting. My passacaglia-like settings of dance tunes are generally (and very ignorantly) described as 'variations'. Since most musicians seem to confound the variation form with the passacaglia form I will here state some of the basic differences between the two:

1. In the variation form the theme is varied, but is not constantly repeated; in the passacaglia form the theme is constantly repeated (in all kinds of tone-heights) but is not varied.
2. In the variation form there are generally pauses between 'verses' (variations); in the passacaglia form there are no such pauses.
3. In the variation form the key and speed and mood of the theme may be altered radically; in the passacaglia form such changes have no place.
4. In the variation form the element of variety is provided by transformations of the theme into new guises; in the passacaglia form the element of variety consists solely in the voices and additions that are woven around the theme, which latter, constantly repeated, remains unaltered. (In short, the only way to mistake the passacaglia form for the variation form is to know nothing about either form.)

With the exception of a momentary break of passage work lasting 8 bars (bars 154-161) the *Green Bushes* tune is heard constantly throughout my passacaglia from the opening of the work to the closing tail-piece, during which latter (bars 602-641) short snatches of the folktune are substituted for complete statements of it.

No key-note modulation at all is undertaken at any time with the folktune itself, which (barring an occasional passing accidental here and there) moves throughout in the mixolydian mode with F as its key-note, with the exception of its appearance in F major for 32 bars (570-601) just before the tail-piece. Though the folktune itself is thus heard throughout the entire work without key-note modulation of any kind, yet the harmonic treatment laid upon it covers a range of 7 or more different keys. This is made possible and natural by the somewhat neutral harmonic color of the mixolydian mode in which the folktune is cast. (The mixolydian mode is exactly like the major scale except that the 7th tone-step is flat in the former instead of sharp, as in the latter.)

During the first 161 bars of my setting the entire texture remains virtually in F mixolydian, but at bar 162 the harmonic treatment shifts into E flat major, and from now on longish sections of the superimposed harmonic treatment (the folksong itself remains, of course, in F) consistently in E flat major, B flat major, F major, F minor and C minor (as well as quickly modulating passages embracing chords in further-off keys) become frequent—generously interlarded, however, with considerable stretches couched in F mixolydian, in which key the tail-piece brings the composition to an end.

The greater part of my passacaglia is many-voiced and free-voiced. Against the folktune I have spun free counter-melodies of my own—top tunes, middle tunes, bass tunes. The aforementioned key-free harmonic neutrality of the folksong's mixolydian mode opens the door to a wondrously free fellowship between the folktune and these grafted-on tunes of mine. One of these latter (the 3rd counter-melody)—carrying with it its entire harmonic background wherever it goes—is heard in E flat major, B flat major and F major in sundry parts of the work, while all the while the *Green Bushes* tune is hammering away stubbornly in F (unchanged during the E flat and B flat episodes, but transposed from F mixolydian into F major and otherwise altered intervallicly during the F major episode).

My *Green Bushes* setting is thus seen to be a strict passacaglia throughout wellnigh its full length. Yet it became a passacaglia unintentionally. In taking the view that the *Green Bushes* tune is a dance-folksong (a type created to form a continuous tone-background to group-dancing) I was naturally led to keep it running like an unbroken thread through my setting, and in feeling prompted to graft upon it modern musical elements expressive of the swish and swirl of dance movements the many-voiced treatment came of itself.

The work is in no sense program-music—in no way does it musically reflect the story told in the verses of the *Green Bushes* song text. It is conceived, and should be listened to, as dance music (it could serve as ballet music to a ballet performance)—as an expression of those athletic and ecstatic intoxications that inspire, and are inspired by, the dance—my new-time harmonies, voice-weavings and form-shapes being lovingly woven around the sterling old-time tune to in some part replace the long-gone but still fondly mind-pictured festive-mooded country-side dancers, their robust looks, body actions and heart-stirs.

Bryan Fairfax, who conducted *Green Bushes* at the Queen Elizabeth Hall, London, during the 1970 Grainger Festival, wrote how 'The effect is hypnotic. Strangely remote harmonies remove, from time to time, a sense of key-centre. The music floats deliriously as the dance gyrates ever on. Pungent, foot-stamping rhythms batter the old tune, which screeches and groans—no time for niceties—with medieval earthiness. The pace is merciless and becomes desperate with increases of tempi; a cymbal roll hisses through a huge glissando and a four-bar fragment of the tune is all that there is time for—the dance is over.'

Of course, it was not only folksongs of British and American origin that Grainger treated in his orchestral works; Danish songs, of which he had personally collected a number, were effectively given his treatment as well.

Grainger's use of the harmonium in *Spoon River, Green Bushes* and many other scores is also reflected in the *Danish Folk-Music Suite*. At the beginning of *The Power of Love*, the first movement in the suite, Grainger is at pains to emphasise that 'in orchestral performance the full effect of this movement can be realised only when a harmonium (or reed organ) is used to accompany the passages for single instruments and an organ (pipe or electric) is used to accompany the passages for massed instruments'. Grainger's usual elastic scoring rules apply, making it suitable for a minimum of 12 instruments up to full orchestra. The table of orchestration opposite prefaces the score.

Grainger's programme note again usefully sets the scene:

(1) THE POWER OF LOVE
   (Danish Folk-Music Settings, No 2)
(2) LORD PETER'S STABLE-BOY
   (Danish Folk-Music Settings, No 1)
(3) THE NIGHTINGALE & THE TWO SISTERS
   (Danish Folk-Music Settings, No 10)
(4) JUTISH MEDLEY
   (Danish Folk-Music Settings, No 9)

Complete Danish Folk-Music Suite for Orchestra, Piano, and Organ
MAKE-UP OF PARTS

For the Entire Suite	For the Separate Numbers			
	The Power of Love	*Lord Peter's Stable-Boy*	*The Nightingale*	*Jutish Medley*
Flute I	Flutes I & II and Piccolo	*Tacet*	Flutes I & II and Piccolo (*ad lib.*)	Flute I
Flute II & Piccolo				Flute II and Piccolo
Oboes I & II	Oboes I & II	*Tacet*	Oboes I & II	Oboes I & II
Clarinets I & II	Clarinets I & II in A	Clarinet in Bb (may be doubled, trebled, or massed)	Clarinets I & II in Bb	Clarinets I & II in Bb
Bass clarinet in Bb	Bass-clarinet in Bb		Bass-clarinet in Bb	Bass clarinet in Bb
Bassoons I & II	Bassoons I & II		Bassoons I & II	Bassoons I & II
Double-bassoon (*ad lib.*)	Double-bassoon (*ad lib.*)	*Tacet*	Double-bassoon (*ad lib.*)	*Tacet*
Baritone Saxophones I & II in Eb (Substitutes for Bassoons I & II)	Baritone Saxophones I & II in Eb (Substitutes for Bassoons I & II)	*Tacet*	Baritone Saxophones I & II in Eb (Substitutes for Bassoons I & II)	Baritone Saxophones I & II in Eb (transposing from part for Bassoons I & II) (Substitutes for Bassoons I & II)
Horns (or Alto Saxophones) I & II in Eb	Horns (or Alto Saxophones) I & II in Eb		Horns I & II in Eb	Horns (or Alto Saxophones) I & II in Eb
Horns I & II in F (Substitutes for Horns I & II in Eb)	Horns I & II in F	Horn in F, or Horn in Eb, or Alto Saxophone in Eb (may be doubled, trebled, or massed)	Horns I & II in F (Substitutes for Horns I & II in Eb)	Horns I & II in F (Substitutes for Horns I & II in Eb)
Horns (or Alto Saxophones) III & IV in Eb	Horns (or Alto Saxophones) III & IV in Eb		Horns III & IV in Eb	Horns (or Alto Saxophones) III & IV in Eb
Horns III & IV in F (Substitutes for Horns III & IV in Eb)	Horns III & IV in F		Horns III & IV in F (Substitutes for Horns III & IV in Eb)	Horns III & IV in F (Substitutes for Horns III & IV in Eb)
Trumpets (or Soprano Saxophones) I & II in Bb	Trumpets (or Soprano Saxophones) I & II in Bb	Trumpet (or Soprano Saxophone) in Bb (may be doubled or trebled)	Trumpets (or Soprano Saxophones) I & II in Bb	Trumpets (or Soprano Saxophones) I & II in Bb
Trumpet (or Soprano Saxophone) III in Bb	Trumpet (or Soprano Saxophone) III in Bb		*Tacet*	Trumpet (or Soprano Saxophone) III in Bb
Trombone (or Tenor Saxophone in Bb) I	Trombone (or Tenor Saxophone in Bb) I	Trombone or Euphonium, or Tenor Saxophone in Bb (may be doubled, trebled, massed)	Trombone (or Tenor Saxophone in Bb) I	Trombone I
Trombone (or Tenor Saxophone in Bb) II	Trombone (or Tenor Saxophone in Bb) II		Trombone (or Tenor Saxophone in Bb) II	Trombone II
Trombone (or Tenor Saxophone in Bb) III	Trombone (or Tenor Saxophone in Bb) III		Trombone III	Trombone III
Euphonium (*ad lib.*)	*Tacet*	Euphonium (*ad lib.*)	*Tacet*	Euphonium (*ad lib.*)
Bass Tuba	Bass Tuba	*Tacet*	Bass Tuba	Bass Tuba
Kettle-drums	Percussion (Kettle-drums, Side-drums, Cymbal)		*Tacet*	Kettle-drums
Percussion (Side-drum, Cymbals, Wood Block, Bass Drum)		Kettle-drums, Cymbal, Bells (Glockenspiel, Xylophone, Staff Bells, Wooden Marimba, Metal Marimba or Vibraharp, *ad lib.*)	*Tacet*	Percussion (Side-drum, Cymbals, Wood Block, Bass Drum)
Metal "Tuneful Percussion" (Glockenspiel, Vibraharp or Metal Marimba, Staff Bells, Tubular Chimes) (*ad lib.*)	Wooden Marimba & Vibraharp (Metal Marimba) (*ad lib.*)		*Tacet*	Glockenspiel (Steel Marimba, Staff Bells, Tubular Chimes, *ad lib.*)
Wooden "Tuneful Percussion" (Xylophone, Wooden Marimba) (*ad lib.*)				Xylophone (Wooden Marimba, *ad lib.*)
Celesta or Dulcitone (or both) (both *ad lib.*)	*Tacet*	*Tacet*	*Tacet*	Celesta or Dulcitone (or both) (*ad lib.*)
Harps (No. II *ad lib.*)	Harps (No. II *ad lib.*)	*Tacet*	Harp	Harp
Piano (2-hands or 4-hands)	Piano (2-hands)	Piano (4-hands or 2-hands)	Piano (2-hands)	Piano (4-hands)
Harmonium (or Reed Organ) (*ad lib.*)	Harmonium (or Reed Organ) (*ad lib.*)	Harmonium (Reed Organ) or Pipe-Organ (obligatory)	Pipe-Organ or Harmonium (or Reed Organ) (obligatory)	Harmonium (or Pipe-Organ)
Pipe (or Electric) Organ (obligatory)	Pipe (or Electric) Organ (obligatory)			
Violin I	Violin I	Violin I	Violin I	Violin I
Violin II	Violin II	Violin II	Violin II	Violin II
Viola	Viola	Viola	Viola	Viola
Violoncello	Violoncello	Violoncello	Violoncello	Violoncello
Double-Bass	Double-Bass	Double-Bass	Double-Bass	Double-Bass

Table of orchestration from the published full score of the Danish Folk-Music Suite.

My *Danish Folk-Music* is based on Danish folk-songs collected in Jutland by me, with the phonograph, during the years 1922-1927, together with Evald Tang Kristensen—Denmark's veteran folklorist. He was 84 years of age at the time of our final gatherings. My part of the collecting was undertaken, partly in order to compare the singing habits of Danish country-side singers (as preserved in minute detail in the phonograph records) with those of English folk-singers similarly recorded with the phonograph by me in the period 1906-1909. This investigation revealed striking similarities in Danish and English folk-singing habits—similarities that might be compared to those existing between Danish and English speech-dialects.

The first movement of the suite is a setting of a folk-song, *The Power of Love,* which tells the story of a maiden who has a clandestine lover. Her seven brothers challenge him to combat, because he has made love to their sister without 'asking their rede'. In the fight that follows he kills the seven brothers.

> 'It's I have struck down thy brothers all seven;
> What answer to that wilt thou give me?'
> 'Yea, hadst thou struck down my father as well,
> I ne'er would be minded to leave thee.'

Of this ballad Mrs Ane Nielsen Post (who sang it to Evald Tang Kristensen and me) remembered only the last verse—so symbolical of love's ruthless sway.

> A green-growing tree in my father's orchard stands,
> I really do believe it is a willow tree.
> From root to crown its branches together bend and twine,
> And likewise so do willing hearts at love's decree.
> (Refrain) In summer-time.

It is the mood of this last verse that is mirrored in my setting.

The tune that underlies the second movement of the suite, *Lord Peter's Stable Boy,* is a sturdy dance-song, cast exclusively in seven-bar phrases. This build of tune is a rare survival from the middle ages.

The ballad of *Lord Peter's Stable-Boy* tells of 'Little Kirsten', who dons male attire because she wants to be a courtier at the Dane-King's castle. On her way thither she meets the Dane-King and Lord Peter as they are riding in the green-wood and she asks the Dane-King for employment as a stable-boy:

> Lord Peter, Lord Peter all to himself he said:
> 'Just by looking at your eyes I can tell you're a maid.'

She becomes Lord Peter's stable-boy and—

> Eight years she rode his young foals out on the lea;
> A stable-boy everyone did deem her to be.

The royal court is much taken aback when, nine years later, this stable-boy gives birth to twins:

> The Dane-King he laughed and he smacked loud his knees:
> 'Now which of my fine stable-boys has given birth to these?'

> 'This morning I had but a stable-boy so bright;
> A groom and a coachman as well are mine to-night!'

Grainger recording Danish folksongs on his Edison phonograph at Lindebo, Hearning, Jylland area of Denmark, 11 September 1925. Evald Tang Kristensen is in the centre photograph, on Grainger's right.

It was no mere chance that the fine tone-works I wrote after my beloved mother's tragic death in April, 1922, were my settings of *Lord Peter's Stable-Boy* and *The Power of Love*. The tune and words of the latter (the more so as grippingly, piercingly, heart-searchingly sung by sixty-year-old Mrs Ane Nielsen Post—a wondrously gifted folk-singer of the very finest type, whose Nordic comeliness, knee-slapping mirth and warm-heartedness, paired with a certain inborn aristocratic holding-back of herself, reminded me of my mother) seemed to me to match my own soul-seared mood of that time—my new-born awareness of the doom-fraught undertow that lurks in all deep love.

I was drawn no less strongly to *Lord Peter's Stable-Boy* on other grounds: for many years my mother and I had read aloud to each other, and doted on, sundry of the rimes in Evald Tang Kristensen's Danish folk-song books. Some of these my mother knew by heart (in Danish). The rimed tale of *Lord Peter's Stable-Boy* had long been one well-liked by both of us. Guess, then, my joy on hearing from Coppersmith Michael Poulsen of Vejle (on August 27, 1922) the manly, ringing melody he sang so well to that ballad. His tune seemed to me to give me a chance to paint a tone-likeness of one side of my mother's nature—sturdy, free, merry, peg-away, farmer-like.

Both these settings are lovingly honor-tokened to my mother's memory.

In the third movement are combined two songs of a fanciful and supernatural character, *The Nightingale* and *The Two Sisters*. Both were sung with winsome singing-grace by the afore-mentioned deeply gifted folk-songstress Mrs Ane Nielsen Post.

The movement is dedicated to Herman Sandby, the champion of Danishness in music, through whom I learned to know and love Danish folk-music as long ago as 1900. The song-words of *The Nightingale* (freely Englished) begin as follows:

> I know a castle, builded of stone,
> Appearing so grand and so stately;
> With silver and the red, red gold
> Bedecked and ornamented ornately.

> And near that castle stands a green tree—
> Its lovely leaves glisten so brightly;
> And in it there dwells a sweet nightingale
> That knows how to carol so lightly.

> A knight rode by and heard the sweet song,
> And greatly it was to his liking;
> But he was astonished to hear it just then,
> For the hour of midnight was striking.

Further verses lay bare the fact that the nightingale is, in reality, a maiden, who has been turned into a nightingale by the spells of a wicked step-mother. When the knight, wanting to break these evil spells, suddenly seizes hold of the nightingale, she is shape-changed into a lion, a bear, 'small snakes', and a 'loathsome dragon'. But the knight does not loosen his grip on her during these shape-changings, and while she is in the dragon-shape he cuts her with his penknife, so that she bleeds. Hereby the evil spell is broken and she stands before him 'a maiden as fair as a flower'.

The first verse of *The Two Sisters* (Englished) runs:

> Two sisters dwelt within our garth,
> Two sisters dwelt within our garth;

The one like sun, the other like earth.
(Refrain) The summer is a most pleasant time.

The verses that follow unfold the story of the older sister (dark as earth) who pushes her younger sister (fair as sun) into the water and lets her drown, because she wants for herself the young man to whom the younger sister is betrothed. Two fiddlers find the younger sister's corpse and make fiddle strings of her hair, fiddle pegs (screws) of her fingers. While the fiddlers are fiddling at the elder sister's wedding the fiddle strings tell of the murder, and the murderess is burnt alive.

Jutish Medley is, as its title implies, a succession of tunes hailing from Jutland. The first, *Choosing the Bride* (sung with fetching liveliness and energy by Mrs Anna Munch, of Fraeer Mark, Skjørping, Jutland) voices a young man's dilemma in choosing between two sweethearts—one rich, one poor—and his reasons for finally taking the poor one. The second melody employed is the sentimental *The Dragoon's Farewell* (likewise sung by Mrs Anna Munch)—supposed to be sung by the dragoon just before setting out for the wars. The third is a very archaic religious songs entitled *The Shoe-maker from Jerusalem,* magnificently rendered by Mrs Marie Tang Kristensen, the wife of the collector. The final ditty in the medley, *Hubby and Wifey,* is a quarreling duet (interpreted with sparkling wit by Jens Christian Jensen, of Albaek, Herning, Jutland) in which the wife brings her obstreperous husband to his senses by means of a spinning spindle skilfully applied to his forehead.

Of these songs, *Choosing the Bride* and *The Dragoon's Farewell* were unearthed by State-Forester Poul Lorenzen (of Mosskovgaard, Skjørping, Jutland), and *Hubby and Wifey* by H P Hansen, Director of the Herning (Jutland) Museum.

The *Jutish Medley* is dedicated to Evald Tang Kristensen as a token of boundless admiration.

Not all Grainger's significant works for orchestra used folk materials. The *Youthful Suite* that he put together in the 1940s from movements written at around the turn of the century, demonstrates quite clearly that he did not have to lean on other men's tunes in order to compose. What is more, he appears to have found his mature style very quickly, as those pieces show. All the movements were at least sketched when Grainger was between the ages of 17 and 19 years. There are five of them: *Northern March, Rustic Dance, Norse Dirge, Eastern Intermezzo* and *English Waltz. Rustic Dance* and *Eastern Intermezzo* were both completed and scored in 1899, while the opening march was complete for all but 36 bars. Grainger later touched up these orchestrations to take account of optional instruments such as harp, piano and tuneful percussion. The openings of the *English Waltz* and the *Norse Dirge* both date from 1901 and 1899 respectively, but they were completed during the Second War, the *Norse Dirge* being finished in 1945.

Grainger felt the *Northern March* to be 'North-English or Scottish' in character owing to its melodic material and rhythms, instancing the flattened seventh minor scale of the opening string tune, or the use of the Scotch snap. *Norse Dirge* reflects Grainger's preoccupation in his teens with the Icelandic sagas, and this music is conceived as a musical counterpart to the drama, a death song for a hero, at once a lament for the dead and a celebration of his life. This is very much a Grainger characteristic, tinging his lamenting with a fierce exultation.

Eastern Intermezzo reminds us of an early interest in oriental music. In its middle section Grainger was inspired by the description of the dance of the

147

elephants in Kipling's story 'Toomai of the Elephants'. In an introductory programme note Grainger was proud to point out how ahead of its time this music had been when he first conceived it, and indeed in his arrangement of the *Intermezzo* for 'tuneful percussion' made in 1933 (recorded by John Hopkins[3]), one is forcibly struck by its personality, even if it is somewhat naive. With how un-Victorian a work did Grainger celebrate the end of the 19th century.

Some of the musical procedures followed in the suite were drastic innovations at the time of their inception and Grainger commented:

> As far as my knowledge goes *Rustic Dance* was the first piece of music ever to end with the triad-with-added-sixth chord (F, C, A, D, F in F major)—the chord which has since become the expectable closing-chord to countless orchestral arrangements of American popular music. (Of course, Debussy closed the second act of *Pelleas and Melisande* with a very similar chord: F sharp, C sharp, A sharp, D sharp, G sharp in F sharp major. But *Pelleas* did not become known to the musical world until 1902.) To the best of my knowledge, extended passages of triads in conjunct motion (as in bars 46-48 of *Northern March*, and in bars 37-41, 98-113 of *Eastern Intermezzo*) were unknown in 1899, as were likewise unbroken sequences of consecutive unresolved sevenths as they appear in bars 9-18, 28-32, 52-53, 56-57, 80-93 of *Eastern Intermezzo*. The whole-tone chords in bars 139-142 of *Northern March* were the result of experiments I undertook with the whole-tone scale and with whole-tone harmony around 1897—several years before Debussy's inspired treatment of this aspect of music reached the musical world.
>
> *English Waltz* reflects, to some extent, popular English waltz-types of the Eighteen-nineties. Some of its phrases are cast in the 5-tone (pentatonic) scale so characteristic of English-speaking melody, instead of the 7-tone (diatonic) scale more usual in Viennese, German, French, Belgian, Spanish and Russian waltzes.

Grainger's wedding on 9 August 1928 reflected that side of his personality which revelled in the gloriously vulgar, celebrated as it was in the Hollywood Bowl in front of an audience of tens of thousands. On that occasion his orchestral bridal song *To a Nordic Princess* was first heard. The work encompasses two moods, the one exemplified by the work's principal tune, which is announced at the very beginning:

Ex 22: 'To A Nordic Princess'.

The other comes in a central section of evocative Delian harmonies and removes us to the world of *The Song of the High Hills,* and reminds us that Grainger is celebrating his bride-to-be's Scandinavian antecedents as well as his love for her. This part of the music needs the orchestral colour for its successful realisation and does not work well as a piano solo. Grainger's plan depends on the way in which the conductor presenting it adheres to his extensive and ever-changing hairpin markings for *crescendi* and *decrescendi.* 'Care should be taken to begin the swells and loudenings *soft* enough' he remarks in his introduction. Grainger prefaces the score with the following notes, first about the music:

The Graingers' wedding, Hollywood Bowl, 9 August 1928 (Insets: the happy couple, a Grainger.)

In mood and type, *To a Nordic Princess* is a thanksgiving song. It begins gently as room-music (17 single instruments—wind, strings, piano, celesta—moving melodically and many-voicedly upon a harmonic background furnished by the harmonium) and swells gatheringly in tonal strength until, about half-way through the piece, the musical stuff of the opening is proudly blazoned forth by the full orchestra (striding melodically and many-voicedly upon a harmonic background furnished by the pipe-organ). This massed restatement leads through an agitated working-up stretch into a strident climax which melts into a tail-piece, quieter and more tender in mood, that closes the work.

He then discusses its subject:

Now and then in Scandinavia may be met a Nordic type of womanhood, half-boyish yet wholly womanly, whose soft, flawless loveliness is like that of a fairy-tale princess; whose wondrous radiance makes real for us the sun-goddesses of the nature-myths; whose broad shoulders, amazon limbs, fearless glance, and freedom of deed and bearing recall the head-strong but noble-natured chieftainesses of the Icelandic sagas; whose cornfield hair and cornflower eyes awaken thoughts of the silent fruitfulness of the soil and of the lowly lives of land-tillers; whose graceful ease in riming, painting, singing, dancing, swimming, is the all-life-embracing giftedness of an unspoiled nature-race.

Such an uncrowned princess may be found in castle or cottage, in town or country-side, amongst high-born or low-born alike; for hers is bed-rock aristocraticness of race, not mere top-layer aristocraticness of class, culture, and breeding. To meet her is to have all one's boy-hood fairy-dreams and hero-dreams come true.

Such a one is my sweet wife-to-be—Ella Viola Ström—and to her this bridal song is offered as a wedding-gift and fondly honor-tokened in impersonal pride of race and personal love.

If in his wedding tribute to his bride Grainger wrote a work which, while sincere in its emotionalism, goes overboard in one direction, he nevertheless produced a score potentially popular by virtue of its melodic appeal. However, his extended score for wind band, string orchestra and organ that he encumbered with the title *The Power of Rome and the Christian Heart,* while equally sincere and passionate in its intention, is not easy music to assess or to come to terms with. Grainger's introductory background note is brief and to the point:

Just as the Early Christians found themselves in conflict with the Power of Ancient Rome so, at all times & places, the Individual Conscience is apt to feel itself threatened or coerced by the Forces of Authority. And especially in war time. Men who hate killing are forced to become soldiers. And other men, though not unwilling to be soldiers, are horrified to find themselves called upon to fight in the ranks of their enemies. The sight of young recruits doing bayonet practice, in the first world war, gave the first impulse to this composition, which, however, is not in any sense programme-music & does not portray the drama of actual events. It is merely the unfoldment of musical feelings that were started by thoughts of the eternal agony of the Individual Soul in conflict with The-Powers-That-Be.

The music is uneven, and without the folk-music or memorable melodic invention of his popular scores it lacks their immediate appeal. The opening is given to the organ, quiet and chromatically falling, which some may find sad or cloying, according to temperament and the registration of the instrument used. This texture is filled out in the wind before the 'Power of Rome

"Florida Princess"

To darling Ella,
from her loving Percy
Sept 16, 1927.
Lilla Vrän, "Passadena Boy"

Morris
Photo

27.

Theme' is given out by all the brass, including horns. These ideas,* and a fanfaring idea in the brass, are worked faster and faster to an impressive *crescendo,* interrupted by quiet intervals on strings or organ (one is marked 'feverishly'). The music ends quietly. There is much to impress in this work, but it is unlikely to find as wide dissemination as most of his scores. Yet, like the *Hill Songs* to which at times it has passing similarity of mood, we must count it to enshrine something of the real Grainger, and so it should not be forgotten.

Another similarly problematic work, though on a much smaller scale, is *The Lonely Desert-Man Sees the Tents of the Happy Tribes.* The thought that Grainger may have viewed this more as a fragmentary study rather than a finished work is prompted by the reappearance of the 'Lonely Desert-Man' theme in section four of *The Warriors.* This fascinating fragment plays for only about 2¼ minutes and comprises two sections—an opening, unbarred, yearning idea over a *tremolando* texture dominated (in most of its varied orchestrations) by the sound of the marimba. There follows the music of the happy tribes ('as if heard from afar—behind platform if possible') in a much faster and happier tempo, to which an ecstatic falling figure derived from the 'Lonely Desert-Man's' theme is briefly added before the work ends quietly. (The fast music is also heard off-stage in *Tribute to Foster.)* The music is notable for Grainger's use of inspired nonsense words** to sing to create the right sound in performance. The passage shown at Ex 23 constitutes the whole of the opening and the beginning of the 'Happy Tribes' music, of which there are another 42 bars in similar vein.

Grainger's alternative scorings vary from voices accompanied by guitars, marimbas, strings and piano to alto saxophone and chamber orchestra. The score is prefaced by a list of ten basic classes of scoring.

One may perhaps pause to wonder the extent to which Grainger identified himself with his 'Lonely Desert-Man', but in the final analysis this works best at the level of a fun-piece, and as such can be commended particularly for school and college use.

Finally, Grainger's Kipling Settings. Grainger produced 33 settings of Kipling, as well as allusions in instrumental works. They cover the whole span of his creative life, and deserve a full-length monograph of their own†. There are 22 numbered 'Kipling Settings' as an identified separate genre in his output. There are also a number of un-numbered settings, and a collection of choral settings as the *Kipling 'Jungle Book' Cycle.*

Grainger set Kipling as solo songs, and as choral works, both *a capella* and with accompaniment. *We Have Fed Our Seas for a Thousand Years* is another Grainger piece against war, though this time dating from the turn of the century. Grainger writes a marching tune, in basically popular idiom, for chorus with accompaniment of strings and brass and generates a remarkable passion by the end. The last of the numbered Kipling settings, No 22, is *The Sea Wife,* another rather more swinging march-tune for mixed chorus

---

* Sir Peter Pears has indicated the first theme is to be called 'Theme of the Lonely Man' (see p 28)

** See Bryan Fairfax's comments, p 100

† See Bibliography, item 20

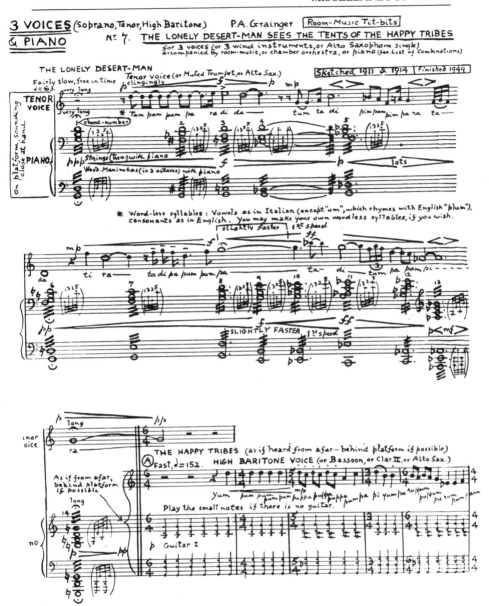

Ex 23: 'The Lonely Desert-Man Sees the Tents of the Happy Tribes'.

accompanied by brass or full orchestra and again moving to a fine climax, almost if it were one of his folk settings.

The *Kipling 'Jungle Book' Cycle* presents eleven choral works intended by Grainger to be a 'protest against civilisation'. The strange part of the procedure is that Grainger mixes accompanied settings with unaccompanied ones, and varies the accompaniments, thus making a complete performance somewhat impracticable*—for only nos 1, 5, (optionally no 7), 10 and 11 require accompaniments, while 3, 6, 8 and 9 require male voices only. However, these practical difficulties considered, the settings themselves are very evocative and distinctive. This is particularly true of the second *(Night-Song in the Jungle),* for either four-part men's chorus or four solo voices; and the word-painting and accentuation of the hunting songs. The strength of the accompanied items, particularly the last, *Mowgli's Song Against People,* again underline the feeling of Grainger identifying himself in passionate terms with the subject of one of his works.

There are many recurrent themes and ideas in Grainger's music, yet one does not have to investigate many of his scores to realise the scope of his achievement—he may not have espoused classical forms, but what he wrote, whether based on folksong or his own invention, presents us with a wholly individual, attractive and invigorating, yet tortured, world. It will surely gain an increasingly important place in our assessment of the music of the present century as time passes.

* See the programme reproduced on p 105

CHAPTER TWELVE

Grainger's 'Free-Music'

Ivar C Dorum

THE term 'free-music' was coined by Percy Grainger himself to cover a life-long concept, the realization of which in terms of actual sound was deferred until he was quite elderly. This aspect of his life's work, accorded a priority of value by him, has until recently received scant attention by others. Percy Grainger's short description of free music is 'scaleless, pulseless music'. He often insisted that its proper expression was by mechanical means, obviating the element of 'interpretation' peculiar to the original sound of any performed or recorded music, and giving us music, as it were, direct from the factory of the composer's mind.

Of the two distinct features of this music, it can be contended that scalelessness was of greater significance than pulselessness. Traditional plainsong was an obvious example of well-established music which had no regularly recurring stress, and as Grainger claimed priority for himself in the modern use of irregular barring and specifically stated in later years that this innovation was his first expression in composition of his free-music ideal, a significant line of research is opened up by this question alone. The case for his priority over other composers in abandoning the progression of melody by precise steps and leaps is much stronger.

Apart from the singer's and string player's *portamento* and the *glissando* which came into prominence with the nineteenth-century cultivation of the virtuoso—both effects being of a short-lived nature in a given composition—there was no precedent in the literature of music for the employment of accurately controlled gliding pitch, no effective notation for controlling such instruments as Professor Thérémin's *Etherophone,* and no significant demand from composers (other than Grainger) for such means of musical expression. Even the *glissando,* which was more frequently heard in piano music than anywhere else, was of course, on this instrument, a faked effect derived from the use of a scale, and the same applied to the harp.

From about 1927 instruments such as the *Theremin,* better known later as the Etherophone after its inventor, became possible sources of gliding pitch, following experimental research of an electronic nature, in its turn the result of the recent widespread application of the thermionic valve to radio circuitry. It was a case where the inventor of the instrument led, and the progressive composer began trying to follow—while his less adventurous colleagues, acknowledging increasing uneasiness over the shortcomings of staff notation in coping with the new experimental scales, did not recognize gliding pitch as part of their business. The important exception provided in jazz creations will be dealt with below.

But it was in 1892 that the young Percy began to wonder why music could not be more like the movement of his boat and of the water which lapped against its side as he was taken for an afternoon out on Melbourne's Albert Park Lake.[1] He was ten years old and had already spent half his life as a student of the piano, yet was able to perceive an analogy between the melodic progressions of piano music and the movement of wind and water in nature, despite the interference with the analogy by a disparate factor. Musical tunes progressed jerkily in pitch, however *legato* the performance, when played on most instruments, but an instantaneous change of water level or of air displacement did not occur in the natural state. (He was not to know that in the latter case the laws of acceleration in mechanics would preclude such a thing from being practical.) It is worthy of note, in passing, that a *legato* passage from one degree of a scale directly to another is at the option of the player of many instruments, such as the violin, and the alternative is to deliberately introduce the *portamento* effect, which consists of a short glide, the control of which is at the artistic discretion of the player. Furthermore, this glide cannot be quite eliminated by the singer (in the *legato* style) nor by the player of the slide trombone. In such cases the performer is in effect trained to cover it up as far as possible so that it passes unnoticed.

These observations were carried more or less consciously in the boy's mind through the days of his formal and informal training at Frankfurt am Main in Germany during his teenage years. Here he studied composition as well as piano at Dr Hoch's conservatory, and had much to do with Cyril Scott, Roger Quilter, Balfour Gardiner and Norman O'Neill as slightly older fellow students. The five of them were later known in London circles as the 'Frankfurt Gang'[2] because of the interchange of musical ideas far more progressive than the rather staid academic approach to the subject offered by their teachers. Of the older ones, Scott was probably the ring-leader in a kind of quiet rebellion against past conventions in composition, with Grainger, who developed a strong friendship for the older youth, not far behind in vigour, and full of his own ideas. It is unlikely that there was much talk of the free-music idea at this stage with so much of other old and new ideas in music to be considered; in any case, whatever there was did not make its way into letters between them for many years to come. It is well to know that the origin of a number of Grainger's works in idioms other than free-music did lie within the period of his life in Germany and were developed after his removal to London, around the turn of the century, although none of these compositions was published until 1911. The cause of this deferment lay in his fear of upsetting his popularity as a pianist, from which pursuit he derived a very good income, by presenting as a composer works likely to shock the bulk of his listeners. So in the early London years he kept to the public image of a conventional virtuoso pianist until he felt secure enough to exhibit his originality. Even then, he produced numerous settings of folksongs which revealed the touch of his mastery as a composer without pushing modernism to the extreme.

Reference has already been made to Grainger's retrospective identification of irregular barring in some of his early writing with a desire to realize a rhythm completely free from metrical time. Of course, there was the immediate problem that in dispensing with bars altogether, concerted music would become impracticable through lack of any co-ordinating factor. The system of harmony that had evolved in music of the European culture required a security of ensemble which, taking its metrical cue from versification of prose, and not unrelated to the regular drum-beat of primitive peoples, was responsible for the dominance of the unchanging time signature in composition from the late seventeenth century until our own. Even during this time, while the written time-signature did not change much during a movement, the urgency for rhythmic conflict produced occasional use of cross-rhythms by devices which returned to the former metrical pattern.

The overt recognition of rhythmic alterations by the use of different time signatures followed the desire for more frequent use of these devices, and it became a matter of notational expediency. The listeners to the first performance in 1913 of Stravinsky's *The Rite of Spring* ballet were largely shocked by the new extents to which this technique was taken, and this tended to associate Stravinsky's name with its introduction in the public mind. It is interesting to compare this writing (and its date) with Grainger's sketch for *Sea Song* (1907), bearing in mind that Grainger could not abandon the barline until he focussed his attention on free-music after World War 2. The opening thirteen bars, marked 'fast', change time signature at every bar in this order:

$$\frac{1}{4} \ \frac{7}{32} \ \frac{3}{32} \ \frac{5}{64} \ \frac{5}{16} \ \frac{3}{8} \ \frac{7}{64} \ \frac{3}{32} \ \frac{5}{64} \ \frac{9}{32} \ \frac{3}{8} \ \frac{7}{64} \ \frac{5}{16}$$

but the writing was experimental in nature, like so much of his output that veers towards free music, and not intended for actual performance by an orchestra. In a letter to Dr Earle Kent, Grainger has short-scored the opening, and his labelling ends with, 'written out for pianola or mechanically played organ (rhythms too complicated for human players)'.[3] Thus the avoidance of interposing the interpreter's art between composer and listener was not the sole reason for his insistence on mechanical music.

One could be forgiven a little scepticism here, were it not for the fact that performers have recently been using some of his lesser-known compositions that are intended for 'human players' and find them well-integrated, worthwhile and significant. In an article by Richard Franko Goldman,[4] reference is made to the compositions *Love Verses from 'The Song of Solomon'* and *Hill Song,* ascribing the varied time-signatures found in these works to the dates 1899 and 1901 respectively.

Another type of research which doubtless influenced both Grainger and other composers in the use of freer rhythm was that dealing with folksong. Folksong shares with plainsong the element of tradition, but is distinguished from it in that no very accurate attempts at notation of the folksong had been made until the youthful and energetic Grainger got to work in Britain. Certainly collections had been printed, and Grainger had studied British folksongs from some of Curwen's publications when he was still a boy in Germany, but the contents of such books were limited. There were many unprinted songs in the memories of old people and unknown outside their own district. When the need for rapid collection of these became apparent, activities were co-ordinated from 1898 by the Folk-Song Society (now the English Folk Dance and Song Society of Cecil Sharp House, London).

Several tunes that had been collected by Grainger were included in the *Journal of the Folk-Song Society* in its 1905 issue; and in the number for May 1908 he had collected three-quarters of the examples given and written most of the text in the 99-page journal as well. Important characteristics of the latter issue were that nearly all Grainger's material had been collected by gramophone recording—he was the first person to do this in England, and the second in the world—and that unprecedented care had been taken in notation. Instead of writing the tune once and the remaining verses separately, the music was written out afresh for each verse, a two-page key to pronunciation was provided for the words of songs throughout the journal, expression marks abounded everywhere, alternative versions of the same section as observed on different occasions, and rarely was the reader left for long without a change in time signature. In a tune collected at Brigg, Lincolnshire, called *Lord Melbourne,* there was a sequence of 31 bars, each with a new signature.

These folksong activities involved Grainger in two considerations which were to recur in his free-music of later years: they were, first, a freedom of rhythm and, second, an adequate method of notating such music which, in both cases, used a form of mechanical reproduction at some stage. It was typical of his insight into things to come to seize on the gramophone for collecting folksong, although the method used for promulgating his findings was the tedious and inaccurate one of converting the recordings to staff notation.[5]

He obtained a 'Standard' Edison Bell phonograph, and soon found that by slowing down the speed of replay by means of the governor provided, much detail of the music could be more readily identified. Whichever name, *phonograph* or *gramophone,* is used, the word reminds us of a link between the sound itself and some graphic record of that sound. To regard the 'graph', that is the sound-track of the wax cylinder, as a form of musical notation, probably did not occur even to Grainger because of the impossibility of a visual 'reading' of it, but today it is regarded as the record in itself, and is capable of being 'read' by the record player. In the free-music machines it will be noted that another kind of graph is always present and this is much closer indeed to a form of notation. At that time, libraries of recordings were unheard of outside the factories which made them, and a version in staff notation was essential for dissemination as there was an understandable prejudice against the gramophone among many musicians.

The most intensive attention was given by Grainger to the development of free-music during the early 1950s, and some account of this will be given below. It is clear from correspondence that he was then seeking to establish the time in his career when an adult interest had begun to manifest itself in the subject of free-music. Another Frankfurt student with whom he maintained life-long friendship and for whose compositions he had high regard, was the Danish cellist Herman Sandby, and in a letter to him[6] Grainger opens with an anecdote about irregular barring:

Around 1907 or 1908 Cyril Scott asked permission of me [PG] to use my 'irregular rhythms', saying that he had got so used to hearing them in my music that he could not compose naturally without them. I answered, 'Use them by all means, as long as you always give Australia credit for the invention of irregular rhythms', Cyril complained to Frederic Austin about this attitude of mine and Austin answered, 'You don't need to give Percy the credit for the irregular rhythms. You could say you got them from Scriabin.' When Cyril told me this I asked, 'But did you get them from Scriabin?' Cyril said, 'No, I got them from you.'

As with so many innovations in science and art, it is often hard to determine who has the first thought about them. Grainger's approach to irregular barring was through his own original patterns of thought, and it is doubtful whether he had much knowledge of the sixteenth-century masters in his younger days, although he investigated this area of knowledge very thoroughly in connexion with his appointment as professor at New York University in 1932. The letter to Sandby continues:

I don't want there to be any needless confusion about the origin of gliding tones in free music—I want the credit to go to Australia, unless somebody else really thought of it first. So I want you to help me, if you can, to remember when I started planning gliding tones. I have just found a letter (dated November 11, 1912), from Holland) to my mother in which I say: 'Heard a new instrument, a "siren", the invention of a Dutchman in Hoorn, which has great possibilities and fills the place I wanted to invent my telegraph wire instrument for. Have written him a warm letter.' What I meant by 'telegraph wire instrument' is an instrument that could imitate the gradually rising tone one hears approaching a telegraph wire, the gradually sinking tone one hears going away from a telegraph wire—in other words, gliding tones. (I enclose a photostat copy of a page of the above letter.) This letter shows I was consciously following the gliding tone idea by 1912. How much earlier may this wish to reproduce gliding tones be traced?

Do you remember when you were staying with mother and me at Hornton Street, Kensington, around 1903 or 1904, and I borrowed your cello to practise on and experiment with, that I would slide with one left-hand finger both up and down and you would say to me (for fun, of course,) 'It is considered very bad taste to slide both up and down. You may slide up to a given note, or slide down to a given note, but you mustn't slide both up and down.'

Do you remember my asking you (because you were so much more 'at home' on the strings than I) if you would slide up and down for me—slide continuously without coming to rest on any note, just remaining in a state of continuous slide?

Can you remember any other details having a bearing on sliding intervals—either anything we did musically at Hornton Street or elsewhere, or anything we talked about, then or at other times, that showed that I was longing to introduce sliding tones into music? For instance, anything in connexion with the cello part of our *La Scandinavie* suites, or passages marked *slide* or *glissando* or *portamento* in the vocal parts of the partsongs we rehearsed at Hornton Street. Of course, an ordinary *portamento* or *glissando* from one note to another would not constitute the beginnings of sliding tones. It would be only if I had said something unusual about sliding such as 'in my music, later on, I will want it to be sliding about all the time.'

This all relates to gliding pitch—the aspect of free-music in which Grainger's early approach is hardly open to challenge. The reference to the siren as a 'new instrument' could be misleading, or the result of ignorance on Grainger's part as of 1912. Actually, sirens were invented towards the close of the eighteenth century by Thomas Seebeck and John Robison for acoustic experiment and warning to ships at sea respectively, and an improved type was constructed in 1819 by Baron Charles Cagniard de la Tour.[7] It could be that the siren of Grainger's unnamed Dutchman was especially designed for musical use, and had some provision for controlling the rate of change of pitch. In his commentary on the remarks made to his mother, one notices the statement 'I was consciously following the gliding tone idea by 1912', and it can well be inferred that this idea had earlier been pushed into the back of his mind in a life known to be crammed with activity as a recitalist and folksong collector.

Even then there was to be a further deferment in furnishing a tangible result, but this was a characteristic of most of his composition of which he was careful to record in the published copies dates of commencement, revision and rearrangement for various chamber orchestra groups. Sometimes these processes would cover a period of 25 or 30 years for one piece.

While the 'controlled freedom' of pitch remained in abeyance, as far as Grainger was concerned, for about 50 years through lack of a suitable instrument, well-known developments, not entirely unrelated, took place elsewhere. In the practice of harmony there was a growing acceptance of more dissonant sound at its face value for the purpose of colouring the texture, rather than demanding resolution or follow-up that progressed to the simpler frequency relationships. So Grieg allowed listeners to enjoy the chord of the major ninth in a more peaceful frame of mind; Debussy, Grainger and Scott between them forgot about the rules laid down for the chord of the added sixth, boldly rounding off their pieces on occasion with the sound of major sixth clashing with perfect fifth and with the addition of either major or minor third; Satie and Scriabin employed their variegated fourths, and so on; and almost concurrently a new revolution was brewing— in the concept of scale.

The division of the octave into degrees, not merely of equal interval but of equal function, disregarding altogether their natural harmonic relationships, is a matter of slightly more recent history. It has been itself one of the biggest changes in musical practice. Yet Grainger's concept of free music is not only directed in sympathy with these trends, but outreaches them all. It was only gradually and intuitively that he came to see his relationship with these movements more clearly. In the entry 'Note-Row' in Percy Scholes' *Oxford Companion to Music,*[8] appears this statement: 'Note-row music is entirely "democratic".' And it will shortly be seen that this idea had a particular appeal to Grainger.

As Professor Grainger, he gave a lecture at Steinway Hall, New York, on 6 December 1932, entitled 'Melody versus Rhythm'.[9] Towards its close he referred to the future of melody in terms of the free glide in pitch. He pointed out that Arthur Fickenscher had constructed at the University of Virginia a harmonium called the *Polytone,* with five divisions to the semi-tone. But when Grainger envisaged scaleless music, he envisaged the limiting case: there were no intervallic divisions, or, to put it another way, the number of divisions was infinite. If Grainger could eulogize, as he did, the harmonies he heard on Fickenscher's instrument, what greater possibilities must there surely be with the harmonies of free-music.

One other matter should not be overlooked. The works of Grainger for more conventional instruments show little influence of jazz. The only one of these idioms used consists of, as with Debussy, an occasional ragtime type of syncopation. This imparts a distinctive character to otherwise non-jazz music in a manner comparable with the use of the 'Scotch snap'. However, Grainger never came near to derogating jazz (a popular pastime with most of his professional colleagues around 1930) and frequently spoke of it in quite glowing terms in newspaper interviews on both sides of the Pacific. He engaged the Duke Ellington orchestra at a lecture in New York University on 25 October 1932, pointing out to the students its merits in the fields of polyphony, ensemble and refinement of tone. Finally, performances of *Creole Rhapsody* and *Creole Love Call* were doubtless included for their slow, controlled *glissandi*. Grainger possessed many Ellington gramophone records, and often referred in subsequent notes and captions to the gliding notes therein. Only in the writings of Ellington, Gershwin and one or two others sympathetic to jazz did he find the true *glissando* used other than in the showy, peremptory flourish of its use in music generally.

In the employment of his ideas of free-music in actual composition, we can see at once the influence of Grainger's compositional trends when writing for more conventional instruments and for voices. Always conscious of his Australian origin, he had associated the quality of democracy particularly with this country, and found in counterpoint a musical expression of this idea. In the development of free-music machines, then, the ultimate aim was to combine strands of such gliding sounds as we have analyzed earlier with a homogeneity of texture scarcely achieved by those in the forefront of today's advancing techniques.

For the construction of the various experimental machines in the progress towards realizing in sound the free-music idea, Grainger had the assistance of Burnett Cross—then a lecturer in physics at the teachers college of the University of Columbia, and many years junior to him. Cross, who has had textbooks published in his own scientific field, first met Grainger because of mutual musical interests, and soon found himself playing under Grainger's conductorship in one of the numerous on-campus activities that Grainger engaged in during and after World War 2. It was when the younger man's knowledge of acoustics was revealed in the course of arranging a concert that Percy Grainger saw his opportunity to obtain some practical assistance, and in a tribute to Burnett Cross written on board the *Queen Mary* on 1 June 1957,[10] he stated that he could not have solved these problems alone. They carried out the constructional work together, with the assistance of Ella Grainger, wife of the composer.

Despite the lack of schooling in his young days, Grainger had no difficulty in grasping the mechanics of what he was doing, and according to Cross, came to the task with a full understanding of Duo-Art piano-roll cutting, in which work he had taken an active interest when recording for that company as a pianist. His father, John Grainger, was an engineer-architect who had successfully designed many public structures in such widely separated places in Australia as Melbourne, Adelaide and Perth. As a young child, Percy ceased to be under his father's direct influence after the separation of his parents, but seems to have been impressed and motivated from the earlier years by the draughtsmanship which was part of his father's profession.

This is curiously reflected not only by the energetic manner in which Percy Grainger would plan his activities at his desk in businesslike style, but also by the detail of improvised mechanical construction apparent in the music machines. Golf balls, vacuum cleaners, sheets of brown paper, yards of string, roller skates, rods of metal, plastic and prepared timber, most of which, together with a few toy balloons, were bought at the hobbies shop not a hundred yards from the front door of his house in White Plains, New York, were all acquired in the urgency of the moment to contribute to the apparatus in hand. Yet there was an unshakeable quality about the finished product—even if its members lacked a conventional brace and only had interlaced string to hold them together.

Burnett Cross was aware that he should have been two people when engaged in this pursuit: one, to do the job of technician that he did, and the other, to record each step of progress in the experiments before moving on to the next. But as each advance was seen ahead, no time was taken to stop and relate for posterity what had just been done. Even Grainger himself found that the eagerness of the quest eclipsed the avidity he had acquired in other aspects of his career for recording in fair detail the stages of its development, with the result that a chronological account of the whole free-music story was never set down. However, an indication of dates of assembly and manufacture is often written on the wooden parts of the machines, other parts have been labelled and photographed, and there are a few diagrams of completed machines.

A letter from Grainger to Mr G Donald Harrison of the Aeolian-Skinner Organ Company in Boston, dated 11 June 1946, shows the beginning of some practical steps in the new direction. In it he referred to the older Aeolian organ with the perforated paper rolls, and it shows that he saw in this the possibility of at least an approximation to gliding pitch. (It will be remembered that the approach to free rhythm, years earlier, was to use another approximation—that of irregular barring.) His proposal for retuning the reeds of the manual keys, which were in turn actuated by the paper roll mechanism, applied in principle to several of the reed-box models he was to undertake in subsequent years. Part of the letter reads:

> To produce my closer intervals, and the impression of gliding intervals, I believe it would be enough if I used three or four divisions (keys) to the half-tone. Thus the notes C, C sharp, D, on the usual keyboard and on the paper roll, would have to be changed to three versions of C on my special machine (producing C, somewhat-raised C, and much-raised C). Similarly the notes D sharp, E, F, on usual keyboard and paper roll, would have to become C sharp, somewhat-raised C sharp, and much-raised C sharp, on my special machine ... With an old instrument of the air-roll-operated Aeolian type, I think I would be able to undertake the necessary preliminary experiments—finding out how close intervals would need to be to produce a gliding effect and many other small details of effect in the new musical medium ...

This was followed by many other letters, reaching their greatest output from 1948 to 1950, in which information was sought on new instruments available, and possible help in connexion with the problems posed by the demands of his imaginative concept. But despite a tremendous production in the United States of manufactured instrumental novelties, in no case did one

Three melanettes harnessed to a Duo-Art player piano.

come anywhere near the total requirements of free-music.

For his machines using the reeds of a reed organ (probably because of their property of holding pitch well), it seems that Grainger soon abandoned the idea of using the intermediary keyboard in favour of a more direct action from paper roll to reeds. However, keyboards were much in evidence in the ·case of the Melanettes in 1948 (see illustration).

Each Melanette had its own keyboard of two-and-a-half octave range with the adjacent intervals of the complete machine tuned one-sixth of a tone apart. Three Melanettes were used to give a good overall pitch-range and their keyboards were coupled to that of a Duo-Art player-piano by cotton threads which were guided by fixed bars to turrets mounted on the keys of the Melanettes. This ensured a perpendicular thrust on the Melanette keys. The piano keyboard was controlled by a paper roll on which the experimenter could cut his perforations. In order to manipulate the paper roll, Ella Grainger had thought of gathering the central threads into a small ring situated between the piano keyboard and the Melanette keyboard above. Thus the threads could still slide independently of each other, but there was plenty of open space to either side of this ring for handling. On this machine an oblique line on the paper roll would produce a slide in pitch, and a plurality of slides in the different registers could be combined, but control over volume was impossible. Sometimes he used a Solovox—a 'single-line' instrument played from a short keyboard and generating its notes electronically—in conjunction with the Melanettes.

During 1951 a Cross-Grainger instrument with reeds was made in which the reeds cells were arranged in a horizontal row on a wind chest to cover a five-octave range. Using a remote vacuum cleaner for power, they could operate on either suction or air-pressure systems. Speech of the reeds was controlled by a paper roll as in a player-piano, but larger, running up some eight feet to overhead rollers which were turned by a manually-operated pulley. At this stage of experiment the graph cut in the rolls was of uniform width.

An important improvement in the cutting of the graph was introduced later by the device of varying the width of the perforated line. A wider section would allow a greater number of adjacent reeds to sound, while a narrower graph-line would affect only three or so. In this way a species of volume control could be achieved by the pitch-producing graph itself. The production of quiet music still remained a problem with these reed instruments, but it was always considered essential to have a 'blend' of adjacent reeds for two reasons. First, the transition of pitch was smoother, as a given reed could contribute to the sound of two slightly different pitch 'settings', and second, the physical phenomenon of beats was greatly reduced. A pair of reeds tuned (as they were in these models) one-sixth of a tone apart would give a very unpleasant beating effect in the middle register, but it was soon found that a multiplicity of reeds, each slightly out of tune with any other, but all approximating to a given average, gave the illusion of a steady note.

Another reed model was built in November 1951, which Grainger labelled the *'Hills and Dales' Air-Blown-Reeds Tone-Tool*. This last substansive was a word of his 'Nordic English' used in private notes, and means 'instrument'. The illustration shows that the reed boxes are arranged vertically. They are blown from a pitch-arm—a tube, the end of which is maintained at the distance of an inch from the reeds. This doubtless gave a mellower tone than the other reed machines. The controlling graph is a continuous cut in a large brown-paper sheet with the upper part removed, and the pitch-arm rides the 'hills and dales' of this graph. There is no provision here for more than one voice at a time.

All machines so far described were of an acoustic nature, and could be driven by the application of human effort, though the application of electricity as motive power was an obvious possibility. Grainger preserved some of these earlier models against the possible occasion of wanting to demonstrate a free-music machine when Cross was not available. He understood how to run them, but professed to have no knowledge of electricity[11] for a confident handling of models employing oscillators or photo-electric cells. The experimental sliding chords tried out on these reed instruments suggest a type of perfection in the use of chordal streams in the earlier twentieth-century harmony.

As Grainger's ideas had been behind the principles of these acoustic machines, so Cross's knowledge of physics came into greater play in 1952

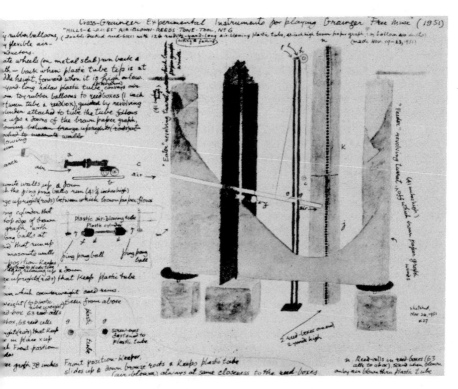

Grainger's sketch of his 'Hills and Dales' Air-Blown-Reeds Tone-Tool No 6 (Cross-Grainger experimental instrument).

with the introduction of electronic frequency generators. In the control of pitch the variable resistance method was preferred to the use of the variable condenser. The problem of establishing a link between composer and controlling unit was dealt with in the *Clothesline Side-ridge* No 1 machine. The pitch-arm of the oscillator, guided by two vertical rods, was made to rest on a sliding bead which was threaded onto the furthermost rod, as in the abacus, but vertical. The bead was supported from sliding down its rod by the clothes line, which was hard by, and rigidly glued onto a large paper roll, in its turn moving horizontally from a feeder to an eater revolving turret. According to the contours of the clothes-line, which were made as it was fixed to the paper, so was the melodic progression.

This led to the construction of the instrument which met Grainger's needs best at the time. He called it the *'Kangaroo-Pouch' Method of Synchronizing and Playing Eight Oscillators* (early 1952). A stiff paper 80 inches high, called the 'main paper', passed horizontally through a metal cage between two revolving turrets. On one side was fixed, at various altitude bands, four 'hill-and-dale' type papers for controlling the pitch of an equal number of oscillator note generators (each with its own speaker). These were interlined with four more papers, the upper edge cut to control the volume of its corresponding pitch-graph. The various controlling papers were sewn to the main paper so as to leave an unattached border at the top, in which a small turret and disc, attached to a control arm, could ride—along the edge of the kangaroo's pouch. Thus control over both pitch and volume was gained for four 'voices' in the musical texture, and this was increased to eight parts by having four more pairs of control papers attached to the other side of the main paper. A part could be silenced by a contact-breaker. This machine is in the Grainger Museum in Melbourne, but is not in working order. It would seem a wise move to have its various papers reproduced in some durable material such as a suitable plastic sheeting, in order to preserve Grainger's experimental fragments.

Other machines were built, including one where each controlling graph was drawn and shaded on one side, thus admitting more or less light to a photo-electric cell governing an oscillator. It must be realized, however, that Grainger never allowed that any of them had passed the experimental stage. For one thing, he did not have time to introduce refinements of tone quality.

In no sense were these machines 'composing machines'. Grainger met with Dr Olsen of the RCA in New York City several times, but felt that many of the examples of electronic music were too remote from the composer. His approach in practice had always been from the conventional to the unconventional, and it should be remembered that his earliest efforts to show the public something of what he was after were in 1934-1935 in Australia. He organized small string groups into giving little fragments on their instruments which he had scored for the purpose and had them included in programmes for the Australian Broadcasting Commission.

In most fields of activity he had a well-trained sense of publicity and promotion, but he did not really ever feel that free-music had 'arrived' and was reluctant to give public demonstrations. Yet his early concept has proved to have had a close relationship to most of the significant changes of the century, and in many ways to have reached beyond them. Today's composers will be wise to acquire knowledge of the principles of Percy Grainger's free-music, for the method of 'hit-or-miss' which has entered into some electronic music is not in the nature of this development. Free-music sprang first in the imagination of the composer, and was baulked in its expression by practical difficulties of the times. Perhaps, in our time, it may come to fulfilment in the hands of other composers, who are not bound to construct their own instruments, nor to use the tall monument to Grainger's effort that lies as if derelict in his museum.

Grainger's free-music machine at White Pl

Statement on Free-Music

Percy Grainger

Music is an art not yet grown up; its condition is comparable to that stage of Egyptian bas-reliefs when the head and legs were shown in profile while the torso appeared 'front face'—the stage of development in which the myriad irregular suggestions of nature can only be taken up in regularized or conventionalized forms. With free music we enter the phase of technical maturity such as that enjoyed by the Greek sculptures when all aspects and attitudes of the human body could be shown in arrested movement.

Existing conventional music (whether 'classical' or popular) is tied down by set scales, a tyrannical (whether metrical or irregular) rhythmic pulse that holds the whole tonal fabric in a vice-like grasp and a set of harmonic procedures (whether key-bound or atonal) that are merely habits, and certainly do not deserve to be called laws. Many composers have loosened, here and there, the cords that tie music down. Cyril Scott and Duke Ellington indulge in sliding tones: Arthur Fickenscher and others use intervals closer than the half tone; Cyril Scott (following my lead) writes very irregular rhythms that have been echoed, on the European continent, by Stravinsky, Hindemith, and others. Schönberg has liberated us from the tyranny of conventional harmony. But no non-Australian composer has been willing to combine *all* these innovations into a consistent whole that can be called *free-music*.

It seems to me absurd to live in an age of flying and yet not be able to execute tonal glides and curves—just as absurd as it would be to have to paint a portrait in little squares (as in the case of mosaic) and not be able to use every type of curved lines. If, in the theatre, several actors (on the stage together) had to continually move in a set metrical relation to one another (to be incapable of individualistic, independent movement) we would think it ridiculous; yet this absurd goose-stepping still persists in music. Out in nature we hear all kinds of lovely and touching 'free' (non-harmonic) combinations of tones; yet we are unable to take up these beauties and expressiveness into the art of music because of our archaic notions of harmony.

Personally I have heard free-music in my head since I was a boy of eleven or twelve in Auburn, Melbourne. It is my only important contribution to music. My impression is that this world of tonal freedom was suggested to me by wave-movements in the sea that I first observed as a young child at Brighton, Victoria, and Albert Park, Melbourne.

Yet the matter of free-music is hardly a personal one. If I do not write it someone else certainly will, for it is the goal that all music is clearly heading for now and has been heading for through the centuries. It seems to me the only music logically suitable to a scientific age.

The first time an example of my free-music was performed on man-played instruments was when Percy Code conducted it (most skilfully and sympathetically) at one of my Melbourne broadcasting lectures for the

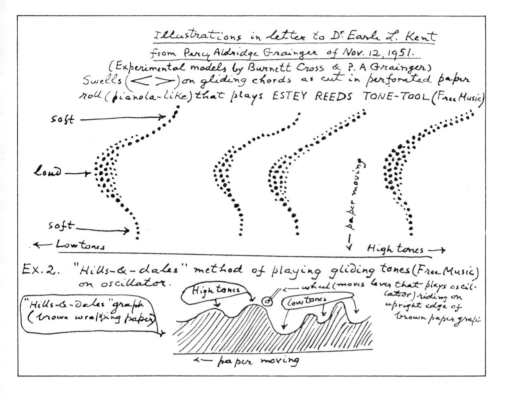

Illustrations in letter to Dr Earle L. Kent from Percy Aldridge Grainger of Nov. 12, 1951.
(Experimental models by Burnett Cross & P. A. Grainger)
Swells (< >) on gliding chords as cut in perforated paper roll (pianola-like) that plays ESTEY REEDS TONE-TOOL (Free Music)

soft

loud

soft

← Low tones

paper moving

High tones →

Ex. 2. "Hills-&-dales" method of playing gliding tones (Free Music) on oscillator.

High tones

"Hills-&-dales" graph (brown wrapping paper)

← wheel (moves lever that plays oscillator) riding on upright edge of brown paper graph.

Low tones

← paper moving

Australian Broadcasting Commission, in January, 1935. But free-music demands a non-human performance. Like most true music, it is an emotional, not a cerebral, product and should pass direct from the imagination of the composer to the ear of the listener by way of delicately controlled musical machines. Too long has music been subject to the limitations of the human hand, and subject to the interfering interpretations of a middle-man: the performer. A composer wants to speak to his public direct. Machines (if properly constructed and properly written for) are capable of niceties of emotional expression impossible to a human performer. That is why I write my free music for theremins—the most perfect tonal instruments I know. In the original scores each voice (both on the pitch-staves and on the sound-strength staves) is written in its own specially coloured ink, so that the voices are easily distinguishable, one from the other.

CHAPTER THIRTEEN

Percy Grainger's Free-Music Machine

Burnett Cross[1]

WHAT Percy Grainger required of a machine to play his free-music can be simply stated. Realising these requirements was not so simple, of course, but their definiteness and straight-forwardness were a great asset: we did not spend time developing features that would be of secondary importance to a composer. Grainger wanted a composer's machine, not one for the concert hall. As he said, he wanted to hear in actuality the sound he had heard in his mind for many years, to determine whether they had the effect he imagined, and to adjust them accordingly.

The free-music machine had to be able to play *any* pitch within its range. It was to be free of the limitations of speaking in half tones, or quarter tones or eighth tones for that matter. Any pitch (or group of pitches within the range of the seven voices planned for the machine shown) was to be available to the composer.

The machine had to be able to go from pitch to pitch by way of a controlled glide as well as by a leap. It was to be free of the limitations of the usual methods of progressing from pitch to pitch.

The machine had to be able to perform complex irregular rhythms accurately, rhythms much too difficult for human beings to execute. It was to be free of the limitations of the human performer, of what Grainger called 'the tyranny of the performer'. Of course, dynamics were to be precisely controlled as well.

The machine had to be workable by the composer. It was not to require a staff of resident engineers to translate the composer's language into the machine's language or to keep the machine in working order.

This last requirement produced, I think, the most striking feature of the machine developed. Grainger had worked out a form of graph notation for free-music many years earlier. The free-music machine developed 'reads' this graph notation, with very little modification required. The pitch-control graph and the volume-control graph are painted in the appropriate bands on the five-foot-wide roll of clear plastic (see Figure 1). Black plastic ink is used. By sliding the portion just painted across the pitch—and volume—control slits, the musical result is heard and any adjustments can be made at once. In fact if one paints on the plastic directly over the pitch-control slit, one can hear the pitch being formed. Happily the plastic ink used is water-soluble, so erasure is easy.

As the pitch-control graph moves across the pitch-control slit, it causes the

...er with free-music machine, White Plains, 1950s.

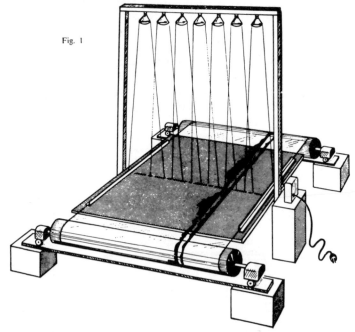

Fig. 1

amount of light entering the slit to vary. This light (from the spotlight above) is reflected from a curved mirror to the pitch-control photocell (see Figure 2). The photocell controls the frequency produced by a transistor oscillator:

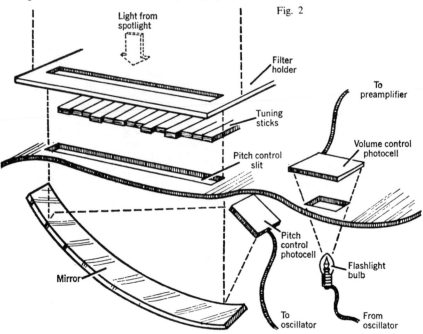

Fig. 2

more light raises the frequency, less light lowers it, and no light at all produces the bottom note of the oscillator range. Thus variations in pitch are obtained.

The output of the oscillator is sent to a common type of flashlight bulb, one that has a tiny filament and a built-in lens. The bulb changes the pulsating current from the oscillator into a pulsating beam of light. This beam is directed upward through the volume-control slit to strike the volume-control photocell. The volume-control graph varies the amount of light reaching this photocell, which is connected to a pre-amplifier-amplifier-speaker circuit. Thus the strength of the oscillator output is varied and control of dynamics achieved.

Imposing on the pitch-control slit a musical scale of whatever sort is desired can be done with the filter and tuning sticks. How these are mounted above the slits, on the tuning bridge, is shown in Figure 3. The tuning bridge rests on the metal guide-rails that steer the flow of the plastic sheet from roller to

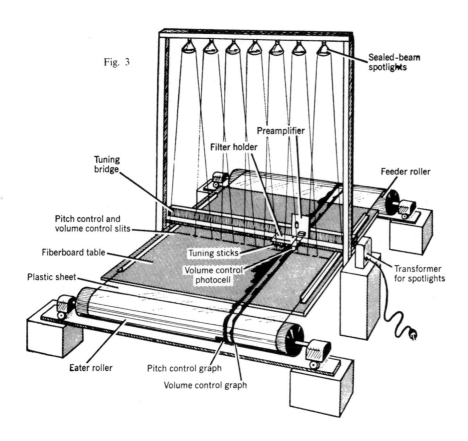

Fig. 3

Sealed-beam spotlights

Preamplifier

Filter holder

Tuning bridge

Feeder roller

Pitch control and volume control slits

Fiberboard table

Tuning sticks

Plastic sheet

Volume control photocell

Transformer for spotlights

Eater roller

Pitch control graph

Volume control graph

roller. A close-up of a filter and tuning sticks is shown in Figure 4. By sliding pieces of exposed photographic film of different densities into the filter holder, the amount of light reaching the pitch-control slit can be crudely controlled and the range placement of the oscillator roughly established, for that particular voice. Then, by moving tuning sticks in or out, the effective width of the slit can be varied. Thus, half-tone reference points (for example) of the scale can be distributed evenly along the length of the pitch-control slit. The narrower the tuning sticks, or in other words the more of them there are along the slit, the finer the adjustment can be. Thanks to transistors in the oscillator and other circuits, the scale imposed is stable enough. Trying to achieve stability with a vacuum tube circuit was a maddening and unsuccessful task. The vacuum tube model turned out to be a very sensitive device for detecting changes in the characteristics of vacuum tubes by means of changes in a musical scale.

Since the spotlights are running on AC, it might be expected that an AC hum would be the principal musical output of the arrangement, but it turns out that this is not so. Apparently the filament of the spotlight is too massive to transmit 60 cycles per second. The power supply for the flashlight bulb, however, has to be pretty smooth DC.

The mirror is made of a strip of copper bent by hand to the desired shape (which was easier than working out the geometry of the thing) and then chrome-plated. A sharp focus on the pitch-control photocell is not necessary. Both photo-cells are shielded with lightproof black cardboard from stray light. The transistor oscillator circuit produces a reedy and not unpleasant quality; a wide range of tone colours could be produced by manipulating the electronics of the oscillator, but Grainger was not at all interested in this at this stage. Command of pitch, duration and intensity were what he wanted, and quality was unimportant.

The feeder and eater rollers, as Grainger called them, are mounted on skate wheels, which allow a roller to move from side to side to compensate for irregularities in the plastic sheeting. Since the plastic sheet is constrained by the guide-rails so that its position relative to the slits will not change, it must be allowed freedom at both ends of its path. An electric motor can be arranged to turn the eater roller by means of a belt, but turning the roller by hand is easy and safe.

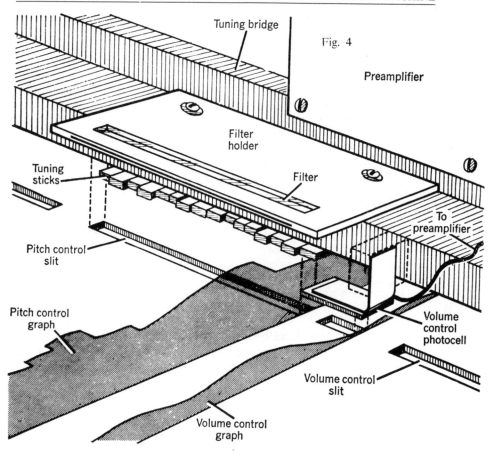

Tuning bridge

Fig. 4

Preamplifier

Filter
holder

Tuning
sticks

Filter

To
preamplifier

Pitch control
slit

Pitch control
graph

Volume
control
photocell

Volume control
slit

Volume control
graph

AEOLIAN HALL

Entrance on 43rd Street

Bet. 5th and 6th Aves.

Saturday Afternoon
November Seventeenth, 1917

at three o'clock

Percy Grainger

Pianist-Composer

FOR THE BENEFIT
OF THE

MANASSAS INDUSTRIAL SCHOOL
FOR COLORED YOUTH

MANASSAS   -   -   -   VIRGINIA

PROGRAM

1.   Fantasia and Fugue in G minor for organ.....................*Bach-Liszt*
      (Arranged for piano)

2. (a) Kulok (Cattle-call) op. 66, No. 1, set by ....*Grieg*

    (b) Folksong from The Valders district, op. 73, set by.................*Grieg*

    (c) "Reflets dans l'eau" (Reflections in the Water) ....*Debussy*

    (d) Prelude in A flat, op. 28, No. 17.............................*Chopin*

    (e) Polonaise in A flat, op. 53 ....*Chopin*

3.   Sonata in G minor ....*Schumann*
        (a) So rasch wie möglich
        (b) Andantino
        (c) Scherzo: Sehr rasch und markirt
        (d) Rondo: Presto

4. (a) "The Whippoorwill"............................*Daniel Gregory Mason*

    (b) "One more day, my John", set by............................*Grainger*
        (BY REQUEST)
    (c) Lullaby from "Tribute to Foster".........................*Grainger*

    (d) Paraphrase on Tschaikowsky's "Flower-waltz" ....*Grainger*
        (From the "Nutcracker's Suite")

STEINWAY PIANO USED EXCLUSIVELY

Management: ANTONIA SAWYER, *Inc., Aeolian Hall, New York City*

Boxes $20.00   Tickets $2.00 to 50 cents

On sale at Box Office or Manager's Office

CHAPTER FOURTEEN

Grainger the Pianist

Joseph Rezits

PERCY Grainger had the 'right ideas' about tone, 'tone-production', touch and tone-quality interrelationships, and so forth, long before Otto Ortmann proved beyond any doubt that tone quality is quantitative.

Grainger's attempt to disseminate this information to his students involved no mere polite academic process. He placed different people at different pianos and put opaque screens in front of each performer so that there could be no visual suggestion to the observers. He had one performer play *fortissimo* with a 'relaxed' touch and another play *fortissimo* with a 'stiff' touch—and challenged the observer-listeners to specify which was which. He would go on (for an hour if necessary) and ask for various levels of volume, for matching qualities and quantities—all to show that relaxation *per se* did not directly produce a 'beautiful tone quality'. Students objected violently (as they would now) but it would seem that Grainger went a long way toward exposing his ultimate point: too much time is spent in thinking about tone quality!

Once Grainger had cleared the air in this way, he was free to discuss some of the more practical qualitative aspects. He claimed that one could avoid harshness in a big sound by making sure that the melody was always in evidence. This process would represent an almost 'automatic' way of ensuring that the tone produced did not transcend the capacity of the instrument. He further claimed that the use of the damper pedal (more about this later) is of utmost importance in creating proper balance.

Grainger always thought of the piano as a truly percussive instrument. After all, if the sound-producing mechanism involves the hitting of tightened wires by felt-covered hammers, how could it be otherwise? Moreover, he believed in a percussive use of the arm; that is, hitting *hard* as opposed to using 'pressure' or 'weight'. He considered this to be a different and useful effect, and labelled it (logically enough) a *double percussion*. This term *double percussion* could also describe the non-legato effect (a high-finger approach) that he loved, especially in Bach and even in some of the Romantic literature where applicable, such as in the last movement of the Chopin B flat minor sonata. One suspects that Grainger was aware of the noise-element that would be inherent in the 'double-percussive' approach; however, I know of no specific reference to this possibility, either written or spoken.

In my own observations of Grainger's playing, I noticed that he often used what might be called a 'high arm preparation' before coming down on the keys in percussive fashion. He sometimes preceded this motion with an upward hand 'snap'. I'm not sure why ... perhaps to ensure having the firm, even rigid hand-position that was necessary to support this kind of motion. In one way or another he often wrote in (by means of instructions to the player) this kind of effect in his own compositions—stiff hand, arm, shoulder, etc. ('When one plays the piano, it is not the time to relax!' he said.) However, he did believe in different degrees of tension, a concept that might be applied especially to the wrist, which 'must be like a spring—tightly or loosely coiled, but a spring nevertheless'.

Strongly related to Grainger's ideas on tension and relaxation are his thoughts on endurance. I firmly believe in his premise (it represents one of the most vivid recollections of my association with him) that lack of endurance is often confused with playing the 'wrong way'. In other words, a player may become discouraged about his inability to play a passage (or an entire composition) and assume that he is doing it with an incorrect approach. In reality, he may not have given himself sufficient opportunity to develop endurance. Muscles sometimes take a long time to become accustomed to certain kinds of technical stresses. It is a form of 'athletic training.'

A case in point might be the learning of the octave passage in the Schumann *Toccata* (or the octaves in the Liszt *Hungarian Rhapsody No 6*). A well-trained but out-of-shape pianist might return to this work after an absence and get through about four bars before flagging, if not breaking down entirely. There may be nothing whatsoever 'wrong' in his technical approach. Slow practicing, gradually increasing in quantity and velocity, would eventually enable the pianist to play the entire passage in tempo, both in isolation and context— not only once, but perhaps *three* times in succession without pause. This operation virtually guarantees that the passage may be played once through in performance regardless of surrounding conditions: tension of performance, resistance of piano mechanism, etc.

In a larger sense, Percy Grainger was concerned, perhaps even obsessed, with the idea of physical fitness. He kept himself in excellent physical shape. Grainger would never walk when he could run; he kept a chinning-bar in his living room and used it frequently. He thought that musicians should not 'protect' their hands but rather use them, even in non-musical ways, as much as possible. He carried heavy bags (sometimes he used a wheelbarrow for this purpose) from his house in White Plains, New York, to the railroad station because he thought this was another means of developing his hands. His hiking, carrying knapsacks, etc, was all part of his plan for physical development. Pianistically speaking, he would create opportunities for developing greater endurance by placing three people at three pianos to play the orchestral reduction of a concerto simultaneously—and as loudly as they possibly could!

Grainger had specific ideas on the major 'areas' of piano technique. Arpeggios were generally played with a non-legato or even detached approach. This approach precluded the use of a conventional 'passing under of the thumb' to create a legato effect. In this way, any distorted lateral motions of the hand were avoided. Actually, Grainger often used what might be called individual miniature hand movements rather than finger movements to play consecutive notes of an arpeggio (or any type of passage-work, for that matter). This approach involved a special measure of control of the larger muscles and very little amplitude in the wrist motion. Extended positions of the hand were avoided whenever possible. It will assist the reader to keep in mind an example such as the Chopin Etude Op 10 No 1, as Grainger advised the player to 'contract as you go, so the hand may always be in its most powerful position—the position of greatest efficiency'.

As stated previously, Grainger preferred non-legato to legato in passage-work. Non-legato, even when pedal was used, produced a more controlled sound and more equality in volume levels. He felt that non-legato was 'cleaner' and more even. Grainger used an 'arm touch' in certain typical examples from French Impressionistic music; that is, the bell-like tones in the upper register of the piano that occur so frequently in the piano music of Debussy. Coming from above rather than approaching from the surface of the keys again offers a greater measure of control, rather than producing a certain 'quality' of sound.

Grainger often redistributed fingering for greater technical efficiency. He divided passages between the hands when necessary, even though the composer might have written it differently. (Some 'purists' would object to this procedure, claiming that the 'sound' would be changed.) Opportunities to utilize this procedure would be found in such examples as the Chopin Etude Op 10 No 12 (re-arranging the left-hand passage-work to include the right hand) and the Chopin Polonaise in A flat, Op 53 (using the right hand whenever possible to relieve the left hand of the continuous octave responsibility).

Grainger would often suggest the use of the thumb for playing a series of melodic notes when optimum position of strength was desired. There was another practical reason for this decision: there is more playing surface on the thumb than on the other fingers, and consequently when the black keys are used one is less likely to strike wrong notes.

Grainger's feeling for a true 'perspective' in the playing of chords is best described in his own words:

What is the need for ever making a note in a chord stand out above its fellows? In all good part-writing, whether for the piano or other instruments or for voices, each voice in a sequence of chords has some melodic value. Many voices have a distinctive melodic value. In the orchestra or in a quartet of strings or of human voices each part has a certain tone color which gives it individuality and distinguishes it from the other parts. But on the piano we have no such contrasting tone colours or tone qualities to work with. What in the orchestra, for instance, is accomplished largely by contrasts of *quality* we on the piano must accomplish by contrasts of *quantity*, or different sound strengths. Don't you see that the only recourse is to individualise the melody in an internal voice by making that melody louder, or by subduing the other notes in the chords? It is quite possible to play a chord in the following fashion:

Ex 24:

That is, the E flat is loud and the D flat and B flat are soft. Nothing is simpler. My own method is to hold my fingers rigidly; with the second finger, which would play the E flat, protruding downwards, while the thumb and the fifth finger, which are to play the D flat and B flat, are kept high, so that the force of the blow descends on to the E flat key (which is pressed down as far as it will go), while the other two keys are only lightly struck (and pressed down only one-third or one-half of the total distance they could descend).[1]

I might add that there is one other way of bringing out a specific tone (or tones) in a vertical structure. If we agree that the way to effect quantitative differences is to alter the speed of the hammer (a faster hammer speed for a a louder sound) then logically, any way to influence the speed of the hammer would be a valid way of altering the quantity of sound. Specifically, the finger that plays the key to be sounded more loudly will simply commence its stroke at a higher distance above the key than the other fingers used in playing the chord. All fingers will play their respective keys simultaneously, but the finger that comes from a higher distance will produce a louder sound. The degree of volume is governed by the height of the finger preceding the stroke. This procedure is especially useful in instances where there are relatively small volume differences among the notes, when the hand spread is wide, and/or when the overall volume level is low. Example: the concluding chord of the Chopin E minor Prelude.

Grainger did not interfere with a student's existing technical approach as long as it worked. This applied to both short-term and long-term teaching. If one could produce what one wanted in one's own way, Grainger made no attempt to change it. Such an approach has been used by other notable teachers, specifically Leschetizky and Hofmann. Grainger especially avoided 'methods' of teaching technique, since he claimed that this would encourage laziness (he did not say whether the laziness was that of the teacher or of the student, or of both!) and in fact it would prevent the pupil from thinking for himself. His overall views on 'technical training' are direct: 'The student can get technical training—after the foundation is laid—in the pieces he studies.' When interviewed by Harriet Brower, as recorded in her book *Piano Mastery*, Grainger stated:

> The technic of an art is, to a certain extent, mainly habit. I do believe in habit. We get used to measuring skips, for instance, with eye and hand, until we can locate them automatically, from habit. It is the same with all sorts of technical figures: we acquire the habit of doing them through constant repetition. When the mechanical part has become automatic, we can give the mind fully to the emotion to be expressed. For I do not believe you can feel the structure of the piece and its emotional message at the same time. For my own part I am not much concerned about how the piece is put together; I think of it as music, as the expression of natural impulses, desires or aspirations.[2]

These views were expressed before 1917, and it is interesting to note the underlying consistency of his thoughts over the years. At a much later time he claimed that 'anyone who *likes* to play scales is an idiot'. He felt that 'abstract' technique did not involve the brain sufficiently . . . it was too easy to go through such exercises without thinking, and 'there *must* be conscious thought at all times'.

Grainger felt that the 'practising' pianist may be compared to a scientist in his laboratory who is constantly experimenting. He thought more was to be learned this way than from specific directions imparted by teachers—and by doing this the individual meets a great obligation to himself. Grainger believed in slow, heavy practising; he claimed that one could practise a rapid work exclusively in this manner for several weeks and then perform it 'a tempo' more successfully than if it had been practised in the conventional manner. He claimed that if everything was 'in the fingers'—and in the mind—there would be no problem.

Percy Grainger himself would often practise well into the night. At intervals he would stretch out flat on the floor for 15 minutes, then resume his work. This was his way of relaxing. To increase his powers of concentration, Grainger would on occasion ask a student to practise on another piano in the same room

FACING PAGE: *Grainger's hands, date unkn*

where he himself was working. In the early years of the century, Grainger declared:

I enjoy teaching immensely: it is such individual work; it is like conducting in its effort to bring out the meaning of the composer by way of another medium or mentality. It is showing others how to express the idea. This is where the true teacher can so greatly assist the student, by being able to show him exactly how various effects are to be made, provided, of course, the pupil is anxious to learn how.[3]

While teaching, Grainger did not always look at the student; he liked to walk around the room, hop up on pieces of furniture, etc. He usually would allow the student to play a composition through completely before starting to correct him. According to Grainger, a teacher must perform: ' . . . otherwise the teacher becomes very pedantic and just tells people what to do'. Of course, one may face the problem of not having sufficient time to practise. Then one must choose: not to play, or to play badly. Grainger felt that the choice must invariably be the former.

Grainger was meticulous about pedalling. Explicit and detailed directions for the use of all three pedals abound in his original compositions, transcriptions, and editions. He pioneered the use of such effects as half-pedalling:

A very striking effect of *diminuendo*, for instance, can be produced by what I call 'half-pedalling.' The problem is to melt from *forte* to *pianissimo* through the use of the pedal. By 'half-pedalling' I mean repeatedly lifting up the damper pedal just so high that the dampers only partially arrest the vibrations of the strings, thereby accomplishing a gradual *diminuendo*.[4]

It must be noted that the effect described above should not be confused with another pedal effect often called 'half-damping'. In this procedure the pedal is depressed to the point of barely releasing the dampers from the strings —giving a partially sustained sound.

His use of the *sostenuto* pedal was extensive. As an exercise he suggested slipping back and forth from *sostenuto* to soft pedal without losing contact

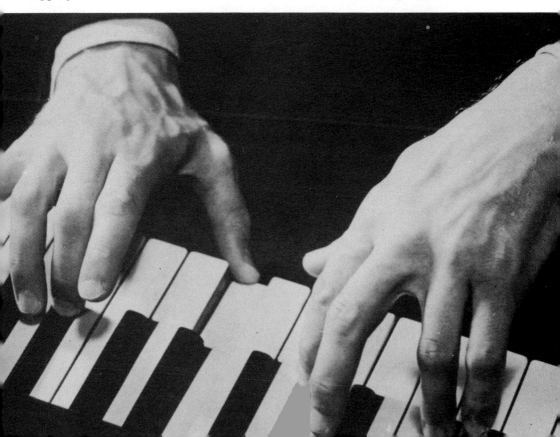

with either one. Girl students complained that their shoes weren't as broad as his! (He wore sandals or army boots.) He used the soft pedal for reasons other than merely making the sound softer; that is, to produce qualitative modifications in louder sections.

In his characteristically thorough manner, Grainger wanted to be sure of his memory, and frequently tested it. It is said that in rehearsing concertos with a second piano, he would have the pianist who was playing the orchestral reduction start at any place in the score, especially within the orchestral tuttis. His statement about memorising is so realistic, significant and thoughtful, it must be quoted here in its entirety:

> It is to be regretted that the custom prevails of playing everything without notes. I think many a fine pianist is greatly worried over the fear of failure of memory. This may affect his playing; it may prevent the freedom of utterance he might have, were he relieved of the fear of forgetting. All pianists agree that it is a great mental strain to perform a long and exacting programme from memory; it is no wonder that even the greatest artists occasionally forget. It is no crime to have a lapse of memory, though it is annoying, especially if one is playing with orchestra. This has never happened to me; if it ever should I think I would treat the situation quite calmly; perhaps I would go and get the notes—I always have them with me—or I would look over the conductor's shoulder, assure myself of the place and then go on. The great thing is to have presence of mind in such an emergency. If one is not very strong physically, or if a great deal depends on the result of one's performance, the strain of performing an exacting programme in public, from memory, is greater. Of course it is not artistic to play badly, so it were much better to have the notes in front of one than to produce poor results. Most artists would play more naturally with notes before them— if accustomed to use them. Fear often destroys the perfection of what might be a fine rendition. The comfortable, the ideal way, I suppose, would be to really know the piece from memory and yet play from the notes.[5]

With reference to the interpretation of his own works, Grainger said: 'If you can make it convincing at *your* tempo, stay with it'. He felt strongly that tempo markings were put up as indicators—not to represent the ultimate tempo. Mrs Dorothy Payne relates the story of a rehearsal of his orchestral work, *The Warriors*. Both Mrs Payne and Eugene Goossens were seated at the second piano. Goossens suggested a tempo and Grainger said, 'That's much too fast'. Goossens replied, 'But look at what you marked it!' Grainger glanced at the score and said, 'Oh well, that was ten years ago!' Grainger insisted that the interpreter must have a *reason* for everything he does; one must find the 'why'—not merely do something because 'it's nice'. The great artist thinks with great clarity. Grainger had his own ideas about interpretation and was not easily swayed. He had a feeling for logic and reason, and every act had a purpose, pianistically or otherwise.

Grainger believed that ensemble playing is one of the most important phases of music-making, but unfortunately it is neglected by pianists in general. He said that no one really could be a good pianist unless he had played with other pianists in instrumental ensembles and also had accompanied singers. Grainger declared that all pianists must be good sight-readers; and to this end he examined his students frequently. He had them follow complex scores as he played, and assigned two-piano music on a regular basis. Grainger also believed in group teaching, holding that its benefits far outweighed any possible disadvantages.

Grainger stated that the greatest performers were composers—for example, Rachmaninov. He thought they had perhaps a greater gift of 'understanding' and that this enabled them to look into a composition and see what the composer meant. Grainger himself divided composers into two categories:

1) those whose own musical ideas and emotions were given preference in their compositions, regardless of the instruments employed. In this classification he placed Bach, Beethoven, Brahms, Wagner, Grieg and Delius; and

2) those who concentrated on the physical nature of the instrument composed for, taking full advantage of colouristic resources. Examples of this latter group were Debussy, Ravel, Albeniz, Couperin, Scarlatti, Chopin and Liszt.

Such classifications, however, seemed to have no particular bearing on his preferences. Some of his own compositions were truly avant-garde for their time (and in my opinion could well be considered avant-garde today), as evidenced by the free-music (that is, music without definite pitch) of his later life, and his experimentation with quarter-steps, even eighth-steps—gliding tones, as he called them. Half-steps, he felt, were 'angular'.

Grainger did much arranging and transcribing of the music of Bach. He arranged fugues for saxophone ensembles, and for harmonium, saxophone, and piano. Solovoxes, which are electronic sound-producing attachments added to conventional pianos, and Hammond organs were also used. Actually, the solovoxes in this case were not attached to pianos but were used on tables—one per person—to represent the different fugal voices. The solovoxes were not capable of producing different timbres, but worked effectively because of their capacity to produce different terraced volume levels. Often he had students play single notes with one finger (on the piano) to stress equality of sound unhandicapped by technical considerations. The one-finger approach also imposed a limit on tempo!

Grainger abhorred what he called 'sewing-machine Bach', and felt that Bach should be played with more rubato than is generally done. As in his approach to the music of many other composers, he stressed the non-legato aspect, using the 'one-finger system' as preparation. Grainger felt that many people did not like or understand the music that preceded Bach. He felt that knowing pre-Bach music was the greatest training, and that Bach's music should be introduced in the actual chronology of its evolution—not 'backwards'—that is, after Beethoven or Mozart, as is so often done.

Beethoven and Mozart were rarely played by Grainger. He simply didn't like their music! He made no secret of his opinion that 'Beethoven was frivolous' and did not compose music of great depth. There seems to be no further documentation of these opinions, but one might guess that Grainger felt that Beethoven's approach was foreign to his own way of composing and thinking about music. Yet, claims Mrs Payne, 'he could play Beethoven beautifully and certainly could teach it'.

Of Brahms, Grainger remarked, 'He had a delicate and tender heart, but was well encased in beer and sausages'. He claimed that Brahms was often performed with insufficient lyrical Romanticism, and that there was too much stress placed on the 'bigness' of his works. He maintained that very careful balance was necessary in the *fortissimo* passages to avoid the effect of harshness; one must be sure that the 'tops' were there.

Chopin's music, Grainger claimed, was interpreted (by most pianists) with insufficient dynamic range. People were often too 'restrained' in playing his music. He qualified this opinion by specifying that a 'different kind of strength' was necessary in accomplishing this; that is 'reserve' rather than 'demonstrated' strength. Perhaps this could be interpreted as one's need to have the means of an absolute control that transcends any technical difficulties.

Percy Grainger's thinking and behaviour were often considered 'different' by his contemporary evaluators. The term 'eccentric' was used not infrequently. These labels were not necessarily used in a derogatory sense, but many had the feeling that he might be (to employ an expression in popular current use) 'listening to a different drummer'. Yet, as one analyzes every facet of his musical and personal endeavours, one finds a supreme logic behind every action, every musical thought or decision. When I am asked the inevitable question, 'In what ways was Percy Grainger eccentric?' I invariably confess that I don't really know. That remark either stops the conversation or commences a new phase.

Grainger conducting at music camp.

CHAPTER FIFTEEN

Grainger the Teacher

Dorothy Payne

OF all the people I have known in the world of music, Percy Grainger was perhaps the greatest teacher. Although he preferred to compose and concertize, he taught occasionally in Chicago, New York, and Interlochen, Michigan, in the summers. I was one of the fortunate ones who attended his classes in all of these places, and, as I knew him through the years, he gave master-classes in my home.

It was in a class of about 60 students held in a small auditorium on the tenth floor at Chicago Musical College in 1929 that I had my initiation into 'Graingerism'. Classes were in the morning, afternoon, and often until 10.30 at night. Promptly on the hour Percy Grainger would come striding in carrying a piano bench, having climbed the stairs for exercise. In addition to learning about music we learned the value of exercise (he didn't own a car) and of spartan living. There was to be no tea, coffee or alcohol. He advised us not to pamper the hands but to use them in all ways to develop strength, to work for long hours, and to be open-minded about all music and methods.

At the beginning of each lesson someone volunteered to play for the class and Mr Grainger listened attentively as he strode around the room, or jumped up on another piano, occasionally watching the student. He always allowed each student to play through, and then came the moment of truth. He was always cautious, smiling kindly at the student as he fixed his electric, penetrating eyes on him, but he then proceeded to take the performance apart. The unpardonable sins were faulty rhythm, careless pedalling, wrong notes, disregard of dynamic signs, excessive rubato, and failure to communicate a musical concept of the work.

Usually the rhythmic errors received the first priority. His general theory was that tempo could vary with different players but that rhythm was written in exact patterns and could only be played one way. He was willing to grant exceptions, since his own music tended toward free rhythmic patterns. The point, then, was to obey the wishes of the composer. There were times when he worked one hour with a student on the correct playing of $\frac{6}{8}$ time in the Saint-Säens concerto in G minor. One time in particular he asked each student in the class to play it; out of 25, only one was correct.

Having taken care of the rhythm aspect, the student already reduced to a nervous wreck, he would proceed to the pedal. It must not cover melodic or harmonic lines; it must enhance them. In his own editions one finds half pedal and sustaining pedal much in evidence. Also soft pedal was used in most *p* and all *pp* passages. As he continued to work with the student, the 'nerves' gradually disappeared and concentration took over. The class and teacher listened to various pedal experiments and offered opinions. On occasion he would comment 'too muddled', or 'too clean', or 'covering the melodic line', etc. Discussion followed and sometimes brisk arguments ensued. Another point was that when two or more notes are struck simultaneously, balance enters in. Harshness in *ff* passages comes from not bringing out the melodic line and from striking all keys equally *ff*. A *pp* passage that simply sounds mushy also has improper balance. After an interruption for such discussions, the student, having returned 'to normal' by this time, was told he might play later in the week after correcting some of the faults.

The next student might play the *Gardens Under the Rain* of Debussy, sometimes confidently, sometimes hesitatingly, trying the additional knowledge he had gained from the last performance. This made him even less secure, since most students require time to incorporate new ideas into their playing. In fact, Mr Grainger stated on one occasion that the mark of a talented player was to be able to change fingerings or musical ideas on the spot. He believed that too often a student refused to admit new ideas readily or was closed-minded about his playing. He thought a student should be ready to try new theories immediately in order to see if they improved performance. He said that practising should resemble a scientist experimenting in a laboratory, trying many experiments until a satisfactory solution was found for a particular problem.

He constantly asked questions of a student, such as, 'Why do you play that so fast?' or 'What mood are you trying to evoke?' or 'Why are your *p*'s and *pp*'s alike?'. This forced the student to think every moment that he practised or performed and not to try to copy a recording or an artist he had heard.

When these questions were put to the student who played the piece by Debussy, he could not put into words what he was trying to convey. Mr Grainger described it as a 'gusty, wind-blown piece' with ever-changing colour and sound ranging from delicate to stormy. In the slow, quiet section the student had an unfortunate way of playing the rolled chords with a thump. In working to correct this, Mr Grainger said, 'That chord stuck out like a bunion!'—not elegant, but certainly to the point.

The first part, describing a pattering of rain, was too loud and percussive. The student tried to correct this but could not achieve the desired result. At this point Mr Grainger observed the position of the hand and arm. Analysis of technical problems was necessary at this point. If a student were able to produce the desired effect in his own way, his technique was not changed. If he failed, suggestions must come from Mr Grainger.

This particular student sat stiffly at the piano, making a relaxed hand very difficult. Mr Grainger observed that he must feel relaxed in the opening and save the tension for later. As the student relaxed and played, the demand was made for softer tone, 'Use soft pedal', 'Don't attack the notes', 'Think of the sound of rain', 'Keep it clear and steady', 'Too much damper pedal ruins the effect'. After much repetition of the first page the student, as well as the class, always agreed that his understanding and performance of the piece had improved.

For the next section, the more 'gusty passages', more strength and excitement were needed. Oddly enough, the pianist who had had too much strength in the first part had too little in this part. The left-hand single notes came out, but the right-hand sixteenth notes did not support the small or large crescendo. He was told to practise the right hand more slowly, with a big tone on every note to develop more strength. Since this is difficult to accomplish, the student realized long hours of practice would be needed. Students were told not to just practise but how to practise to achieve results. Everyone had sore fingers during the first two weeks of classes but they eventually toughened up.

After working with the very delicate middle part, Mr Grainger turned his' attention to the last two pages. The tremolo was started with alternate right and left hand for strength and evenness, and then as tone diminished the left hand took over. This produced a good sound—again, the ultimate goal.

Next came dynamics; each mark was to be observed meticulously. A sign over four notes must be played in just that way but must also be related to other marks, mood, and meaning. If *pp*'s were not soft enough, then Mr Grainger demonstrated his idea of *pp*'s—a heavenly soft tone. He insisted that all such markings be heard in the mind and then conveyed to the keyboard. He asserted, 'One could play softly with one's foot if the mind were in command'. Immediately challenged by his students, he demonstrated that this could be done. It was a bit awkward, but it proved the point.

He was the first teacher I knew who insisted that all tone related to quantity rather than to quality. No one could alter the personality of an individual touch but quantity and balance could be controlled by teaching. This idea was challenged by many students who had been taught to relax in order to produce a better tone-quality. Mr Grainger agreed that relaxation for some effects was indeed necessary, but he also favoured a stiff arm and wrist for other effects. As was his way, he said, 'Let's prove the original statement'.

There were many pianos in the studio, and screens were placed around two of them. Two students were chosen to play, one *ff* with a stiff arm and one *ff* relaxed. The class was to decide on quality. After they had played, the class in chorus responded that the first was louder, not knowing which was relaxed. This was tried again and one was always found to be louder. Then just one pianist played, with the same results. We proceeded to *p* and *pp* with the same conclusions. After an hour of this, Mr Grainger, smiling, said, 'You see, we cannot even get quantity regulated, now when shall we talk about quality?' Scientists later proved his theory that the hammer hits the string in such a way that the key could be struck with an umbrella without affecting the tone.

When Mr Grainger demonstrated a passage for a student it came alive with colour, or excitement, or delicacy—whatever was desired. By contrast, the students' playing sounded pale, and all of us felt extremely inferior. It was not that Mr Grainger meant this to happen. Indeed, he constantly referred to his inadequate playing and never felt that he was a great pianist. Nevertheless, listeners were enthralled by his beautiful interpretations and counted him among the truly great performers. But his modesty was sincere, and he always placed himself in a position where the students could easily reach him.

The one thing that convinced me that I must study with Percy Grainger was his playing of Bach. I had heard him play the *G Minor Fantasia* for organ, transcribed by Liszt, and never had I been so uplifted and thrilled. Then and there I was determined to study with this artist. I worked up my own interpretation of the *Fantasia*, and at my first lesson in Chicago I played it for him. He listened politely and then began his usual analysis. Since it was a transcription he felt free to add some of his own ideas, and his changes improved it enormously. The organ sound was really there, the majestic quality of the *Fantasia*. What a revelation for me.

Later, during additional work on Bach, Mr Grainger reminded us of the religious fervour so evident in all Bach's music and warned us against what he called 'the "sewing machine" style' of playing Bach.

When it came to the four-voiced fugue of the *Fantasia in G minor* he placed four students at separate pianos, each playing one voice, at times doubling it with two hands. We were encouraged to practise Bach themes using the same finger for every note to develop steadiness and equality of tone. When the playing of the fugue by one performer took place, it lacked life, nerve, tone and intensity. To get the feeling for the theme, Mr Grainger would proceed to dance it. He would jump up on the first note and down on the second and then take a series of steps until the next jump. This illustration remains vividly in my memory and has always influenced my own playing of this fugue.

Bach was Grainger's great love; and he said that as a child he performed, but was not touched by, music until he discovered Bach. This was music—inspired, logical, perfect and meaningful. As a young boy he also had a passion for stories of knights in armour and was given a suit of armour. While quite young he began to concertize, but he only consented to do so if he could have his suit of armour on stage while he played. What a combination—the little Grainger, Bach and armour.

Though Percy Grainger was a teacher with the ability to work patiently with the most minute details of rhythm, dynamics, balance, pedal, precision, and tempo, he also managed to impart a feeling of the broader sense of the music. For example, he said many times that one should not play music of any period without knowing the history of that time, the art, the literature, the dress, the architecture, and the customs. In addition, one should familiarize oneself with the life of the composer and his works. He asserted that one does not compose in a vacuum and that the artist is influenced by the times in which he lives. In this way the student can come to know the composer better and to understand, for example, the influence of Italian opera on Mozart and to hear the many ornaments in the terms of a fine Italian soprano or tenor. One should also know what kinds of instruments were played in different periods and why Beethoven bass notes with pedal are often too heavy on modern pianos but probably sounded well on his instrument.

It was from Mr Grainger that I learned so much of musical and historical interest; in addition, however, I recall those capsule impressions he left with me of each composer. We know that each Brahms piece is a separate and inspired composition. However, Grainger's description of Brahms—'a delicate and tender heart, well-encased in beer and sausages'—conveys the feel of this composer. The fact that Brahms loved to read folklore and ballads of knights in armour rescuing fair maidens is also apparent in many compositions.

As for Chopin, we are aware of those delicate, lovely ethereal moments, but the sheer power and strength of the scherzi, ballads, sonatas, and polonaises is also a factor in playing fine Chopin. Mr Grainger likened this power to a partially sleeping lion. A mouse approaches timidly at first, then becomes more daring and comes closer. The lion lifts one huge paw and comes down on the mouse, killing it. There is seemingly no display of power, but one is aware that enormous strength is present.

I remember one unfortunate student who thundered his way through the *Ab Polonaise* with no regard for balance, pedal, or contrast. At the conclusion, Mr Grainger said mildly, 'That was a veritable bloodbath'. 'Let's see how we can make it a musical composition.' And, as always, he did just that.

Among his many accomplishments, Percy Grainger was noted for collecting folk-music, arranging it, recording it, etc. Long before this was a popular art he would , in his usual thorough way, travel to some obscure island—the Faeroe Islands, for example—and live there for some months absorbing the culture, ideas, language, and collecting folk-songs on recordings. Out of this was to come the lovely duet *Fair Is Play on the Greensward,* also known as *Let's Dance Gay in Green Meadow.* This reflected the energy, hardiness and gaiety of people who could dance for eight hours without missing a footfall. Again, his theory of background became essential to the performance of the music.

I studied many of his beautiful arrangements of folk-tunes and found them satisfying musically and pianistically. He much preferred them for orchestra and chamber groups and jotted on the piano score 'dished up for piano or pianos'. He marked every detail so carefully that one could reproduce the spirit of the folk-tune but could never manage to make it sound like Grainger's own performance. In one class he remarked that the simplicity was the greatest beauty of a fine folk-tune. Unfortunately, composers seemed compelled to arrange such music for chorus or orchestra.

In arranging American and English folksongs it was his aim to perpetuate them and allow more people to hear them. Think of the millions of people who have heard the Grainger arrangement of *Country Gardens* who might otherwise never have known that such a charming tune existed.

Our class in Chicago assisted in presenting a programme of Grainger arrangements, with the composer conducting. For example, the lovely *Spoon River* was given to the group of pianists, of which I was one. He chose some for two pianos, others for xylophone, and I was to play marimba with Ella Grainger. When I explained that I had never played the instrument, he said brusquely, 'Oh, it's like the keyboard; you can do it'. One didn't argue; one played. On the day of the performance we had played several pages when Mr Grainger stopped us and said casually, 'It really is too slow'. 'Let's start again at a livelier tempo.' So we did and miraculously finished together.

His approach to playing was casual, and he disliked any kind of formality. Concerts became much more free—and unpredictable. Today, years later, this has come about in a way that would have delighted him.

In teaching piano, Mr Grainger was a master of the keyboard and its vast literature. But above all he stressed that playing the piano was a part of the great world of music. We sightread extensively; made use of two and four pianos simultaneously; played chamber music with various instruments; constantly discussed backgrounds of composers and their music; analysed form; and considered the meaning of music.

Master-classes with Mr Grainger in Chicago, Interlochen, Northwestern University, New York, and in Cincinnati at my own home altered my entire approach to teaching, playing and the understanding of music. It was a most inspirational and wonderful experience.

CHAPTER SIXTEEN

Grainger on Record

John Bird

CONSIDERABLE research over the last decade or so has helped to dispel the legends which encrusted the figure of Grainger, happily to reveal a fuller, more rounded character, whose rich and extensive musical legacy speaks of a man of great warmth and human integrity—a reality which need not dredge the sediment of legend for its timelessness. What has also occasionally emerged, I feel, in some 'live' as well as some recorded performances, is a discernible quality that one might call a 'Grainger spirit'. This spirit is born of the music itself, of course, but translating it into performable values is not the easiest of tasks.

The 'spirit' of a composer is elusive enough, probably impossible, to define, let alone to communicate. The 'absolutist' view does not help here. Both Toscanini and Fürtwangler, for example, opened doors to their 'own' Beethoven with different keys, both of which revealed great 'truths', but neither of whom could have claimed to have been the owner of the only key. Sincerity on its own would seem to be of little help in our quest. As Oscar Wilde said, this is dangerous enough in small doses; a great deal of it is absolutely fatal. Experience tells us also that mere virtuosity is of no use. Technique, though a useful tool, is not a key.

One would do well, with Grainger, to try to understand some of the facts of his life, his artistic beliefs, his hopes and frustrations, his range and limitations, the human and artistic influences which were assimilated and those which were rejected.

One of Grainger's concerns was that his music would survive him, and partly because of this he took his art and his craft very seriously indeed, with a kind of passion to which only a born iconoclast can lay claim. He was a man not wholly unacquainted with tragedy and, perhaps largely as a result of this, produced many works of great tenderness, sadness and even ferocity, admitting only on occasions a boyish sense of fun.

Grainger was not, as was once thought in some circles, a musical *farceur,* and whenever he is approached as a 'light music' composer, the point is missed and he is done no little injustice. Too often, when his music is played today, it suggests the atmosphere of, say, a pleasant afternoon tea down by the river at Henley-on-Thames. Works are sometimes under-rehearsed (audible even on records) when, to their great and belated astonishment, musicians discover that they present enormous technical and interpretative challenges. One writer recently made the astute observation that 'His music, which sounds so spontaneous, is full of problems for the performer, however; in rehearsal it often seems too repetitive but it absolutely demands a "performance"; a routine play-through is always a disaster'.[1]

Further keys to the spirit of Grainger lie in the instinctive use of sensitive phrasing, sympathy for the subtleties of his counterpoint, and a spontaneous exuberance derived from cross-rhythms, syncopation and a general rhythmic 'snap'. Though in the end these things can hardly be taught, one is given every help in page after page of his scores, which bristle with meticulously detailed instructions and suggestions which, if understood, show that at least Grainger knew exactly what he wanted as regards sound, atmosphere and feeling.

There has been for some time a great quantity of recordings in circulation of 'live' and 'off-the-air' performances given by Grainger as conductor, pianist and even guitarist in his own and other composers' works. It is not difficult for any diligent musician or record collector to track these down, and in doing so he can learn much. We will never know exactly how Bach used ornaments, how Chopin used *rubato* and how Liszt may or may not have embellished his piano scores, and so the controversies will always rage. With Grainger, as with other 20th-century composers, we have this splendid opportunity of gaining insights into their feelings about their own and other composers' works. It would be boorish to advocate a slavish copying of a composer's view of his own works, but it would be equally undesirable to propose a complete break with these incipient traditions. A sense of balance is clearly required. It is also interesting to hear where Grainger departed from his scores, which he did from time to time.

The renaissance of Grainger as a recorded composer really begins in the 1950s, at a time in his life when his letters would seem to portray a man faced with the kind of neglect which at times brought him to the brink of despair. Leopold Stokowski and Frederick Fennell issued some discs which have remained to this day key items in the recording canon. During a period when Grainger suffered general ill-health and battered spirits, these two conductors, from widely differing disciplines and backgrounds, took the trouble of actually going to see Grainger at his home in White Plains to discuss with him the interpretation of his works. The amount of joy and restoration of self-confidence this renewal of interest and respect gave to the composer can never be measured.

First came Stokowski with a request to Grainger that he take down some of his scores and 'make an entirely new version of them . . . that each time a theme is repeated, fresh instruments would play, [and] that such instruments as vibraharps, marimbaphones, saxophones, celestes—and in fact all the colourful instruments of the modern orchestra—could be employed'.[2] At first, Grainger took the request as something of a slight because he felt it suggested that his existing arrangements were not good enough to record, and indeed he had already pioneered the orchestral use of some of these 'colourful instruments'. When eventually he made these dazzling re-arrangements and the ensuing records, however, he changed his mind, and a few years later looked back on the venture with pride, writing to Stokowski: 'I am tempted to say that my ears have never before heard such a coming-together of lovely skills and mastery of diversified details in a gramophone record'.[3] The arrangements are, needless to say, quite the most extravagant (some would say 'perverse') to have come from Grainger's pen, and the performances which Stokowski gives them (despite some cuts) are pure magic. This conductor's ability to command huge forces without a loss of detail and clarity (essential with Grainger) is nowhere better to be seen than on this record. These recordings (re-issued now on RCA VRL10168) are historical documents of great importance, not only because of the close collaboration between composer and conductor but also because of the presence of Grainger as the pianist in *Country Gardens, Shepherd's Hey* and *Handel in the Strand*. The uniquely beautiful *Early One Morning* on this record has, to my knowledge, never been performed on any other occasion.

From this side of the Atlantic it is almost impossible to measure the importance of Frederick Fennell in the musical life of America. Almost single-handedly this pupil of Koussevitsky injected new life into that peculiarly American instrumental grouping known as the wind ensemble. In America he is a living legend, a man often as not able to command a fully-deserved hero-worship and, more importantly, brilliant performances from the thousands of musicians who have served their musical apprenticeships and subsequently worked under him. He is the only man in the world of the wind ensemble through whom all previous and subsequent traditions lead.

The turning point for Fennell came in 1952, when he founded the Eastman Wind Ensemble and began to make a series of 25 supreme records for Mercury, one of which was an all-Grainger album and two more of which contained works by Grainger. This pioneer and unique creation of Fennell's set new standards and created new traditions without ignoring the synthesising role of all that had gone before it. With Fennell the wind ensemble was moved from the high-school gymnasium to the international concert stage, thereby acting as the perfect vehicle for creative pioneers from Gabrielli to Grainger, who had been hanging around, so to speak, awaiting their ideal medium.

Not only was Fennell's ensemble quite clearly the finest in the world, but by great good fortune Mercury had hit upon a single-microphone recording technique which at a stroke cast all previous, and practically all subsequent, recording techniques into the shade. My own copies (mono, if you please), pressed in the late 1950s, are grey with use and one can all but see the turntable through the grooves, yet the clarity and detail of the individual instruments and the fullness of the sound throughout the entire audio spectrum are far better than anything produced today in stereo, with the possible exception of some of the new direct-cut and digital discs. A damning indictment on modern multi-microphone techniques, I feel. May I offer up a prayer that if and when Phonogram (in whom, I believe, the rights reside) re-issue these precious recordings in the UK they do not commit that most heinous of crimes and produce those that have original mono master-tapes in electronically recreated stereo.

Over the years these masterly recordings have made appearances on a multitude of different labels and catalogue numbers, but whatever the disguise they are performances which any Grainger devotee must cherish and are yardsticks against which subsequent performances can be judged.

Fennell sought the advice of Grainger in preparing these recordings and there is a consequent degree of authenticity in them which few can rival.

When Grainger first heard these records he wrote to a friend: 'Another reason for restored optimism is Frederick Fennell's disc recording of *Lincolnshire Posy*. Never have I heard music of mine played half so well. In fact what he has done is simply magical . . . The main thing is that he sees everything fiercely, loudly, savagely—just what I have always wanted . . . But it is all part of the strange enthusiasm that the younger bandleaders feel for my music—something that I cannot explain at all . . . Don't you think that F. Fennell's recording of *Colonial Song* is wonderfully fine—so rich and glowing. He is a wonder.'[4] To which I can add nothing except 'Here, Here!'

Frederick Fennell's more recent recording of the *Lincolnshire Posy* with the Cleveland Symphonic Winds on Telarc Digital Stereo DG-10050 takes a more mature, rounded look at the work. The musicians involved seem to lend a more professional polish to their playing, yet to me it seems to lack just a little of the youthful dash and bite so much a characteristic of the old Mercury performances. The quality of sound is superb, but it must be stated that only when played through the very best equipment will the digital improvements be heard. *Shepherd's Hey* is thrown in as a filler and it is given a bright and glittering performance. The acoustic properties of New York's Eastman Theatre, in which the Mercury recordings were made, seem altogether more pleasing than the somewhat hollow and empty hall of Cleveland, Ohio, where the Telarc record was made.

In a letter to the present writer, Frederick Fennell pointed out these facts:

> The recordings made by the Eastman Wind Ensemble of *Lincolnshire Posy* and *Hill Song 2* were played by a *completely student* group, all being full-time students at the Eastman School of Music—and none being beyond the age of 24—and, of course, all professionals as well. David Hall, Editor of *Stereo Review*, recently selected the *Posy* recording as 'one of the 50 best recordings in the first century of the Phonograph'—a great testament to those really marvellous young players. The group is frequently confused with the Eastman-Rochester Orchestra, which recorded the Grainger orchestral pieces, and those musicians were the Wind Ensemble's players' teachers and the professional orchestra of Rochester, recording under two names at once: Rochester Philharmonic and Eastman Rochester.

For the benefit of future conductors and students of Grainger, reference must be made to the May, September and October 1980 editions of *The Instrumentalist,* which carry a brilliant three-part essay on *Lincolnshire Posy* by Frederick Fennell. It is in the form of a performer's analysis and corrects many of the mistakes which managed to creep into the published edition. Yet it is more than that: it is a masterpiece of scholarship and one which reflects a life-long devotion to and love for the music of Grainger.

Further cornerstones for every Grainger collection should be the two Decca records SXL 6410 and SLX 6872, which together form Volumes One and Two of their 'Salute to Percy Grainger'. The first is conducted by Benjamin Britten, the second by Steuart Bedford—a worthy successor. Britten was another pioneer in the championship of Grainger's music and he regarded the Australian as his master in the art of folksong setting. That is as far as his admiration went, but in this field the identification was profound and scholarly.

As far as Grainger's feeling for folksong is concerned, I have recently been drawn to the conclusion that he could well have looked upon his work in this field *not* as a kind of musical archaeology, but more with the thought that folk-music (in its unique tonal structures, in its improvisatory use of ornament and irregular rhythms, and its general striving for freedom) was the most *advanced* music he had encountered up to that time. It could be that Bartók, Kodály, Grieg and even Dvořák felt exactly the same.

Grainger invests his settings with a love and a reverence for the original work as did no other composer, and Britten, Pears, Bedford, Shirley-Quirk, and the ECO provide us with all the interpretative joys to which we have grown accustomed from these artists. These two Decca records, made to their highest technical standards, also include exciting explorations of previously unrecorded and sometimes unperformed works. Peter Pears knew Grainger and performed under his direction several times. His singing, therefore, is authoritative, impeccable and always deeply moving. The first volume has the bonus of letting us hear Britten as a pianist—always a rare treat. John Shirley-Quirk's powerful and heart-rending performances of the sea-chanties *Shallow Brown, Shenandoah, Dollar and a Half a Day* and *Stormy* are memorable in every way. The arrangement of *Irish Tune from County Derry* used in Volume Two is not in the harmonisation we all know and love but a completely different version written in 1920. With this performance I think we can begin to understand a vital key to the Grainger spirit when he wrote:

> The object of my music is not to entertain, but to agonize ... My efforts even in my young days, was [sic] to wrench the listener's heart with my chords. It is a subtle matter for music is not made agonizing merely by sharp discords any more than literature is made agonizing by crude events. It is the contrast between the sweet and the harsh that is heart-rending. On the whole I think the whole musical world is oblivious of all the bitterness, resentment, iconoclasm and denunciation that lies behind my music. The worth of my music will never be guessed or its value to mankind felt until the approach to it is consciously undertaken as a pilgrimage to sorrows.[5]

Leading the way for a time with piano recording was Daniel Adni on EMI HQS 1363, but this was because it was at the time the only record of its kind in the catalogues. It was a wholly wrong-headed choice to get this talented young pianist to record Grainger's music, for he seems to miss the point in practically every piece. In fact the only worthy track is Grainger's setting of Fauré's lovely song *Nell,* though I suspect this might have been born more of a sympathy for Fauré than for Grainger.

EMI improved matters by reissuing Australian recordings by David Stanhope and Leslie Howard on HQS 1402. A fine performance of the two-piano/four-handed version of *Lincolnshire Posy* is complemented by spirited and well-considered solo performances by Leslie Howard. Their joint playing of Grainger's *English Waltz* is a huge romp from beginning to end. As I write, news has just reached me, however, which indicates that I should be using the past tense for this paragraph because it would seem that, perfectly in character with the idiotic ways in which record companies act,

British EMI have deleted the splendid Stanhope/Howard recording and retained in their catalogue the uninspired Adni efforts. What does one do? Tear one's hair, gnash one's teeth, throw up one's hands in Oliver Hardy-like despair and run screaming!

For the British and American buyer, however, the only hope is to hop around to your local import record dealer (yet again) and invest in the three magnificent Australian World Record Club discs R 03433 (solo works—Leslie Howard), R 06332 (two pianos, four hands: Leslie Howard and David Stanhope) and R 06333 (two pianos, six hands: Leslie Howard, Geoffrey Parsons and David Stanhope with the Adelaide Brass Quintet and guests). It is unlikely that these records will have peers for a very long time to come. The recording quality is very good indeed and the multi-pianist items are played with a high degree of unity of thought and skill, thus enabling the listener to follow the complicated warp and weft of Grainger's counterpoint, more easily perhaps even than in the orchestral editions.

For some years the conductor John Hopkins had built up an antipodean reputation as Grainger's most enterprising champion, and I myself had attended some very enjoyable concerts which included Grainger's works in both Sydney and Melbourne (which often left the audience either wildly enthusiastic or utterly stunned), but his records until quite recently I felt were woefully inadequate. He was first recorded on the Australian Broadcasting Commission's own label, Australian World Record Club and Australian EMI, but much of this constituted a poor showing.

The Australian Broadcasting Commission's own recording of *The Warriors,* with John Hopkins conducting the Melbourne Symphony Orchestra (RRCS 131), was an energetic but not perhaps completely successful performance of this, one of Grainger's most difficult scores. The Leslie Howard/David Stanhope/Geoffrey Parsons two-piano/six-handed performance with off-stage brass is a far more coherent and enlightening performance (World Record Club (Australia) R 06333) but one hopes that eventually John Hopkins will be given another chance to take a fresh look at the full orchestral version.

Australian EMI, however, would now seem to have taken the whole project by the scruff of the neck and begun at square one with a properly planned series of records which, one hopes, might eventually include all Grainger's orchestral works. (Since Australian choirs have a reputation rivalling that of the Welsh, let us hope that it will also include the magnificent choral music of Grainger.) The Symphony Orchestras of Melbourne, Sydney and Adelaide play as if they liked Grainger's music, and the love and care which John Hopkins has obviously invested in the preparation of these scores (works which in many cases have never been recorded or even performed before) leaves no doubts in my mind as to his abilities as a Grainger conductor.

There are too many goodies on these records to receive individual, critical attention in an article of this length, but outstanding are the 'Tuneful Percussion' items (*Eastern Intermezzo* and *La Vallée des Cloches*), the three big suites (*Danish Folk-Music, Youthful, In a Nutshell*) and a spanking concert performance of *Tribute to Foster*. The fine voices of Rhonda Bruce (sop) and Christopher Field (bar)—new names to me—grace several works, in all of which the soloists have been chosen with care. The technical standards of the Australian recordings compare well with the best from Europe and USA.

On the reverse side of the RCA record containing the re-issue of the Stokowski/Grainger items mentioned earlier is a performance of the Grieg Piano Concerto played by a 'doctored' version of Grainger's own Duo-Art reproducing piano roll installed in electronic robot equipment which in turn is offered up to the keyboard of a modern concert grand piano, whilst John Hopkins and the Sydney Symphony Orchestra provide valiant accompaniment (if you see what I mean). The controversy surrounding the authenticity of these machines from the early part of this century will continue to rage, and doubtless this record will sell well and add fuel to the flames. I don't propose to delve into the pros and cons other than by acknowledging John Hopkins's splendid efforts and the technical ingenuity of Denis Condon and Peter Phillips, the creators of this endlessly fascinating machine, but I remain aurally unconvinced. There is a restraint and, for me, an unnerving mechanicalness about the present performance which make it in the end a feeble imitation of the real thing. Besides, it would take a formidable piece of electro-pneumatic wizardry to generate the necessary wattage for a true Grainger forte. Stylistically it bears only a passing resemblance to the real live piano-playing of Grainger, with which I am as familiar as I am with my own toes. I am told that a similar project is being prepared with a roll (this time one which was cut in the early 1920s with this kind of performance expressly in mind) of the Tchaikovsky Piano Concerto No 1 and I shall reserve my judgement till then. For the moment I prefer the real thing (preserved in live performances to be discussed later), wrong notes and incompetent orchestras withal. For similar reasons I urge anyone to avoid the already issued solo recordings of Grainger's Duo-Art rolls. The day has yet to come for the production of a satisfactory recording of Grainger's reproducing piano rolls.

Also from the RCA stable is a record of a mixed selection of popular and lesser-known pieces played by the Bournemouth Sinfonietta under Kenneth Montgomery on RL 25198. Unfortunately the impression that some of this is sadly under-rehearsed is inescapable. I did, however, enjoy Moray Welsh's strong and loving interpretation of *Youthful Rapture*.

Not to be outclassed in the Grainger stakes, EMI have produced their own all-Grainger orchestral record containing world première recorded performances of *Danish Folk-Music* and *In a Nutshell* suites. One certainly gets the feeling that the conductor, Neville Dilkes, gave much thought to these difficult pieces, but neither he nor his orchestra produces much more than bland and joyless performances, and often worse. So many sections could have benefited from greater drive and contrast, and a sharper pointing with more prominence perhaps to the keyboard and tuneful percussion instruments.

One of the big mistakes often made by conductors (though not on this record especially) is that they tend to approach Grainger's music as if it had been written by Vaughan Williams or Holst. Disaster always ensues because Grainger had a completely different view of the constitution of his orchestral groupings, and in fact he despised the conventional symphony orchestra.

To play much of Grainger's music with what amounts to an augmented symphony orchestra can be quite at variance with what he had in mind as regards balance, colour, texture and counterpoint. One only has to listen to Grainger's own orchestral recordings of *Shepherd's Hey, The Power of Love, Gum-suckers' March* and *Lord Peter's Stable-Boy* made for American Columbia in 1927 (with clean copies the sound is still amazing) to hear this. His essay 'To Conductors'[6] should be compulsory reading for anyone embarking on a performance of his music, because this vexing problem of texture and balance is something which cannot be avoided, especially with large forces tackling the music. Britten, Fennell, Stokowski and now Hopkins have faced the problem with success, but others too often tend to lose the exquisite details in hopeless turgidity. Grainger's music is hard to perform for two reasons: first, it is not always easy to assemble the right number of instrumentalists for the correct balance, and second, his music makes conductors think.

Bits and pieces of Grainger's music lurk here and there on odd tracks of records devoted in part to works by other composers. Denis Wick and the London Wind Orchestra on the late Enigma label (K 53574) recently produced a first-rate recording of *Lincolnshire Posy*. It also included one of the best performances of *Molly on the Shore* I have ever heard—tight, energetic and well pointed. Ian Partridge, with the Elizabethan Singers under Louis Halsey, recorded a memorable *Brigg Fair* on Argo ZRG 5496—an album devoted to British folksong choral settings. The young and gifted tenor, Robin Doveton, in a well-chosen collection of folksong settings by Vaughan Williams, Holst and Grainger (most ably assisted by Victoria Hartung at the piano), provides us with some beautifully passionate and sensitive singing on the now defunct Prelude label (PMS 1502). George Weldon, Sir Adrian Boult and Sir Vivian Dunn have all recorded selections of popular Grainger pieces, but they are all deficient in one way or another—mainly with this recurring question of balance and texture.

A good LP transfer of some of Grainger's acoustic recordings is to be found on the Pearl label (GEM 143). Much more interesting, however, is an LP of two 'live' performances of the Grieg Concerto; the earlier recording with Stokowski at his outrageous worst in the Hollywood Bowl and Grainger playing in a Sunday-best, dull style, and the other with the Southeast Iowa Symphony Orchestra, an orchestra wholly unable to cope, but with Grainger as wild and fiery as one could wish him to be. The record also includes a transfer of some impeccable private performances Grainger made of extracts from Grieg's Op 17. A hearty and youthful interpretation of *Lads of Wamphray March* performed by the Cornell University Symphonic Band under Marice Stith is still available from that University. Major Peter Parkes, conducting the band of the Grenadier Guards, gives a lively and colourful performance of the *Children's March 'Over the Hills and Far Away'* on Decca (SB 706). It is sad to reflect that so few British bands have made recordings of Grainger's music, indeed it ought to be a cause of some considerable shame that the finest recorded performances of the great British band classics have as often as not come to us from American bands. Let us hope that Major Parkes's efforts will establish a precedent.

The University of Illinois Symphonic Band conducted by Harry Begian

Photo by Morse, N. Y.

PERCY GRAINGER
(Exclusive Columbia Artist)

Pianist--Composer

Management: ANTONIA SAWYER, INC. Box 446, White Plains, New

Leaflet advertising some of Grainger's 78rpm recordings.

PERCY GRAINGER, *Pianist,*
makes records exclusively for Columbia

PERCY GRAINGER is undoubtedly one of the most unique personalities before the musical public to-day. This great vital genius of the pianoforte is an exclusive Columbia artist. It may be there is some remarkable quality in the touch of Grainger, but no such piano tone has ever been equalled in recorded music before. Grainger has revived many old English and Irish Selections by a re-arrangement of the music.

MASTERWORKS SET NO. 32

Chopin: Sonata in B Minor, for Pianoforte, Opus 58. In six parts on three 12-inch double-disc records enclosed in a permanent and appropriate record album........................$4.50 complete

12-INCH, $1.50

7002M	Wedding Day at Troldhaugen (Grieg)
	Paraphrase on Tschaikowsky's Flower Waltz (Grainger)
7000M	Valse in A Flat (Brahms) Juba Dance (Dett)
	Prelude in A Flat, Op. 28, No. 17 (Chopin)
7001M	Country Gardens; Shepherds Hey (English Morris Dances)
	(Set by Percy Grainger)
	Norwegian Bridal Procession (Grieg)
7003M	Polonaise in E Major, Part I (Liszt)
	Polonaise in E Major, Part II (Liszt)
7109M	Etude in C Minor, Op. 25, No. 12 (Chopin) Waltz in A Flat (Brahms)
	Prelude in A Flat Major (Chopin)
7104M	Scotch Strathspey and Reel, Parts I and II (Grainger)
	Grainger Singers and Players (Conducted by Frank Kasschau)

10-INCH, $1.00

2000M	Cradle Song (Brahms-Grainger)
	Spoon River (Masters-Grainger)
2001M	Golliwogg's Cake Walk (Debussy)
	Gavotte (Gluck-Brahms)
2002M	Gum-Suckers March (Grainger)
	Turkey in the Straw (Arranged by Guion)
2003M	Rustle of Spring (Sinding)
	To a Water-Lily (MacDowell)
2004M	Water Music: Hornpipe (Handel-Grainger)
	Why? (Warum?) (Schumann, Op. 12)
2025M	Scherzo, Op. 31, No. 2 (Chopin) Part I
	Scherzo, Op. 31, No. 2 (Chopin) Part II

Once you have played a Columbia New Process Record on your Phonograph, or heard a Columbia New Process Record played anywhere, you will never again be satisfied with a tone less round, rich, or natural. They are the only records without scratch. Hear one Columbia New Process Record and we have told our story.

COLUMBIA PHONOGRAPH COMPANY
NEW YORK CITY
DEALERS EVERYWHERE

5 M (9-26)   Printed in U. S. A.

produced some years ago a two-record all-Grainger collection. Begian's predecessor, Mark Hindsley, had earlier begun a recording project with this band and issued three records (now unavailable) which included items of Grainger; this new set is a continuation and in a sense a culmination of these endeavours. As with many American student bands, one need not make allowances for the youthfulness of the musicians involved, and indeed these performances (some more successful than others) have much to offer. Though they play with a praiseworthy degree of professionalism, they remain (thankfully) amateur performances in the best sense of the word and on the whole are very rewarding. Perhaps the only serious drawback is the sheer size and consequent unwieldiness of the forces used—occasionally inhospitable to the demands of clarity and precision of attack in Grainger's music. Pure massiveness of sound is rarely required for Grainger's scores. The sleeve-notes of this highly recommended set of records leave much to be desired where historical accuracy is concerned.

I must also mention the shortest but in some ways the most remarkable item to have come my way for some time. On the Australian Move label (MS3027) it consists of an electronic realisation by Barry Conyngham of what Grainger called his *Free Music 1 & 2,* originally written out on a roll of graph paper with meticulous detail by the composer in 1934 but probably conceived many years earlier.

A critical assessment of this realisation is not easy, but a familiarity with the home-recordings made by Grainger's colleague, Burnett Cross, of performances by the free-music instruments which they jointly built, leads me to believe that this performance may not be quite what Grainger had in mind. I wonder if the fault lies, perhaps, not so much with Barry Conyngham but more with the over-sophistication of his instruments?

For those just discovering him, however, Grainger's life may seem full of apparent contradictions and the thought that this was by the same man who wrote *Country Gardens* never ceases to amaze me.

Another chapter could possibly be written (and many tears shed) about the large number of records of Grainger's music now irredeemably lost from the catalogues. For my own listening pleasure I play these records (many of them ancient 78 rpm records) with as great a frequency as I do the currently available recordings. With the present tightening-of-belts in the recording industry it seems unlikely that many or indeed any will see new life for some time to come. I have listed these recordings at the end of the discography. One area which I feel it would be criminal to ignore (especially in the centenary year 1982) is Grainger's own recorded output of his own and other composers' works—a treasure-trove indeed, containing some of the high points in the history of recorded piano-playing.

Perhaps the most sadly missed departure from the catalogue is the lavishly produced album called 'Unto Brigg Fair' from Leader Sound Ltd. The record included transfers of the nine issued and three unissued Gramophone Company recordings made in 1908 by Joseph Taylor and other cylinders made by Taylor, Thomson, Leaning, Gouldthorpe, Wray and Robinson, Grainger's leading Lincolnshire singers. One cannot overstate the importance of this record for anyone wishing to gain an insight into the traditions of folk-singing which Grainger found alive in Lincolnshire just after the turn of the century. The transfers are excellent, the notes and illustrations copious and scholarly, and the singing, of course, incomparably beautiful. It is very instructive too, to be able to listen to the original singer and his song and to be able to follow it immediately with a recording of one's choice of a Grainger setting of the tune.

An extensive collection of sound recordings is in the British Institute of Recorded Sound[7]. The Grainger Society sound archive includes many of these, together with private recordings of Grainger performing and conducting. There is a windband performance of *The Power of Rome and the Christian Heart* under the composer's baton, a 1942 performance of the *'Jungle Book' Cycle,* a 1914 cylinder recording of the composer playing his own transcription of *Died for Love* for piano solo, various home experiments with 'free-music', and much more. Though not exactly hi-fi recordings, these are invaluable for their insight into Grainger's interpretation of his own compositions. The British Music Information Centre now holds over nine hours of such material.

If I were to be asked for what I thought to be the most urgent suggestions for the future I would begin by hustling the best choir available into a studio and getting them to record the *'Jungle Book' Cycle* and then some of the works which demand combined orchestral, vocal and/or choral forces such as *Sir Eglamore, The Bride's Tragedy, Father and Daughter, The Lads of Wamphray, Love Verses from 'The Song of Solomon,' Marching Song of Democracy, Marching Tune, The Merry Wedding,* or any of the non-*'Jungle Book' cycle* Kipling settings. There is much purely vocal and piano material begging to be recorded and one would also like to see some of the splendid 'cello and piano material recorded or at least performed which Grainger wrote with his friend Herman Sandby in mind. One would also welcome a record devoted wholly to his original compositions—an area generally neglected hitherto to the advantage of the folksong arrangements. Duplication of rare material at this stage would do no harm. What is, however, boring in the extreme is to see the catalogue becoming overloaded with multiple and rarely good performances of the same old *chevaux de bataille.* There is still much that could be done by an enterprising record company or companies.

201

tensions in the making, Nov. 8, 1938 *Photo*

P.G. (kneeling) with Frank Hansen a 5 men

On site: extensions to the Grainger Museum, Melbourne.

CHAPTER SEVENTEEN

Sources for Grainger Research

David Tall

THE unravelling of the complex web of Grainger's manuscripts and personal effects is a daunting task which is nowhere near completion. The more specific quest to identify a particular arrangement of one of Grainger's pieces and to obtain the parts for a performance can also present unforseen problems. In this article I shall attempt to outline the root causes for these difficulties, specify the movements of the major collections of Grainger's music and guide the interested reader into the appropriate channel to find a particular source of information or music.

Grainger tried throughout his life to retain his manuscripts in various states of completion, carefully dated down to minor changes in individual bars. He kept enormous collections of the trivia of his everyday activities: bills, programmes, press-cuttings, letters, details of his inventions, scrap-books, diaries, records of his thoughts about others, piano rolls, phonograph cylinders of folksingers, folksong notations, domestic items, clothes, souvenirs of his travels, music of other composers, and so on. This was all part of a grand plan to preserve not only his music and that of others but to leave a collection that would give an insight into the extraneous factors that could affect the development of a composer.

It was Grainger's ambition that his entire collection of manuscripts, letters and memorabilia should be housed in the Grainger Museum, which he founded in Melbourne in 1934 and finished building in 1938. During the latter part of his life he made several large shipments of his effects to the Museum and on his death left the completion of the task to the executor of his will, his widow Ella.

She was faced with an appalling dilemma. Despite Grainger's efforts there was insufficient funding then available for the Museum, and she felt that it would be unable to cope. She was not then to know of the renaissance that would occur in the Museum's activities more than a decade later. Concerned only with the preservation of her husband's manuscripts at a time when she was over 70 years old herself, she took the decision to send packages of manuscripts to established libraries in places which could claim some connection with the music. Irish folksong settings would go to the National Library of Ireland, Scotch settings to the National Library of Scotland, manuscripts with English connections would go to the British Museum, and so on. In 1962, aided by Gustave Reese, she sent consignments of manuscripts to the following institutions:

The Library of Congress, Washington, USA;

The Research Library of the Performing Arts, Lincoln Center,
New York, USA;

The Sibley Library of the Eastman School of Music, Rochester,
New York, USA;

The British Library, London, England;

The National Library of Scotland, Edinburgh;

The National Library of Ireland, Dublin;

The Elder Conservatorium, University of Adelaide, Australia;

The Grainger Museum, Melbourne, Australia.

By far the largest of these collections is in the Grainger Museum. A glance at any of the other collections will show that not only were specially chosen manuscripts sent to each library, there was also a concerted effort to make sure that each place had a representative collection of work. For instance, the Scottish collection not only had Scotch folksong settings (such as three manuscripts of *Lord Maxwell's Goodnight* and oddments from *Ye Banks and Braes O' Bonnie Doon*), it had original compositions with Scotch words (*The Lads of Wamphray* and *Twa Corbies*), compositions with Scottish links (various parts for *Walking Tune* which was originally conceived on a walking holiday in Scotland) and a number of manuscripts with no obvious links with Scotland whatsoever (such as a set of trial parts of *The Rival Brothers* based on a Faeroe Island text, a free setting for piano of Fauré's *Nell*, string quartet transcriptions of Bach and Scarlatti, and a variety of recorder sketches).[1]

Perusal of just one set of parts is enough to sow the seeds of confusion. The *Walking Tune* manuscripts include the outside pages of a manuscript for piano duet, with the inner leaf missing. There is an original set of parts for the wind quintet version, three transcriptions for alternative instruments, a revision of the score for bars 18-25 and a corresponding set of four parts for these bars of revision (the flute part being unchanged).

Copying from a short typed description of these parts, Thomas Slattery noted these items in his thesis[2] to consist of 'sketches, room music score; twelve parts'. Reference to this list might intimate that there was a completely different setting of *Walking Tune* to be found in Scotland. Such a conclusion would not be shaken without reference to the actual parts, and further confusion could not be avoided without looking at several other collections. The Sibley Library claimed ownership[3] of a *Walking Tune* score which turned out to be in someone else's hand; the Library of Congress had[4] a full version for piano duet differing in detail from the Scottish manuscript; the Elder Conservatorium[5][6] had some parts for 'sound trials' and a manuscript Mustel organ part to be added to the wind quintet!

The story of *Walking Tune* can be repeated time and again for other pieces. It has led to the raising of false hopes until a 'new' manuscript turned out to be another sketch or a copy of a known one. On the other hand, a number of genuinely different versions awaited discovery. *Six Dukes Went A-fishin'* was published in its final version for voice and piano in 1912. There are two earlier versions—one for four voices (1905/6) in the Grainger Museum and one for four voices and flute (1908) in the British Library. Anyone consulting only the Grainger Museum collection would find the early quartet version to be the same length as the published one. But reference to the British Library, either

CHORAL COMPOSITIONS
By PERCY ALDRIDGE GRAINGER

MIXED CHORUS WITH INSTRUMENTAL ACCOMPANIMENT
(Symphony or chamber orchestra, or pipe-organ, or harmonium, or piano, or piano duet, or 2 pianos)   Price (in U. S. A.)

Marching Song of Democracy, 4-part (7½ mins.)	.60
The Bride's Tragedy (*Swinburne*), 4-part (7¼ mins.)	1.00
Tribute to Foster, 6 solo voices and 4-part chorus (9¾ mins.)	.20
Father and Daughter, 5 solo men's voices and 13-part double chorus (3 mins.). Complete vocal score	1.25
Women 1st chorus, Women 2nd chorus, Men 1st chorus, Men 2nd chorus, each	.20
Love Verses from "The Song of Solomon," 1 or 2 solo voices and 4-part chorus, accompanied by room-music or piano duet (6 mins.). (*In preparation.*)	
The Merry Wedding, 9 solo voices and 5-part chorus (6⅛ mins.)	1.00
Irish Tune from County Derry (British Folk-Music Settings, Nr. 29), 5-part (5½ mins.)	.20
I'm Seventeen Come Sunday (English Folk-Song), 4-part (2¼ mins.)	.20
Marching Tune (English Folk-Song), 5-part (3 mins.)	.20
Sir Eglamore (English Folk-Song), double chorus, 11-part (4 mins.)	.50
The Camp (Welsh Fighting-Song), 6-part (2 mins.)	.20
The March of the Men of Harlech (Welsh Fighting-Song), 3-part (2 mins.)	.15
The Hunter in His Career, unison chorus, 2-piano accompaniment (1½ mins.)	.12
2nd Piano Part	.20
Shallow Brown (Sea Chanty), unison chorus, solo voice *ad lib.* (3½ mins.)	.15
We Have Fed Our Sea for a Thousand Years (*Kipling*), 7-part (2¾ mins.)	.30
The Fall of the Stone (*Kipling*), 8-part (1¾ mins.)	.30
The Peora Hunt (*Kipling*), 5-part (0.¾ min.)	.30
Mowgli's Song against People (*Kipling*), 6-part (2¾ mins.)	.30
Recessional (*Kipling*), 5-part (2¾ mins.)	.15

MIXED CHORUS—A CAPPELLA

Australian Up-Country Song, 6-part (1½ mins.)	.12
Irish Tune from County Derry (British Folk-Music Settings, Nr. 5), 6-part (3½ mins.)	.12
Brigg Fair (English Folk-Song), tenor solo and 5-part chorus (2 mins.)	.20
A Song of Vermeland (Swedish Folk-Song), 5-part (3 mins.)	.30
At Twilight, tenor solo and 6-part chorus (3 mins.)	.40
Morning Song in the Jungle (*Kipling*), 10-part (2¾ mins.)	.30
The Inuit (*Kipling*), 6-part (1 min.)	.30
The Peora Hunt (*Kipling*), 5-part (0.¾ min.)	.30
Soldier, Soldier, 7-part (2 mins.)	.30
Recessional (*Kipling*), 5-part (2¾ mins.)	.15

WOMEN'S VOICES WITH INSTRUMENTAL ACCOMPANIMENT

Irish Tune from County Derry (British Folk-Music Settings, Nr. 29), 4-part (5½ mins.)	.20
Shallow Brown (Sea Chanty), unison chorus, solo voice, *ad lib.* (3½ mins.)	.15
The Power of Love (Danish Folk-Song), soprano solo and unison chorus; piano accomp. or room-music accomp. (3¾ mins.). (*In preparation.*)	

WOMEN'S VOICES—A CAPPELLA

There was a Pig Went Out to Dig (Chrissimas Day in the Morning) (English Folk-Song), 4-part (2 mins.)	.30

MEN'S VOICES WITH INSTRUMENTAL ACCOMPANIMENT

The Lads of Wamphray, 2-piano accomp. 3-part (6½ mins.)	.35
The Hunter in His Career, 2-piano accomp., unison chorus (1½ mins.)	.15
Scotch Strathspey and Reel, 4-part, and 16 instruments (6 mins.)	1.50
Shallow Brown (Sea Chanty), unison chorus, solo voice *ad lib.* (3½ mins.)	.15
Danny Deever (*Kipling*), 5-part (2½ mins.)	.30
Anchor Song (*Kipling*), baritone solo and 4-part chorus (3 mins.)	.30
The Widow's Party (*Kipling*), unison chorus (3½ mins.)	.30

MEN'S VOICES—A CAPPELLA

Dollar and a Half a Day (Sea Chanty), 10-part (2½ mins.)	.25
Tiger-Tiger (*Kipling*), 8-part (1 min.)	.30
Night Song in the Jungle (*Kipling*), 4-part (0.¾ min.)	.20
The Running of Shindand (*Kipling*), 6-part (1 min.)	.20
The Hunting Song of the Seeonee Pack (*Kipling*), 4-part (1 min.)	.30

UNISON CHORUSES (Women's Voices, or Children's Voices, or Men's Voices or Mixed Voices)

The Power of Love (Danish Folk-Song), piano accomp. or room-music accomp. (3¾ mins.). (*In preparation.*)	
The Hunter in His Career, 2-piano accomp. (1½ mins.)	.12
Shallow Brown (Sea Chanty), piano accomp. or chamber orchestra accomp. (3½ mins.)	.15
The Widow's Party (*Kipling*), piano-duet accomp., or chamber orchestra accomp. (3½ mins.)	.30
Ye Banks and Braes o' Bonnie Doon (Women's or Children's, or both's—unison chorus, accompanied by 4 men's voices—singly or massed—and whistlers)	.12
Harvest Hymn, for one or more single voices or for unison chorus and piano duet (3½ mins.)	.10

Published by or obtainable from
G. SCHIRMER Inc., New York
(N. B.—All prices apply to vocal scores unless otherwise specified)

1930s advertisement for Grainger's music.

205

through visiting the place or waiting several months to obtain an expensive photocopy by post, reveals that the version for four voices and flute has two more verses, a find of considerable interest.

Even when all the scores of a single work are apparently in a single centre, their status may be misinterpreted. When I visited the Scottish collection I found three scores for *Lord Maxwell's Goodnight*, dating from 1904, 1912 and a complete sketch in 1947. Since the 1947 sketch had not been fully inked-in and the 1912 score had been tidied up shortly after the 1947 sketch had been done, I concluded[7] that Grainger was probably dissatisfied with the 1947 version and had reverted to the 1912 score. On visiting White Plains I found the error of my ways, for there was to be found a complete set of parts identical to the 1947 score, together with a set of photostated additional parts which would make the arrangement suitable for full orchestra. This chastening experience shows that until the entire collection is housed under one roof there cannot be a scholarly listing of Grainger's known output.

Two early catalogues of Grainger's work appeared in the 'seventies: an appendix to Thomas Slattery's biography of the composer[8] in 1974 and a *Complete Catalogue of the Works of Percy Grainger* by Teresa Balough[9] in 1975. These brave attempts at grasping the whole opus of this complex composer were, of course, limited by the information available from widely dispersed sources. These included information retained at the composer's home, published details from several libraries and private information from other librarians[10].

Notable omissions in the Balough catalogue include the arrangements made for the Stokowski recording and a number of piano solos; in particular, only ten items are mentioned out of over two dozen compiled for a projected beginner's album, *The Easy Grainger*. On the other side of the coin, the style of printing gives equal prominence to brief sketches and completed works, giving undue emphasis to incomplete items which are merely a few bars in length. In addition to the inescapable errors that arise in the manner I mentioned earlier, there seem to be a number of entries which have somehow become misaligned. The scoring for *Willow, Willow* (voice, guitar and strings) appears also under *Molly on the Shore*, allegedly published by Schott, although the publisher disclaims all knowledge of such an arrangement. *I'm Seventeen Come Sunday* reputedly appears in *Linconshire Posy*, which it doesn't. And the scoring for *Irish Tune from County Derry, British Folk-Music Setting* (BFMS 29), gets transferred to a completely different setting (BFMS 20), there to be given the copyright date of yet a third version, a brass-band arrangement by Denis Wright. Two sets of corrections have been made and published in the journal *Studies in Music*[11].

Thomas Slattery's briefer listing suffers from the same strengths and weaknesses. His earlier cataloguing procedures were severely criticised by David Josephson in a series of articles on Grainger scholarship[12]. Whilst every criticism was entirely relevant, the stand which Professor Josephson took was weakened by his reference to a 'version of *Scotch Strathspey and Reel* for piano, flute, oboe, clarinet, bass clarinet and bassoon' in the National Library of Scotland which he suggested should be added to a catalogue of chamber music with winds[13]. There is no such version. The manuscripts in Scotland consist of the piano solo arrangement and a separate collection of excerpts from a preliminary instrumental setting for use as 'sound trials'. Professor Josephson fell victim to the same faulty sources of information that he criticised.

There are two ways to tackle Grainger's enormous output. One is the flair and imagination of Balough and Slattery, which gets the great majority of material right but falls down on many details. On the other hand, one can catalogue only that portion of the music which is known to be correct. In his Grainger biography,[14] John Bird took the second line and concentrated on the published material, a method which is more accurate and more restricted (though he fell into the same trap over the instrumentation of BFMS 20 and listed the mysterious 'voice, strings and guitar' version of *Molly on the Shore* mentioned in the Balough catalogue). This apart, the Bird list is a sensible step forward.

The first major piece of scholarship in listing Grainger's compositions came from the Grainger Museum when the archivist, Kay Dreyfus, listed the entire contents relating to Grainger's published works and manuscripts[15]. The strength of this method is that, at last, we have a fully reliable source of information. Its weakness is that, by its very nature not all of Grainger's work is represented in the catalogue because it is not all in the museum.

As I have already said, there is only one solution for this confused state of affairs: the manuscripts must be collected in one place for a proper scholarly inventory. In 1975 the archivist of the Grainger Museum visited the Adelaide collection and a substantial portion was transferred to Melbourne.[16] On the death of Ella Grainger in 1979 she was succeeded as executor of the composer's original will by Burnett Cross, who set about the task of recovering the dispersed manuscripts to despatch them to the revitalised Grainger Museum. By the end of 1980 the White Plains manuscripts and the collections from the Lincoln Center, the Library of Congress and the Sibley Library had all been transferred. The National Library of Scotland refused to comply with Mr Cross's request, citing a letter from Ella Grainger which stated that she and Percy had discussed the project to send Scottish manuscripts to them. The final decision as to where the three British Isles collections will be housed may well have changed by the time this book is in print.

The Grainger Museum hope to have a supplement to their original catalogue, detailing all these new acquisitions in time for the centenary year, 1982. Meanwhile, faced with the practical problem of assembling collections of music for actual performances, several distinct initiatives were taken. As Grainger's American publisher took less interest in maintaining his works in their catalogue, the Percy Grainger Library Society in White Plains set about providing a source of information and parts for performance. Enquiries may be addressed to the Archivist, Stewart Manville, who was left the copyright of Grainger's works in Ella Grainger's will, and deals with business matters relating to the Grainger Estate.

In London, Grainger's publishers, Schott & Co, have prepared an inventory of music available for sale or hire. This includes photocopies of out-of-print items which are available on request. Thames Publishing are publishing two volumes of folksong arrangements simultaneously with this book.

The Percy Grainger Society was inaugurated in London in 1978. It publishes a biannual journal containing articles of scholarship and up-to-date information. For an annual subscription members receive the journal and have access to extensive music and sound archives. Recent items in the journal have included in-depth studies of Grainger manuscript collections intended to eradicate the source errors mentioned earlier.[17] The music archive contains items otherwise only available from the Grainger Library in White Plains or in the manuscript collections. It includes virtually all the choral music and songs, most of the piano music and a wide selection of instrumental and orchestral items. The purpose of the Grainger Society archive is to complement the activities of Schott & Co, providing photocopies of music which is either out of print and otherwise unavailable or is in manuscript only. A surprisingly large proportion of Grainger's commercially available recordings includes music in these forms. For instance, of the items on the *Salute to Percy Grainger* volume 2 recording issued in 1978 by Decca, five have never been published and all seven of the special arrangements for the Stokowski recording of 1950 remain in manuscript. All the scores of these items are in the Grainger Society Archive, along with many other intriguing compositions.

Other items in Grainger's vast collection are in various states of organisation. The folksong collection and phonograph recordings have been mentioned in chapter 11. A listing of Grainger piano rolls has been made by Gerald Stonehill.[18] The Grainger collection of arts from the Pacific has been exhibited and a catalogue was produced for the occasion.[19] But these items and the Grainger costume collection are just two projects which are in progress at the Grainger Museum. Information concerning the vast proportion of Grainger's music, letters and memorabilia is held there.

There is much to do in Grainger research over the next few years and the centre of this activity will be in the museum that Grainger built for the purpose. A growing band of research workers are stationed there, cataloguing, analysing and publishing information relating to this fascinating and multi-talented personality.

Notes

and

Appendices

Notes

Chapter I: Editor's Introduction (Lewis Foreman)

1. CAMERON, Basil: Reminiscence of Grainger IN John Amis' 'Talking About Music'; BBC Transciption disc 106543.
2. GRIFFITHS, Paul: *A Concise History of Modern Music from Debussy to Boulez.* Thames & Hudson, 1978.
3. WHITTALL, Arnold: *Music Since the First World War.* Dent, 1977.
4. SAMPSON, Jim: *Music in Transition—a study of tonal expansion and atonality, 1900-1920.* Dent, 1977.
5. DAVIES, Laurence: *Paths to Modern Music.* Barrie & Jenkins, 1971.
6. STERNFELD, F W ed: *A History of Western Music—V Music in the Modern Age.* Weidenfeld & Nicolson, 1973.
7. New Oxford History of Music X: *The Modern Age 1890-1960,* edited by Martin Cooper, OUP, 1974.

Chapter II: Grainger 'In a Nutshell' (Stephen Lloyd)

1. *Percy Aldridge Grainger.* An unpublished type-script by Rolf Gardiner.
2. BIRD, John: *Percy Grainger,* Elek, 1976.
3. *The Daily Telegraph,* 14 March 1912.
4. It has not been finally established which *Hill Song* was played in Balfour Gardiner's concerts, Slattery (see pp 103-4, and note 7, p 213) also feels it was probably No 2. Balfour Gardiner had in 1911 (not 1907 as stated by Bird) provided the means for Grainger to hear the materials used in the *Hill Songs,* and is known to have preferred No. 2. *Hill Song No 1* did not receive its first European performance until 6 Dec. 1949 (RAH, Philharmonia Orch., George Weldon deputizing as conductor for Richard Austin); a *Times* review mentions the orchestra included 'oboes, saxophones, a piano and harmonium.'
5. CAMERON, Basil: 'Memories of Percy Grainger', from BBC Transcription disc 106543.
6. Diary entry for 3 March 1933; from *Benjamin Britten: Pictures from a Life 1913-1976,* Faber & Faber, 1978.
7. MITCHELL, Donald: Interval talk to BBC broadcast of Aldeburgh Festival 'Tribute to Percy Grainger', 12 June 1966.

Chapter III: A Personal Introduction to Percy Grainger (Sir Peter Pears)

1. Edited text of a lecture given on 16 February 1970 at the British Institute of Recorded Sound, published in *Recorded Sound* Jan-April 1972 pp 11-15, and further revised for its appearance here.
2. ELWES, W *and* R: *Gervase Elwes—the story of his life.* Grayson, 1935, p 157.
3. ibid p 163.
4. ibid p 164.

Chapter IV: Impulsive Friend: Grainger and Delius (Lionel Carley)

1. Letter to Henry Clews, 20 June, 1918.
2. Delius to his wife 21 April, 1907.
3. Quoted in: Röntgen, Julius: *Edvard Grieg.* ('Beroemde Musici': XIX) Kruseman, Den Haag, 2nd edition, n.d. The letter was written from Troldhaugen and dated 23 August, 1907.
4. The outcome of Delius's proposal is unknown: I have not found a reply from Grainger and no MS piano arrangement by him of *Paris* has been discovered.
5. Haym's daughter, the late Eva Haym-Simons, contributes a reminiscence of Grainger: 'I do indeed in a "young girl-way" remember Percy Grainger in Elberfeld. I wish only I had been there with a more grown-up mind! He must have played in one of the Soloist-Concerts ... Might he have played Chopin? or was that not the particular field? I was fascinated by his "beauty" which might even have been carrying some vanity and some feminine touch. Anyway I kept drawing his profile on blotting paper and school copybooks ad infinitum to the interest and amusement of my classmates'. (Letter, written in English, to the author, 30 November, 1971).
6. Letter to Eric Fenby, 6 December, 1936.

7. Among Grainger's writings on Delius over the years may be mentioned: 'The Genius of Frederick Delius', *Musical Courier* (New York), *71,* No 20, 1915; 'The Personality of Frederick Delius', *The Australian Musical News* (Melbourne), 1 July, 1934 (reprinted later that year in the *Musical Courier)*; and 'About Delius', in Peter Warlock: *Frederick Delius,* revised edition, The Bodley Head, London 1952. A translation, 'Das Genie Delius', was published in *Musikblätter des Anbruch* (Vienna) 5 Jan., 1923.
8. Leopold Stokowski to Andrew Wheeler, 25 September, 1916. A typed copy of this letter is in the Colton/Clews Accession in the Delius Trust Archive.
9. Grainger's autograph manuscript is now in the British Museum (Add MS 50886). It was published by Universal-Edition (No 7142).
10. Autograph manuscripts of this unpublished Grainger arrangement are in the Music Archive of the Delius Trust, London (Vol 23); the Percy Grainger Library Society, White Plains, New York; and the Grainger Centre, Melbourne.
11. The autograph manuscript of this arrangement, which again remains unpublished, was sold at Sotheby's to B Quaritch Ltd on 16 December, 1964.
12. 'Høifagerli', at Lesjaskog, in Gudbradsdalen.
13. Sketches in Grainger's hand for the 'Dance' from *Hassan* are to be found in the British Museum (Add MS 50879). If one uses the presently available published vocal score as a guide, this draft takes us from the *Allegro* of p 28 to the end of the movement on p 33 Grainger later claimed that he could not remember whether he actually used any of Delius's thematic material or not.
14. The improvised chair, showing evidence of Grainger's carpentry, is still there, as I found on a visit to the Øverli farm at Lesjaskog in 1976. See my photograph on p 43.
15. I was privileged to hear these piano-roll recordings by Grainger on more than one occasion at the London home of Mr and Mrs Gerald Stonehill. Subsequently Robert Threlfall confirmed that Grainger had used the Singer transcription of the Delius concerto. The two rolls now recorded on LP are *Brigg Fair* on Larrikin Records LRF 034 and *North Country Sketches on* Klavier KS 132.
16. Letter, dated 5 February, 1927, to the editor of the London *Evening Standard.* A typed copy of this is among Grainger papers in the Library of Congress.
17. Quoted from notes made at the time by the artist, Ernest Procter, one of whose portraits of Delius may be seen in the National Portrait Gallery, London.
18. I am indebted to these institutions for most of my original (and evidently widely-scattered) source-material for this essay; notably the large correspondence between the Graingers ;and Deliuses. See also David Tall's chapter on Sources for Grainger Research, p 203.
19. Letter to Mrs Henry S Richmond, 23 September, 1943.

Chapter V: Grainger and Frankfurt (Cyril Scott)

No sources cited.

Chapter VI: Grainger and Folksong (David Tall)

1. DREYFUS, Kay, *Music by Percy Aldridge Grainger.* University of Melbourne, 1978 pp 290-296.
2. Information from 'The Music Lover's Grainger', 25 Sept 1951, a manuscript in the National Library of Scotland, accession 3391.
3. In the *Australian Musical News* of 1st April 1934, page 7, Grainger wrote:
   'My admiration for Haydn as a composer of active music is proved by the extent to which I have based many of my own folkmusic settings,(*Molly on the Shore, Shepherd's Hey* and the like) on his style'.
4. Manuscript in the National Library of Scotland, accession 3391, quoted in David Tall: 'Percy Grainger & Scotland', *The Grainger Journal, 1* no 2, Dec 1978; pp 29, 30.
5. On this matter John Bird, Grainger's biographer, disagrees with me, referring to Grainger's fondness for listening to hymns whilst standing outside St Columb's Church. Grainger's early compositions are often hymn-like, sounding like a latter-day John Bacchus Dykes, but my own musical antennae detect no influence of church modes. Listening to hymns is quite a different matter from being brought up in the Anglican church, with its emphasis on sung plainsong and Tudor settings of the English service.
6. *O Mistress Mine* remains in manuscript with the legend 'settings of Folksongs and popular tunes' added by the composer.
7. See the first section of catalogue (1) above. Vocal scores of all these items are in the Grainger Society archive.
8. *Proceedings of the Musical Association 31,* pp 89-109 is a transcript of the lecture and the ensuing discussion.
9. See 'Interview with Percy Grainger' by John Amis, a BBC transcription, published in *Studies in Music 10* (1976) 4-7 reprinted in *The Grainger Journal 2* no 2; Feb 1980; pp 12-18.
10. See (1) MG 13/1-7.

11. *Hermundur Illi* and *Let's Dance Gay in Green Meadow.*
12. Recalled in the preface to the *Danish Folk-Music Suite* published by Schott & Schirmer.
13. Referred to in Grainger's unpublished draft introduction to his 'British Folk-Music Settings' in the British Library, Add Ms 50884.
14. Quoted in BIRD John: *Percy Grainger.* Elek, 1976, p 108.
15. *Journal of the Folk-Song Society 2* (1905-6) pp 79-81.
16. These quotations come from pages 164-5 of Grainger's main article in the *Journal of the Folk-Song Society 3* (1908-9) pp 147-242. They are reproduced, with minor changes, in the preface of the *Lincolnshire Posy.*
17. From the article mentioned in (16), page 158.
18. Mentioned in PEGG, Bob: *Folk.* Wildwood House, 1976. p 13.
19. See (8) above, pp 107-8.
20. Introduction to article (16), page 147.
21. Article (16).
22. Article (16) page 187.
23. Detailed in Grainger's typewritten list of phonograph cylinders.
24. *Percy Grainger & Arts of the Pacific,* Grainger Museum, 1979, p 28.
25. See (1), MG 13/4.
26. See (1), MG 13/2.
27. Preface to the *Danish Folk-Music Suite.*
28. Note on Grainger's typewritten list of phonograph cylinders.
29. Published by Bayley and Ferguson, London (1937).
30. See (1), section 13.
31. THOMSON, R.S.: 'Songs from the Grainger Collection'. *Folk Music Journal* (1974); pp 335-351.
32. O'SHAUGHNESSY, Patrick: 'The English Folk Song Collection' *The Grainger Journal, 1* no 1; Spring 1978; pp 31-36.

Chapter VII: Orchestral Music (Bryan Fairfax)

No sources cited.

Chapter VIII: Music for Wind Instruments (Thomas C Slattery)

1. GOLDMAN, Richard Franko: *The Wind Band.* Boston, Allyn & Bacon, Inc. 1961, p225.
2. The first performance of the original setting for double reeds occurred at Northwestern University, Evanston, Ill., in May, 1969. New parts were prepared from the original score and barrings edited by Professor Alan Stout.
3. The desire to write music which is free from a basic pulse may be seen throughout Grainger's compositions. It is especially apparent in the opening of movement five of the *Lincolnshire Posy,* and in Grainger's later experiments in 'free music'.
4. Percy. A. Grainger, *Hill Song No 1* Universal Edition, 1924.
5. GRAINGER: 'Notes on Hill Song No 1', printed in *Grainger Journal,* Dec. 1978, pp 14-23.
6. Instrumental families of *Hill Song No 2:* flute family—2 flutes, 1 piccolo; clarinet family—1 E-flat, 2 B-flat, 1 A, 1 alto, 1 bass; saxophone family—1 soprano, 1 alto, 1 tenor, 1 baritone; double-reeds—2 oboes, 1 English horn, 2 bassoons, 1 contra-bassoon; brass family—2 cornets, 2 horns.
7. Although the 'Hillsong (for Winds and Percussion), First Performance,' which appeared in Balfour Gardiner's Choral and Orchestral Concert on February 25, 1913, was most probably *Hill Song No 2,* Grainger gives credit to the July 25, 1929 performance as the premiere. See also note 4 to Chapter II.
8. GRAINGER, *Hill Song No 2.* Leeds Music Corp, 1950.
9. GOLDMAN, Richard Franko: *The Band's Music.* New York, Pitman Publ. Co., 1938, p 31.
10. Grainger was one of the first composers to use the term, 'wind band'. Later, during his military service, he adapted the more common phrase 'military band'. He coined the term 'wind ensemble' to apply to his larger wind chamber pieces, such as *Hill Song No 2.*
11. GOLDMAN: *The Wind Band,* p 225.
12. Grainger: *Lads of Wamphray.* New York: C. Fischer.
13. Grainger, *I'm Seventeen Come Sunday.* London: Schott & Co., 1913; and *Marching Tune* London: Schott & Co., 1911.
★14. Grainger, 'Notes on Hill Song No 1.' *op. cit., Grainger Journal* p 23.
15. Letter to Frederick Fennell from Percy Grainger, White Plains, New York, dated 1959. Quoted in programme notes compiled by Fennell for the record jacket of Mercury MG50219.

16. *Ibid.*
17. Grainger was fond of sarrusophones, but knew that their continued use was limited. As late as 1927, Ricordi Press published arrangements with sarrusophone parts.
19. Later Grainger assigned his royalties from *Country Gardens,* also a Morris tune collected by Sharp, to finance publication of Sharp's *English Folk Songs of the Southern Appalachian Mountains.* Sharp had originally refused to take any profits from *Country Gardens* for himself, but in the year of his death was persuaded by Maud Karpeles to accept the continuing offer to help finance his last project.
19. Stanford, Sir C V ed: *The Complete Collection of Irish Music as noted by George Petrie,* 3 vols, Boosey & Co., 1902-05.
20. The root form of *Lost Lady Found,* the sixth movement of *Lincolnshire Posy,* was scored in 1910 for mixed chorus, two trumpets, two horns, strings, and percussion. It conforms to Grainger's utilisation of small instrumental combinations to accompany vocal works. This song was collected by Lucy Broadwood and not by Grainger.
21. Grainger, 'Programme Notes' to *Lincolnshire Posy.* New York: Schirmer, 1940.
22. Grainger, 'Round Letter to Kin and Friends' (unpublished typescript, Sept. 3, 1943).
23. The 1931 military band arrangement of *County Gardens* was by Tom Clark.
24. Two entries numbered 41 resulted when the publisher assigned the number without the knowledge that Grainger had already assigned No 41 to an existing manuscript. We adopt the now accepted numbering of 43 (see catalogue p 219).
25. Four male voices, four double reeds, concertino, xylophone, two guitars, and eight strings.
26. Letter to Basil Cameron from Percy Grainger, White Plains, New York, dated March 10, 1957.

Chapter IX: Grainger and the Piano (Ronald Stevenson)

1. *Musical Quarterly,* July 1915.
2. *Brieven van Julius Röntgen.* Amsterdam, H J Paris, 1934, p 251.
3. NY, Schirmer, 1933.
4. NY, Schirmer, 1894.
5. Cf Ronald Stevenson: 'Busoni—Doktor Faust of the Keyboard' in *Piano Journal of the European Piano Teachers' Association, vol 1, no 1,* 1980, pp 14-15.
6. NY, Schirmer, 1920.
7. The Teresa Balough *Complete Catalogue of the Works of Percy Grainger,* University of Western Australia, 1975, erroneously states (footnote, p 104) that my arrangements in *The Young Pianist's Grainger,* Schott, London, 1967, are 'more difficult' than those in the unpublished *Easy Grainger.* The reverse is true.
8. Published in *The Grainger Journal, vol 3, no 1,* August 1980, pp 14-15.
9. J B T Marsh: *The Story of the Jubilee Singers including their Songs.* Hodder & Stoughton. London, 1899.
10. 4 books: *Hampton Series,* NY, Schirmer 1918-19.
11. Quoted in Natalie Curtis Burlin (ed.): *Negro Folk-Songs, Hampton Series, Book I.* Schirmer, NY, 1918, p 9.
12. Fürstner/Schirmer, 1928.
13. Schirmer, 1916.
14. Schirmer, 1918.
15. Schott, 1931.
16. Chappell/NY Gershwin Pub. Co., 1946.
17. Schott/Schirmer, 1922.
18. Published in *The Grainger Journal, vol I, no 2.* Dec 1978, p 2.

Chapter X: Grainger's Songs (David Wilson-Johnson)

No sources cited.

Chapter XI: Miscellaneous Works (Lewis Foreman)

1. HMV 10" 78: B 2478.
2. Slattery (PhD thesis p 34) quotes a financial statement from Schirmer to Grainger showing that as late as 1942 the royalties on this one piece were over $13,000 annually.
3. Australian HMV 12" Stereo LP: OASD 7606.

Chapter XII: Grainger's 'Free-Music' (Ivar C Dorum)

1. Grainger Museum file, GM84: details from interview at White Plains, N.Y., 29 Jan. 1953.
2. The term 'Frankfurt Gang' is given as 'known' alternative to 'Frankfurt Group' in Sir

Thomas Armstrong's paper, 'The Frankfurt Group'. *Proceedings of the Royal Musical Association LXXXV* 1958/59.

3. GM441-2, p.3; illustrations in the letter dated 12 Nov 1951. See illustration p 70.
4. 'Percy Grainger's "Free Music",' *The Juilliard Review,* Fall 1955.
5. Paradoxically, the same invention proved best in preserving what could be saved of the old folksongs as had precipitated the crisis which demanded their salvage so quickly, for the gramophone and the music-hall songs between them were to cause an eclipse of public interest in the individual folksinger.
6. GM89 (1952,4): letter dated 31 July 1952. The copy of this letter is labelled 'Questionnaire to Herman Sandby re gliding tones in free music'.
7. *Encyclopaedia Britannica* (Chicago, 1961), vol 4, p 531; vol 14, p 97.
8. Ninth ed., OUP, 1955.
9. This lecture, in modified form, appeared as one in the series 'A Commonsense View of All Music', which he gave for the Australian Broadcasting Commission in 1935.
10. GM413-6.
11. GM160 (1954, 1): postscript of round letter (PG to kin and friends), 4 Sept 1954.

Statement on Free-Music (Percy Grainger)

12. Grainger's Statement on Free Music, 6 December 1938 in exhibition case at the Grainger Museum, University of Melbourne, Victoria, Australia, reproduced by kind permission of the late Mrs Ella Grainger and Curator.

Chapter XIII: Percy Grainger's Free-Music Machine (Burnett Cross).
1. Previously published in *Recorded Sound* Jan-April 1972

Chapter XIV: Grainger the Pianist (Joseph Rezits)

1. COOKE, James Francis: *Great Pianists on Piano Playing,* Philadelphia, Theodore Presser Co 1913; pp 369-70.
2. BROWER, Harriette: *Piano Mastery—Second Series.* New York, Frederick A Stokes Co, 1917.
3. BROWER, *op cit*; p 5.
4. COOKE, *op cit*; p 372.
5. BROWER, *op cit*; p 7.

Chapter XV: Grainger the Teacher (Dorothy Payne)

No sources cited.

Chapter XVI: Recordings of Grainger (John Bird)

1. Programme notes for *The Third Festival of English Music,* Bracknell, July 18, 19 and 20, 1980.
2. Letter from Leopold Stokowski to Percy Grainger, January 17, 1949.
3. Letter from Percy Grainger to Leopold Stokowski, May 16, 1952.
4. Letter from Percy Grainger to John H Petersen, October 27, 1958.
5. Grainger, Percy A: 'Grainger's Anecdotes', being a handwritten collection of autobiographical jottings variously dated between 1949 and 1954, located Grainger Archives, White Plains.
6. Grainger, Percy A: 'To Conductors and to Those Forming, or in Charge of, Amateur Orchestras, High School, College and Music School Orchestras and Chamber-Music Bodies', being the prefatory essay published with his composition *Spoon River.*
7. See *Recorded Sound* Jan-April 1972.

Chapter XVII: Sources for Grainger Research (David Tall)

1. See the article TALL, David: 'Percy Grainger and Scotland' *The Grainger Journal, 1* no 2, 1978, pp 24-32.
2. SLATTERY, Thomas: *The Wind Music of Percy Aldridge Grainger,* available from Ann Arbor: University Microfilms (UM order no. 67-9104, 1967) and University Microfilms Ltd, High Wycombe, England.
3. WATANABE, Ruth: 'The Percy Grainger Manuscripts', *The University of Rochester Library Bulletin,* 1964, pp 21-26. (This is reproduced in *The Grainger Journal, 2* no 1, (1979).)
4. WATERS, Edward N.: 'Music', *The Library of Congress Quarterly Journal of Current Acquisitions XX/I* (1962), pp 21-26.
5. DREYFUS, Kay: 'The Adelaide Collection Transferred to the Grainger Museum,

University of Melbourne', *Miscellanea Musicologica* (Adelaide Studies in Musicology) *9*, (1977), pp 49-71.

6. DREYFUS, Kay: 'Music by Percy Aldridge Grainger', University of Melbourne, (1978). MG 15/2-11.

7. See (1) above.

8. SLATTERY, Thomas, *Percy Grainger*, Evanston, The Instrumentalist Co., 1974.

9. BALOUGH, Teresa: *A Complete Catalogue of the Works of Percy Grainger,* University of Western Australia, 1975.

10. Published sources available at the time were (3), (4), above together with Pamela Willett's articles 'An Autograph Manuscript of Percy Grainger', *The British Museum Quarterly,* XXV (1962) 18-19; 'The Percy Grainger Collection', *The British Museum Quarterly* XXVII/3-4 pp 66-71 (Winter 1963-4), and Philip L. Miller, 'Percy Grainger Gift', Bulletin of the New York Public Library 66 (1962) 415-6.

11. WRIGHT, Elizabeth: 'Additions to Teresa Balough's Cataloguing of Percy Aldridge Grainger's Compositions for Piano Solo' *Studies in Music, 13,* (1979), pp 77-91. There is a list of corrections by Teresa Balough in the press for the 1980 edition of *Studies in Music.*

12. JOSEPHSON, David: 'Percy Grainger: Country Gardens & Other Curses', *Current Musicology, 15* (1973), pp 56-63, 'Thomas Slattery—The Wind Music of Percy Aldridge Grainger' *Current Musicology, 16* (1973), pp 79-91, 'Margaret Hee-Leng Tan—The Free Music of Percy Grainger' *Current Musicology 17* (1974) pp 130-133.

13. See *Current Musicology 16* (1973) page 88.

14. BIRD, John: *Percy Grainger,* Elek, 1976.

15. See (6) above.

16. See (5) above.

17. See (1) above and DREYFUS, Kay: 'The Grainger Manuscripts in the Sibley Library—A Commentary, *The Grainger Journal 2,* No. 2 (1980), pp 19-32, *The Grainger Journal 3,* No 1 (1980) pp 24-27.

18. STONEHILL, Gerald: 'Piano Rolls played by Percy Grainger', *Recorded Sound, 45-46* (1972), pp 49, reprinted as an appendix to (8).

19. 'Percy Grainger & the Arts of the Pacific' *Grainger Museum,* 24 September-5 October 1979.

Catalogue of Works

Edited by David Tall

List of abbreviations

Grainger's generic headings

AFMS American Folk-Music Settings.
BFMS British Folk-Music Settings.
DFMS Danish Folk-Music Settings.
FI Faeroe Island Dance Folk-Song Settings.
JBC Jungle Book Cycle.
KS Kipling Settings.
OEPM Settings of Songs and Tunes from William
         Chappell's *Old English Popular Music.*
RMTB Room-Music Tit-Bits.
S Sentimentals.
SCS Sea Chanty Settings.

Publishers

SL Schott, London.
SM Schott, Mainz.
US Schirmer, USA.
A Allan, Australia.
TP Thames, London.

Sources

SS Schott, London: items for sale.
SH Schott, London: items for hire or file
      copies available for photocopying.
GS Grainger Society Archive.
MG Grainger Museum, Melbourne (an entry
      beginning MG . . . is taken from Kay Dreyfus's
      catalogue—item 19 in the bibliography).
NLS National Library of Scotland.
BL British Library (Additional Manuscript number as quoted).

(a) ORIGINAL COMPOSITIONS AND FOLKSONG SETTINGS

Manuscripts in White Plains, the Library of Congress, the Sibley Library, Rochester, New York, and the New York Public Library prior to 1980 have all been transferred to the Grainger Museum and will subsequently be catalogued.

Music required for performance should, in the first instance, be sought from the publisher. Items otherwise unavailable which are in the Grainger Society Archive are available through the Grainger Society.

This list is based on a card index prepared by John Bird, Leslie Howard and David Stanhope, the contents of the Grainger Society Archive (sheet music and photocopies of manuscripts, mainly donated by Stewart Manville of the Grainger Library Society, White Plains), a list of file copies and hire material prepared for Schott's, London, by Alan Woolgar, visits to the National Library of Scotland, the British Library and White Plains, and photocopies provided by the Grainger Museum, the Grainger Library Society, the National Library of Scotland, the British Library, John Bird, Ronald Stevenson, Burnett Cross, Barry Ould, Stewart Manville, Kay Dreyfus, Helen Griffiths, Leslie Howard and others.

The scholarly listing of Grainger's compositions will take many more years. It certainly cannot be achieved until all manuscripts and copies of sheet music are assembled in one place: the Grainger Museum. For the moment this list is intended to serve a practical purpose: an outline of the material at Schott, London, and in the Grainger Society Archive available for performance. Both sources are constantly being updated, with interchange of materials between various collections.

Apart from a few pieces published by a firm other than Schott in Europe or Schirmer in America, it may be taken that each acted as the other's agent in the appropriate country. In some instances both companies engraved a particular piece, but more often than not they imported each other's materials. Where there is no indication of a British or American publisher, then it may be taken to be Schott or Schirmer, respectively. Where possible, the date given is that of publication rather than copyright, using the valuable information in the Dreyfus catalogue of Grainger's compositions. The absence of an edition for any piece may simply indicate that no copy is available in the Museum, the Society Archive or at Schott, London. The complete picture of first editions is by no means clear yet.

To give some indication to the reader of the relative importance of pieces, all incomplete sketches and compositions before 1900 have been listed in lower-case letters and all complete later works in capital letters. A number of ethnic transciptions are also included, which do not really belong. Grainger's works are difficult to categorise and the precise line between settings and transcriptions is sometimes difficult to draw. Purely arbitrarily a number of single-line recorder melodies at present in the National Library of Scotland are excluded on the grounds that their inclusion might give them more importance than a straight melodic transcription might deserve. *Tribute to Foster* is included as an original work on Stephen Foster's melody, but *Blithe Bells,* based on Bach's *Sheep May Safely Graze,* is included in list (b), as are many other works based on other composers' music which includes varying contributions from Grainger. Dowland's *Now O Now I Needs Must Part* has a second verse harmonized by Grainger, Gershwin's *Love Walked In* has delicious Graingeresque touches, whilst his *The Man I Love* is almost a straight transcription of 16 bars of the song plus the Gershwin piano transcription. Where does one draw the line? List (a) simply excludes works based mainly on those of others. These include a handful of works of Ella Grainger, in which Grainger himself played a large part. That is the frustration and delight in trying to categorize Grainger's music: the boundaries between classes are not strict, they drift one into another. This list is therefore only a practical stop-gap until the entire Grainger output is assembled for scholastic consideration. Even then he will defeat those who try to classify him. The best hope is a computer listing with multiple classifications, so that any requirements can be keyed-in and the appropriate class of compositions can be sifted out by the computer. Until that time, reference for information should be addressed to the publisher, as appropriate, or the relevant archive.*

*   *   *

Afterword (1910-11, Dec 1 1957), sketch for mixed unison chorus and brass, MG7/1.

Afton Water (Nov 2-4 1898?), voice and piano, MG3/102-6-6:3, GS.

Agincourt Song (BFMS), mixed chorus, sketch MG3/1, BL 50883.

ANCHOR SONG (KS6) (1899, 1905, 1915, 1921)
i) voice and piano (ms 1899), MG3/102-9-7 GS;
ii) solo baritone, 4-part male chorus and piano or 4 men's single voice and piano (SL 1922) SH, GS.

ARRIVAL PLATFORM HUMLET (RMTBM7) (1908, 1910, 1912, scored 1916)
i) piano solo (US 1916) SH, GS;
ii) orchestra and piano (US 1916) SH;   } incorporated into
iii) 2 pianos 4 hands (US 1917) SH, GS;)   *In a Nutshell Suite*
iv) unaccompanied viola (SL 1926) SH, GS. }

AS SALLY SAT A-WEEPING (BFMS) see 'TWO MUSICAL RELICS OF MY MOTHER'.

AT TWILIGHT (1900-1909).
i) unaccompanied mixed chorus (1928) (SL 1930), SS, GS;
ii) unaccompanied mixed chorus and tenor solo (SL 1913), SH, GS;
iii) piano solo (Easy Grainger) (1939) MG3/21:3, GS.

AUSTRALIAN UP-COUNTRY SONG (based on tune also used in *Colonial Song* and *Gum-suckers' March*) (tune 1905)
i) unaccompanied mixed chorus (1928) (SL 1930), SS, GS;
ii) piano solo (Easy Grainger) (1932), MG3/21:3, GS.

Bahariyale V. Palaniyandi (Jalaratarangan), transcription for Indian cup bells, harmonium and 3 or 4 hand-drums (1935).

Ballad of Clampherdown (KS), baritone and piano or orchestra sketches (1899), BL50871, GS.

Ballad of the 'Bolivar' (KS), male chorus and large orchestra (1901), BL 50871, GS.

BEACHES OF LUKANNON (KS20, JBC5) (1898, 1941), chorus, 9 strings, optional. harmonium (SL 1958), vocal score, SH, GS (parts in preparation).

BEAUTIFUL FRESH FLOWER (Chinese, harmonised Joseph Yasser), piano (1935) GS.

Binu Adami: African transcription.

Birthday Gift to Mother (1893), MG3/9.

BOLD WILLIAM TAYLOR (BFMS43) (1908), voice and piano or room-music, SH, GS, TP.

The Bridegroom Grat (BFMS), ms sketch 1902, MG3/101:4, GS.

BRIDE'S TRAGEDY, THE (1908, 1909, 1913, scored 1914), double or single chorus and orchestra or piano (SL 1914), SH, GS (vocal score), score MG3/8-1, MG7/4.

BRIGG FAIR (BFMS7) (1906), tenor solo and mixed chorus (Forsyth 1906, SL 1911), SS, GS.

Bristol Town — see *In Bristol Town.*

BRITISH WATERSIDE (THE JOLLY SAILOR) (BFMS26) (1920), voice and piano (high key and low (original) key) SH, GS, TP.

Bush Music (1900/22), sketch GS.

Charging Irishrey (see also *Train Music),* orchestral sketches GS.

CHILDREN'S MARCH: OVER THE HILLS & FAR AWAY (RMTB4) (1916, 1918)
i) piano(s) & military band (US 1919);
ii) 2 pianos 4 hands (SL 1920) SH;
iii) piano (excerpt) (US, SL 1918) SH, GS.
(also arr. theatre orchestra (Schmid) (US19??))

COLLEEN DHAS (or 'The Valley Lay Smiling') (BFMS) (1904), room-music, MG3/12, GS.

* Addresses appear on p 258.

COLONIAL SONG (Sentimental 1) (1905, 1911, scored 1912, rescored 1913, band 1918)
   i) 2 voices (optional), harp or 3 strings and orchestra (SL 1913).
   ii) violin, cello, piano and 2 optional voices (SL 1913) SH, GS;
   iii) piano solo, 2 optional voices (SL 1913) SH, GS;
   iv) piano solo (US, A 1921) SH, GS;
   v) military band (Fischer 1921) SH;
   vi) theatre orchestra (US 1928).
COUNTRY GARDENS (BFMS22) (sketched 1908 for whistlers and instruments)
   i) piano (1918) (US 1919, SL 1919, A 1923, Hansen 1923), SS, GS;
   ii) piano — easy version (1930) (SL 1931 US 19??), SS, GS;
   iii) piano — especially easy version (1932) (US 1943 SL 19??), SS. GS;
   iv) band (ed and arr Clark) (US 1931);
   v) 2 pianos 4 hands (1932) (US 1932 SL 1937), SS, GS;
   vi) 1 piano 4 hands (1936) (US 1937 SL 19??), SS, GS;
   vii) 2 pianos 8 hands (1936) (US 1937 SL 19??), SH, GS;
   viii) descant and treble recorder (1947) NLS 3390, GS;
   ix) 2 descant recorders (1947), NLS 3390, GS.
      (other versions include: domestic orchestra (arr Schmid US 1932), salon orchestra (arr
      Artok SM 1931) accordion (arr Diero), recorders and piano (arr Bergmann))
COUNTRY GARDENS (2nd version)
   i) orchestra (for Stokowski recording (1949/50) MG11/1, GS;
   ii) large room music (1952) (whereabouts unknown, incomplete set of parts GS);
   iii) wind band (1953) BL: 50883.
COUNTY DERRY AIR (BFMS29) (Same melody as Irish Tune from County Derry)
      (1920), elastic setting for harmonium, optional female chorus, optional unison men's
      chorus, and 3 bass parts played by 3 single instruments up to full orchestra or wind band.
      (1930), SH, GS.
CREEPING JANE (BFMS) (1920/1), Voice and piano, MG3/15, SH, GS, TP.
Crew of the Long Serpent, for orchestra (1898) or piano duet (1940), MG3/102-1.
DANISH FOLK-MUSIC SUITE (See *Power of Love, Lord Peter's Stable-Boy, Nightingale and Two Sisters, Jutish Medley*), SH, GS. See p 143.
DANNY DEEVER (KS12) (1903/22/24), Men's double chorus and orchestra or baritone,
      men's chorus and piano (SL 1924), vocal score SH, GS.
      SH, GS.
DAVID OF THE WHITE ROCK (BFMS) (1954), voice and piano (SL 1963), SH, GS.
Death Song for Hjalmar Thuren (1916/17), sketch MG3/16.
DEDICATION (KS1) (1901), high voice and piano (SL 1912), SH, GS.
DIED FOR LOVE (BFMS10) (1906/7)
   i) woman's voice and piano or instrumental trio (SL 1912), SH, GS, TP;
   ii) piano solo, BL 50883, GS;
   iii) string orchestra GS.
DOLLAR AND A HALF A DAY (SCS2) (1908/9), male chorus (US 1922, SL 1923), SH,
   GS.
Drei Klavierstucke (1897).
DUBLIN BAY, see LISBON.
DUKE OF MARLBOROUGH FANFARE (BFMS36) (1939), Brass (SL 1949), SH, GS,
      (A first piano part of a setting for two pianos in the British Library.)
EARLY ONE MORNING (BFMS) (early setting 1899, sketches 1901, 1939)
   i) 2 players at 1 harmonium (Easy Grainger) (1939), MG3/21:4, GS;
   ii) elastic version for optional soprano and room-music or orchestra, GS;
   iii) soprano and piano (1940), GS, TP;
   iv) reed organ and 2 solovoxes (1950), NLS for solovox parts, GS for organ;
   v) orchestra (for Stokowski recording) (1950), MG11/2, GS.
Early settings of Folksongs & Popular Tunes (1899), voice and piano, MG3/102-7-2, GS.
EASTERN INTERMEZZO (1898 or 1899) for small orchestra (SL 1950) as part of *Youthful Suite* SH, GS
   ii) piano solo (1922) (US 1922) GS;
   iii) 2 pianos 4 hands (1922) (US 1922), SH, GS;
   iv) tuneful percussion (1933), GS.

Echo Song (1945), short sound trial for projected room-music version of Ella Grainger's *To Echo.*

ENGLISH DANCE (composed 1899, 1901, 1902, reworked and scored 1906-9, arr 2 pianos 1921). (room-music 9-some (incomplete?) MG15/12). Rescored 1924-25.

  i) orchestra with organ (US 1929) SH, GS; see p 91.

  ii) 2 pianos 6 hands (SL 1924) SH, GS;

  iii) elastic scoring using (ii) and parts from (i);

  iv) room-music (1952) for piano 4 hands, harmonium, solovox, organ, 4 or 5 strings (some parts GS).

ENGLISH WALTZ

  i) orchestra (1899-1901, rev. 1940-1943) (SL 1950 as part of *Youthful Suite),* SH, GS;

  ii) piano (1943/5), BL 50879;

  iii) 2 pianos 4 hands (SL 1948), SH, GS.

Evan Banks (1898), voice and piano, MG3/102-8-10, GS.

FAEROE ISLAND DANCE, see LET'S DANCE GAY IN GREEN MEADOW.

FALL OF THE STONE, THE (KS16 JBC1) (1901-4, rev. 1923, parts 1957-8), chorus and room music (SL 1924), GS, SH (parts in preparation).

FATHER & DAUGHTER (FI 1) (1908-9, parts 1911), five men's solos, double mixed chorus, strings, brass, percussion (SL 1912), SH.

First Chantey, The (1899) (KS), voice and piano, MG3/102-9-6, GS (sketch for baritone, men's chorus and instruments (1903) MG3/83).

Fisher's Boarding House (KS) (1899), orchestra, MG3/102-2-7-5.

Fourteen Scottish Folksongs, see *Songs of the North.*

FREE MUSIC 1: sample for string 4-some (1935), MG5/21-1, graph (1937), MG5/21-3.

FREE MUSIC 2: for 6 theremins (1935/6?), MG5/21-2, graph MG5/21-4.

Gamelan Anklung: transcription of Balinese ceremonial music (1936), MG10/1, GS.

Ganges Pilot (KS) (1899), baritone and piano, MG3/101-2.

GAY BUT WISTFUL (composed 1912, worked out and scored 1915-16), incorporated in *In a Nutshell* Suite.

  i) piano solo (US 1916) SH, GS;

  ii) orchestra and piano (US 1917) SH, GS.

  iii) 2 pianos 4 hands (US 1917) SH, GS.

GIPSY'S WEDDING DAY (BFMS) (1906), four voices, BL 50884, GS.

GREEN BUSHES (BFMS12,25) (small orchestra 1905/6 SH (parts only))

  i) room-music or orchestra (BFMS12) (revised 1921) (SM 1931), SH;

  ii) 2 pianos 6 hands (BFMS25) (1919-21) (US 1921 SL 1923), GS.

GUM-SUCKERS' MARCH (originally *Cornstalk's March)* (1905/7/11, scored 1914)

  i) piano (US 1916) SH, GS;

  ii) orchestra and piano (US 1917) SH, GS;   } incorporated into

  iii) 2 pianos 4 hands (US 1917) SH, GS;   *In A Nutshell* Suite.

  iv) piano and band (1942).

HANDEL IN THE STRAND (CLOG DANCE) (RMTB2) (1911-12)

  i) piano, violin, optional viola, cello or massed pianos and strings (SL 1912), SS, GS;

  ii) piano (1930) (SL US 1930), SS, GS;

  iii) 2 pianos 4 hands (1947) (SL 1948);

  iv) as rescored for Stokowski (1949) GS;

  v) large room-music (1952);

    (also orchestra arr H Wood, SH, GS; band arr R F Goldman (Galaxy))

HARD-HEARTED BARB'RA [H]ELLEN (BFMS) sketched between 1906 and 1914)

  i) piano (Easy Grainger) in F# (1932), MG3/21:5, GS;

  ii) piano (Easy Grainger) in F, GS;

  iii) voice and piano (1946) MG3/30, GS, TP.

HARVEST HYMN (bars 1-17, entitled *Hymny Tune,* sketched 1905, completed 1932, arr piano 1936, arr 2 pianos 1938)

  i) chamber orchestra (original version), 18 single instruments or orchestra with or without voices; or elastic scoring from 2 instruments upwards, including string quartet or string ensemble & harmonium. (US 1940), SH;

  ii) piano solo (US 1940 A 1942), GS;

  iii) violin and piano (included in (i)) (A 1942), SH, GS;

  iv) 1 piano 4 hands (US 1940 A 1942) SH, GS;

   v) voice(s) and piano duet (US 1940), SH, GS;
   Note: all the above versions may be freely combined
HERMUNDUR ILLI(FI) see 'TWO MUSICAL RELICS OF MY MOTHER'.
HILL SONG No 1 (composed 1901-2, rescored 1921, revised 1923, 2-piano revision 1921).
   i) version for 21 woodwinds BL 50867;   } See p 87.
   ii) room-music 22-some (Universal 1924), GS;
   iii) 2 pianos 4 hands (US 1922) GS.
HILL SONG No 2 (composed 1901-7, scored 1907, minor revisions 1911/40/42/46, arr 2
   pianos 1907)
   i) solo wind ensemble (23 or 24 instruments) or band or symphony orchestra (Leeds Music
      Corps 1950), GS; See p 87.
   iii) 2 pianos 4 hands (US 1922) GS.
HUNTER IN HIS CAREER, THE (set 1903, reworked 1929 as OEPM3)
   i) double men's chorus, 2 pianos (or orchestra?) (Vincent 1904), GS;
   ii) unison men's chorus and 2 pianos (OEPM3) (US SL 1930), SH, GS;
   iii) piano (OEPM4) (US SL 1930), SH, GS.
HUNTING SONG OF THE SEEONEE PACK, THE (KS8, JBC818) (1899, rev. 1922)
      4-part male chorus (SL 1922), optional strings added 1956, SH, GS (parts in preparation).
Hunt is Up, The (BFMS), sketch 1901, MG3/101:2, GS.
HUSBAND & WIFE (DFMS5), 2 voices, 2 guitars, cello, timpani (1923), GS (melody
   incorporated into *Jutish Medley*).
IMMOVABLE DO, THE (The Ciphering C) (1933-40), elastic scoring for 9 single strings, or
   string orchestra or full orchestra (US 1942), SH, GS;
   ii) military band or woodwind or clarinet or saxophone choir (US 1941), GS;
   iii) organ (US 1940), GS;
   iv) mixed chorus (US 1940), SH, GS;
   v) piano (US 1940), SH, GS;
   .any of the above may be performed together.
I'M SEVENTEEN COME SUNDAY (BFMS8) (1905-12), mixed chorus and brass (or piano)
   (SL 1912), vocal score SS, parts SH, GS (strings in lieu of brass, GS).
IN A NUTSHELL SUITE for orchestra or 2 pianos 4 hands, see individual movements:
      1. Arrival Platform Humlet.
      2. Gay but Wistful   } See p 97.
      3. Pastoral
      4. Gum-suckers' March.
IN BRISTOL TOWN (BFMS), sketch for voice and room-music (1906), GS; sketch for viola
   and organ (1947) BL 50884, GS;
   i) piano (Easy Grainger) 1951, GS;
   ii) piano 6 hands (Easy Grainger) 1951, GS.
IN DAHOMEY piano (1903-9), MG3/40, GS.
INUIT, THE (KS5 JBC4) (1902), mixed chorus (SL 1912) SH, GS.
IRISH TUNE FROM COUNTY DERRY (BFMS 5, 6, 15, 20. See also COUNTY DERRY
   AIR, BFMS29).
   i) chorus (1902): published as *Old Irish Tune* by Vincent 1904, GS, revised and published as
      BFMS 5 (SL 1912 US 19?? A 1927), SS, GS;
   ii) piano (BFMS 6) (1911) (SL 1911 US 1917? A1921), SS, GS;
   iii) 10 strings or string orchestra (1 or 2 horns ad lib) (BFMS15) (1913) (SL 1913), SS, GS;
   iv) wind band (BFMS20) (1918) (Fischer 1918), SH;
   v) orchestra (for Stokowski recording) (1949), MG11/4, score GS;
   vi) large room-music (1952), GS (complete?)
(other versions include brass band (arr Wright), theatre orchestra (arr Schmid)).
JUTISH MEDLEY
   i) piano solo (DFMS8) (1927) (SL US 1928), SH, GS;
   ii) elastic scoring (DFMS9) (1923, 1928-9) (SL US 1930), SH, GS;
   iii) 2 pianos 6 hands (DFMS9) (SL US 1930) (may be used as part of (ii)) SH, GS.
      Note: (ii) is part of the *Danish Folk-Music Suite*. The tunes of (i) are *Choosing the
      Bride, The Dragoon's Farewell, The Shoemaker from Jerusalem, Husband & Wife,
      Lord Peter's Stable-Boy.* The tunes of (ii) & (iii) are as (i) but with *Lord Peter's
      Stableboy* omitted.

Keel Row, The (BFMS), sketch (1901), MG3/101:4, GS.

KIPLING 'JUNGLE BOOK' CYCLE: a compilation of 11 Kipling settings as follows:
1. The Fall of the Stone (KS16)+
2. Morning Song in the Jungle (KS3)
3. Night Song in the Jungle (KS17)
4. The Inuit (KS5)
5. The Beaches of Lukannon (KS20)+ 9 str, horn.
6. The Red Dog (KS19)
7. The Peora Hunt (KS14)+
8. Hunting Song of the Seeonee Pack (KS8)
9. Tiger, Tiger (KS4)
10. The Only Son (KS21)+ solos +
11. Mowgli's Song Against People (KS15). + 4 men + 10 insts
  (complete score SH, GS, parts in preparation)
Klavierstucke (various) (1898), MG3/45, MG3/46 (etc?) GS(?).
Kleine Variationen-Form (1898), MG3/102-7-6.
KNIGHT & SHEPHERD'S DAUGHTER (BFMS18) (1918), piano (US 1918 SL 1919), SH, GS.
LADS OF WAMPHRAY, THE (composed 1904 for chorus, brass and reed version 1904-5)
  i) men's chorus and band (1904-7), MG3/49;
  ii) brass and reed band (1905), MG5/38;
  iii) men's chorus and orchestra or 2 pianos (vocal score US 1925), vocal score SH, GS;
  iv) choral parts arr for women's (or children's) voices NLS;
  v) wind band (revised 1937-8) (Fischer 1941), GS.
Land o' the Seal (BFMS) (1901), sketch, MG3/101:4, GS;
LET'S DANCE GAY IN GREEN MEADOW (FI) chorus sketch 1905?
  i) 3 players at 1 harmonium (Easy Grainger) (1932), GS;
  ii) 1 piano 4 hands (1943) (Faber 1967), GS;
  iii) band (1954) (US 1969).
LINCOLNSHIRE POSY (BFMS34&35) (set & scored 1937 using earlier sketches) (movements are: 1. Lisbon (Dublin Bay), 2. Horkstow Grange, 3. Rufford Park Poachers, 4. The Brisk Young Sailor, 5. Lord Melbourne, 6. The Lost Lady Found).
  i) wind band (BFMS34) (1937) (SL 1940), SS, GS; see p 101.
  ii) 2 pianos 4 hands (BFMS35) (1938) (SL 1940), SH, GS;
  iii) movements 1 and 4 arr for piano (Easy Grainger), GS.
LISBON (Dublin Bay) (BFMS40) chorus sketch 1906?
  i) wind quintet (BFMS40) (1937) (SL 1971), SS, GS;
  ii) piano (Easy Grainger) (2 versions) (1932, 1946), GS;
  iii) in Lincolnshire Posy (see above);
  iv) saxophone quintet (1943) BL 50884, GS;
  v) recorders, 2 descant, 1 treble (1947), NLS, GS.
LONELY DESERT-MAN SEES THE TENTS OF THE HAPPY TRIBES, THE (RMTB 9)
  i) room-music and 3 solo voices or solo instruments or saxophone, or voices and piano (sketched 1911, 1914, set 1949), GS;
  ii) 2 pianists at 1 piano (Easy Grainger) (1950-4), GS.
LORD MAXWELL'S GOODNIGHT (BFMS 14 and 42)
  i) tenor and 4 strings or piano (BFMS42) (1904, piano 1958), score NLS, piano part MG7/13-2, score and parts GS; TP
  ii) baritone and string orchestra (1914) (intended BFMS14?), score NLS, GS;
  iii) baritone and strings (1947) (BFMS14), sketch score NLS, GS;
  iv) optional baritone or unison male chorus and strings or orchestra (1947?) (BFMS14), parts GS.
LORD PETER'S STABLE-BOY (DFMS1 AND 7)
  i) elastic scoring (4 instruments up to orchestra or band) (DFMS1) (1922/23/25/27) (US 1930), SH, GS;
  ii) voices and room-music (DFMS7) (??).
LOST LADY FOUND, THE (BFMS33) (set 1910, 1938), mixed chorus or voice(s) with a variety of accompaniments (SL 1949), SH, GS.
Lot of Rot, A : early title for *Youthful Rapture*.

LOVE SONG OF HAR DYAL (KS11) (1901),
i) voice and piano (SL 1923), SH, GS;
ii) voice and room-music (1957), parts GS.

LOVE VERSES FROM 'THE SONG OF SOLOMON' (composed and scored 1899-1900, rescored 1931) 4 solos, chorus, chamber orchestra or piano (SL US 1931) OUP? vocal score and parts GS (sketch of 'part V' of the *Song of Solomon* for mixed choir & large orchestra, quite different from published material, MG3/86, GS). See p 87.

LULLABY FROM 'TRIBUTE TO FOSTER' piano (1915) (US 1917 SL 1921), SH, GS.
ii) piano (Easy Grainger) (1932), MG3/21:6, GS.

MAIDEN & THE FROG, THE (DFMS), cello and piano (?).

MARCH OF THE MEN OF HARLECH, see TWO WELSH FIGHTING SONGS.

MARCHING SONG OF DEMOCRACY (1901/08/15, scored 1915-17).
i) orchestra, organ, mixed chorus (chorus and piano score US 1916, Universal 1925, 'compressed full score' Universal Leipzig 1916, score Universal 1927) GS; see p 99.
ii) band (1948) MG3/57-2.

MARCHING TUNE (BFMS9), chorus and brass (or piano) (1905) (Forsyth 1906 SL 1911), SH, voal score GS.

MARY THOMSON (BFMS), 4-part mixed voices (1909-10?), MG3/58, GS.

MEN OF THE SEA (KS 10) (1899) Voice and piano (SL 1923) SH, GS.

Merchantmen, The (KS) (1902/3/9) sketch for voices and instruments MG3/59.

Merciful Town (KS) (1899), MG3/102-9-9.

MERRY KING, THE (BFMS38 and 39), sketched 1905/6 (for chorus)
i) piano (1936-9) (BFMS38) (US 1939), SH, GS;
ii) piano, harmonium (ad lib) and strings or wind or both (BFMS39), GS.

MERRY WEDDING, THE (Faeroe Island Setting) (12-13, scored 1915), 9 solo voices, mixed chorus (ad lib) and orchestra or 9 strings or piano (Ditson 1915), score G S (OUP?).

MOCK MORRIS (RMTB1) begun 1910.
i) 6 or 7 strings (SL 1911 US 1914), SS, score GS;
ii) piano, concert version (SL 1912), SS, GS;
iii) piano, popular version (SL 1912/13), SS, GS;
iv) 2 pianos, 4 hands (1910), BL 50877;
v) theatre orchestra (SL 1914), SH;
vi) violin and piano (SL 1914) (= piano and violin parts of (v)), SS, GS;
vii) orchestra (for Stokowski recording) (1950), MG11/5, score GS;
viii) large room-music (1952) (?);
(also arr violin and piano (Kreisler), brass band (Wright), salon orchestra (Artok), orchestra (Langey)).

MOLLY ON THE SHORE (BFMS1, 19, 23) (set 1907)
i) 4 strings or string orchestra (BFMS1) (1907) (SL 1911), SS, GS;
ii) pianola (1914 or earlier) (ms MG15/12-6);
iii) full or theatre orchestra (BFMS1) (1914) (SL 1914), score GS;
iv) violin and piano (= parts from (iii)), SH, GS;
v) piano (BFMS19) (1918) (US 1918 SL 1919), SS,GS;
vi) wind band (BFMS23) (1920) (Fischer 1921?) SH (incomplete);
vii) 2 pianos 4 hands (BFMS1) (1947) (SL 19??), SG, GS;
viii) orchestra (for Stokowski recording) (1949), MG11/6, score GS;
(other arrangements: violin and piano (Kreisler), domestic orchestra (Langey), piano (Stevenson), 2 pianos 4 hands (Bull)).

MORNING SONG IN THE JUNGLE (KS3 JBC3) (1903 revised 1907/23/56), mixed chorus (SL 1912), SH, GS.

MOWGLI'S SONG AGAINST PEOPLE (KS15 JBC11) (1903, revised 1907/23/41/56), 4 men's solos, mixed chorus, 10 or more instruments (vocal score SL 1925) SH, GS.

MY LOVE'S IN GERMANY (BFMS) (1903), mixed voices, complete sketch MG3/83, GS.

MY ROBIN IS TO THE GREENWOOD GONE (OEPM2) (1912)
i) 6 strings, flute, cor anglais (SL 1912), SH, GS;
ii) piano (SL 1912), SH, GS;
iii) violin, cello, piano (SL 1912), SH GS.

NEAR WOODSTOCK TOWN (BFMS) (1903/42).
i) mixed chorus, GS;
ii) piano (Easy Grainger) (1951), MG3/21:11, GS.

NIGHTINGALE & THE TWO SISTERS, THE (DFMS10) (1923-30)
  i) elastic scoring (US 1931), SH, GS;
  ii) piano (1949), GS.
NIGHT-SONG IN THE JUNGLE (KS17 JBC3) (1898, 1905, 1924), 4-part men's voices (SL 1925), SH, GS.
Nornagesti Rima, sketch for chorus based on Faeroe Island Ballad.
NORSE DIRGE (1899, 1942/3), orchestra (3rd movement of *Youthful Suite*) (SL 1950), SH, GS.
Northern Ballad (KS) (1898/9) voice and piano, MG3/100-4, GS.
NORTHERN MARCH (1899-1901) orchestra (1st movement of *Youthful Suite*) (SL 1950), SH, GS. See p 147.
Norwegian Idyll (1910), sketch MG5/55.
O MISTRESS MINE ('BFMS') (1903), mixed chorus MG3/83, GS.
OLD IRISH TUNE: early title for IRISH TUNE FROM COUNTY DERRY.
Old Little English Dance (1899), orchestra, MG3/23.
OLD WOMAN AT THE CHRISTENING, THE (DFMS11) (1925), voice, piano, harmonium, GS.
ONE MORE DAY MY JOHN (SCS1) (1915),
  i) piano (US 19?? SL 1921, Universal 1924), SH, GS;
  ii) piano (Easy Grainger) (1932), MG3/21:7, GS.
ONLY SON, THE (KS21 JBC10) 1945-7, revised 1953), soprano, tenor, optional chorus, room music (SL 1958), SH, GS.
PASTORAL (1917?, 1915-16)
  i) piano (US 1916) SH, GS;
  ii) orchestra and piano (US 1916), SH, GS; } incorporated into *In a Nutshell Suite*
  iii) 2 pianos 4 hands (US 1916), SH, GS.
Peace and Saxon Twi-play (1898), 2 PIECES for piano, MG3/102-8-2, GS.
PEORA HUNT, THE (KS13, JBC7) (1901/06/41/58), mixed choirs and a variety of optional accompaniments (SL 1924), SH, GS.
Piano Concerto ('Klavier Concerto') (1896), 2 pianos, MG3/102-8-3,4.
POWER OF LOVE, THE (DFMS2 and 4)
  i) soprano(s) and room-music or pianos (DFMS4 (originally DFMS2)) (1922), vocal score and odd parts, GS; TP.
  ii) elastic scoring (DFMS2) (1922 rev. 1941) (US SL 1950), SH, GS (first movement of *Danish Folk-Music Suite*)
POWER OF ROME & THE CHRISTIAN HEART, THE (1918-1943), band, organ, optional strings (Mills 1953), score GS.
PRETTY MAID MILKIN' HER COW, THE (BFMS27) (1920), voice and piano (high (original) and low keys) (US SL 1921/2), SH, GS, TP.
Pritteling, Pratteling, Pretty Poll Parrot: early version of *Gum-suckers' March*.
RANDOM ROUND (RMTB8) (1912-14/43/54), a 'join-in-when-you-like' round
  i) random version for guitar, a few voices and a few instruments (1943), GS;
  ii) set version (flute, violin, viola, cello, soprano, alto, tenor, mandoline (or ukelele), wood marimba, steel guitar, guitar, xylophone) (1943), GS;
  iii) 5 or 6 pianists at 2 pianos (Easy Grainger) (1954), GS.
Rarotongan Transcriptions (1909/47).
RECESSIONAL (KS18) (sketched 1905), scored 1929, mixed chorus unaccompanied or with a variety of accompaniments (SL US 1930), vocal score SH, GS. But see p 242!
RED DOG (KS19 JBC6) (1941), 4-part men (SL 1958), SH, GS.
REIVER'S NECK-VERSE, A (1908), voice and piano (SL 1911), SH, GS.
Rhyme of the Three Sealers, The (KS) (1900/01), 4-part men & boys, MG5/58.
Ride with an Idle Whip (KS) (1899), voice and piano, BL 50876, GS.
RIMMER & GOLDCASTLE (DFMS3),
  i) chorus ? (ms unknown);
  ii) piano solo (Easy Grainger) (1951), NLS, GS.
RIVAL BROTHERS, THE (Faeroe Island Setting),
  i) sketched for voices and room-music (1905/31/38/40/43) NLS, GS, MG3/75;
  ii) piano (Easy Grainger) 1932/43), MG3/21:12, GS;
  iii) piano 4 hands (Easy Grainger) (1932), MG3/21:8, GS.
Rondo (1897), piano 4 hands, MG3/102-6-4, GS; piano quartet (unfinished) MG3/

102-6-5.

RUFFORD PARK POACHERS: see *Lincolnshire Posy.*

RUNNING OF SHINDAND, THE (KS9) (1901-4?).
   i) men's chorus (SL 1922), SH, GS;
   ii) 5 cellos (1946), GS.

RUSTIC DANCE (1899), orchestra (SL 1950) (second movement of *Youthful Suite*), SH, GS.

Saga of King Olaf (1898/9), voice and piano sketches, MG3/102-8-7.

Sailor's Chanty (1901), men's chorus or tenor solo and piano, MG3/102-2, GS.

SAILOR'S SONG (1900-1954), sketch for orchestra 1900, MG3/76;
   i) bells and tuneful percussion (1954) MG9/21;
   ii) piano (1954), GS;
   iii) piano (simplified version) (1954), GS.

Saxon Twi-play : see *Peace & Saxon Twi-play.*

SCANDINAVIE, LA (Scandinavian Suite) (1902), cello and piano (SM 190?), GS;
   1. Swedish Air & Dance
   2. A Song of Vermeland (Swedish)
   3. Norwegian Polka
   5. Danish Melody
   5. Air & Finale on Norwegian Dances.

SCOTCH STRATHSPEY & REEL (BFMS28 & 37) (early setting 'BAND WITH STRINGS', sketch 1901-2, MG3/101:3, GS)
   i) 4-part men & room-music 20-some (21 at will) (BFMS28) (1901-11) (SM 1924), SH, GS;
   ii) piano (BFMS37) (1937 or 8 - 1939) (US 1939), SH, GS.

Sea Song (1907/22/46), sketches for 'beatless music', MG3/79, GS.

SEA WIFE, THE (KS22) (1898, 1905, 1947)
   i) voice & piano (1898) MG3/102-9-10.
   ii) mixed chorus and various room-music accompaniments (SL 1948), SH, GS.

Secret of the Sea, The (1898), voice and piano, MG3/102-7-3, GS.

Sekar Gadung (Javanese), transcription for tuneful percussion and voices (1932/3), MG15/6, GS.

SHALLOW BROWN (SCS3) (1910, rev. 1923/5) voice(s) and room-music or piano (US 1927), SH, GS.

SHENANDOAH (SCS) (1907), male voices, MG3/102-8-7, GS.

SHEPHERD'S HEY (BFMS3,4,16,21) (set 1908-9, revised 1911)
   i) room-music (BFMS3) (1908/9) (SL 1911), SH, score GS;
   ii) piano (BFMS4) (1911, revised 1913) (SL 1911, 1914), SS, GS;
   iii) full orchestra (BFMS16) (1913) (SL 1913), SH, score GS;
   iv) violin, cello, piano 'working copies' (1913), MG15/10-2-2;
   v) wind band (BFMS21) (1918?) (Fischer 1918), SH, score GS;
   vi) piano (simplified) (BFMS4) (1937) (SL US 1937), SS, GS.
   vii) 2 pianos 4 hands (BFMS16) (1947) (SL 19??), SH, GS;
   viii) orchestra (for Stokowski recording) (1949), MG11/7, score GS;
      (other versions include: brass band (arr Wright), theatre orchestra (arr Langey), recorders and piano (arr Bonsor)).

SHOEMAKER FROM JERUSALEM, THE (DFMS6) (1929), room-music (piano 4 hands, cello, flute, trumpet, violin, viola, bass), incorporated into *Jutish Medley,* G.S.

SIR EGLAMORE (BFMS13) (1904, 1912), chorus, brass, strings, percussion (Vincent 1904) (SL 1912), SH, vocal score GS.

SIX DUKES WENT A-FISHIN' (BFMS11) (1905-12)
   i) 4 voices (1905-6), MG15/1-5-2, GS;
   ii) 4 voices and flute (1905-10), BL 50883, GS;
   iii) voice and piano (high and low keys) (BFMS11) (1905-12) (SL 1913), SH, GS, TP.

SOLDIER SOLDIER (KS13),
   i) early setting(s) for voice and piano (1898/9), MG3/102-9-2, MG3/102-9-8. BL 50871. GS;
   ii) 6 soloists, mixed chorus, optional harmonium (KS13) (1907-8) (SL 1925), SH, GS.

SONG OF AUTUMN, A (1899), voice and piano (SL 1923), SH, GS.

SONG OF SOLOMON: see *Love Verses from the Song of Solomon.*

SONG OF VERMELAND, A (1904??), mixed chorus (Vincent 1904 SL ?), GS.

SONGS OF THE NORTH (1900), 1-12 for voice and piano, 13, 14 for chorus and piano; 3 may be performed with solo, unison chorus & piano.
1. Willie's gone to Melville Castle
2. Weaving Song
3. Skye Boat Song
4. This is No My Plaid
5. Turn Ye to Me
6. Drowned
7. Fair Young Mary (Cmairi Bhan Ogd)
8. Leezie Lindsay
9. The Women are a' Gane Wud
10. My Faithful Fond One (Mo Run Geal Dileas)
11. Bonnie George Campbell
12. O'er the Moor
13. O Gin I Were Where Gowrie Rins
14. Mo Nighean Dhu (My Dark-Haired Maid)
1-14 MG3/77, GS;
8,13,14 arranged for piano (1954) GS.

SPOON RIVER (AFMS1,2,3) (1919, 1922, 1941)
  i) piano (AFMS1) (US 1922), SH, GS;
  ii) elastic scoring, 3 instruments to orchestra (AFMS2) (scored 1929) (US 1930), SH, GS;
  iii) 2 pianos 4 hands (AFMS3) (1922) (US 1932 x 1936), SH, GS;
  iv) band (1941). See p 109.

SPRIG OF THYME, THE (BFMS24) (1907/20), voice and piano (high and low keys) (US SL 1921/22), SH, GS, TP.

STALT VESSELIL (Proud Vesselil) (DFMS),
  i) sketch for voice, room-music (1951), GS;
  ii) piano solo (Easy Grainger) (1951), GS.

STORMY (PUMPING CHANTY) (SCS) (1907), male voices, MG3/102-8-8, GS.

SUSSEX MUMMERS' CHRISTMAS CAROL, THE (BFMS2 and 17)
  i) piano (BFMS2) (1905-11) (SL 1911), SH, GS;
  ii) cello (or violin) and piano (BFMS17) (1905-15) (US 1916 SL 1921), SH, GS;
  iii) band (completed and scored by R F Goldman) (Galaxy 1965) (also sketches for organ, 1915, chorus, orchestra, organ, 1917 (voices?), organ, orchestra 1943, MG9/24, MG5/66, GS).

THANKSGIVING SONG (1945), 5 voices and about 30 instruments, MG9/25, GS.

Theme and Variation (containing 'Der Pfeifender Reiter' tune) (1898), string quartet, MG3/102-4, GS.

THERE WAS A PIG WENT OUT TO DIG (BFMS18) (1905, revised 1910), 4-part female voices (US 1915 SL 1923), SS, GS.

There were three friends (KS) (1898/9), orchestra, MG3/102-8-5, GS.

Thora Von Rimol (part of the Saga of King Olaf) (1898/9), voice and piano sketch, MG3/102-8-6.

THOU GRACIOUS POWER (1952), chorus (adapted from Near Woodstock Town), GS.

THREE RAVENS, THE (BFMS41) (1902/42/43/50)), baritone, mixed chorus and 5 wood-winds, (SL 1950), vocal score SH, Score and parts, GS.

THREE SCOTTISH FOLKSONGS FOR PIANO: see Songs of the North.

TIGER TIGER (KS4 JBC9) (1905).
  i) men's chorus, optional solo (SL 1912), SH, GS.
  ii) piano solo (Easy Grainger) (1939) MG3/21:9, GS;
  iii) 2 players at 1 harmonium (Easy Grainger) GS;
  iv) cello ensemble (1946), GS.

TO A NORDIC PRINCESS (early title Bridal Song) (1927-8)
  i) orchestra (organ ad lib) (US 1929/30), SH, GS;
  ii) piano (excerpt) (US SL 1929), SH, GS.

To Wolcott Balestier (KS), sketch for contralto (?), male voices, organ pedals, MG3/102-9-4, GS.

TRAIN MUSIC (1901/07/57), large orchestra sketches, MG5/70, GS, simplified piano version (1957), GS.

TRIBUTE TO FOSTER (1913-14, scored 1931), soloists, chorus, orchestra, musical glasses and bowls (or pianos to substitute for orchestra) (US 1932 OUP 1934), SH, GS (see also *Lullaby from Tribute to Foster*). See p 92.

TWA CORBIES, THE (1903, scored 1909), voice and 7 strings or piano (US 1924), SH, GS, TP.

TWO MUSICAL RELICS OF MY MOTHER, 2 pianos 4 hands;
  a) Hermundur Illi (FI) (1905/11);
  b) As Sally Sat a-Weeping (BFMS) (1908/12) (US 1924), GS.

TWO WELSH FIGHTING SONGS (BFMS) (1904)
  a) THE CAMP (Y GADLYS), 2 men's choruses, guitars and brass (Vincent 1904, Winthrop Rogers 1922), vlocal score GS;
  b) MARCH OF THE MEN OF HARLECH, double mixed chorus and drums (Vincent 1904, Winthrop Rogers 1922), vocal score GS.

UNDER EN BRO (UNDER A BRIDGE) (DFMS12) (1945/6), soprano, baritone, flute, trumpet, piano, tuneful percussion, GS.

WALKING TUNE (RMTB3) (1900/05/11/12 etc)
  i) wind fivesome (SL 1912), SS, GS;
  ii) piano (1911) (SL 1912), SS, GS;
  iii) piano duet (Easy Grainger) (simpler version than (v) below) (1932), GS.
  iv) piano (Easy Grainger) (1939), MG3/21:10, GS;
  v) piano duet (Easy Grainger) (1939, 1957), GS;
  vi) symphonic wind choir (1940), SH, GS.

WARRIORS, THE (1913-16, 1922)
  i) orchestra & 3 pianos (SM 1924/6) SH, GS; see p 94.
  ii) 2 pianos 6 hands and optional brass (1922) (SM 1923), GS.

We be three poor mariners (BFMS), 3 sketch settings (1901), MG3/101:1, GS.

WE HAVE FED OUR SEAS FOR A THOUSAND YEARS (KS2) (1900-1904, rescored 1911), 6-part mixed chorus, brass (strings ad lib) (SL 1912), SH, score GS.

We Were Dreamers (KS) (1899),
  i) 4-part chorus, sketches MG3/98, MG3/102-9-1;
  ii) orchestra MG3/102-7-4. GS.

WHEN THE WORLD WAS YOUNG (1910/11/50/59), 2 pianos 4 hands, BL 50879, GS.

Who Built De Ark?, solo voice, 3 male voices, guitar sketch 1911.

WIDOW'S PARTY, THE (KS7) (1906/23/26/29)
  i) men's chorus and orchestra or piano duet or massed pianos in G or band in A♭ (vocal score SL 1923, full score SL 1929), SH, GS;
  ii) voice and piano ?? (1906?), BL 50872? MG5/87-16;
  iii) piano duet (1939)?;
  iv) piano (Easy Grainger) 1954, GS.

WILLOW WILLOW (OEPM1) (1902-11) voice, and piano or 4 strings and guitar (SL 1912), SH, GS, TP.

WRAITH OF ODIN, THE (1903/22/47)
  i) orchestra and double mixed chorus (1903), MG5/87-17;
  ii) 2 pianos 4 hands (1922), MG5/87-18;
  iii) chorus & piano 1947.

YE BANKS & BRAES O' BONNIE DOON (BFMS30,31,32) (1901/32/37 etc)
  i) unison women, 4-part men, whistlers, harmonium (scored 1932) (BFMS 30) (SL 1936 US 1937), SH GS;
  ii) elastic scoring (BFMS31) (scored 1932) (SL 1937), SH, GS;
  iii) band or wind choirs (SL 1937, US 1949);
  iv) 1 piano 4 hands (Easy Grainger) (1953), GS;
  v) 1 piano 6 hands (Easy Grainger) (1957), GS.

You Wild & Mossy Mountains (1898), voice and piano, MG3/102-6-6, GS.

Young British Soldier (KS) (1899), voice and piano, MG3/102-9-5, GS.

YOUTHFUL RAPTURE (1901, scored 1901, scored 1929), cello and piano or room-music (SM 1930), SH, GS.

YOUTHFUL SUITE (1899-1945), orchestra (SL 1950) (see individual movements: *Northern March, Rustic Dance, Norse Dirge, Eastern Intermezzo, English Waltz*), SH, GS.

ZANZIBAR BOAT SONG (RMTB6) (1902), 1 piano 6 hands (SL 1923), SS, GS.

(b) ARRANGEMENTS OF OTHER COMPOSERS' WORKS

Percy Grainger was an eminently practical musician. For many years he attended summer music camps, particularly at Interlochen. He would be quite happy to make an arrangement of a favourite piece of music for a concert. It might be a Debussy piano piece for a small ensemble, a piece of English Gothic music for wind band, clarinet choir or saxophone choir, an arrangement of Dowland for tuneful percussion or just a transposition of continuo part into a new key.

On the other hand, he would often spice his piano recitals with his own transcriptions: a Fauré song, a Handel hornpipe, a Strauss aria. Or he would encourage ensemble playing amongst his piano pupils with multi-piano versions of Bach fugues.

His gift for languages was put to good use in translating the words of choruses by Grieg and the Norwegian folksongs of Sparre Olsen.

In every aspect of music-making the key word was *involvement*. His participation would vary according to the task in hand. The two-piano edition of the Grieg Piano Converto is a model of scholarship, carefully distinguishing between new suggestions by Grieg, suggestions by Grainger approved by Grieg, and suggestions by Grainger not submitted to Grieg. At the other extreme he would happily write a 'ramble', loosely based on the work of another composer.

The items in the list which follow are many and varied. The full tale cannot yet be told. After Grainger's death a large proportion of these arrangements remained in the United States, although most of them have now been transferred to the Grainger Museum, where they will be catalogued and sorted into appropriate categories. Until this happens the catalogues produced by the American musicologists Teresa Balough and Thomas Slattery are the most satisfactory sources, as they had direct access to most of the manuscripts at the time.

CGS:	Chosen Gems for Strings (a collection of pieces for string ensembles)
CGW:	Chosen Gems for Wind (a collection of pieces for small wind ensembles)
CT:	Concert Transcriptions of Favourite Concertos for piano solo
DC:	Dolmetsch Collection of English Consorts (edited for viols by Dolmetsch, transcribed for modern strings by Grainger)
EGM:	English Gothic Music (transcriptions of early music for voices and instruments)
FS:	Free Settings of Favourite Melodies (for piano)

ADDINSELL, RICHARD
FESTIVAL, two pianos (MS 1954).
WARSAW CONCERTO, two pianos (Keith Prowse, 1946), MG2/1,GS.
ALFORD KENNETH J
COLONEL BOGEY, see *Bridge on the River Kwai* by Malcolm Arnold.
ANON
RAGTIME GIRL, THE (popular American Song), arr. piano (with voice?) (1901), GS.
ANON (EGM)
AD CANTUM LAETITIAE, voices, with winds or strings MS (sketch?).

ALLELUIA PSALLAT (arrangement & English text by Grainger).
  i) voices acc. by strings and/or winds, or keyboard (US 1943), vocal score.
  ii) arr. saxophone, clarinet and brass trios or choirs (MS?) MG2/2, SH, GS;
  iii) arr. 3 descant recorders (sketch score, MS 1947?); National Library of Scotland, GS;
  iv) arr. 2 desc. and 1 treble recorders, parts (MS 1947?) National Library of Scotland, GS.
ANGELUS AD VIRGINEM (arrangement and English text by Grainger)
  i) voices acc. by strings and/or winds, or keyboard (US 1943, revised 1952) vocal score MG2/3, SH, GS.
  ii) arr. brass, clarinet, saxophone choirs (MS 1942) (CGW).
  iii) arr. 2 descants and treble recorder (MS nd 1947?) National Library of Scotland, GS.
  iv) arr. piano (MS 1937).
  v) band (MS) (CGW)
BEATA VISCERA
  i) voices acc. by strings and/or winds or single voice acc. by harp, lute or guitar—or keyboard (US, 1943), MG2/4, vocal score SH, GS,;
  ii) arr. clarinet, saxophone choirs, or woodwind and horns (MS 1942);
  iii) arr. 2 descant and treble recorder score (MS nd 1947?) National Library of Scotland, GS
  iv) arr. 3 descant recorders, score (MS nd 1947?) National Library of Scotland, GS.
CREDO, a Gregorian cantus firmus arr. for 3 voices (MS 1934), optional wind or strings acc.
EDI BEO THU, 2 voices, wind or strings, MS 1939.
FOWELES IN THE FRITH, 2 voices, MS 1933.
FULGET COELESTIS CURIA, 3 voices, 3 violins, harmonium (MS sketches, 1936, written out 1950) MG 12/2-15, GS.
HAC IN ANNI JANUA, 3-part chorus (MS 1939).
JUBILEMUS OMNES UNA, chorus, MS nd.
MARIONETTE DOUCE, voices acc. by strings and/or winds, or keyboard (US 1950) vocal score, MG 2/5, SS, GS;
PRINCESSE OF YOUTH, voices, acc. by harmonium, organ, or accordion (MS 1937), vocal score GS.
PRO BEATI PAULI—O PRAECLARA PATRIAE, 4 celli/stg orch, MS 1939.
PUELLARE GREMIUM voices, acc. by strings and/or winds, or keyboard (US 1950), vocal score, MG 2/6, GS, SH.
WORCESTER SANCTUS, 3-part women's (or 3-part men's) voices, or
  i) 6-part mixed voices in C major (MS 1939);
  ii) 3-part mixed voices, or 3-part men's voices with male alto, strings in Eb (MS 1939;.
ARNE, THOMAS
RULE BRITANNIA, arranged c. 1917 small orchestra(?), location of MS unknown.
ARNOLD, MALCOLM
BRIDGE ON THE RIVER KWAI, MARCHES (being an amalgamation of *Colonel Bogey March* by Kenneth J Alford with a counter-theme by Malcolm Arnold entitled *River Kwai March*, set circa 1959, three pianists at 1,2 or 3 pianos (MS undated), GS.
BACH, J S
AIR from SUITE No 3 in D major, BWV 1068, continuo part only, transcribed into E^b for harp or piano (MA 1937).
BLITHE BELLS (Bach-Grainger) free ramble on Bach's *Schafe Können sicher weiden* from the Cantata BVW 208, *Was mir behagt*, MG 2/8, set 1930-31
  i) elastic scoring (US, 1932), GS, SH;
  ii) piano solo (US, SL 1931), GS, SH;
  iii) piano solo easy version (US, SL 1931), GS;
  v) military band and tuneful percussion (MS 1931).
BRANDENBURG CONCERTO No 3 in G, arr. strings, piano, MS.
FUGUE in A minor, No 20 (Book 1, WTK)
  i) arr. piano, harpsichord style (MS nd), MG 4/3;
  ii) 2 pf 8 hands (massed pianos) (US 1930), GS.
FUGUE No 1 in C major (WTK) arr. 2 harmoniums (MS 1927).
FUGUE in C# minor, No 4 (Book 1, WTK), saxophone sixsome (MS 1943).
FUGUE in D# minor (WTK II No 8) arr. two pianos (MS 1928).
FUGUE in E major, (WTK II No 9) arr. 4 pianos, octave study (MS 1928). GS; 2 pf 8 hands (MS 1950) GS; pf solo MS (unfinished?).
MARCH in D (from the *Notenbuch der Anna Magdalena Bach*) (CGW) arr. saxophone,.

clarinet, brass, wind choirs and wind band (MS 1946), GS.

O MENSCH, BEWEIN DEIN SÜNDE GROSS (Organ Choral arr. brass choir, wind band (MS 1937, 1942).

O PRAISE THE LORD ALL YE HEATHENS, vocal parts MS MG 15/6-2.

PRELUDE AND FUGUE (WTK I (unidentified)) (CGW), sax/brass/wind choirs, MS?

PRELUDE AND FUGUE No 5 in D major (WTK II), BWV 874,
   i) string foursome (parts in both D and E) (MS 1927) National Library of Scotland
   ii) saxophone foursome MS 1943, GS.

SEHET, WAS DIE LIEBE TUT! from Cantata No 85, band, (MS 1937), 2 versions, in Eb, Db.

TOCCATA in F FOR ORGAN, BWV 540, for 3 pianos 6 hands (or massed pianos) US 1939), MG 2/10.

TOCCATA and FUGUE in D MINOR FOR ORGAN BWV 565, arr. pianos MS? date?, based in part upon transciptions by Ferruccio Busoni and Karl Tausig. Grainger played various combinations with his versions of several passages; two pages of excerpts (1950), MG 4/4, GS.

BALAKIREV, MILY ALEXEYEVICH

TAMARA, — symphonic poem, arranged for 2 pianos, 8 hands (MS?).

BIRD, GEORGE

MELODY, harmonisation (MS 1945).

BRADE, WILLIAM

ALLEMANDE, transcribed for strings, MG 15/6-2.

BRAHMS, JOHANNES

CRADLE SONG, Opus 49, No 4 (FS1) piano solo (US, SL 1923); SH, GS.

VARIATION No 12 from Paganini Variations Op. 35, II, piano, simplified (MS 1957).

BROCKWAY, HOWARD

sketches for *Folksongs from Kentucky,* (MS 1945) MG 4/7.

BULL, OLE

THE DAIRYMAID'S LAMENT, arr. 2 violas, 2 cellos.

BYRD, WILLIAM

CARMAN'S WHISTLE, THE, piano (MS 1947), GS.

CABEZON, ANTONIO DE

PRELUDE IN THE DORIAN MODE
   i) 2 violas, 2 'cellos (MS 1935) (CGS) MG 4/8.
   ii) 10 strings or string orchestra
   iii) 4 tone-strands, for wind band (MS 1941) (CGW) MG 8/3, GS.
   iv) arr. saxophone choir (MS 1943)

CHEATHAM, KITTY

HARVEST SONG, 4 part mixed voices, violin, harp (or piano), organ (or piano), MG 2/12.

CURTIS-BURLIN, NATALIE

LULLABY (Negro Folksong) (CGS), arr. for mixed voices, optional strings (MS mimeograph, 1934) vocal score, MG 12/2-3, GS.

MATACHINA DANCE, orchestration of her scoring sketches (MS 1925).

SANGRE de CRISTO (Lenten Chant), orchestration of her scoring sketches (MS 1925).

DEBUSSY, CLAUDE ACHILLE

BRUYÈRES (HEATHER BELLS) arr. wind ensemble (MS 1918), parts (complete?), GS.

PAGODES, arr. tuneful percussion and harmonium (MS 1928), score GS.

DELIUS, FREDERICK

AIR AND DANCE, see p 212: ch IV note 11.

DANCE RHAPSODY, No 1, arr. for 2 pianos, 4 hands (Universal Ed. 1923), GS.

SONG OF THE HIGH HILLS, THE, arr. 2 pianos (MS 1923) (Delius Trust), MG 6/9, GS.

HASSAN: part of 'General Dance' composed by Grainger.

DES PRÉS: see Josquin

DOWLAND, JOHN

NOW, O NOW I NEEDS MUST PART (FS 5 and 6 in USA, FS 3 and 4 in UK)
   i) piano solo, easy version (US 1937, FS5) (SL 1937, FS3), SH, GS;
   iii) piano solo, concert version (US 1937, FS6) (SL 1937, FS4) SH, GS;
   iii) original additional voice part (MS) GS.
   iv) 'Bell Piece', tuneful percussion and small band sketched 1948, 1953, parts variously dated 1951, 1953, 1954 (MS).

DUFAY, GUILLAUME
LE JOUR S'ENDORT (CGS), mezzo soprano, violin, viola (or cello), cello (MS, nd).
DUNSTABLE, JOHN
O ROSA BELLA, (EGM), 4-6 mixed voice, unacc. or supported by instruments (SL, 1963)
    MG8/4, SS, GS.
REGINA COELI, (EGM), unfinished MS.
VENI SANCTE SPIRITUS (EGM)
    i) 4 mixed voices or 4-part woman, ad lib tuneful percussion and keyboard (MS 1939), MG
      12/1, GS;
    ii) orchestra (MS 1956)
    iii) strings
ELGAR, SIR EDWARD
NIMROD VARIATION (Enigma Variations, Op 36) arr. piano solo (MS 1953), GS.
FAURÉ, GABRIEL
APRÈS UN RÊVE, Op 7 No 1 (FS 7) arr. piano (US 1940), MG 2/15, GS.
FUNERARY CHANT, parts (incomplete) MG8/5.
PIANO QUARTET no. 2 in G minor, Op 45, arr. 2 pianos (MS nd, complete?).
NELL, Op. 18/1 (FS 3) arr. piano (1924) (US 1925), MG2/16, GS.
TUSCAN SERENADE, Op 3, No 2, arr. piano, band (MS 1937).

FERRABOSCO II, ALFONSO
FOUR-NOTE PAVAN (DC1)
    i) strings (US 1944) (CGS) MG2/17, score GS;
    ii) wind choir, brass choir, saxophone (MS 1940) (CGW), GS.
FINCK, HEINRICH
O SCHÖNES WEIB (CGS), tenor and string trio (MS 1934/1940). MG4/11.
FRANCK, CÉSAR
CHORALE (for organ), scored for band (MS 1942).
GARDINER, BALFOUR
ENGLISH DANCE, arr. 2 pianos (MS 1925), British Museum.
FLOWING MELODY (1900-4) (given to Grainger for completion) MS sketch 1947, GS.
GARDINERIANA RHAPSODY, sketches 1947, GS.
JOYFUL HOMECOMING, MS sketches 1946.
LONDON BRIDGE, arr. 2 pianos, harmonium and tuneful percussion.
MOVEMENT FOR STRINGS in C minor, (Schott, 1949), bass part MG6/10, GS.
PRELUDE, DE PROFUNDIS (Guide to virtuosity, No 1), edited Percy Grainger (US 1927),
    MG2/18, GS.
GERSHWIN, GEORGE
EMBRACEABLE YOU, arr. piano duet, MS 1951, GS.
LOVE WALKED IN, arranged piano solo 1945 (Gershwin Pub Corp, 1946), MG2/19, GS.
MAN I LOVE, THE, concert adaptation of Gershwin's own transcription (piano), New World
    Music Corp. 1944, MG2/20, GS.
PORGY AND BESS, fantasy for 2 pianos (Gershwin & Co. 1951), MG2/21, GS.
O, LORD I'M ON MY WAY (PORGY AND BESS), MS sketch 1950.
OH, I CAN'T SIT DOWN (PORGY AND BESS), 1 piano 6 hands, (MS 1950), GS.
GOOSSENS, SIR EUGENE
FOLKTUNE, arr. band (MS 1942), MG10/6, score GS.
GRAINGER, ELLA
BIGELOW, MARCH OF 1940, piano MG10/7, GS.
CRYING FOR THE MOON,
    i) contralto voice and tuneful percussion group, harmonised and scored by P G (MS 1946),
      GS.
    ii) contralto and piano, GS.
FAREWELL TO AN ATOLL
    i) voice and piano—harmonised by P G (MS 1944), GS;
    ii) soprano, mixed chorus (optional), and orchestra (MS 1945), GS.
HEARTLESS, mezzo sop, mixed chorus, room music ad lib, (MS 1947-8), vocal score GS.
HONEY-POT BEE
    i) mezzo sop, room music (5 strings, harp, piano, harmonium, vibraharp), (MS 1947), sketch
      score GS;
    ii) voice and piano, GS. (MS 1948)

LOVE AT FIRST SIGHT,
 i) unaccompanied women's chorus and soprano soloist (optional baritone soloist as well)—harmonised by P G (US 1946), MG2/22-2, GS;
 ii) unaccompanied mixed chorus with soprano solo, harmonised by P G (US 1946), MG2/22-1, GS;
 iii) voice and piano or organ, GS.
THE MERMAID
 i) mezzo soprano plus soprano, sax, MS c. 1947;
 ii) voice and piano, MS 1947, GS.
PLAYING ON HEART STRINGS, alto solo, tenor solo, mixed chorus or woman's chorus, (MS 1950), score GS.
TO ECHO, voice, with piano or 7 instruments (scored by P G) (MS 1945-46), GS

GRIEG, EDVARD
ALBUM FOR MALE CHORUS, Op 30, nos 1, 2, 3, 4, 5, 6, 10, 12 unaccompanied chorus (Peters, 1925), edited by Grainger, MG2/23, GS.
FOUR PSALMS, Op 74, baritone solo, mixed voices *a capella* (Peters, 1925, 1949, 1953), edited by Grainger, MG2/24, GS.
KNUT LURÆSENS HALLING II, arr 2 pianos (MS 1921), MG4/13, GS.
NORWEGIAN BRIDAL PROCESSION, Op 19, No 2, edited and fingered by Grainger (Theo Presser Co, 1920) (SL, 1920), MG2/25, GS.
PIANO CONCERTO in A minor, Op 16
 i) two-piano edition (complete) (US, 1920 Peters, 1920), MG2/26, GS.
 ii) piano transcription of main themes and episodes of 1st movement (CT) (US 1945), MG2/27, GS
SYMPHONY in E minor (orchestration of opening of Sonata in E minor, Op 7) MS sketch, 1944.
THREE LYRIC PIECES, from Book 1, Op 12, Nos 2,4 and 5, orchestration by Grainger (MS 1898), MG4/14, score GS.

HANDEL, GEORGE FRIDERIC
HARMONIOUS BLACKSMITH, THE (Harpsichord Suite, No 5) variations, voice or bass fiddle and piano (MS 1911) (see also *Clog Dance* and *Handel in the Strand*), MG6/12, GS.
HORNPIPE (from *Water Music*), (FS2), arr. piano (US, SL 1923) (A 1926), MG2/28, GS

HARRIS, CHARLES K.
AFTER THE BALL WAS OVER, sketch for whistlers and strings, MS 1901, MG 3/101:1, (BL 50884).

JAPPART, JEAN
NENCIOZZA MIA (CGS), for strings (2 violas, 2 cellos), (MS 1934), MG15/6-6.

JENKINS, JOHN
FANTASY No 1 in D (or 5-part fantasy)
 i) room-music ensemble (strings) (US 1944) (DC2) (CGS), MG2/29
 ii) wind band, brass band, sax choir, clarinet choir, etc (MS 1933, 1937, 1941, 1953).

LE JEUNE, CLAUDE
LA BEL ARONDE (Pretty Swallow)
 i) 6 singing voices (transposable), MS mimeo, MG 12/2-1, GS;
 ii) saxophone, brass, clarinet, wind choirs (MS 1942);
 iii) 2 harmoniums 1932, GS;
 iv) piano duet 1932, GS.

JOSQUIN DES PRÉS
LA BERNARDINA
 i) violin, viola, cello (MS 1934), (CGS), MG15/6-5.
 ii) 3 violins (MS)
 iii) brass trio, clarinet trip (MS 1943);
 iv) band, wind ensemble, brass (MS 1943) (CGW) GS score and parts.
A L'HEURE QUE JE VOUS (CGS)
 i) 2 violins, viola, cello (MS 1934?), MG15/6-4;
 ii) string ensemble (MS 1939?).
ROYAL FANFARE (CGW), brass 5-tet (MS 1937).

LAWES, WILLIAM
6-PART FANTASY AND AIR No 1 (English Consorts, No 3) (DC3) (CGS)
 i) strings (US 1944)/GS score and parts, MG2/30;

ii) wind choir, bass choir, clar choir, sax choir, band (MS 1932, 1937, 1944) (CGW), GS;

iii) piano (MS 1932).

iv) 2 pianos (MS 1932).

LINEVA, EUGENIE

FLOWERS THAT BLOOMED IN THE FIELD, THE, 4 mixed voices, or 4-part mixed choir edited by P G (MS mimeo 1934), MG12/2-7.

KINDLING WOOD, 3 women's voices, or 3-part women's chorus (MS mimeo, 1934), MG12/2-8, GS.

LISZT, FRANZ

FANTASY ON HUNGARIAN FOLK-SONGS, arr band and piano (MS 1959?), MG4/14.

MACHAUT, GUILLAUME DE

BALLADE No 17

i) 3-part for singers (MS mimeo 1934), MG12/2-5;

ii) strings, (CGS), MG15/6-7;

iii) brass or wind ensemble (CGW) (MS 1937/42)

iv) brass choir, saxophone choir (MS 1940, 1942) (CGW).

RONDEAU No 14 (CGS), 3 to 6 strings (MS), MG4/18.

MASON, DANIEL G

FREE & EASY FIVE-STEP (arr. Harwood Simmons for band), sketch score PG, MG4/32.

MOHR, HALSEY K

LIBERTY BELL (arr. band by G. F. Breigel), re-arr. band P.G. (MS), Library of Congress, MG4/36

MORLEY, THOMAS

O MISTRESS MINE, mixed chorus (MS 1903), GS.

OLSEN, SPARRE

MOUNTAIN-NORWAY (or SPIRIT OF NORWAY)

i) mixed chorus and piano (MS mimeo 1934), MG 12/2-9, chorus parts GS;

ii) orchestral accompaniment MG4/19,20.

NORWEGIAN FOLKSONGS: foreword and translations by PG (Norsk Musikforlag 1946), GS.

WHEN YULETIDE COMES,

i) soprano alto, men's voices (1937) MG4/21;

ii) 3 saxophones (MS 1943).

PARKER, KATHERINE

DOWN LONGFORD WAY, set early 1935, elastic scoring (3 instruments to full orchestra) (Boosey & Hawkes 1936), MG2/31.

PISADOR, DIEGO

PASEABASE. THE MOORISH KING (CGS), 3 strings (or lute), baritone (piano ad lib) (MS nd), MG15/6-8.

POWER, LYONEL

ANIMA MEA LIQUEFACTA EST. (EGM), 3 strings, mezzo soprano (MS nd), MG4/23.

SANCTUS, (EGM), 3 voices with optional accompaniment by strings and/or winds, or keyboard (US 1950), MG12/2-16, vocal score GS.

PURCELL, HENRY

FOUR-PART FANTASY, No 8.,

i) strings and harmonium (MS nd);

ii) massed pianos and harmonium (MS?).

RACHMANINOV, SERGE

PIANO CONCERTO No 2 (CT), transcription by PG of main themes and episodes from last movement (US 1946), GS.

RAVEL, MAURICE

LA VALLEE DES CLOCHES, parts for tuneful percussion (MS 1944), MG 10/9, GS.

ROSS, ORVIS

AWAY IN A MANGER, arr cello and piano.

SANDBY, HERMAN

CHANT (Solemn Chant) (or 'The Page's Song')

i) scored for room-music (MS 1900);

ii) violin, cello, harmonium, piano (MS nd).

ELV ERHØJ, song sketch 1937.

INTERMEZZO, arr band.
LOVE SONG (CGS) arr for strings (MS 1939).
2 PIECES arranged for celli (MS 1899).
2 PIECES arranged for piano (MS 1901).
SCARLATTI, DOMENICO
QUIET BROOK, THE, Sonata in B minor, L.33 (CGS)
  i) arr string quartet (US 1930) (MS parts National Library of Scotland) MG6/13;
  ii) arr clarinet choir (MS 1942) (CGW).
SCHUMANN, ROBERT
PIANO CONCERTO, transcription from main themes and episodes from 1st movement for
  piano (US 1947). GS
SCOTT, CYRIL
AUBADE, harmonium, MS 1932, MG4/24.
HANDELIAN RHAPSODY, piano transcription (Elkin and Co 1909), MG2/35.
SOLEMN DANCE, arr strings, harmonium, piano, percussion (MS 1933), MG4/25.
3 SYMPHONIC DANCES, arranged for 2 pianos, 4 hands (SM 1922), MG2/36, GS.
STANFORD, SIR CHARLES VILLIERS
FOUR IRISH DANCES (from '*The Complete Petrie Collection of Ancient Irish Music*')
1) A March Jig (Maguire's Kick) ⎫
2) A Slow Dance   ⎬ arr for piano   (published separately, (Houghton c1907, Fischer 1916) MG 2/37-MG 2/40, GS)
3) The Leprechaun's Dance ⎪
4) A Reel   ⎭
STRAUSS, RICHARD
RAMBLE ON LOVE (FS4) arr for piano of final duet, *Rosenkavalier*, Act III, (Fürstner, 1928) (US 1928), MG2/41, GS.
STOKEM, JOHANNES
HARRAYTRE AMOURS (CGS), violin, viola, cello (MS 1934).
TCHAIKOVSKY, PYOTR I.
FLOWER WALTZ PARAPHRASE (*Nutcracker*, Op 71)ᴵ, 1904, piano (Forsyth 1905) (SL 1916), MG2/42, SH, GS.
PIANO CONCERTO (FS 8, CT) opening of 1st concerto transcribed (US 1943), MG2/43, GS.
WILLAERT, ADRIAN
O SALUTARIS HOSTIA (CGW)
  i) 2 voices and 4 instruments, (MS 1941) MG12/2-12, GS;
  ii) brass choir, 2 clarinets or 2 voices.

BY APPOINTMENT TO
H.M. QUEEN ALEXANDRA

GRAMOPHONE

RECORDS OF
PERCY GRAINGER'S COLLECTION OF
English Traditional Folk-Songs
sung by Genuine Peasant Folksinger

Photo by E. Hill
MR. JOSEPH TAYLOR,
of Saxby-All-Saints, North Lincolnshire.

Cover of Gramophone Company brochure, 1908. (See p 29 for the contents.)

Current Discography

John Bird

A scholarly discography of Percy Grainger appeared in 'Recorded Sound' in 1972[1], and was reprinted in Slattery's book on the composer[2]. What follows is largely a list of currently available recordings mentioned in Chapter XVI, plus a personal selection of out-of-print material as a separate sequence at the end. British, Australian and American record numbers are given.

CURRENT RECORDINGS

'Salute to Percy Grainger'. Benjamin Britten, Peter Pears, John Shirley-Quirk, the Ambrosian Singers (Chorus Master: John McCarthy), Viola Tunnard, English Chamber Orchestra: *Shepherd's Hey, Willow Willow, I'm Seventeen Come Sunday, Bold William Taylor, There was a Pig went out to Dig, My Robin is to the Greenwood gone, Lord Maxwell's Goodnight, The Duke of Marlborough Fanfare, Let's Dance Gay in Green Meadow, Scotch Strathspey and Reel, The Pretty Maid milkin' her Cow, Lisbon, The Lost Lady Found, Shallow Brown.* Decca (UK) SXL 6410, Decca (Australia) SXLA 6410, London (USA) CS 6632.

'Salute to Percy Grainger Vol. 2'. Peter Pears, John Shirley-Quirk, Anna Reynolds, Wandsworth Boys Choir, Linden Singers, English Chamber Orchestra, Steuart Bedford: *Molly on the Shore, Shenandoah, Under a Bridge, Dollar and a Half a Day, The Merry King, Six Dukes went Afishin', Stormy, Irish Tune from County Derry, Brigg Fair, Green Bushes, The Three Ravens, Died for Love, Country Gardens, The Power of Love, The Hunter in His Career.* Decca (UK) SXL 6872.

'Australian Digital Music'. *Free Music I and II* (Sketches for an electronic piece). (Realised by Barry Conyngham). Included on Move (Australia) MS 3027. While only playing for 1' 53", these are fascinating fragments dating from 1934-35 which have been realised on the Music V system running at the Computer Music Project at the University of Melbourne.

'Piano Music of Percy Grainger'. Daniel Adni: *Country Gardens, Nell Op. 18 No. 1. (Fauré arr. Grainger), Irish Tune from County Derry, Molly on the Shore, To a Nordic Princess (Bridal Song), Lullaby (from Tribute to Foster), Over the Hills and Far Away (Children's March), Handel in the Strand (Clog Dance), Walking Tune, Knight and Shepherd's Daughter, Love walked in (Gershwin arr. Grainger), The man I love (Gershwin arr. Grainger), Shepherd's Hey, Sailor's Song, Eastern Intermezzo.* EMI (UK) HQS 1363, Seraphim (USA) S-60295.

'Room-Music Tit-bits & Other Tone Stuffs'. Leslie Howard: *Shepherd's Hey, Harvest Hymn, One more day, my John, The Sussex Mummers' Christmas Carol, Jutish Medley, Country Gardens, The Merry King, Handel in the Stand.* Leslie Howard and David Stanhope: *Children's March 'Over the Hills and Far Away', Lincolnshire Posy, English Waltz.* EMI (UK) HQS 1402.

'Musicians of Australia Vol. 15—Percy Grainger: Piano Music for Two Hands Vol. 1'. Leslie Howard: *Shepherd's Hey, Harvest Hymn, One more day, my John, The Sussex Mummers' Christmas Carol, Molly on the Shore, To a Nordic Princess, Handel in the Strand, Jutish Medley, Irish Tune from County Derry, Knight and Shepherd's Daughter, The Merry King, Colonial Song, Country Gardens.* World Record Club (Australia) R03433.

'Percy Grainger Piano Settings, Vol. 2: Two Pianos, Four Hands'. Leslie Howard and David Stanhope: *Shepherd's Hey, Hermundur Illi, As Sally sat a-weeping, Hill Song No 1, Hill Song No 2, Suite: In a Nutshell.* World Record Club (Australia) R06332.

'**Percy Grainger Piano Settings, Vol. 3: Two Pianos, Six Hands**'. Leslie Howard, David Stanhope and Geoffrey Parsons, With the Adelaide Brass Quintet and guests: *Jutish Medley, English Dance, Green Bushes, The Warriors*. World Record Club (Australia) R06333.

'**The Orchestral Works of Percy Grainger. Vol. 1**'. John Hopkins conducting the Sydney Symphony Orchestra: *Country Gardens, Harvest Hymn (for string orchestra), Under En Bro, Children's March: 'Over the Hills and Far Away', The lonely desert man sees the tents of the happy tribes, Colonial Song, Duke of Marlborough Fanfare, Shallow Brown, Handel in the Strand, Harvest Hymn (for 18 single instruments), La Vallee des Cloches (arr. from Ravel), Scotch Strathspey and Reel.* EMI (UK) EMD 5514 (now deleted), EMI (Australia) EMD 5514.

'**To a Nordic Princess—The Orchestral Works of Percy Grainger—Vol. 2.**' John Hopkins conducting the Melbourne Symphony Orchestra: *To A Nordic Princess (Bridal Song), Willow Willow, My Robin is to the Greenwood gone, Shepherd's Hey, Eastern Intermezzo* (for tuneful percussion), *Farewell to an Atoll* (words and melody by Ella Grainger; harmonized and scored for soprano solo and orchestra by P A Grainger), *Molly on the Shore, Hill Song No 2, Spoon River.* EMI (Australia) OASD 7606.

'**The Orchestral Works of Percy Grainger. Vol. 3**'. John Hopkins conducting the Adelaide Symphony Orchestra. *Blithe Bells (free ramble on 'Sheep may safely graze' from Bach's cantata 'Was mir behagt BWV 208), We were Dreamers, There were three Friends, Walking Tune* (played by the Adelaide Wind Quintet), *The Immovable Do (or the Cyphering C), Suite: In a Nutshell.* EMI (Australia) OASD 7607.

'**The Orchestral Works of Percy Grainger. Vol. 4**'. John Hopkins conducting the Sydney Symphony Orchestra: *Danish Folk-Music Suite, Tribute to Foster, Youthful Suite.* EMI (Australia) OASD 7608.

Percy Grainger (Duo-Art piano roll) with John Hopkins conducting the Sydney Symphony Orchestra: *Grieg: Piano Concerto in A minor, Op. 16.* 'Leopold Stokowski Conducts Percy Grainger Favorites': *Handel in the Strand,* Irish Tune from County Derry, Country Gardens,** Shepherd's Hey,** Mock Morris, Molly on the Shore, Early one Morning.* Leopold Stokowski and his Symphony Orchestra with Percy Grainger piano soloist, * orchestral piano. ** RCA (UK) VRL1 0168, RCA (USA) ARL1 3059, RCA (Australia) VRL1 0168 (The Stokowski items were once included—in a different order of play—on RCA (USA) LM 1238, and *Molly on the Shore, Handel in the Strand, Mock Morris Dance* and *Irish Tune from County Derry* were once issued on HMV (UK) (45 rpm) 7ER 5046).

The Cornell University Wind Ensemble conducted by Marice Stith: *Lads of Wamphray*. Included on Silver Crest Custom (USA) CUWE-B (Available from the Band Office, Lincoln Hall, Cornell University, Ithaca, NY 14850, USA).

'**English Folk Songs**'. Robin Doveton acc. by Victoria Hartung: *The Sprig of Thyme, Willow Willow, British Waterside or The Jolly Sailor, Six Dukes went Afishin', The Pretty Maid milkin' her Cow, Shallow Brown, Died for Love, The Lost Lady Found.* Included on Prelude (UK) PMS 1502.

'**Over the Hills and Far Away**'—the music of Percy Aldridge Grainger. Harry Begian conducting the University of Illinois Symphonic Band: *Children's March, Over the Hills and Far Away, Colonial Song, Lads of Wamphray, Lincolnshire Posy, Irish Tune from County Derry, Shepherd's Hey, Country Gardens, Ye Banks and Braes O' Bonnie Doon, Handel in the Strand, Spoon River, Hill Song No 2, Duke of Marlborough Fanfare, The Immovable Do, Power of Rome and the Christian Heart.* Two untitled stereo records. Nos 74 and 75. (Available by writing to University of Illinois Bands, 1103, S Sixth, Champaign, Illinois. 61820, USA).

'**Marching Through History**'. Major Peter Parkes conducting the Band of The Grenadier Guards: *Over the Hills and Far Away.* Included on Decca (UK) SB 706.

'**Sir Adrian Boult conducts Marches**'. *Over the Hills and Far Away (Children's March).* Included on Lyrita (UK) SRCS 71.

'**I Love My Love**'. Ian Partridge (tenor solo) and Louis Halsey conducting The Elizabethan Singers: *Brigg Fair.* Included on Argo (UK) ZRG 5496.

'**Grainger on the Shore**'. Neville Dilkes conducting the English Sinfonia: *Suite: In a Nutshell, Molly on the Shore, Irish Tune from County Derry, Danish Folk-Music Suite, The Immovable 'Do'.* EMI (UK) ASD 3651.

'**By Plane From Paris**'. Denis Wick conducting the London Wind Orchestra: *Molly on the Shore, Irish Tune from County Derry, Shepherd's Hey, Lincolnshire Posy.* Included on Enigma (UK) K 53574.

'**British Concert Pops**'. George Weldon conducting the Philharmonia Orchestra: *Mock Morris.* Included on HMV Concert Classics (UK) SXLP 30123.

'**Free Rambles, Room-music Tit Bits and...**'. Kenneth Montgomery conducting the Bournemouth Sinfonietta: *Rustic Dance* and *Eastern Intermezzo* from *Youthful Suite, Blithe Bells, Spoon River, My Robin is to the Greenwood gone, Green Bushes, Country Gardens (arr. Adolf Schmid), Mock Morris, Youthful Rapture* (solo cello: Moray Welsh), *Shepherd's Hey, Walking Tune, Molly on the Shore, Handel in the Strand* (orch. Henry J Wood). RCA (UK) RL 25198 (cassette).

Sir Vivian Dunn conducting The Light Music Society Orchestra: *Country Gardens (arr. Artok), Molly on the Shore, Londonderry Air (Air from County Derry), Handel in the Strand, Mock Morris, Shepherd's Hey.* Included on Columbia (UK) TWO 295.

'**Folksong Suites & Other British Band Classics**'. Frederick Fennell conducting the Eastman Wind Ensemble: *Hill Song No 2.* Included on Mercury (USA) SR90388, Fontana (UK) 6747177.

'**Winds in Hi-Fi**'. Frederick Fennell conducting the Eastman Wind Ensemble: *Lincolnshire Posy.* Included on Mercury, Golden Imports (pressed and printed in Holland for USA markets). SRI 75093.

'**Country Gardens and Other Favorites**'. Frederick Fennell conducting the Eastman-Rochester 'Pops' Orchestra: *Country Gardens, Shepherd's Hey, Colonial Song, Children's March, The Immovable Do, Mock Morris, Handel in the Strand, Irish Tune from County Derry, Spoon River, My Robin is to the Greenwood gone, Molly on the Shore.* Mercury, Golden Imports (USA) SRI 95102.

Frederick Fennell conducting The Cleveland Symphonic Winds: *Lincolnshire Posy, Shepherd's Hey.* Included on Telarc Digital (USA) DG-10050.

'**Percy Grainger plays Grieg**'. *Concerto in A minor, Op 16.* Hollywood Bowl Symphony Orchestra conducted by Leopold Stokowski (15 vii 45). *Cadenza only from First Movement of Concerto in A minor, Op.16.* (16 v 08), *Concerto in A minor, Op16.* Southeast Iowa Symphony Orchestra conducted by Richard A Morse (27 x 56), *Three Norwegian Folksongs from Op 17.* International Piano Archives (USA) IPA 508. (Available from the IPA, c/o The Department of Music, University of Maryland, College Park, Maryland 20742, USA).

Percy Grainger plays: Chopin: *Polonaise in A flat, Op.53. (abridged),* Chopin: *Prelude in A flat, Op.28 No.17,* Liszt: *Polonaise No. 2 in E major,* Liszt: *Hungarian Fantasia (abridged)* with unidentified orchestra, Debussy: *Toccata (from 'Pour le Piano'),* Grieg: *Wedding Day at Troldhaugen,* Grieg: *To Spring,* Tchaikovsky-Grainger: *'Valse des Fleurs' paraphrase (abridged),* Brahms- Grainger: *Cradle Song,* Grainger: *Mock Morris Dances,* Grainger: *Gum-Suckers March,* Grainger: *Spoon River,* Grainger *Shepherd's Hey.* Pearl (UK) GEM 143.

'Landmarks Of Recorded Pianism'. Volume 1. Acoustic Recordings (1889-1924). Percy Grainger plays a previously unissued US Columbia recording of Liszt: *Hungarian Rhapsody No. 15, 'Rakoczy March' (Abridged)* (3 viii 22). Included on Desmar (USA) IPA 117.

HISTORICAL RECORDINGS

The following recordings have long been withdrawn from the catalogues. This list is not, of course, complete but merely reflects the taste of its compiler, nor can any guide be given as to their procurement except perhaps as a result of a diligent scouring of the second-hand record shops or second-hand record dealers' lists.

Grieg: *Piano Concerto in A minor, Op.16*. Percy Grainger with Per Dreier conducting the Aarhus Municipal Orchestra (25 ii 57). Grainger: *Country Gardens* (25 ii 57) played by Percy Grainger. Strauss-Grainger: *Ramble on Love* (25 ii 57) played by Grainger. Grainger: *Suite on Danish Folk Songs for Orchestra* [sic] played by Percy Grainger with Per Dreier conducting the Aarhus Municipal Orchestra. Vanguard (USA) VRS-1098.

'Band Masterpieces'. Richard Franko Goldman conducting the Goldman Band: *Children's March: 'Over the Hills and Far Away'* (Percy Grainger at the piano). Decca (USA) DL 78633.

P. Pears (ten), B. Britten (pf): *Six Dukes went Afishin'*. HMV (UK) DA 2023 (10" 78 rpm) 7P268 (7" 45 rpm), 7EP7071 (7" 45 rpm). EMI (UK) RLS 748.

Philadelphia Wind Quintet: *Walking Tune*. Included on Columbia (US) MS 6584.

Watson Forbes (vla): *Arrival Platform Humlet* (unacc)/*Sussex Mummers' Christmas Carol* (with E de Chaulnieu (pf)). Decca (UK) M 540 (10" 78 rpm), Decca (Australia) Y5977 (10" 78 rpm). (Impeccable performances of the only commercial recording of these arrangements).

Beatrice Harrison (vlc) with orchestra conducted by M. Sargent: *Youthful Rapture*. HMV (UK) C 1929 (12" 78 rpm). (A stylish and impassioned performance by an artist obviously committed to the work).

N. Stone (ten) with Charles Kennedy Scott conducting the Oriana Madrigal Singers: *Brigg Fair*. HMV (UK) E 473 (10" 78 rpm). (An elegant and soulful performance which Grainger himself knew, owned and loved).

Ossip Gabrilowitsch (pf): *Shepherd's Hey*. Victor (USA) 1095, HMV (UK) DA 717 (10" 78 rpm) also included on RCA (USA) LM 2824, RCA (UK) VIC 1210. (A somewhat precious but nonetheless aristocratic performance which sheds new light on this frequently performed work).

Eugene Ormandy conducting the Minneapolis Symphony Orchestra: *Londonderry Air, Molly on the Shore*. HMV (UK, India and Australia) DB 2685, Victor (USA) 8734. (Until Fennell's Mercury came along, this was Grainger's own personal favourite. A highly idiosyncratic but perfectly valid interpretation with rich and fulsome string sound).

'Unto Brigg Fair': Joseph Taylor and other traditional Lincolnshire singers recorded in 1908 by Percy Grainger. Joseph Taylor (Gramophone Company recordings): *Sprig o' thyme, Died for love, Brigg Fair, The white hair, Lord Bateman, Rufford Park poachers, The gipsy's wedding day, Worcester City, Creeping Jane, Murder of Maria Martin, Sprig o' thyme, Bold William Taylor*. (Cylinders made by Percy Grainger). Mr Thomson: *Lord Bateman*, Joseph Leaning: *Green Bushes, The Sheffield apprentice*, George Goulthorpe: *Horkstow Grange*, Joseph Taylor: *Landlord and tenant, Bold Nevison*, George Wray: *Lord Melbourne*, Dean Robinson: *Bold Robin Hood, T'owd yowe wi' one horn*. Leader (UK) LEA 4050.

Grainger in the BBC Archives

Lewis Foreman

Owing to the extent of the detailed records and archives that it has preserved, the BBC is an important source for many aspects of historical research in the present century; those relating to music are particularly valuable, and surprisingly little-used. The following attempts to guide the reader to those parts of the BBC where there is Grainger material, give some indication of what is held, and indicate appropriate procedure for gaining access to it.

In dealing with the BBC, we are interested in four separate areas:

(i)   BBC Written Archives
(ii) BBC Script Registry and Programme Index
(iii) BBC Sound Archives, including Transcription Discs
(iv) BBC Film Library.

(i) BBC WRITTEN ARCHIVES

The BBC Written Archives Centre is at Caversham, a suburb of Reading, Berkshire. It consists of a small reading room where researchers are accommodated by appointment only. Material is looked-out for visitors according to their specification of requirements supplied when making an appointment. Research can be carried out for readers unable to attend, on a published scale of charges. Copyright can be a complex matter with all BBC material, and written permission is required to copy material relating both to privately-owned copyright and to that of the BBC. A photocopy service is available.

The BBC Written Archives have two Percy Grainger files; neither is very large, but they are of some interest as the material is unlikely to have been duplicated elsewhere. The first file, relating to Grainger as composer, includes 10 letters, three postcards and two telegrams written by Grainger himself, plus a good number of carbon copies of letters to him and BBC memoranda about him. The second file relates to the BBC's engagement of Grainger as a performing artist, and is slimmer, including eight letters written by Grainger, plus two postcards and a telegram, and BBC material similar to the first file. The following account is intended to give an idea of the substance of the more interesting items through a chronological series of extracts and summaries.

The composer file is dated 1928-1962, but in fact only includes material up to 1957. The first document on it is a BBC 'Internal Circulating Memo' dated 25 July 1928 from the conductor Stanford Robinson to the BBC Library:

> I should very much like to perform 'Sir Eglamore' ... two years ago I put it down ... [but] we had to cancel it because Schott's said they had not got the orchestral parts ...

One presumes the BBC no longer attempts to preserve every library request from their music staff, but it is fortunate that they have done so here, because this request resulted in their first formal contact with Percy Grainger, to whom a letter of enquiry was soon directed, Schott's clearly still not having the parts requested.

The first letter in the hand of Percy Grainger to have been preserved is dated Aug 6 1931 and is written from Lilla Vrán, Pevensey Bay, Sussex, to Stanford Robinson:

... I have written to Mr Watt (Mr Kipling's agent) to ask if they will give broadcasting permission to you for some such Kipling group as

(a) The Fall of the Stone
(b) Morning Song in the Jungle
(c) The Peora Hunt
(d) Tiger-Tiger
(e) Mowgli's Song against People

I am asking Schott & Co to send you *The Lads of Wamphray, The Bride's Tragedy, At Twilight, Shallow Brown* and *Scotch Strathspey & Reel,* as ... I attach especial importance to these works.

... *Shallow Brown & Scotch Strathspey—Reel* ... can be given without the guitars ...

Percy Grainger to Stanford Robinson
Aug 17 1931 Lilla Vràn, Pevensey Bay, Sussex.
... the BBC choir ... to give the Grainger-Kipling group on 26th September ... you will, I suppose need the *chamber orchestrations* ... Recessional has only organ accompaniment (unless you pref to add yr own orchestral accomp ...)

Percy Grainger to Stanford Robinson
Sep 22, 1931 Seven Cromwell Place, White Plains, New York
I have found the score of *Sir Eglamore,* but cannot find a trace of the orchestral parts—tho they existed, as I used them several times between 1904 & 1913 ...
[there follow notes about the orchestration of *Sir Eglamore*]

Percy Grainger to Leslie Woodgate
Sept 13, 1936 Lilla Vràn, Pevensey Bay, Sussex.
..... I am ordering over £40 worth of Chime bells from Hawkes for use in March. Song of Dem., Spoon River ... and also seeing that the proper vibraphone, wooden marimba, etc is available (on Hire from Hawkes) for use in Blithe Bells, Spoon River, etc ...

Percy Grainger to Walter Yeomans, Decca Record Company Ltd.
[carbon copy]
Sept 18, 1936 c/o Schott & Co Ltd, 48 Great Marlborough Street, London W.1.
I was saying to Mr Leslie Woodgate how much I admired your delightful Decca record of Sir Henry Wood's recording of my 'Mock Morris' and 'Handel in the Strand', and how much I wished such records could be made of some of my choral compositions as sung so superbly by the BBC Chorus under Mr Leslie Woodgate ... On Nov. 5 the BBC are giving a 75

minute All-Grainger choral and orchestral programme . . . I would not want any fee for playing the solo piano parts or for conducting . . .

Percy Grainger to Leslie Woodgate

Oct 22, 1936 Lilla Vrån
. . . I am distressed to find my metronome markings wrong again—*always too fast!!* . . .

There is a very interesting exchange in January 1937 between Douglas Kennedy, Director of the English Folk Dance and Song Society, and Horace Dann of the BBC. Kennedy wrote (12 January) to say that he has received many complaints over the BBC's practice of describing *Shepherd's Hey* as 'Percy Grainger's *Shepherd's Hey*', 'as if he had composed the work' rather than merely arranging it. However, the BBC refuse to change their practice, writing on 27 January that Grainger's works are 'definitely compositions and not arrangements'.

Around Christmas 1936 Grainger sent two scores to the BBC, underlining his interest in the then contemporary American composers. The music was Loeffler's *Ode to One That Fell in Battle* for eight-part unaccompanied chorus and Ives's song *General William Booth enters into Heaven*. About the latter the BBC wrote that it was 'the kind of piece that . . . we couldn't broadcast owing to its subject matter . . .'.

Grainger appears to have faded from interest over the subsequent few years, for the next material on the file dates from 1942 and takes the form of enquiries by the BBC to establish Grainger's status in Australia. They are assured that he is regarded as a famous Australian.

In 1948 the BBC included Grainger's *Danish Suite* in the Promenade Concerts, a work that they again considered in 1950, but were not able to 'offer any definite date'.

We now jump to a memo dated 8 Jan 1957 in which Leslie Woodgate notes Grainger's forthcoming 75th birthday. 'The last time we gave a full concert of Grainger's works was on 5th November 1936. Grainger may not be a "major" composer, but is a worthy and worthwhile—and entertaining—personality.' However, he was not to be successful. For example, the Head of Light Music (Sound) did not feel 'this department could embark on a full programme . . . it might be rather indigestible for the light music audience in general . . .'.

At the beginning of 1957 the Graingers were back at Lilla Vrån and Kenneth A Wright reported on 28 January: 'Grainger and his wife are staying in seclusion at Pevensey . . . Grainger has not been well, is very lame . . . and has aged considerably in the last three years . . .'.

The Grainger composer file ends with an impassioned appeal by Stanford Robinson for a Grainger programme to be mounted to mark the 75th birthday, but there was 'little now to be done . . .'.

The file of Percy Grainger as performer starts with arrangements and the contract for the 1936 concert of his music, in which he participated (fee: 8 gns). In the middle of these arrangements Grainger suddenly writes to Leslie Woodgate asking if he can try through 'Dom Anselm Hughes things, which he and I have now fully prepared', and were apparently played. The BBC's arrangements for the concert include letters clearing with the Home Office and the Ministry of Labour, Aliens Branch, Grainger's right to perform.

The file now jumps to 1948 and deals with the Promenade Concert on August 21, at which Basil Cameron conducted the first English performance of the *Danish Folk-Music* suite, with Percy Grainger taking the first piano part.

The BBC Promenade concert file that includes this concert has two cuttings, from *The Times* and the *Glasgow Herald,* both for 23 August 1948. The latter describes the performing forces as a large orchestra, with organ and piano duet, and including wooden marimba, 'vibroharp' and harmonium (though 'its presence was not discernible to eye or ear').

Later there was a concert of Grainger's music with the composer conducting the BBC Theatre Orchestra broadcast on 21 November 1948, while on 15th of that month he had recorded a three-minute talk about *Brigg Fair* for use in a schools 'Adventures in Music' programme. Lastly are the arrangements for John Amis's 1957 interview.

(ii) BBC SCRIPT REGISTRY AND PROGRAMME INDEX

The Script Registry files the written texts of BBC programmes. The Programme Index consists of a large card-index, mostly on cassetted microfilm, of works broadcast, arranged by composer. The following notes only apply to the Script Registry. There are only a few items relating to Grainger:

1 March 1949 (Home Service) 'The Story of Brigg Fair' (for schools)
5 March 1952 (Home Service) 'Shepherd's Hey . . .' (for schools)
12 June 1966 (Radio 3) 'The Originality of Percy Grainger' (by Donald Mitchell)
17 Jan 1970 (Radio 3) Programme on Grainger narrated by Ates Orga
25 June 1971 (Radio 4) 'The Composer Plays' (recorded programme introduced by Denis Matthews)

(iii) BBC SOUND ARCHIVES

Material broadcast by the BBC may have been preserved in three different ways. It might have been recorded off the air by the British Institute of Recorded Sound (BIRS) (and be available for listening at the Institute). It might have been disseminated on BBC Transcription discs to foreign radio stations, or it might have been added to the BBC Sound Archives.

The material issued on transcription discs and also that recorded off the air at the BIRS was included in Eric Hughes's discography of Grainger published in *Recordèd Sound* (Bibliography item 37). This encompasses the BBC's eight programmes of Grainger's music broadcast in 1970, most of which are also preserved in the BBC Sound Archives. The earlier material in the Sound Archives is, by and large, of fairly routine repertoire, the earliest recordings represented being *Country Gardens* (BBC Revue O/Groves: 23 Feb 1944) and *Gum-suckers' March* (RAF Central Band: 19 Sept 1944).

Possibly of most documentary interest are those recordings of Grainger's voice, and of others reminiscing about him. Perhaps John Amis's interview with Grainger, which appears, together with reminiscence by Basil Cameron, on 'Talking About Music No 20' (31 May 1961: LP 27562), is the most convenient source, though Grainger also appears on 'Portrait of a Prima Donna—Melba' (15 Dec 1960: LP 27971-2). Grainger is remembered by Eric Fenby (25 Nov 1961: LP 27566 and May 1965: LP 29775), by Eileen Joyce (22 Dec 1964: LP 29142), by Ella Grainger (14 March 1970: LP 32999), by Cyril Scott (14 June 1962: LP 32634) and by Ronald Stevenson (22 Sept 1972: St T 36563).

All enquiries in this area should be first made to the BIRS.

(iv) BBC FILM LIBRARY

Two films relating to Grainger are preserved by the BBC, and are of programmes originally broadcast in 1957 and 1970 respectively. These may be best be noted from their billings in the *Radio Times:*

Percy Grainger
APPEARS IN
CONCERT HOUR

Some of his works are performed by men of the
BBC Midland Chorus
and the composer at the piano
WITH THE
BBC Midland
Light Orchestra
(*Leader, James Hutcheon*)
Conductor, Gerald Gentry
AND
Ralph Holmes (violin)
Introduced by
Sidney Harrison
Presented by David Martin
and Peter Haysom Craddy
From the BBC's Midland
Television studio
AT 2.45

19 May 1957

9.5 pm *Colour*
Music on 2
Percy Grainger
with the voices of
RAY BARRETT as Narrator
and
ROBIN RAMSAY as Percy Grainger
Nothing of the sounds, nothing of the happenings of life should be forgotten, Of all bad habits the worst, to me, is to let resplendent things fade away
Tonight's film biography has drawn on the vast collection of material Grainger made relating to his life, and it is the first detailed study of this unusual composer-pianist.
As a child in Melbourne, Percy Grainger (1882-1961) imagined a new musical sound which would be 'as free as the waves on the shore.' But his talent as a pianist prevented him from developing this 'free music' until he was in his 60s.
Written by BASIL DEANE
Photography DAVID PROSSER
and MICHAEL FRANKLIN
Film editor COLIN HILL
Produced and directed by
WILLIAM FITZWATER †

1 March 1970

In the former, Grainger plays Grieg's *To the Spring,* and with the orchestra, *Handel In The Strand,* while the men of the BBC Midland Chorus conducted by Gerald Gentry sing *The Hunting Song of the Seeonee Pack.*

In the later film, many dubbed discs are used, but of especial interest are: free-music realisation (BBC Radiophonic Workshop), 15"; the youthful *Piano Concerto* (Ruth Nye and Martin Goldstein), 1' 03"; the *Love Verses from 'The Song of Solomon'* (Ambrosian Singers/Polyphonia Orchestra), 1' 30"; Free-music for Theremins (BBC Radiophonic Workshop, as are the remaining items), 36"; Butterfly Piano, 36"; *Sea Song*, 19" and various free-music experiments, 1' 16" and 1' 27".

The film includes interior shots of Grainger's home at White Plains.

The Percy Grainger Library Society

Stewart Manville

At the time of the founding of the Percy Grainger Library Society, the following purposes were spelled out in a preliminary charter dated June 26th, 1964:

(a) *to maintain a music research library;*
(b) *to foster knowledge and appreciation of the music of the late Percy Grainger and others and to encourage the performance of music;*
(c) *to make financial grants to orchestras and musical institutions.*

The society was registered as a New York State educational corporation under its first president, Ella Grainger. Its business has been steered by a board of directors, with day-to-day affairs in the hands of its archivist.

In practice, inevitably, the society became involved in unforseen ways that were not mentioned in the charter. For instance, as archivist my primary and most time-consuming task came to be the management of business aspects of a body of music that has attained considerable artistic and commercial success; for example, the copyrighting of music, negotiations with publishers, and supplying music to professional and amateur performers otherwise unable to obtain material.

Instead of finding it necessary to encourage the performance of music relating to Grainger, I have reached the pleasant, if occasionally trying, condition of having to attempt, sometimes at short notice and considerable expense, to keep pace with demands for performing material on the part of music festivals, recording artists, music faculties, *et al.* While in some instances this has been necessary because publishers have allowed music to go out of print, in others works have achieved a degree of popularity or actually been recorded without ever being published.

The Grainger residence at 7 Cromwell Place, White Plains, New York 10601, USA, was the home of the composer for 40 years (1921-1961) and his wife Ella lived there for 51 years, from 1928 until her death, at the age of 90, in 1979.

Ella and I acted as curators, and it is the existence of this remarkably functional house and its practical usefulness to the Percy Grainger Library Society that enabled us to continue our work without necessity of financing expensive office and storage facilities. There is a place for everything:

(a) archive copies of Percy Grainger's published work;
(b) files of his unpublished work, reproduceable by Xerox, photostat, or microfilm facilities (of differing types for differing requirements) just steps away from the house;
(c) performing material; and
(e) a vast store of diverse memorabilia, some of it still to be organised and catalogued.

The Grainger archive is somewhat different in nature from that of the Grainger Museum. In particular the Library Society's involvement in the business side of Grainger's music and its library facilities naturally complement the activities of the museum.

The existence of two fireproof vaults in the cellar of the house, installed by Grainger for the safekeeping of materials whose loss would be disastrous, is perhaps greatest among its physical assets. Still intact in the fireproof basement is the darkroom in which Grainger made his own duplicate copies of music from beautifully prepared transparencies.

People—more of them all the time, some from Great Britain and Australia—ask to see the house.

Those who had an opportunity to view the TV film about Grainger presented by the BBC early in 1970 were given a generous glimpse of 7 Cromwell Place, seen through the eyes (or lens) of Bill Fitzwater, producer of the film.*

My curatorial efforts involve an application of historic preservation techniques in resolving certain questions concerning the visual aspects of the (room) interiors—which could provide material for an entire article.

The composer's widow and I edited surviving recorded material chiefly from acetate discs, some from rehearsals and old broadcasts, for its preservation on tape. An ongoing, evergrowing sound archive is maintained—both on tape and disc—with the aim of ultimately assembling all of Grainger's compositions. In this project valuable assistance has been given by the Yale Collection of Historical Sound Recordings, Yale University Library.

On a number of occasions, house concerts have been organised in order (partly) to familiarize ourselves with some of the less-frequently performed works of Percy Grainger.

Ella and I have provided access to Grainger material for such researchers as Balough, Bird, Blanton, Callaway, Campbell, Carley, Counsell, Dreyfus, Ermey, Hopkins, Dorum, Josephson, O'Brien, Rezits, Slattery, Stang, Stevenson, Tan, Thomson, and Warren. [If by chance I have failed to mention anyone who should have been included, forgive my oversight, which can be blamed on an overcrowded memory.] These have included biographers (not only of Grainger, but of such former colleagues as Arnold Dolmetsch), film producers, writers of dissertations, conductors, professors of musicology, the curator of the Grainger Museum, the archivist of the Delius Trust, and the editor of *Studies in Music*.

As time goes by, various member of the Library Society board have taken an interest in one or other aspects of Grainger scholarship. Let me mention briefly:

—Teresa Balough's catalogue of Grainger's works, her study of Grainger and Kipling, and her work on English Gothic Music deriving from Grainger's association with Dom Anselm Hughes;

—David Josephson's interest in Grainger's piano repertory, his compositional procedures, and his relationship to the cultural, musical and intellectual milieus in which he lived;

—Ralph Stang's research into the literary sources of Grainger's songs—and later efforts (which continue) to have various of Ella's poems set to music;

—and the Yale Library (Richard Warren's) effort to assemble a more complete set of Grainger's piano recordings than the artist himself managed to keep on hand.

* See p 245

In the course of my work with Ella, I succeeded in having her write down a number of reminiscences. Rather than become nostalgic—which would have been fine, but wasn't Ella's manner—she tended toward the useful or practical. Let me include an example—only one of several that can't all be accommodated at this writing but which will ultimately invest a more extended work concerning Ella's life. Here she discusses the assembling of suitable glassware for the 'musical glasses' effect in Grainger's *Tribute to Foster*:

* * *

In Search of the Perfect Note

by Ella Grainger

Percy Grainger had a taste for unusual instruments, which he included in his compositions, such as staff bells, marimbas, xylophones, drums—on which I had been partaking in concerts. So when he mentioned musical glasses, for which he had been writing parts for the chorus in his composition, *Tribute to Stephen Foster,* I was all ready and willing to assist him in finding them.

We went to many stores and warehouses that specialized in glass, and there we had to explain our problem of finding glasses of the right note. Hence a great number of glasses were assembled and offered for us to try out. Assistants in the various warehouses and shops were really quite intrigued and helpful. When we also demanded buckets of water for use in tuning, they were equally willing to rush around with pots and cans for that purpose. They were patient with us. Each glass that we tried had to be either one note or another: C sharp, D sharp, E sharp, F sharp, G sharp, A sharp—all six sharps in several octaves.

Eighty glasses, one each for a chorus of 80, and more, if needed. Each glass had to have a small amount of water, for the sake of dipping the finger-tips, because one had to have a wet finger with which to rub the rim of the glass. Also, water was to be added to make the note of the right pitch, more or less, to make it sharp or flat. If a glass was too sharp, a certain amount of water added would make it less sharp. Hence our labour lasted some hours.

That the assistants in the shops were willing to give us so much time and serious attention was due to their kindness and perseverance, plus the 'Grainger charm' perhaps? Percy had this invincible quality of charm (plus insistence) that was very difficult to resist. I experienced it from time to time in many various ways. And, when asked by some friend if Percy did not mesmerize me, my answer was, 'Yes, if someone very clever and charming persuades one into doing something one would not otherwise do, then indeed he mesmerizes me'.

Thus a great many glasses were gradually assembled, and they had to be tuned, as I said above, and the tuning waterline had to be painted on each glass in black oil paint, which was an easy task for me, who had been an art student and therefore glad to wield a paint brush.

The *tone* of a musical glass is produced by rubbing the rim of the glass with a wet finger-tip. For that purpose there should be a small quantity of water (as well as for the proper 'tuning').

Then, in order to let each member of the chorus have a glass steady enough to make the note ring, every glass had to have a foot so that it could be held safely on the knee or on a chair (or sometimes on a table). These feet were cut out of sturdy cardboard, each with an identifying note written on it. Later the cardboard feet were replaced by more sturdy wooden bases.

In order to be *certain* to produce tone, the finger should be re-moistened from time to time. There is no tone from a dry finger-tip. Also, the fingers should be clean. No hand cream, please, because a slightly greasy finger-tip will prevent tone.

When the 80 (or more) glasses enter at the lull of the orchestra, at bars 77, 81, 91, 102, etc., they make quite a breathtaking effect, something like the drone of insects on a summer's eve.

Select, annotated bibliography

Lewis Foreman

Substantial bibliographies of Grainger have been appended to several of the items cited below (items 8, 32, 38-40, 73, 75) and these should be consulted for further literature, especially by Grainger himself. The following is intended to cover only those items that the compiler has found to be most valuable, up-to-date, or difficult to trace through other channels. Some forthcoming items have been included.

AMIS, John *see* 80.
1. ANDERSON, Peter James: *The Innovative Music of Percy Grainger—an examination of the origins and development of free-music*. MM Thesis, University of Melbourne, 1979 134pp.
    Part I explores Grainger's attitudes to music, not so much by analysing his music, but rather his writings. Part II shows how Free-Music was the culmination of his musical philosophy—what he believed to be the 'ideal music of the future'. Part III analyses the free-music pieces in the light of their realization at the University of Melbourne. Appendices include the score of *Free Music No 1* and *No 2*.
2. ARMSTRONG, *Sir* Thomas: 'The Frankfort Group' *Proceedings of the Royal Musical Association LXXXV* 1958/59 pp 1-16, Paper read on 17 November 1958.
3. BALOUGH, Teresa: *A Complete Catalogue of the Works of Percy Grainger*. Nedlands, University of Western Australia, Dept. of Music, 1975. XVI, 258pp *(Music Monograph No 2.)* In three sequences: 'Alphabetical Listing and Index of Works'; 'Generic Headings'; 'Instrumentation [classified list]'. This was the first really extensive scholarly listing of Grainger's music, and in spite of certain omissions a notable achievement. *See also* 89.
4. —'The English Gothic Music of Dom Anselm Hughes and Percy Grainger' *Studies in Music 13* 1979 pp 63-65.
5. —'Kipling and Grainger' *Studies in Music II* 1979 pp 74-110. Includes table of 'comparative dates of musical and poetical compositions' [pp 104-5] and 'chronological dates of composition for Grainger's Kipling settings' [pp 109-110].
6. —'Percy Grainger' *Grainger Journal I* no 1 Spring 1978 pp 5-8. Excellent short introduction to the man and his ideas, citing a range of largely unfamiliar sources.
6A.—*A Musical Genius from Australia: selected writings by and about Percy Grainger*. Nedlands, University of Western Australia, Dept. of Music, *forthcoming*. *(Music Monograph No 4.)*
7. BAUER, M: *Iwan Knorr—ein gedenkblatt*. Frankfurt am Main, Reitz und Koehler, 1916. 35pp. While not discussing Grainger, provides a good brief portrait of his teacher. In German.
8. BIRD, John: *Percy Grainger*, Paul Elek, 1976. xvi, 317pp (A paperback edition is announced by Faber for 1982). The standard musical biography. Prefaced by brief notes signed by Benjamin Britten and Peter Pears, and by Leopold Stokowski. Appendices include a catalogue of Grainger's published compositions; Grainger's statement on 'Free Music' dated December 6, 1938; Grainger's essay (from the Preface to *Spoon River*) 'To Conductors and to Those Forming, or in Charge of, Amateur Orchestras, High School, College and Music School Orchestras and Chamber-Music Bodies'; discographies of performances by Grainger and by others, and a catalogue of Duo-Art piano rolls. *See also* 9.
9. —'Percy Grainger—a postscript' *Studies in Music II* 1979 pp 111-114. Concerned with the persisting problems of scattered sources for the study of Grainger, and traces how the present interest in him originated. 'The more I learned about Grainger the more I viewed his life as a tragedy. I hope that by tracing some of the misfortunes and mistakes of his career it will perhaps act as a pointer for the future rescue and restoration operation needed before Grainger's artistic genius can be fully appreciated.'

10. —'Percy Grainger's Concert Repertoire' *Grainger Journal 1* no 2 December 1978 pp 33-43. List of works played and conducted by Grainger, compiled from surviving programmes, and Grainger's own recordings. A list of additions compiled by Elizabeth Wright appeared in *Grainger Journal 2* no 1 July 1979 pp 20-23.

11. BOWEN, Richard: 'The Musical Rebel' *Music & Musicians* July 1955 p 9.

12. BRITISH INSTITUTE OF RECORDED SOUND: 'Grainger, Percy (Aldridge)' IN THEIR *Music by British Composers of the Twentieth Century–a handlist of tape recordings in the Institute's collection.* BIRS, 1967 pp 22-23. A typescript listing, the precursor of Eric Hughes' later discography (37) but still useful for the dates and times of the original broadcasts, or other sources.

13. CAHN, Peter: *Das Hoch'sche Konservatorium in Frankfurt am Main (1878-1978)* Frankfurt am Main, Verlag Waldemar Kramer, 1979 394pp. In German.

14. —'Percy Grainger's Frankfurt Years' *Studies in Music 12* 1978 pp 110-113. Valuable research in German-language sources, translated for the first time by Professor Martin Lindsay of the University of Western Australia. Includes two appendices—-I [p 110] 'study periods and teachers' of Scott, O'Neill, Gardiner, Grainger, Quilter, Braunfels, Franckenstein, Hodapp, Sandby, Carlo Fischer, Johanna Renck, Zilcher, Pauline Klimsch and Mimi Kwast (guest listener); II [p 111] 'Early Criticism of Grainger from *General-Anzeiger* and *Frankfurter Zeitung*.'

COVELL, Roger *see* 80.

CROSS, Burnett *see* 80.

15. DREYFUS, Kay: 'The Adelaide Grainger Collection Transferred to the Grainger Museum' *Miscellanea Musicologica 9* 1977 pp 49-71.

16. —'The Grainger Manuscripts in the Sibley Library—a commentary [part I]' *Grainger Journal 2* no 2 February 1980 pp 19-32. Annotated list of manuscripts held in the Sibley Music Library, pointing comparisons and asking questions. The works mentioned include: *The First Chantey, Green Bushes, The Hunter in his Career, In a Nutshell, The Merry King, The Merry Wedding, A Reiver's Neck-Verse, Shallow Brown, Sir Eglamore,* and *Walking Tune.*

17. —'The Grainger Manuscripts in the Sibley Library—a commentary part II' *Grainger Journal 3* no 1 August 1980 pp 24-28. Notes on sketches and fragments of *The Lonely Desert Man Sees the Tents of the Happy Tribes, Norwegian Idyll, The Rival Brothers, Molly on the Shore, Song of Solomon,* and arrangements of six works by other composers.

18. —'The Grainger Museum' *APRA Journal 2* no. 1 January 1976; reprinted in *Grainger Journal 1* no 1 Spring 1978 pp 9-13.

19. —*Music by Percy Aldridge Grainger.* Parkville [Victoria, Australia] University of Melbourne, Grainger Museum, 1978 336pp (*Percy Grainger Music Collection Part I*). The first of a projected series of catalogues. Arranged in fifteen groups: 'Published Music—Original Compositions and Folksong Settings' and 'Selective Listing of Sets of Parts'; 'Published Music—Arrangements, Transcriptions, Paraphrases and Editions of Other Composer's Music' and 'Selective Listing of Sets of Parts'; 'Manuscripts—Original Compositions and Folksong Settings'; 'Manuscripts—Arrangements, Transcriptions, Paraphrases and Editions of Other Composers' Music'; 'Photostat Copies of Manuscripts—Original Compositions and Folksong Settings'; 'Photostat Copies of Manuscripts—Arrangements, Transcriptions, Paraphrases and Editions of Other Composers' Music'; 'Dieline Transparencies—Original Compositions and Folksong Settings'; 'Dieline Transparencies—Arrangements, Transcriptions, Paraphrases and Editions of Other Composers' Music'; 'Dieline Print-offs—Original Compositions and Folksong Settings'; 'Dieline Print-offs—Arrangements, Transcriptions, Paraphrases and Editions of Other Composers' Music'; 'Stokowski Orchestrations'; 'Adelaide Stencilled Music'; 'Folksong Collections'; 'Music for Roller Desk'; 'Adelaide Grainger Collection Transferred to the Grainger Museum December 1975'.

20. —*Percy Grainger's Kipling Settings–a study of the manuscript sources.* Nedlands, University of Western Australia, Dept. of Music, announced for 1981. viii, 132pp (*Music Monograph No 3.*)

A general consideration of the bibliographic problems affecting a study of Percy Aldridge Grainger's vast, scattered, and to some extent confusing legacy of music manuscripts is followed by a specific study of the manuscripts of his settings of texts by Rudyard Kipling. The layout of this latter 'bibliographic chronology' reflects a two-fold aim. In its chronological organisation it emphasises *compositional* patterns, presenting a picture of

Grainger's involvement with Kipling 'as it happened', enabling observation of periods of preoccupation with particular texts or types of setting, the intensity or otherwise of compositional activity and so on. In its bibliographic aspects, it emphasises the unfolding history of each setting as seen in relation to surviving manuscript material. Full publication details are given where appropriate, and the locations of manuscripts are specified. Some reference is made to the performance histories of the settings, though this is not a central concern of the study. Supporting annotations are drawn from Grainger's correspondence, and other ancillary material. Though concerned only with one group of Grainger's compositions, the study points towards more general aspects of his aspirations and development as a composer.

21. FENNELL, Frederick: 'Basic Band Repertory—Lincolnshire Posy' *The Instrumentalist* May 1980 pp 42-48 ['Lisbon' and 'Horkstow Grange']; September 1980 pp 15-20 ['Rufford Park Poachers']; October 1980 pp 28-36 ['The Brisk Young Sailor', 'Lord Melbourne', 'The Lost Lady Found'].

22. FRED, Herbert W: 'Percy Grainger's Music for Wind Band' *Journal of Band Research I* no 1 Autumn 1964 pp 10-16.

23. GOLDMAN, Richard Franko: *The Band's Music* Pitman, 1939 xviii, 442pp. With a foreword by Percy Grainger [pp ix-xv] and notes on Grainger's works for band [pp 204-210].

24. —'Percy Grainger's "Free Music" ' *Juilliard Review II* Fall 1955 pp 37-47. *See also 80.*

25. GOOSSENS, Sir Eugene: 'The Unconventional Composer' *Music & Musicians* April 1961 pp 9, 41. Includes a photograph of Grainger, Goossens and Cyril Scott together during 1958.

26. GRAINGER, Percy A: 'Collecting With The Phonograph—the old singers and the new method' *Journal of the Folk-Song Society III* no 12 May 1908. pp 147-162. Apart from the first and the last two leaves the whole issue is by Grainger (paged 147-242). The article cited is followed by 'The Impress of Personality in Traditional Singing' [pp 163-166] which includes notes on Joseph Taylor, George Gouldthorpe and George Wray. After a note on 'signs and accents used in this journal' [pp 167-169] there follow transcriptions of 20 folksongs collected by Grainger, with extensive notes and variant versions. The tunes are: 'Six Dukes Went A-Fishin' ' (3 versions); 'The "Rainbow" '; 'The North Country Maid'; 'Rufford Park Poachers'; 'I Wish My Baby It Was Born'; 'The White Hare'; 'Geordie'; 'Lord Bateman' (2 versions); 'Lord Melbourne (The Duke of Marlborough)'; 'Merican Frigate or, Paul Jones'; 'Bold William Taylor'; (2 versions); 'The Gipsy's Wedding Day'; 'Shepherd's Daughter'; 'The Merry King'; 'Storm Along'; 'Stormy Lowlands'; 'Dollar and a 'Alf a Day'; 'Santa Anna' (2 versions); 'Tom's Gone to Ilo' (2 versions); and, 'Shallow Brown'.

27. —'Foreword to "Bold William Taylor" ' *Grainger Journal 3* no 1 August 1980 pp 7-9. The foreword hitherto only available in typescript with the unpublished Grainger setting (announced for Thames' second volume of Grainger songs). Here without Grainger's 'Key to Dialect Pronunciation'.

28. —'Impress of Personality in Unwritten Music' *Musical Quarterly* July 1915 pp 416-435. Includes two plates [facsimiles of 'excerpt from "Random Round" ' and from 'a March for Piano and Orchestra by Percy Grainger']. This is a wide-ranging and passionate survey. '... let us make noble efforts to preserve ... adequate printed records of what now still remains of a phase of music which ... can never be reborn again'. *See also 61*

29. —'P.A. Grainger's Remarks About His Hill Song No 1' *Grainger Journal 1* no 2 December 1978 pp 14-23. Dated September 1949, an extended statement with musical examples, of various technical procedures that were innovatory at the time the work was conceived and scored.

30. —*Photos of Rose Grainger and Three Short Accounts of Her Life by Herself in Her Own Handwriting, reproduced by Percy Grainger* ... Privately printed, 1923 46ff.

31. GRIFFITHS, Helen: 'Notes from the Grainger Museum' *Grainger Journal 3* no 1 August 1980 pp 3-4. An appeal for funds to preserve the garments and personal effects in the museum.

32. GUEMPLE, Mary Jolliff: *Percy Grainger's Contributions to the Musical World.* MM Thesis, Baylor University, 1959 164pp. Includes a 'Glossary of Blue-eyed English' [pp 137-142] and an early attempt at a Grainger catalogue of works [pp 143-154].

33. HOPKINS, John: 'Percy Grainger (1882-1961)' IN *Australian Composition in the Twentieth Century* edited by Frank Callaway and David Tunley. Melbourne, OUP 1978 pp

18-28. Good short account by conductor of Grainger's music. Followed by useful source notes and an 80-item discography valuable for its inclusion of Australian recordings and ABC unpublished material.

34. HOWES, Frank: [Grainger] IN HIS *The English Musical Renaissance*. Secker & Warburg, 1966 pp 196-197. Written by an admirer of Grainger, though of an earlier generation who did not fully understand him. 'His accompaniment ... to ... *Six Dukes went a-fishing* is impervious to changes of taste ... After he settled in America (1914) he produced some choral music, which has not crossed the ocean ... he made a distinctive if small contribution to the musical life of his time.'

35. —'Percy Grainger' *Recorded Sound* Summer 1961 pp 96-98.

36. HUGHES, Charles W: 'Percy Grainger, Cosmopolitan Composer' *Musical Quarterly* April 1937 pp 127-136. Includes plates of 'Percy Grainger composing at his Bilhorn Reed Organ' and facsimile of 'Page 1 of the manuscript of Percy Grainger's *Hill Song No 1* (dated March 16, 1901) ...'

37. HUGHES, Eric: 'The Recorded Works of Percy Grainger' *Recorded Sound* no 45-46 January-April 1972 pp 38-43. Reprinted in reduced facsimile in 72. 'This list of recordings of Grainger's music attempts to include all important commercially published discs, but some omissions are made in the case of frequently encountered works.'

38. JOSEPHSON, David: 'Grainger, (George) Percy (Aldridge)' IN *The New Grove 7* pp 614-619. An excellent up-to-date account with an extended catalogue of works and a good bibliography.

39. —'Percy Grainger—Country Gardens and Other Curses' *Current Musicology 15* 1973 pp 56-63. 'A more immediately fruitful approach to understanding Grainger is bibliographical ... Much of it, however, was laudatory and repetitive, and marred by garbled stories and outright misinformation. We must be careful even with primary materials.' A well-informed and reliable bibliographical study, with a valuable list of sources cited.

40. —'Thomas Carl Slattery—The Wind Music of Percy Aldridge Grainger' [a review] *Current Musicology 16* 1973 pp 79-91. A very long and detailed review. 'Pioneering and admirable in its breadth, the dissertation is nevertheless deeply flawed and terribly uneven'. The review, however, is of more value for its further exploration of bibliographical questions than for its probing of any shortcomings in the thesis.

41. —'Margaret Hee-Leng Tan—The Free-Music of Percy Grainger' [a review]*Current Musicology 17* 1974 pp 130-133. Critical review which challenges the standard of scholarship in it.

42. —'Percy Grainger—some problems and approaches' *Current Musicology 18* 1974 pp 55-68. 'We have good reason to suspect that Grainger was aware of a waning of his creative impulse by mid-life, even though he seems never to have acknowledged it'. 'This is the fourth and last in a series of writings conceived ... as an essay in bibliography, seeking to provide the foundation for a thorough and broadly-based study of the life and music of Percy Grainger.
—See also 81

LAUNCHBURY, Simon *see 62*.

43. LAWRENCE, A F R: 'Records of Percy Grainger as an Interpreter' *Recorded Sound* no 45-46 January-April 1972 pp 43-48. Includes an 'Index to Composers and Titles of Works Recorded by Grainger ...', and 'Gramophone records made from piano rolls played by Percy Grainger'. Reprinted in reduced facsimile in 72.

44. LOWE, Rachel: *A Descriptive catalogue with checklists of the Letters and Related Documents in the Delius collection of the Grainger Museum ...* Delius Trust, [Boosey & Hawkes], 1981. vi, 323 pp. (Numbered edition of 500 copies.)
Checklists, chronology and calendars of the letters of Percy, Rose and Ella Grainger to Frederick and Jelka Delius, with appendices of Percy Grainger's footnotes/marginalia, Related documents found with the letters and a list of newsclippings. Opening sentences have been quoted for all Delius' letters for identification purposes, but in the case of Grainger the Grainger Museum preferred that salient sentences should be quoted, regardless of their position in the text.

45. MURRAY-SMITH, Stephen: 'Intellectual Vandalism at University' *The Age* 8 June 1979. Reprinted in *Grainger Journal 2* no 1 July 1979 p 24. Newspaper story of a move by

the University of Melbourne to demolish the Grainger Museum to make way for new university buildings.

NYAGAARD, Kaare K *see* 80.

46. O'BRIEN, Jane R: *Percy Grainger: English folk song and the Grainger English folk song collection.* PhD Thesis, La Trobe University, 1979.

47. OLSEN, Sparre: *Percy Grainger.* Oslo, Det Norske Samlaget, 1963 93pp In Norwegian. Personal, well-illustrated account by Grainger's Norwegian composer friend. Handicapped by its lack of an index. An English translation, in typescript, by Bent Vanberg edited by Stewart Manville, is available from the Grainger Library Society.

48. ORGA, Ates: 'Percy Grainger 1882-1961' *Music & Musicians* March 1970 pp 28-36, 70. When it first appeared it was the best account of Grainger's achievement that had appeared. Pages 33, 35 and 37 contain advertisements, the first and last relating to Grainger. The song *A Song of Autumn* follows on pp 38-40.

O'SHAUGHNESSY, Patrick *see* 80.

49. OULD, Barry Peter: 'Ella Grainger' *Grainger Journal 2* no 1 July 1979 pp 4-5. Includes a list of Ella Grainger's music and poetry.

50. PALMER, Christopher: 'Delius and Percy Grainger' *Music & Letters* October 1971 pp 418-425. 'In the last analysis, however, the main spiritual force which impelled Grainger and Delius towards each other was undoubtedly their common response to folk art.' Some of this article is recast in 51.

51. —[Grainger] IN HIS *Delius—Portrait of a cosmopolitan* Duckworth, 1976 pp 78-92. Extended comparison of Delius and Grainger includes evocative and knowledgeable account of Grainger. 'Grainger was like Delius a nomad, a footless wanderer, a cosmopolitan'.

52. —'Grainger on Record' IN *Building a Library 2–a listener's guide to record collecting,* edited by John Lade. OUP, 1980 pp 161-166. Edited transcript of talk on BBC 'Record Review' programme.

53. PARKER, Douglas Charles: *Percy Aldridge Grainger–a study.* New York, G Schirmer nd [1918] 36pp.

54. —'Grainger's *Colonial Song' Musical Standard* 5 May 1917 p 297.

55. —'Grainger the Experimentalist' *Musical Opinion* May 1917 p 483. 'The enormous popularity of one or two of Grainger's short compositions . . . is calculated to obscure the fact that he is one of the most eager and curious experimentalists of the present day.'

56. —'Percy Grainger' *Grainger Journal 2* no 1 July 1979 pp 14-19. A chapter from the previously unpublished 'Memoirs' of the Glasgow critic.

57. PEARS, [Sir] Peter: 'A Note on Percy Grainger' *Musical Times* March 1970 pp 267-268. A brief personal account written before the 1970 London 'Grainger Festival'.

58. —'Percy Grainger—the Kipling of Music' *The American Review of Reviews* September 1916 pp 332-333. Notes Grainger's establishment in the US and summarises Cyril Scott's article (69).

REESE, Gustav *see* 80.

59. ROCKWELL, Joan: *Evald Tang Kristensen–a lifelong adventure in folksong* Danish Folklore Society (c/o Danish Folklore Archives, Birketinget 6, DK-2300 Copenhagen S, Denmark.) 1981 500pp.

60. 'Salute to Percy Grainger, Volume 2' *Grainger Journal 1* no 1 1978 pp 27-30. Eye-opening account of the forces used in the recording of Decca SXL 6872, adapting the music to the forces available and procuring the performing materials.

61. SAPIR, E: 'Discussion and Correspondence—Percy Grainger and Primitive Music' *American Anthropologist* October 1916 pp 592-597. Commentary on, and extensive quotation from, Grainger's article in the *Musical Quarterly* (28). 'Grainger's ideal falls nowise short of that of the scientific ethnologist . . . Grainger's enthusiastic proposal doubtless meets with little more than a humorous smile from the average musician. To the ethnologist it opens up a vista full of interest and profit.'

62. SCHOTT & Co: [Two typescript, photocopied, lists.]
(1) *A Listing of Works by Percy Grainger held in the archives of Scott & Co. Ltd.,* compiled by Alan Woolgar, 9ff.
(2) *Grainger: works for orchestra and chamber ensemble etc.*
'This listing has been prepared to indicate the instrumentation of available versions of

works. Prepared by Simon Launchbury, Schott & Co Ltd Hire Library.' September 1980 26ff.

63. SCOTT, Cyril: 'Egotism and Landladies' IN HIS *My Years of Indiscretion* Mills & Boon, 1924 pp 24-31. Includes background to the Frankfort Group and Grainger.

64. —'The Frankfurt Group' IN HIS *Bone of Contention–life story and confessions* The Aquarian Press, 1969 pp 68-73.

65. —'Grainger, Percy Aldridge' IN *Cobbett's Cyclopedia of Chamber Music* OUP, 1929, 1963 Vol 1 pp 486-488.

66. —'Percy Grainger' *Musical Times* April 1961 p 245.

67. —*Percy Grainger–a course in contemporary musical biography* NY, G Schirmer, 1919.

68. —'Percy Grainger—the man and the music' *Musical Times* July 1957 pp 368-369. 'Grainger likes and believes in the "vulgar" . . . he likes it with the same ardour that he dislikes to be associated with anything that might be termed "artistic".'

69. —'Percy Grainger, The Music and the Man' *Musical Quarterley II* 1916 pp 425-433.

70. —'Percy Grainger—the music and the man [Appendix III] IN HIS *The Philosophy of Modernism–its connection with music* Kegan Paul, nd; The Waverley Book Co., nd pp 125-135.

71. SLATTERY, Thomas C: 'The Life and Work of Percy Grainger' *The Instrumentalist* November 1967 pp 42-43; December 1967 pp 47-49; January 1968 pp 36-38.

72. —*Percy Grainger–the inveterate innovator* Evanston, Illinois, The Instrumentalist Co., 1974 xi, 308pp. The first full-length published account of Grainger's life and work; draws some material from 74. Includes reprint of 37, 43, 79. With an extended bibliography and a pioneering catalogue of works. Includes Grainger's Will as an appendix. No index.

73. —'Two Hill Songs—an analystical study' *Journal of Band Research* Fall 1971.

74. —*The Wind Music of Percy Aldridge Grainger*. Ph D Thesis: University of Iowa, February 1967. UM 67-9104. xii 252pp. Reviewed at 40.

75. STANG, Ralph: 'Eulogy—for a very dear friend' *Grainger Journal 2* no 2 February 1980 pp 3-7. The funeral oration for Ella Grainger, White Plains, New York, 20 July 1979.

76. STANHOPE, David: 'Correspondence' *Grainger Journal 2* no 2 February 1980 pp 10-11. 'New performances continue to make the same old blunders . . . *Rufford Park Poachers* . . . says one *crochet* equals 132, whereas it should be one *quaver* . . . two piano version of *Lincolnshire Posy* is riddled with mistakes—the opening verse of *Lisbon* is even in the wrong key . . . *Pastoral* from *Nutshell Suite* . . . *The Two Sisters* from the *Danish Folk-Music Suite* . . .'

77. —'Understanding Grainger' *Grainger Journal 3* no 1 pp 16-20 Excerpt from a radio talk given in Adelaide in 1979.

78. STEVENSON, Ronald: 'Random Relics of Percy Grainger by one of his pen-pals' *Grainger Journal 1* no 2 December 1978 pp 12-13 Brief notes on Grainger's letters to Stevenson.

79. STONEHILL, Gerald: 'Piano Rolls played by Percy Grainger' *Recorded Sound* no 45-46 January-April 1971 p 49. Reprinted in 72.

80. *STUDIES IN MUSIC*: [first Grainger issue] *10* 1976. Contains: 'Interview with Percy Grainger' by John Amis pp 4-8. (reprinted in *Grainger Journal 2* no 2 pp 12-15, 18 with the addition of musical examples not used in the original; from BBC Transcription disc 106543).
'A Consideration of Grainger' by David Josephson pp 8-10.
'Some Notes on Percy Grainger' by Richard Franko Goldman pp 10-11.
'Percy Grainger—a personal view' by Roger Covell pp 12-13.
'Percy Grainger and Early Music' by Gustave Reese pp 13-14.
Photograph of sculptured head of Grainger by Dr Kaare K Nyagaard
'Grainger as I Saw Him' by Burnett Cross p 16 (captions) p 17-18 (photographs).
'Percy Grainger—the English folk-song collection' by Patrick O'Shaughnessy pp 19-24; reprinted in *Grainger Journal 1* no 1 Spring 1978 pp 31-36.

81. TALL, David: 'Percy Grainger and Scotland' *Grainger Journal 1* no 2 December 1978 pp 24-32. Reviews Grainger's musical links with Scotland and considers the extent to which they are covered by the Grainger material in the National Library of Scotland. Notes on individual items.

82. TAN, Margaret Hee- Leng: *The Free-Music of Percy Grainger*. DMA Thesis: Juilliard School of Music, 1971 258pp. The substance of the text published as 'Free-Music of Percy Grainger' *Recorded Sound* no 45-46 January-April 1972 pp 21-38. Includes Grainger's

1949 notes on Hill Song No 1. Reviewed in 41.

83. TAYLOR, Robert Lewis: *The Running Pianist* New York, Doubleday, 1950 (Originally published in *The New Yorker* 31 January 1948 pp 29-32; 7 February 1948 pp 32-36; 14 February 1948 pp 32-34).

84. THACKER, E C: *Catalogue Raisonné of Material Concerning Percy Grainger and his music which is housed in the Music and Percy Grainger Museum, Melbourne.* MA Thesis: Melbourne University, 1965.

85. THOMSON, Bob: *Unto Brigg Fair* 19-page essay bound into the sleeve of 12" LP record (Leadersound LEA 4050). Includes many photographs and the words of the songs.

86. WATANABE, Ruth: 'The Grainger Manuscripts in the Sibley Library' *Grainger Journal 2* no 1 July 1979 pp 9-13.

87. WILLETTS, Pamela J: 'An Autograph Manuscript of Percy Grainger' *British Museum Quarterly XXV* 1962 pp 18-19. About the autograph piano score of 'Country Gardens', Add MSS 50823.

88. —'The Percy Grainger Collection' *British Museum Quarterly XXVII* Winter 1963-64 pp 65-71.
'Mrs Ella Grainger . . . has generously added to her previous gift of the piano score of Country Gardens a large and representative collection of autograph manuscripts . . .Add MSS 50867-87.' (List of manuscripts pp 69-71.)
WOOLGAR, Alan *see* 62.

89. WRIGHT, Elizabeth: 'Additions to Teresa Balough's Catalogue of Percy Aldridge Grainger's Compositions for Piano Solo' *Studies in Music 13* 1979 pp 77-81.
List of 18 items. *See* 3, 10 (note).

Addresses

The following list of addresses gives the main points of contact for those requiring to research or perform Grainger's music. In cases of difficulty the Grainger Society will often be able to assist. A few addresses relating to recordings issued by college performers are only available from the issuing bodies, and these addresses are given after the appropriate entries in the discography. Current addresses of UK record companies may be found in the *Gramophone Classical Catalogue*.

PRIMARY CONTACTS

Percy Grainger Library
　Stewart Manville
　7 Cromwell Place
　White Plains
　New York 10601
　USA

Percy Grainger Society
　Chairman and Editor
　The Grainger Journal:
　David Tall
　21 Laburnum Avenue
　Kenilworth
　Warwickshire CV8 2DR

　Secretary and Music Archive:
　Barry Peter Ould
　84A Coltman Street
　Hull HU3 2SJ
　North Humberside

　Publicity and Grainger
　Centenary Co-ordinator:
　Stephen Lloyd
　41 Marlborough Road
　Luton
　Beds

　Sound Archivist: John Bird
　56 Leathwaite Road
　London SW11 6RS

Grainger Museum
　University of Melbourne
　Parkville
　Victoria 3052
　Australia

PUBLISHERS
　Schott & Co Ltd
　48 Great Marlborough Street
　London W1V 2BN

　Schott Sohne
　Weihergarten 65
　Mainz
　W Germany

G Schirmer Inc
866 Third Avenue
New York
N Y 10022
USA

Boosey & Hawkes Music Publishers Ltd
295 Regent Street
London W1R 8JH

Faber Music Ltd
3 Queen Square
London WC1N 3AU

Oxford University Press
Music Dept
Ely House
37 Dover Street
London W1X 4AH

Thames Publishing
14 Barlby Road
London W1O 6AR

Universal Edition
2/3 Fareham Street
Dean Street
London W1V 4DU

LIBRARIES AND ARCHIVES
BBC
Broadcasting House
London W1A 1AA

BBC Film Library
Windmill Road
Brentford
Middlesex

BBC Written Archives Centre
Caversham Park
Reading
Berks RG4 8TZ

British Institute of Recorded Sound
29 Exhibition Road
London SW7

British Library
Department of Manuscripts
British Museum
Bloomsbury
London W1N 9AE

British Music Information Centre
10 Stratford Place
London W1N 9AE

Central Music Library
160 Buckingham Palace Road
London SW1

English Folk Dance and Song Society
Cecil Sharp House
2 Regents Park Road
London NW1

Det Kongelige Bibliotek (Royal Library)
Christians Brygge 8
DK-1219 Copenhagen
Denmark

Library of Congress
Music Division
Washington DC 20540
USA

National Library of Scotland
George IV Bridge
Edinburgh
Scotland

New York Public Library
Music Division at Lincoln Center
111 Amsterdam Avenue
New York
N Y 10023
USA

Sibley Music Library
Eastman School of Music
26 Gibbs Street
Rochester
New York 14604
USA

Welholme Galleries
Welholme Road
Great Grimsby
South Humberside DN32 9LP

Yale Historical Sound
  Recordings Collection
Yale Community
98 Wall Street
New Haven
Connecticut 06520
USA

PUBLISHERS OF BOOKS AND JOURNALS

The Instrumentalist Co
1418 Lake Street
Evanston
Illinois 60204
USA

Studies in Music
University of Western Australia
Department of Music
Nedlands
Western Australia 6009

University Microfilms
300 North Zeeb Road
Ann Arbor
Michigan 48106
USA
or 18 Bedford Row
London WC1R 4EJ

see also: Grainger Society,
Grainger Museum

SOURCES OF RECORDINGS

Australian World Record Club
605 Camberwell Road
Hartwell
Victoria 3124
Australia

Direction Dean Street
97-99 Dean Street
Oxford Street
London W1
(British dealer which stocks
Australian imports)

International Piano Archives
c/o Department of Music
University of Maryland
College Park
Maryland 20742
USA

Move Records
Box 266
Carlton South 3053
Australia

Records International
PO Box 1140
Goleta
California 93116
USA
(US dealer who covers Australian imports)

See also: Grainger Society,
British Institute of Recorded
Sound

INDEX

In this index the works and arrangements of Percy Grainger are entered directly in their own right, and are italicised. Folksongs are similarly entered but within single quotation marks and are not italicised. Works by other composers are entered under that composer's name. Italicised page-numbers refer to illustrations and not to textual matter.

The catalogue of works and the discography are not included in the index, but the bibliography and the annotations thereto are.

Dett, N, *20, 39, 199*
Dialect, 66, 130, 144
Died for Love, 30, 54, 63, 109, 124, 201
Dilkes, Neville, 197
Diton, Carl R, 39
Dollar and a half a day,
Dolmetsch family, 68; Arnold, 148
Doveton, Robin, 198
Dowland, John, 109, 218, 231
Dreyfus, Kay, 207, 218, 248, 252
Dublin Bay, 110, see also *Lincolnshire Posy*
Dufay, Guillaume, 231
Duke of Marlborough, 107
Dulcitone, 81
Dunn, Sir Vivian, 198
Dunstable, John, 232
Duo-Art Reproducing piano, 44, 114, 161, 162, *163,* 197, 251, 256
Dvorak, Antonin, 195
Dykes, John Bacchus, 212

Early music, 256
Early One Morning (vocal), 124; (orchestra), 193
Eastern Intermezzo, 196; see also *Youthful Suite*
Eastman Rochester Orchestra, 194
Eastman School of Music, 194, 204
Eastman Wind Ensemble, 193
Easy Grainger, The, 206
Edison Bell phonograph, 19, 55, 58, 59, 114, 118, 145, 158
Egyptian double reeds, 103
Elastic scoring, 75ff, 138, 139ff
Elberfeld Concert Society, 34
Elder Conservatory, *see* Adelaide
Electronic music, 74, 111
Elgar, Sir Edward, 98, 232
Elizabethan Singers, 198
Ellington, Duke, 161, 168; *Creole Love Call, Creole Rhapsody,* 161
Elwes, Gervase, 28, 29, 30, 131
England: Grainger comes to, 26
English Chamber Orchestra, 195
English Church Music, 56
English Dance, 19, 34, 91ff, *105*
English dialects, 144
English Folk Dance and Song Society, 158, 243
English Folksongs and Popular Tunes, 55
English Gothic Music, 109, 111, 248, 251
English Morris Dance, see Shepherd's Hey
English song, 135
English Waltz, 195, see also *Youthful Suite*
Ermey, 248
Etherophone, 155
Ethnology, 255
Evan Banks, 123
Experiments, 79ff, 255

Fair is the Play on the Greensward, see *Let's Dance Gay in Green Meadow*
Fairfax, Bryan, 71ff, 142

Faeroe Islands, 56, 189, 204
Father and Daughter, 19, 34, 54, 78, 83, 201
Faure, Gabriel, 109, 195, 229, 232; *Nell,* 204, 232
Feilding, Everard, 61
Fenby, Eric, 46, 49, 211, 245
Fennell, Frederick, 106, 192, 193, 194, 198, 253
Ferrabosco, Alfonso, 111, 232
Fickenscher, Arthur, 160, 168
Field, Christopher, 196
Fijians, 95
Finck, H 232
First Chantey, 121, 252
Fischer, Carlo, 118, 252
Fitzwater, William, 245, 248
Flecker, James Elroy, 40
Folkeminde Samling, see Kongelige Bibliotek
Folk-fiddlers, 114
Folk Music Journal, 68
Folksong, 69, 123, 195; British, 142, 157; collecting 19, 29, 55ff, 63, 256; English 68; Jutland, 64; notation, 30; Swedish, 56
Folk-song Society, 19, 58, 59, 157
See also Journal of the . . .
Fort Jay, 107
Foster, Stephen, 16, 106, 218; *Campdown Races,* 92; see also *Tribute to Foster*
France, 38
Franck, Cesar, 109, 232
Franckenstein, Clemens von, 252
Frankfurt, 25, 39, 40, 55, 100, 113, 118, 123, 155, 252 *see also* Hoch'sche Konservatorium
Frankfurt group, 16, 20, 21, 51, 156, 251, 256
Fred, Herbert W, 253
Free-music, 21, 56, 66, 73, 74, 79, 155ff, 166, 171, 201, 214, 246, 251, 254, 256
Free Music I and II, 200, 251
Furtwangler, Wilhelm, 191

Gabrielli, G, 193
Gamelan, 81, 84
Gamelan Anklung, 65
Ganges Pilot, 124
Gardiner, Balfour, 12, 20, 26, 39, 44, *45,* 49, 54, 123, 156, 232, 252; choral and orchestra concerts, 19, 54, 213
Gardiner, Rolf, 211
Gauguin, Paul, 33
Gay but Wistful, 98ff; see also *In a Nutshell*
Germany, 34
Gershwin, George, 160, 232; *Love Walked In,* 121, 218; *The Man I Love,* 218
'The Gipsy's Wedding Day', 57
Glasses, musical, 23, 77, 93, 249, 250
Glissando, performance of, 121
Gloucestershire, 59, 63
Godowsky, Leopold, 121
Goldman, Edwin Franko, 108
Goldman, Richard Franko, 109, 157, 213, 253, 256
Goossens, Eugene, 182, 232, 253
Gordon, Adam Lindsay, 123, 125

BACK ENDPAPER:

(from top left hand corner) Ella and Percy on the Loing; Tang Kristensen and Grainger; Jelka Delius, Alexandre Barjanski and Percy Grainger on the Loing; Percy and Ella at Highgate, 1927; Grainger late 1920s.

(right hand page)

'Percy Grainger as he really looked – aged 61 (1943 Indianapolis)' [photograph: W H Bass, Indianapolis]